The Cambridge Companion to French Art Song

The twenty-first century has witnessed a surge of scholarly interest in the French art song, or *mélodie*, with a flood of new books, articles, and editions. This Companion draws on the best of this new research, with chapters by world-renowned scholars and performers examining French art song through the practicality of performance, both pianistic and vocal. The book surveys the repertory chronologically from the 1820s into the 1950s, covering all the central composers (Berlioz, Gounod, Fauré, Debussy, Duparc, Chausson, Ravel, Poulenc, Messiaen, and many more). It includes chapters on the role of women in the creation, performance, and diffusion of French song; the analysis of French prosody and poetic forms; the position of the *mélodie* in French literary history; and the interpretation of *mélodie* in performance. Scholars, students, performers, and music lovers will find thorough and up-to-date resources to enable them to explore this crucial yet understudied song repertory.

STEPHEN RUMPH is Professor of Music History at the University of Washington. His publications include *Mozart and Enlightenment Semiotics* (2011), *The Fauré Song Cycles: Poetry and Music, 1861–1921* (2020), and the co-edited Cambridge *Fauré Studies* (2021).

Cambridge Companions to Music

Topics

The Cambridge Companion to Ballet
Edited by Marion Kant

The Cambridge Companion to Blues and Gospel Music
Edited by Allan Moore

The Cambridge Companion to Caribbean Music
Edited by Nanette de Jong

The Cambridge Companion to Choral Music
Edited by André de Quadros

The Cambridge Companion to Composition
Edited by Toby Young

The Cambridge Companion to the Concerto
Edited by Simon P. Keefe

The Cambridge Companion to Conducting
Edited by José Antonio Bowen

The Cambridge Companion to Eighteenth-Century Opera
Edited by Anthony R. DelDonna and Pierpaolo Polzonetti

The Cambridge Companion to Electronic Music, second edition
Edited by Nick Collins and Julio D'Escriván

The Cambridge Companion to the 'Eroica' Symphony
Edited by Nancy November

The Cambridge Companion to Film Music
Edited by Mervyn Cooke and Fiona Ford

The Cambridge Companion to French Music
Edited by Simon Trezise

The Cambridge Companion to French Art Song
Edited by Stephen Rumph

The Cambridge Companion to Grand Opera
Edited by David Charlton

The Cambridge Companion to Hip-Hop
Edited by Justin A. Williams

The Cambridge Companion to Jazz
Edited by Mervyn Cooke and David Horn

The Cambridge Companion to Jewish Music
Edited by Joshua S. Walden

The Cambridge Companion to K-Pop
Edited by Suk-Young Kim

The Cambridge Companion to Krautrock
Edited by Uwe Schütte

The Cambridge Companion to the Lied
Edited by James Parsons

The Cambridge Companion to The Magic Flute
Edited by Jessica Waldoff

The Cambridge Companion to Medieval Music
Edited by Mark Everist

The Cambridge Companion to Metal Music
Edited by Jan-Peter Herbst

The Cambridge Companion to Music and Romanticism
Edited by Benedict Taylor

The Cambridge Companion to Music in Australia
Edited by Amanda Harris and Clint Bracknell

The Cambridge Companion to Music in Digital Culture
Edited by Nicholas Cook, Monique Ingalls and David Trippett

The Cambridge Companion to the Musical, third edition
Edited by William Everett and Paul Laird

The Cambridge Companion to Opera Studies
Edited by Nicholas Till

The Cambridge Companion to Operetta
Edited by Anastasia Belina and Derek B. Scott

The Cambridge Companion to the Orchestra
Edited by Colin Lawson

The Cambridge Companion to Pop and Rock
Edited by Simon Frith, Will Straw and John Street

The Cambridge Companion to Recorded Music
Edited by Eric Clarke, Nicholas Cook, Daniel Leech-Wilkinson and John Rink

The Cambridge Companion to Rhythm
Edited by Russell Hartenberger and Ryan McClelland

The Cambridge Companion to The Rite of Spring
Edited by Davinia Caddy

The Cambridge Companion to Schubert's 'Winterreise'
Edited by Marjorie W. Hirsch and Lisa Feurzeig

The Cambridge Companion to Serialism
Edited by Martin Iddon

The Cambridge Companion to Seventeenth-Century Opera
Edited by Jacqueline Waeber

The Cambridge Companion to the Singer-Songwriter
Edited by Katherine Williams and Justin A. Williams

The Cambridge Companion to the String Quartet
Edited by Robin Stowell

The Cambridge Companion to the Symphony
Edited by Julian Horton

The Cambridge Companion to Tango
Edited by Kristin Wendland and Kacey Link

The Cambridge Companion to Twentieth-Century Opera
Edited by Mervyn Cooke

The Cambridge Companion to Video Game Music
Edited by Melanie Fritsch and Tim Summers

The Cambridge Companion to Wagner's Der Ring des Nibelungen
Edited by Mark Berry and Nicholas Vazsonyi

The Cambridge Companion to West Side Story
Edited by Paul R. Laird and Elizabeth A. Wells

The Cambridge Companion to Women Composers
Edited by Matthew Head and Susan Wollenberg

The Cambridge Companion to Women in Music since 1900
Edited by Laura Hamer

Composers

The Cambridge Companion to Bach
Edited by John Butt

The Cambridge Companion to Bartók
Edited by Amanda Bayley

The Cambridge Companion to Amy Beach
Edited by E. Douglas Bomberger

The Cambridge Companion to the Beatles
Edited by Kenneth Womack

The Cambridge Companion to Beethoven
Edited by Glenn Stanley

The Cambridge Companion to Berg
Edited by Anthony Pople

The Cambridge Companion to Berlioz
Edited by Peter Bloom

The Cambridge Companion to Brahms
Edited by Michael Musgrave

The Cambridge Companion to Benjamin Britten
Edited by Mervyn Cooke

The Cambridge Companion to Bruckner
Edited by John Williamson

The Cambridge Companion to John Cage
Edited by David Nicholls

The Cambridge Companion to Chopin
Edited by Jim Samson

The Cambridge Companion to Debussy
Edited by Simon Trezise

The Cambridge Companion to Elgar
Edited by Daniel M. Grimley and Julian Rushton

The Cambridge Companion to Duke Ellington
Edited by Edward Green

The Cambridge Companion to Gershwin
Edited by Anna Celenza

The Cambridge Companion to Gilbert and Sullivan
Edited by David Eden and Meinhard Saremba

The Cambridge Companion to Handel
Edited by Donald Burrows

The Cambridge Companion to Haydn
Edited by Caryl Clark

The Cambridge Companion to Liszt
Edited by Kenneth Hamilton

The Cambridge Companion to Mahler
Edited by Jeremy Barham

The Cambridge Companion to Mendelssohn
Edited by Peter Mercer-Taylor

The Cambridge Companion to Monteverdi
Edited by John Whenham and Richard Wistreich

The Cambridge Companion to Mozart
Edited by Simon P. Keefe

The Cambridge Companion to Arvo Pärt
Edited by Andrew Shenton

The Cambridge Companion to Ravel
Edited by Deborah Mawer

The Cambridge Companion to the Rolling Stones
Edited by Victor Coelho and John Covach

The Cambridge Companion to Rossini
Edited by Emanuele Senici

The Cambridge Companion to Schoenberg
Edited by Jennifer Shaw and Joseph Auner

The Cambridge Companion to Schubert
Edited by Christopher Gibbs

The Cambridge Companion to Schumann
Edited by Beate Perrey

The Cambridge Companion to Shostakovich
Edited by Pauline Fairclough and David Fanning

The Cambridge Companion to Sibelius
Edited by Daniel M. Grimley

The Cambridge Companion to Richard Strauss
Edited by Charles Youmans

The Cambridge Companion to Stravinsky
Edited by Jonathan Cross

The Cambridge Companion to Michael Tippett
Edited by Kenneth Gloag and Nicholas Jones

The Cambridge Companion to Vaughan Williams
Edited by Alain Frogley and Aiden J. Thomson

The Cambridge Companion to Verdi
Edited by Scott L. Balthazar

The Cambridge Companion to Wagner
Edited by Thomas S. Grey

Instruments

The Cambridge Companion to Brass Instruments
Edited by Trevor Herbert and John Wallace

The Cambridge Companion to the Cello
Edited by Robin Stowell

The Cambridge Companion to the Clarinet
Edited by Colin Lawson

The Cambridge Companion to the Drum Kit
Edited by Matt Brennan, Joseph Michael Pignato and Daniel Akir a Stadnicki

The Cambridge Companion to the Electric Guitar
Edited by Jan-Peter Herbst and Steve Waksman

The Cambridge Companion to the Guitar
Edited by Victor Coelho

The Cambridge Companion to the Harpsichord
Edited by Mark Kroll

The Cambridge Companion to the Organ
Edited by Nicholas Thistlethwaite and Geoffrey Webber

The Cambridge Companion to Percussion
Edited by Russell Hartenberger

The Cambridge Companion to the Piano
Edited by David Rowland

The Cambridge Companion to the Saxophone
Edited by Richard Ingham

The Cambridge Companion to Singing
Edited by John Potter

The Cambridge Companion to the Violin
Edited by Robin Stowell

The Cambridge Companion to French Art Song

Edited by
STEPHEN RUMPH
University of Washington

CAMBRIDGE UNIVERSITY PRESS

Shaftesbury Road, Cambridge CB2 8EA, United Kingdom

One Liberty Plaza, 20th Floor, New York, NY 10006, USA

477 Williamstown Road, Port Melbourne, VIC 3207, Australia

314–321, 3rd Floor, Plot 3, Splendor Forum, Jasola District Centre,
New Delhi – 110025, India

103 Penang Road, #05–06/07, Visioncrest Commercial, Singapore 238467

Cambridge University Press is part of Cambridge University Press & Assessment,
a department of the University of Cambridge.

We share the University's mission to contribute to society through the pursuit of education, learning and research at the highest international levels of excellence.

www.cambridge.org
Information on this title: www.cambridge.org/9781316514474

DOI: 10.1017/9781009083386

© Cambridge University Press & Assessment 2026

This publication is in copyright. Subject to statutory exception and to the provisions of relevant collective licensing agreements, no reproduction of any part may take place without the written permission of Cambridge University Press & Assessment.

When citing this work, please include a reference to the DOI 10.1017/9781009083386

First published 2026

A catalogue record for this publication is available from the British Library

A Cataloging-in-Publication data record for this book is available from the Library of Congress

ISBN 978-1-316-51447-4 Hardback
ISBN 978-1-009-08757-5 Paperback

Cambridge University Press & Assessment has no responsibility for the persistence or accuracy of URLs for external or third-party internet websites referred to in this publication and does not guarantee that any content on such websites is, or will remain, accurate or appropriate.

For EU product safety concerns, contact us at Calle de José Abascal, 56, 1°, 28003 Madrid, Spain, or email eugpsr@cambridge.org.

For my family

Contents

List of Figures [*page* xiii]
List of Music Examples [xiv]
List of Contributors [xvii]
Preface [xxi]
Acknowledgements [xxiv]

1 Song and the French Poetic Tradition
  VINCENT VIVÈS [1]

2 French Versification and Song: Interconnected Worlds
  DAVID HUNTER [20]

3 *Romance* to *mélodie*? The Trajectory of Berlioz's Songs
  JULIAN RUSHTON [38]

4 The *Mélodie* Comes of Age (Gounod, Saint-Saëns, Bizet, Massenet)
  STEVEN HUEBNER [60]

5 Fauré's Individual Songs and Collections
  ROY HOWAT [91]

6 Debussy's Early Songs: Finding His Compositional Voice
  MARIE ROLF [111]

7 The Franckist-Wagnerian Strain (Duparc, Chausson, Chabrier)
  ANDREW PAU [146]

8 Women and French Song
  ANNEGRET FAUSER [168]

9 Fauré's Song Cycles
  STEPHEN RUMPH [189]

10 Debussy's Mature Songs
   DENIS HERLIN [214]

11 Ravel and His Contemporaries
   EMILY KILPATRICK [240]

12　Poulenc and His Circle: *Le style quotidien*
　　BYRON ADAMS　　[264]

13　Olivier Messiaen
　　STEPHEN BROAD AND DAVID EVANS　　[283]

14　Interpreting French Art Song
　　FRANÇOIS LE ROUX　　[306]

Guide to Further Reading　[319]
Index　[328]

Figures

6.1 [online only*] Songs and poetic texts studied   [*page* 113]
6.2 Poetic and musical structure of Debussy, 'Caprice'   [122]

---

* Figures and music examples labelled as 'online only' can be viewed at www.cambridge.org/9781316514474 under the 'Resources' tab.

Music Examples

3.1 Jean-Paul Égide Martini, 'Plaisir d'amour', refrain [*page* 40]
3.2 Hector Berlioz, 'Le dépit de la bergère', comparison of first and last stanzas [43]
3.3 [online only] Berlioz, 'L'Origine de la Harpe' (*Neuf mélodies irlandaises*), introduction and comparison of stanzas 1 and 4 [46]
3.4 Berlioz, 'Le pêcheur', comparison of stanzas, beginning at m. 11 [48]
3.5 Berlioz, 'Sur les Lagunes' (*Les Nuits d'été*) [52]
    a) Opening [52]
    b) Refrain [53]
3.6 Berlioz, 'L'île inconnue' (*Les Nuits d'été*), mm. 93–111 (voice only) [54]
4.1 Charles Gounod, 'Ce que je suis sans toi', mm. 1–9 [64]
4.2 Gounod, 'Le soir', mm. 1–16 [68]
4.3 Gounod, 'Venise', mm. 31–46 [71]
4.4 [online only] Camille Saint-Saëns, 'Guitare', mm. 4–13 [74]
4.5a Saint-Saëns, 'Extase', mm. 1–15 [76]
4.5b Saint-Saëns, 'Extase', mm. 52–5 [77]
4.6 Saint-Saëns, 'Sabre en main', mm. 1–8 [78]
4.7 Georges Bizet, 'Guitare', mm. 5–16 [81]
4.8 Jules Massenet, 'Septembre' [86]
    a) [online only] Mm. 3–11 [86]
    b) Mm. 19–26 [86]
4.9 Massenet, 'Enchantement' [88]
    a) Mm. 1–6 [88]
    b) [online only] Mm. 14–22 [88]
5.1 Gabriel Fauré, 'Chant d'automne', mm. 56–9 [93]
5.2 Voice-piano dialogue in Fauré's Sully Prudhomme settings [97]
    a) 'Ici-bas', mm. 21–4 [97]
    b) 'Au bord de l'eau', mm. 2–6 [97]
5.3 Fauré, 'Le papillon et la fleur' (first published key), mm. 10–17 [99]

5.4   Rhythmically differentiated line starts in Fauré's early Hugo settings   [100]
   a) 'Puisque j'ai mis ma lèvre' (final manuscript key), mm. 8–13   [100]
   b) 'Mai' (manuscript key), mm. 3–6   [100]
   c) 'S'il est un charmant gazon' (1864 autograph version), mm. 9–12   [100]
   d) 'L'aurore', mm. 1–3   [100]
5.5   Fauré, 'Les berceaux', mm. 19–20   [104]
6.1   Figural variation in Claude Debussy, 'Nuit d'étoiles'   [116]
   a) First refrain   [116]
   b) Second refrain   [116]
   c) Third refrain   [116]
6.2   Debussy, refrain of 'Flots, palmes, sables'   [118]
6.3   Debussy, 'Caprice', mm. 20–34   [123]
6.4   Debussy, 'Caprice', mm. 1–8   [124]
6.5   Prosody in Debussy, 'Clair de lune' (1882 and 1891 versions)   [128]
6.6   Debussy, 'Clair de lune' (1882), mm. 1–11   [129]
6.7   Debussy, 'Clair de lune' (1882), mm. 24–9   [129]
6.8   Debussy, 'Clair de lune' (1882), mm. 39–53   [130]
6.9   Debussy, 'Clair de lune' (1882), mm. 75–84   [131]
6.10 Debussy, 'Clair de lune' (*Fêtes galantes I*, 1891), mm. 1–6   [133]
6.11 Motivic juxtapositions in Debussy, 'Clair de lune' (1891)   [134]
   a) Introduction, m. 1   [134]
   b) Quatrain 1, mm. 9–10   [134]
   c) Quatrain 2, m. 16   [134]
   d) Quatrain 2, mm. 19–20   [134]
   e) Quatrain 3, mm. 21–22   [134]
6.12 Debussy, 'Clair de lune' (1891), mm. 25–6   [135]
6.13 Debussy, 'Clair de lune' (1891), mm. 27–32   [135]
6.14 Appearances of the motto in Debussy, 'Spleen' (*Ariettes*)   [138]
   a) Introduction, mm. 1–4   [138]
   b) Couplet 1, mm. 9–10   [138]
   c) Couplet 4, mm. 18–19   [138]
   d) Couplet 5, mm. 22–3   [138]
   e) Couplet 5, mm. 24–5   [138]
   f) Couplet 6, mm. 28–9   [138]
   g) Couplet 6, mm. 30–1   [139]
6.15 Debussy, 'Spleen', mm. 4–8   [140]
6.16 Enharmonic vocal entries in Debussy, 'Spleen'   [140]
   a) Couplet 2, mm. 9–11   [140]
   b) Couplet 3, mm. 14–15   [140]

7.1 César Franck, 'Lied', mm. 1–11   [147]
7.2 Contrasting chromatic practice in Wagner and Duparc   [148]
   a) Richard Wagner, 'Träume' (*Wesendonck Lieder*), mm. 1–12   [148]
   b) Henri Duparc, 'Phidylé', mm. 46–9   [148]
7.3 Duparc, 'L'invitation au voyage', mm. 3–10   [152]
7.4 Ernest Chausson, *Poème de l'amour et de la mer*   [159]
   a) 'La fleur des eaux', mm. 19–22   [159]
   b) 'La mort de l'amour', mm. 32–42   [159]
9.1 Motivic recollection in Gabriel Fauré, *Poème d'un jour*   [193]
   a) 'Rencontre', mm. 2–4   [193]
   b) 'Adieu', mm. 5–8   [193]
9.2 Motivic counterpoint in Fauré, 'J'allais par des chemins perfides' (*La bonne chanson*), mm. 48–54   [199]
9.3 Theatrical song in *La chanson d'Ève*   [204]
   a) Fauré, 'The King's Three Blind Daughters' (incidental music to *Pelléas et Mélisande*), mm. 3–7   [204]
   b) Fauré, 'O Mort, poussière d'étoiles' (*La chanson d'Ève*), mm. 18–19   [204]
9.4 Fauré, 'Danseuse' (*Mirages*), mm. 1–6   [210]
10.1 Claude Debussy, 'Clair de lune' (*Fêtes galantes I*), mm. 19–22   [226]
11.1 Maurice Ravel, 'Sainte', mm. 20–24   [247]
11.2 Charles Koechlin's homage to Ravel's *Shéhérazade*   [250]
   a) Ravel, 'Asie' (*Shéhérazade*), mm. 1–2   [250]
   b) Charles Koechlin, 'Le voyage' (*Shéhérazade*, Op. 84, no. 2), mm. 1–2   [250]
   c) Koechlin, 'Le voyage', m. (4)   [250]
11.3 Albert Roussel, 'Le jardin mouillé' (*Quatre poèmes de Régnier*, Op. 3), mm. 46–50   [252]
11.4 Lili Boulanger, 'Nous nous aimerons tant' (*Clairières dans le ciel*), mm. 17–26   [258]
12.1 Francis Poulenc, 'Bonne journée' (*Tel jour telle nuit*), mm. 1–4   [277]
12.2 Poulenc, 'Sanglots' (*Banalités*), mm. 15–18   [278]
14.1 Tone row in Henri Dutilleux, 'J'ai rêvé que je vous portais entre mes bras' (*Sonnets de Jean Cassou*), mm. 1–4   [311]
14.2 Henri Duparc, 'La vie antérieure', mm. 44–8   [314]
14.3 Francis Poulenc, 'Aussi bien que les cigales' (*Calligrammes*), piano postlude   [316]

Contributors

BYRON ADAMS is Distinguished Professor of Musicology, Emeritus at the University of California, Riverside. He edited *Edward Elgar and His World* (Princeton University Press, 2007) and co-edited *Ralph Vaughan Williams and His World* (University of Chicago Press, 2023). An associate editor of *The Musical Quarterly*, Byron Adams has contributed chapters to *Jean Sibelius and His World* (Princeton University Press, 2011), *The Cambridge Companion to Elgar* (2011), and the Cambridge *Fauré Studies* (2021).

STEPHEN BROAD is Professor of Music at the Royal Conservatoire of Scotland. His publications include *Olivier Messiaen: Journalism 1935–1939* (Ashgate, 2012), as well as essays in *Messiaen Perspectives* (Ashgate, 2013), *Olivier Messiaen und die 'französische Tradition'* (Verlag Dohr, 2013), and *Olivier Messiaen: Music, Art and Literature* (Ashgate, 2007).

DAVID EVANS is Reader in French at the University of St Andrews. His publications include *Théodore de Banville: Constructing Poetic Value in Nineteenth-Century France* (Legenda, 2014) and essays on Charles Baudelaire, Paul Verlaine, Marie Krysinska, and other poets in *Nineteenth-Century French Studies*, the *Routledge Companion to Music and Modern Literature* (2022), *Revue Verlaine*, and *French Ecocriticism: From the Early Modern Period to the Twenty-First Century* (Peter Lang, 2017).

ANNEGRET FAUSER is Cary C. Boshamer Distinguished Professor of Music, Emerita at the University of North Carolina at Chapel Hill. Her books include *Sounds of War: Music in the United States during World War II* (Oxford University Press, 2013), *The Politics of Musical Identity* (Routledge, 2015), *Musical Encounters at the 1889 Paris World's Fair* (Boydell & Brewer, 2005), and *Der Orchestergesang in Frankreich zwischen 1870 und 1920* (Laaber, 1994). She is an Honorary Member of the American Musicological Society and was awarded the Edward J. Dent Medal of the Royal Musical Association.

DENIS HERLIN is Director of Research at IReMUSC (Institut de recherche en musicologie), Paris. His many publications on French music include *Claude Debussy: Portraits et études* (Georg Olms Verlag, 2021) and the critical edition with F. Lesure of the Debussy *Correspondance: 1872–1918* (Gallimard, 2005). He is editor-in-chief of the *Œuvres complètes de Claude Debussy* (Durand, 1985–) and co-editor of the *Catalogue thématique des œuvres de Jean-Philippe Rameau* (CNRS Éditions, 2003–).

ROY HOWAT is a concert pianist and Research Fellow at the Royal Academy of Music and Royal Conservatoire of Scotland. One of the founding editors of the *Œuvres complètes de Claude Debussy*, he has produced critical editions of major works by Debussy, Chabrier, and Fauré (including the complete Fauré songs for Edition Peters, co-edited with Emily Kilpatrick). He is the author of *Debussy in Proportion: A Musical Analysis* (Cambridge University Press, 1983), *The Art of French Piano Music* (Yale University Press, 2009), and a forthcoming Cambridge Handbook on Chopin's Etudes.

STEVEN HUEBNER is Professor of Musicology at McGill University. A leading authority on French opera, his publications include *The Operas of Charles Gounod* (Clarendon, 1990), *French Opera at the Fin de Siècle: Wagnerism, Nationalism, and Style* (Oxford University Press, 1999), and *Les Opéras de Verdi: Éléments d'un langage musico-dramatique* (Presses de l'Université de Montréal, 2016). He co-edited *Debussy's Resonance* (Boydell & Brewer, 2018).

DAVID HUNTER is an independent writer and editor. He is the author of *Understanding French Verse: A Guide for Singers* (Oxford University Press, 2005) and *Apollinaire in the Great War, 1914–18* (Peter Owen Publishers, 2015).

EMILY KILPATRICK is Associate Professor in Academic Studies at the Royal Academy of Music. She is the author of *The Operas of Maurice Ravel* (Cambridge University Press, 2015) and *French Art Song: History of a New Music, 1870–1914* (University of Rochester Press, 2022), together with numerous articles and chapters on the vocal music of Fauré and Ravel. She co-edited the Urtext edition *Gabriel Fauré: Complete Songs* (Peters Edition, 2013–22) and recorded, with tenor Tony Boutté, Fauré's *La bonne chanson* for Peters Sounds (2015).

FRANÇOIS LE ROUX is an internationally renowned operatic baritone, famous for his portrayal of Debussy's Pelléas (*Pelléas et Mélisande*), and a foremost interpreter of the *mélodie*. He has recorded widely on EMI, Naxos, Hyperion, and other labels and is the author of *Le chant intime: The Interpretation of French Art Song* (Oxford University Press, 2021). He is a Chevalier in the Ordre des Arts et des Lettres.

ANDREW PAU is Associate Professor of Music Theory at the Oberlin Conservatory of Music. He focusses on nineteenth-century French music and theory, and his publications explore chromatic harmony, text-setting, phrase structure, and musical meaning and narrative in Bizet, Debussy, Fauré, and Duparc.

MARIE ROLF is Professor of Music Theory, Emerita at the Eastman School of Music. She translated and revised François Lesure's *Claude Debussy: A Critical Biography* (University of Rochester Press, 2019) and is a founding member of the editorial board for the *Œuvres complètes de Claude Debussy* (Durand), for which she has prepared critical editions of *La Mer* and a volume of *mélodies*.

STEPHEN RUMPH is Professor of Music History at the University of Washington. His publications include *Beethoven after Napoleon: Political Romanticism in the Late Works* (University of California Press, 2004), *Mozart and Enlightenment Semiotics* (University of California Press, 2011), *The Fauré Song Cycles: Poetry and Music, 1861–1921* (University of California Press, 2020), and *Cambridge Fauré Studies* (2021), co-edited with Carlo Caballero.

JULIAN RUSHTON is Professor of Music, Emeritus at the University of Leeds. His books include *Berlioz: 'Roméo et Juliette'* (Cambridge University Press, 1994), *The Music of Berlioz* (Oxford University Press, 2001), and *The Musical Language of Berlioz* (Cambridge University Press, 2008). He edits the *Berlioz Society Bulletin*.

VINCENT VIVÈS is Professor of Literature at the Université Polytechnique Hauts-de-France. He co-authored *Histoire et poétique de la mélodie française* (CNRS Éditions, 2000). His other publications include *Vox Humana: Poésie, musique, individuation* (Presses universitaires de Provence, 2006), *La Règle du jeu* (Fiorini, 2007), and editions, studies, and anthologies of Victor Hugo, Leconte de Lisle, Arthur Rimbaud, Guillaume Apollinaire, and other French poets.

Preface

Charles Baudelaire's poem 'L'invitation au voyage', set unforgettably by Henri Duparc, envisions a distant land where 'all is nothing but order and beauty, / Abundance, calm, and voluptuous delight'. French art song certainly belongs to such a land. The golden age of the *mélodie*, as the genre became known, occurred during the Belle Époque, that astonishing flowering of literature, music, and visual arts bounded by the Franco-Prussian War of 1870–1 and the outbreak of the First World War in 1914. The *mélodie* epitomises the rich interplay of arts in fin-de-siècle France: visionary poets called forth undreamt-of music, while daring composers inspired poets to reimagine their art. The result was a fusion of word and tone unique in the history of Western art music, and a repertoire of inexhaustible beauty and fascination.

Nevertheless, French song can present challenges to listeners more familiar with the Austro-Germanic *Lied* and other song repertories. More than any national tradition, French song springs from its linguistic soil. Language has served as a key source of political and cultural identity in modern France from the foundation of the Académie française in 1635 to the present day. Composers of *mélodies* collaborated closely with poets, moulding their settings to the distinctive rhythms and properties of their native tongue. The literary theorist Roland Barthes could even write that 'the historical meaning of the *mélodie* is a certain culture of the French language'.[1] Accordingly, this book opens with Vincent Vivès' panoramic survey of French poetry and song across the nineteenth and twentieth centuries. David Hunter then unlocks the secrets of French prosody and poetic form, indispensable knowledge for singers, coaches, and scholars alike. François Le Roux's concluding chapter on interpretation returns to the centrality of poetic understanding and sensibility for performers of French song.

A further challenge may lie in the beguiling modesty of the *mélodie*. French song by no means lacks passion or drama, as witness Gabriel

---

[1] Barthes, 'The Grain of the Voice', in *Image, Music, Text*, trans. Stephen Heath (New York: Hill and Wang, 1977), 186.

Fauré's *La bonne chanson*, Duparc's Baudelaire settings, or the last song of Francis Poulenc's *Banalités*. But French composers painted with a subtle palette; they did not wear their hearts on their sleeves. The *mélodie* flowered after the humiliating defeat by Prussia, at a time when many French composers were distancing themselves from Germanic music and its quest for self-expression, profundity, and the monumental. The 'Ars gallica' championed by the new Société nationale de musique distinguished itself more through elegance, refinement, wit, and understatement. Listeners accustomed to the thundering hoofbeats of Schubert's 'Erlkönig' or the passionate effusions of Schumann's *Dichterliebe* will need to fine-tune their hearing, attending to the subtle gesture, the exquisite melodic shape or harmony, the sensitive rendering of the poetic text.

Finally, much of the poetry set by *mélodie* composers deliberately avoids the confessional tone and soul-baring that make Goethe or Heine so accessible. The Parnassian poets embraced by Fauré and Duparc rejected Romantic enthusiasm in favour of formal perfection, erudition, and classical serenity. The Symbolist movement that swept up Claude Debussy questioned representation itself, cultivating a mysterious, allusive language content with its own inner play. And the Surrealists, inspiration for Poulenc and other composers after the First World War, further scrambled the message with illogical juxtapositions, wild typography, and even automatic writing. Stephen Rumph's chapter on Fauré's song cycles and Byron Adams' on Poulenc and his circle probe the ways in which composers responded to these fascinating and elusive poetic trends.

The history of French art song begins long before the Belle Époque and stretches well after the Great War. Nineteenth-century French song actually entwines two genres: the native *romance* and the more highbrow *mélodie* that emerged in the 1820s. The chapters by Julian Rushton and Steven Huebner trace the coexistence of these genres from Hector Berlioz to Jules Massenet, and the gradual ascendancy of the *mélodie*. Andrew Pau explores the pervasive influence of Richard Wagner on French song composers, focussing on César Franck and his pupils. Two composers have merited multiple chapters in this book: the complementary survey of Fauré's individual songs by Roy Howat and the twin essays on Debussy by Marie Rolf and Denis Herlin recognise the prestige, breadth, and influence of these master *mélodistes*. Meanwhile, the chapters by Emily Kilpatrick and Annegret Fauser explore broader themes in the history of French art song. Kilpatrick's survey of Maurice Ravel and his contemporaries traces the evolution of the *mélodie* from a salon delicacy to a serious concert genre, while Fauser's 'herstory' reveals the crucial role of women in the creation, performance, and diffusion of French song.

Olivier Messiaen, who composed *mélodies* into the 1940s, provides an arbitrary but appropriate conclusion to our repertoire survey. As Stephen Broad and David Evans demonstrate, Messiaen was immersed in the literary tradition that nourished the *mélodie*, as the son of a poet and the author of his own song texts. While his works stand at a dizzying stylistic remove from the early *mélodies* of Berlioz and Charles Gounod, they cap a long tradition united by the same quest: the pursuit of new, imaginative fusions of music and poetry. This book invites readers to deepen their knowledge, appreciation, and interpretation of this remarkable French tradition.

The examples in the following chapters give only a taste of the music, but readers can easily access scores and recordings online. The essential French art song repertory is available in open score archives, and recordings of most of the songs are also readily accessible, along with reliable translations. The Guide to Further Reading lists online resources, as well as a wealth of scholarly sources on all the topics covered in this book. Happy reading and *bon voyage*!

Acknowledgements

My first thanks go to the authors of this volume, who rose to the occasion with such insightful and wide-ranging essays. I am also deeply grateful to Kate Brett, Abigail Sears, and the rest of the team at Cambridge University Press for their encouragement, support, and patience in shepherding this book through the publication process.

The Floyd and Delores Jones Endowed Fund for the Arts provided a generous subvention for this book. The University of Washington also provided valuable funding.

We remember with gratitude our friend and colleague David Code, a brilliant Debussy scholar who assisted in the planning of this volume. His sophisticated, original research animates the following discussion of both Debussy and Fauré.

Finally, I acknowledge with great affection my large transatlantic family, both living and deceased. This book is dedicated to them for all their love, support, and passion for music.

1 | Song and the French Poetic Tradition

VINCENT VIVÈS

> 'Voici, pour ma part, comment je définirai la mélodie française: c'est le champ (ou le chant) de célébration de la langue française cultivée.'
> Roland Barthes[1]

The aesthetic of the French *mélodie* crystallises a rich network of historical, political, and social influences that crisscross the fields of language, literature, and music. The precise birthplace of the *mélodie* lies neither here nor there, but rather in the intersection of multiple shifting aesthetic terrains whose sediment forms a space of representation, a period of stylistic practice, an aesthetic landscape. The *mélodie* took shape gradually, not in lonely isolation but as a variegated and fluid phenomenon, recalling at times the older genre of the *romance* and dialoguing intermittently with the Austro-Germanic *Lied*. Labile in conception and compositional practice, the *mélodie* would gravitate to still other forms to reinvent itself, or vanish entirely, following the general tendency of the twentieth century to dissolve the traces of art and its elements (syntax, genre, material). It would also fashion itself in opposition to certain aesthetics on the margins of the major genres (opera, cantata, symphony). As we untangle this skein, we shall establish genealogies and ruptures, bifurcations, some invariants, and much diversity. The *mélodie*, which arrived so late among the nineteenth-century arts during an epoch of richly burgeoning genres, created through its dialogue of musical and poetic materials the conditions for a salon art (the dominant model of the *mélodie* for voice and piano) that steadily freed itself from social contingencies to rethink the connection between music and poetry, individual sensibility and critical awareness.

Toward an Aesthetic of the *Mélodie*

The difference in languages, most notably between French and English, cannot alone explain the aesthetic distance that separates the *mélodie* from other contemporary European art forms that unite poetry and music. Neither the conception of 'song', as used in anglophone circles, nor of *Lied* (and its derivatives *Volkslied* and *Kunstlied*) has a precise equivalent in the French domain, where the generic term *mélodie* demarcates a serious tradition in opposition, above all, to the genres of the *romance* and *chanson*. The name traces its lineage to the crucible of Romanticism, which during the years 1820–30 ceaselessly birthed new forms and genres in both literature and music. In this regard, Berlioz's *Mélodies irlandaises* (1829–30, to translations of Thomas Moore) and their reception certainly exercised an influence:

> At the outset of the century, the word 'melody' was not an exact equivalent of 'song'. Moore clearly reached for a more erudite meaning to call greater attention to the distinct beauty of the sonorous heritage, as learned as it was popular, of his conquered island. Repatriated in French, the term *mélodie* preserves its intended character. Or better, everything follows as if the rare side, the precious side of this word had predestined its associated genre for elitist ends.[2]

The French *mélodie* did not escape the nationalist influences that roiled the nineteenth century. But it engaged with a tradition that imaginatively positioned itself against other European traditions as universal and unbound by such contingencies. Heir to a courtly tradition, the *mélodie* distinguished itself as an art rooted solely in the aesthetic realm. For Roland Barthes, it was a 'site where language works for free, that is, in perversion':

> This sung writing of language is, to my mind, what the French *mélodie* has sometimes striven to achieve. I am well aware that the German *Lied* is often bound intimately to the German language through the mediation of the Romantic poem; I also know that Schumann's poetic cultivation was immense and that he himself said of Schubert that, had he lived longer, he would have set all German literature to music; nevertheless, I believe that the historic meaning of the *Lied* must be located on the side of music (by virtue of its popular origins). In contrast, the historic meaning of the French *mélodie* is a certain culture of the French language ... what is involved in these works is more than musical style, but rather a practical reflection (if one can use the phrase) on language; there is a progressive assumption of language by poem, of poem by *mélodie*, and of *mélodie* by performance. This means that the *mélodie* (French) owes very little to musical history and very much to theories of the text.[3]

The French language, through the phonological traits and cultural meanings, both political and social, with which it was charged throughout its history, established a distinctive aesthetic sphere. André Boucourechliev, having chosen in 1984 to contrast the German and French languages by setting Paul Celan's 'Schneebett' in both the original and in translation, described this distinction:

French is a language that very much dominates the musician. French prosody has at times something quite authoritative about it to which it is hard not to conform ... In the German language, I could allow myself to break up some words – hence, vocalises. Yet I felt bound – and I return to the authority of the French language – to take account of the prosody ... the French element corresponds to a certain aura of the French language that is more supple, more luminous.[4]

The influence of the French language, depending on the literature and the poetry that enfolds and nourishes it, grants the *mélodie* a clear rapport with singing: the declamation yields its place to the art of diction, the play of drama to the experience of musical reading. The enunciation becomes neutral in its precision, irrespective of the gender of performer or poetic subject. What we hear in Fauré's setting of Verlaine's 'Clair de lune' or Duparc's treatment of Baudelaire's 'L'invitation au voyage' is a certain rapport between language and poetry, and not a story. A sentimental romantic tale is far less troublesome than this emotion that writing awakens in a subject, a speaker, a reader who delights in its own dissolution in the depths of aesthetic experience.

Towards a French Tradition: Linguistic Aesthetics and Politics

One of the main influences on the *mélodie* undoubtedly lies in the status of the French language, which from early on played a role in constructing a centralised political space in France. Among the milestones that mark this connection between the French language and state-building, we should mention the 1539 ordinance of Villers-Cotterêts by which Francis I imposed two articles (never revoked) that replaced Latin with French as the legal and administrative language of his realm. We must cite next, of course, the celebrated institution of the Académie française founded a century later by Richelieu in 1635 and validated by letters of patent signed by Louis XIII. The Académie set out to 'give definite rules for our language and to render it pure, eloquent, and fit for the arts and sciences'. One of the first members of this academy, the grammarian Claude Favre de Vaugelas, found part of his theoretical inspiration in the poet François de Malherbe whose efforts to simplify expression and strip away rhetoric, breaking with the magnificence of what would later be called Baroque poetry, imposed upon an entire century the model of a polished, perfected language, whose aesthetic ideal was inextricably bound to a policed and political mastery of language. The ideal of French classicism owes much to a political model in which language, in the context of courtly culture, had become a major weapon in the arsenal of power. By the late seventeenth century, France had already conjured the dream of being an exceptional culture among the nations. Its growing power in the centre of Europe required a narrative of military pre-eminence, which meant inflating the moral superiority and artistic excellence of its protagonist. France also demanded an art that was not merely an Italian tributary. It needed to define its particularity and establish an idea of primacy. The *tragédie lyrique* was thus fashioned as the antipode of Italian opera. At the heart of this opposition lay the question of taste and *mesure*, supposedly possessed by the French, versus Italian extravagance. This aesthetic distinction was expressed in large measure through the status granted to language, or put differently, through the position it enjoyed through its relationship with moderation, mastery, order, law. Italian Baroque opera subordinated language to music, taste to emotion; the *tragédie lyrique* subordinated music to the controlled diction of the language and the measured declamation of the verse. From this vantage point, the alexandrine, whose metric structure was founded on balance and symmetry (twelve syllables divided into equal hemistichs by a caesura), established a model of formal perfection that enshrined a moral and intellectual perfection, a historic ideal of distinctly French origin among whose most beautiful ornaments we may count the *mélodie*. This notion of a form that enshrined the ideal, whose beauty exteriorised the wholesome and good (*du bien et du bon*), a heritage of Ancient Greece (just as the French *mesure* was heir to *sophrosunê*, or temperance), was energetically perpetuated as a distinctive trait of what would become *l'esprit français*, characterised by Marcel Proust in the third volume of *À la recherche du temps perdu* (*In Search of Lost Time*, 1920):

> All the same, it is a pleasant thing, and probably exclusively French, that what is beautiful in equitable judgment, what has value according to the spirit and the heart, should first be charming to the eyes, painted with grace, chiselled with care, also expressing within its material and form an inner perfection.[5]

The great *mélodie* singer Pierre Bernac would uphold the same ideal: 'Debussy speaks of the "clarity of expression, of precision, of terseness in the form of French music" in contrast to the German musical genius, which excels in long sentimental effusions; lyricism and even passion are not lacking in French music, but reason and the mind control the emotions'.[6] We thus cannot understand the *mélodie* without examining this linguistic imaginary that descended in a straight line from the work of the Académie française and assumed its place among the accepted truths about the perfection of the French language, a perfection postulated as a universal law all the more so as French became the international language of the nobility and diplomacy, albeit a law that would be challenged after the defeat of Napoleon at Waterloo by the British, Dutch, German, and Prussian armies.

State of the Language

The *mélodie* is inextricably tied to the history of the French language and, more practically, to the state of that language in the nineteenth century, and thus to the highly distinctive French phonological system that impacted song. An offspring of Latin, the French language nevertheless departed greatly from its progenitor. It abandoned the accentual system of Latin, based on the word, for a more flexible system based on syntax. Whereas Latin accentuation is grounded in the volumetric mass of the individual word, that of French is organised according to the place of the words within syntactic units. At the same time, the French language progressively developed a tense, frontal phonetics. It is distinguished by an articulation placed chiefly at the front of the buccal cavity, aiming for forward resonance space, and by the muscular energy exerted in tensing the muscle groups involved in phonation – this is not a relaxed mode of phonation that requires little movement and muscular force. This phonatory system led to the dissolution of diphthongs (still heard in the eighteenth century) and was distinguished by the premium placed on articulation, which meant giving consonants their precise character and sharply differentiating vowels. The articulatory system of modern French, which resulted from the evolution of practices shot through with political ideology, joined a literature that, in part, took upon itself the same defining traits – precision, elegance, and so forth. So many rigid features that French literature of the erudite tradition accepted, passed on! So many features from which it sought to free itself as well, in a poetry that counted the names of Lamartine, Hugo, and, later, Verlaine and Rimbaud.

(R)evolution in Prosody

A happy accident would conjoin the histories of poetry and music in the sphere of metre, a coincidence that can explain both the miracle of the *mélodie* and its distinction from the poetic-musical creations of other European countries. Indeed, with Louis Quicherat's *Traité de versification française* (1838), metrical theory underwent a decisive modification, which drew support from contemporary poetic practice and would impact the way that later poets viewed the issue.[7] It involved a shift from an arithmetic and syllabic conception of French verse to a rhythmic-accentual conception, based on the arrangement of accented and unaccented syllables. This change of perspective prompted an evolution in thinking about the alexandrine (the axiomatic model of the French metric universe since its classic age in the seventeenth century) from a symmetric binary structure (6 + 6) toward a quadripartite conception, in which the two principal accents (at the caesura and the rhyme) were joined by two secondary and mobile accents within the two hemistichs. Thus, in both theory and the most modern practice, French nineteenth-century verse took on new colours as a rhythmic experience that simultaneously liberated classical metre and thrived in the sonorous space close to music (Stéphane Mallarmé would even speak of the tinkling (*pianotage*) of twelve tones in the alexandrine).

In the Romantic Cauldron

To understand both how music took charge of poetry and how poetry imposed itself upon music in the *mélodie*, we must unavoidably return to the moment of its birth, to the larger aesthetic movement from which it sprang: Romanticism. Romanticism was a European movement that, for political reasons, took on different colours in France than the Romanticisms that developed in England, Scotland, Ireland, and the German-speaking lands (from the dissolution of the Holy Roman Empire in 1806 through the Napoleonic protectorate to the German Federation after 1815 led by Prussia and Austria). The situation in France owed its distinct quality to the French Revolution and its aftermath in the Napoleonic Empire. For more than twenty years, France set itself in opposition to its neighbouring monarchies. It did this by rejecting the political, religious, and aesthetic outlook of the kingdoms that banded together against it and, for some, became its prey.

An aesthetic divide opened: revolutionary and imperial France constructed its universalist discourse by continuing the aesthetics of neoclassicism, a European movement that had emerged during the 1750s. The revolutionaries of 1789 rediscovered in neoclassicism the glories attending the birth of the Enlightenment, while Napoleon projected upon it the glorious dream of imperial Rome. Some French authors who, in different ways, inaugurated what would be known as Romanticism chose exile (René de Chateaubriand to England) or were exiled (Germaine de Staël in Switzerland and Germany). Jean-Jacques Rousseau's influence also had more impact across the Rhine than in France. The theories of the sublime that accompanied the emergence of Romanticism circulated freely in England and Germany where they often took on a counter-revolutionary aspect, and they comprised a new aesthetic that was, in effect, censored in France. Edmund Burke's *Philosophical Inquiry into the Origin of Our Ideas of the Sublime and the Beautiful* (1757) had spread widely at the end of the century: after influencing Diderot, the idea of the sublime would nourish the reflections of Immanuel Kant (*Critique of Judgment*, 1790), Friedrich Schiller (*On the Sublime*, 1793, and *Concerning the Sublime*, 1798), and Johann Gottfried Herder (*Kalligone*, 1800). Yet as this concept voyaged through space and time (time marked by the French Revolution), it underwent a sea change. Burke's sublime, based on emotion, bears the impress of sensualism: the sublime is nothing more for him than an effect, born of a shock that nature imprints on the senses. Kant critiqued this conception and gave it an idealist slant. What remained for Burke a matter of physiology must now be thought of in aesthetic terms, but as an aesthetic that engages a sense of negativity inscribed within the feeling and consciousness of humanity's deficiency in the face of its surroundings (nature, cosmos, God). Certainly, the experience of human finitude is what allows humanity to transcend the senses ('*Sublime is what even to be able to think proves that the mind has a power surpassing any standard of sense*').[8] But this experience shades easily into a sorrowful feeling – despondency before an unattainable truth, abnegation in the face of a reality in which one cannot participate.

Obviously, the *mélodie*, which freely embraced a minor aesthetic (short form, less demonstrative literary subjects), distanced itself from the 'delicious terror' that, according to Burke's own expression, lay at the heart of the sublime, a major category of Romanticism that permeated Romantic opera from Gaetano Donizetti's *Lucia di Lammermoor* to Hector Berlioz's *La damnation de Faust* (this also marks a divergence from the *romance*, a genre more attuned to the spirit of the times, which had become tainted with the sublime during the Reign of Terror). Nevertheless, the *mélodie* participated in the modernist rupture that developed out of the aesthetic crisis out of which it was born – in part, as in the *Lied*, through the experience of loss (the theme of the dead beloved, of absence), but also in the radical transformation of meaning. The self that sings is no longer the spokesman for a community; it is not the 'voices of the nations in songs' disclosed by Herder, the grand deeds of the ballads that comprised the moralising historic mythology and geopolitical dreams of a nation, or the 'soul' that across the Rhine could join in a collective religious song, the chorale, as in Schubert's 'Ave Maria' or many of Brahms' religious *Lieder*.[9] The self that reveals itself in the *mélodie* is an interpreter: he or she delivers the poem, expresses himself or herself in delivering the poem. He or she indistinctly delivers a poem that, above all, speaks of poetry itself since it removes everything serious (the grandiose, grandiloquent, and pathetic) that could anchor it to thematic subjects.

Poetic Revival

Contrary to what one might imagine, Romantic literature fashioned itself after prose works of a philosophical bent. Chateaubriand, Madame de Staël, Benjamin Constant, Senancour – so many authors explored the modern world, with its tragic character and flaws, in essays and novels. Not until 1820 with Alphonse de Lamartine (and Marceline Desbordes-Valmore in roughly the same years) did poetry return to the French landscape, and it returned under a completely new guise:

That which, in our view, marks the distinction and importance of Lamartine is that at the moment in which poetry had vanished from sight and after at least two centuries of 'functionality' in French verse – between the bedside and the salon, the backstreets and the Académie – he revived the demands of poetry and restored its serious nature. Shattering precisely that which hitherto had allowed it to function superficially above its still cadaver, he began from the premise that poetry was dead – that it no longer existed, that one must begin anew from this death and silence, from its absence or its chattering counterfeit (neoclassical poetry, descriptive or didactic, the conventionally lyrical). Language was no more. A new one must thus be found. In this condition, Lamartine's intervention could hardly be other than radical, as indeed it was.[10]

His *Méditations poétiques* (1820) aimed to invest this sclerotic form with delicate movement. The 1849 preface noted their novelty: 'I am the first who has brought poetry down from Parnassus, who has given to what one called the Muse not a lyre with seven conventional strings but the very fibres of the human heart, touched and stirred by the uncountable frissons of the soul and nature'. Poetry would henceforth be something created outside the rhetorical forms, beyond the rules and customary practice of what had passed for verse art in the previous century. It would also seek to assuage the uncertainty and wavering of the shivering self before whom the chasm opened in 1789. In Lamartine, the mystic exaltations no longer return to religious certainties, but are ventures beyond. For him the infinite opens onto the void, enthusiasm onto exhaustion or dispossession. The themes themselves, seemingly spiritual, vaporous, or amorous, remain vague. The poem that might be seen as the touchstone of his poetics, 'Le lac', culminates in the emergence of a word prior to language (a groan, a sigh) that succeeds in suspending the laws governing the material world. The result is a distancing from psychological reference (prosopopoeia instead of direct address, 'they' instead of 'we') and an attention to the poetic act itself (what 'everything says'):

O time! Suspend your flight, and you, propitious hours!
    Suspend your course:
Let the wind that moans, the reed that sighs,
Let the faint perfume of the fragrant air,
Let everything that one hears, sees, or breathes
    All say: They loved!

We should note the evolution of the poem's title, which went from 'Ode au lac du Bourget' to 'Le lac de B.' and, finally, 'Le lac' (Mallarmé would proceed similarly with 'Sainte Cécile', which became the poem 'Sainte' that inspired Maurice Ravel), as the fundamental movement that initiates the ideal – and the practice – of a poetry rent from, or resistant to, the fixed referents that hem in the arts. Indeed, Aurélie Loiseleur identified in the *Méditations* a 'progressive "desertification"', as if the cancellation of the image, just as it emerges, must give free rein to the feeling for the infinite', or again of a world 'less encumbered', 'dedicated to infinitude and effacement', demonstrating the reinterpretation of the sublime as negativity.[11] Lamartine initiated the experience of writing as mediation, that is, as the felt experience (the *frisson*: sensory impression) of a double negation: absence itself, and the lack of an existing form of expression prior to the poetic act. With Lamartine we must think of poetry as the invention of *another* language, a language altered, alternative, 'a language more penetrating, more harmonious, more sensual, more abounding in images, more exclaimed, more song than its usual language', as the poet wrote in his *Cours familier de littérature*.[12]

It is important to note how much this idea of poetry, whether French poets embraced or opposed it, influenced both the *mélodie* and the formal relationship that music maintained with poetry. Even in 1820, Louis Niedermeyer was inspired by the poem 'Le lac' (the song was composed in 1821, published in 1825). Having no other name at hand, Lamartine described the song as a 'romance' or 'ode', but Camille Saint-Saëns underlined its novel character: 'Niedermeyer was, above all, a precursor. He broke the mould of the tired old French *romance* and, inspired by the beautiful poems of Lamartine and Victor Hugo, created a new genre, a superior art analogous to the German *Lied*; the resounding success of "Le lac" cleared the way for M. Gounod and all the others who followed him on this path'.[13] Gabriel Fauré, at the end of his life, returned to it:

> The name of Louis Niedermeyer, for the preceding two or three generations, hardly awoke any memory but that of the celebrated song: 'Le lac'. It is very likely that his name has no other meaning for the present generation. Such oblivion is a grave injustice. Even if we count only 'Le lac' – or 'Automne' or 'L'isolement', also by Niedermeyer – we cannot fail to acknowledge the profound change to what was in France around 1835 the representative genre of music sung with piano or guitar accompaniment ... This transformation appears in the choice of poems, in the introduction of full recitatives before the *couplets*, in the style so greatly elevated by comparison with that characteristic of the 'Romance' of the time.[14]

Lamartine's poetic works also inaugurated a new way of thinking about poetry in France. Based on 'negative objects' (the term appears in Chateaubriand's *Le génie du christianisme* of 1802), they shun descriptive poetry and didactic literature (philosophic, encomiastic, theoretic, scientific). Inscribed within the history of a sensibility, they eschew circumstantial markings and divest themselves of the narrative features that are the fundamental elements of the traditional *romance*. In these works, poetics suspends any collaboration with the general order of discourse. The *méditation* thus wavers between a theme and a poetic genre, and this hesitation shifts the centre of gravity of the poetic act, in large measure, toward the literary act itself, toward poetic self-reflection. At the heart of this self-reflection, the metaphor of music – connecting a religious, mystical, and harmonic discourse to a reinterpretation of the poetic voice – unfolds. It enjoins a specific use of language (named 'song') that tends less to embrace actual music (vocal or instrumental) than to distance itself from the domain of logic and the assertions of language. We can already hear the 'fading' of poetry that would inspire the *mélodie* at its zenith with Paul Verlaine.

It is from this key impulse, introduced by Lamartine, by which poetry reflects on itself and reveals itself through equivocation, achieved by effacing lyrical situations, topical humour, politics, and indeed, at times, by even renouncing the external world, that the *mélodie* derived its aesthetic. From Hugo, it chose the vein mined in 1829 by *Les orientales*, ignoring the political *Odes*; it favoured *Les voix intérieures* and *Les chants du crépuscule*, while neglecting *Les châtiments* or the *La Légende des siècles*. From Hugo, who was all and wrote about all, the *mélodie* discarded both the political odes and the *ballades* of medieval inspiration, narratives that better suit the *romance*, a form itself based on narration. (There are always exceptions: 'Le pas d'armes du Roi Jean' inspired one of Saint-Saëns' most celebrated *mélodies*, but this highly ironic ballad has less to do with grand chivalric deeds than with the virtuosity of Hugo's poetic craft.) The *mélodie* disdained Hugo's grand satiric or tragic political effusions, the epic and metaphysical works, and the fulsome developments, deferring instead to seemingly minor poems in subject and length where verse art seems to play freely, without getting in its own way.

It is this tendency that reappears radicalised under the pen of Théophile Gautier, 'impeccable poet, the consummate magician of French letters' (Baudelaire's dedication to *Les Fleurs du Mal*), promoting an 'art for art's sake' that beneath the cover of poetic play affirms the ethical autonomy of literature's aesthetic sphere. To be sure, Gautier is not Lamartine. Because Gautier no longer needed to defend the territory of poetry, his art tends to shrink to stylistic craftsmanship, and his irony inverts the idea of poetry's liberation: in Gautier anti-bourgeois art remains, in its stubborn resistance to the bourgeois values of his age, partly indebted to those same values. From the heart of this irony sprang *La Comédie de la mort* (1838), a collection that inspired many composers (Gounod, Fauré, Duparc, Chausson) and from which Hector Berlioz drew six poems whose musical setting would play an important role in the evolution of the genre that became the *mélodie*. His cycle *Les Nuits d'été*, composed for voice and piano in 1840–1 and orchestrated from 1843 to 1856, belongs to the aesthetic laboratory in which Berlioz conducted his work. Berlioz renounced neither the somewhat faded art of the *romance* nor even the exoticism through which Romanticism sought through the idea of *couleur locale* to plumb the diverse states of human sensibility. Three years after the publication of Hugo's *Les orientales* (1829), he set 'La captive' for voice and instrumental ensemble. The added orchestra is crucial: it draws the poetic-verbal element into the realm of music in the serious tradition and subtly alters the manner of conceiving its relationship to the poetic material, from specific issues of prosody (already severely mauled, as Rousseau had observed, in the *romance*) to the more general literary quality. *Les Nuits d'été* reinforces and deepens this distinction and marks a key stage in the construction of the aesthetic of the newly emerging genre. Berlioz was attempting a form of discursive deconstruction: his nights are not nocturnes; the poems do not form a suite, thematic grouping, or narrative; they were not even intended originally for one and the same voice. Ultimately, they structure a double space that strives to reveal a quality of language, Gautier's, as it presses forward to confront a musical aesthetic. If *Les Nuits d'été* marks a fundamental and foundational moment for the *mélodie*, it is surely because Berlioz marked it by an absence of programme (contrary to his tendency in symphonic music), an absence that became a privileged space of aesthetic renewal and rupture, insofar as formal invention is emancipated, by limiting the psychological and dramatic scope and intentionality that had fed the Romantic aesthetic prevailing in both France and Germany.

Revolutions in Poetic Language

The seriousness with which French music began to treat poetry is inseparable from the seriousness with which, rejecting the imperious demands and primacy of opera as a career path for musicians, it reconsidered its own future in a metapoetic movement focussed on instrumental music, both orchestral and chamber. The care that Gounod took in the choice of poems and their prosodic treatment must be viewed in light of his demand for a new symphonic conception of the orchestral material in his own operas. This rigour, owing in part to the influence of German and Austrian music, only intensified during the Second Empire (1851–70) and the first decades of the Third Republic. The influence of Schubert, Schumann, and Brahms in the spheres of the *Lied* and chamber music (sonatas, trios, and quartets), or even Wagner in the matter of musical syntax, is undeniable, even if they met resistance based largely on the political rivalry that culminated in the Franco-Prussian War of 1870. The creation of the Société nationale de musique in 1871, with its motto 'Ars gallica', signalled both the renewal of French music and the autonomy that it sought from Italian opera and the Wagnerian models that through the influence of Charles Baudelaire, among others, had infiltrated French music. This society of French composers (founded by Camille Saint-Saëns, César Franck, Jules Massenet, Henri Duparc, and Gabriel Fauré), striving to support French musical composition, wrought an evolution in the status of poetic-musical works that, moving away from both opera and the template of the *romance*, impelled the *mélodie* toward a resolutely erudite art, less bound to the spirit of the salon – structural and harmonic complexity in the piano accompaniment, orchestral development, expansion of the vocal writing beyond the scope of intimate bourgeois performance. But also, conjointly, it involved a search for poets and poetry from the grand tradition of serious French verse: Jean-Antoine de Baïf, Pierre de Ronsard, Charles d'Orléans, François Villon, Tristan l'Hermite, and so on. As the *mélodie* reinvented its relationship to poetry, it became ever more interested in both the works that constituted the history of French verse and the contemporary poets that were lighting its future path.

It was during the Second Empire that the *mélodie* fully shed its old skin, owing to both an evolution in the concept of music and revolutions in poetry. In 1854 Eduard Hanslick's (anti-Wagnerian) essay *On the Musically Beautiful* exempted music from the category of the sublime. His conception of music, which he defined as an autonomous art whose expressivity owed to its own inherent means (and not to pathetic, sentimental, or dramatic effects), inverted the Romantic tendency to saturate works with intentions and effects that were not immanent in the musical material (collective unconscious, transcendence of the medium, emotions avowed or not by an authorial voice, etc.). Two years earlier, this rupture had occurred within poetry with Charles-Marie Leconte de Lisle and his *Poèmes antiques*, whose preface breaks with Romantic conceptions. To be sure, 'art for art's sake' had already granted art its autonomy, but in ambivalent terms. With Leconte de Lisle the break is cleaner: poetry should become a form of study. Inspiration no longer has any place. Poetic writing is called upon to revive, with philological care, the way in which the human spirit manifests itself in ideas and forms. Fauré, laying aside the grand metaphysical pessimism of Leconte de Lisle's long poems, retained only those lyrics where his musical 'Atticism' could find nourishment. 'Lydia', inspired in 1871 by a short 'Latin study' from the *Poèmes antiques*, realises a new aesthetic ideal, hailed as innovative by Camille Saint-Saëns – concision of expression and means; a learned art whose erudition hides behind a mask of sensual discourse; a restrained sensuality that, finding employment in neither a narrative scheme nor a private psychological experience, records the seductions of the linguistic and musical material. We should note that it was by following the formal studies of Leconte de Lisle (think of 'Les roses d'Ispahan', with its constricted rhyme scheme) that Fauré effected an ever-greater autonomy of the *mélodie* from other musical-verbal genres.

Nevertheless, it was with Verlaine that the *mélodie* reached its full aesthetic stature. As often noted, 'La lune blanche luit dans les bois' from *La bonne chanson* has been set to music more often than any other French poem. As Theodor Adorno remarked in his posthumous *Aesthetic Theory* (1970), in perhaps the best summation of the *mélodie*, the meeting between the poet and Claude Debussy gave birth to the very essence of French art, just as the *mélodie* reached its zenith:

> The meaning of a poem such as Verlaine's 'Clair de lune' cannot be univocally established, yet this is not to say that its meaning does not reach beyond the incomparable resonance of the verses. The poem's sensuality is itself an element of intention: Happiness and sadness, which accompany sexuality as soon as it descends into itself and negates spirit as ascetic, are the poem's content [*Gehalt*]; the flawlessly presented idea of sensuality divorced from sensuousness is the meaning. This trait, central to the whole of late nineteenth- and early twentieth-century French art, including Debussy, contains the potential of radical modernism.[15]

Vladimir Jankélévitch began his essay on *Fauré and the Inexpressible* (1974) thus:

> There are privileged moments in history where one sees poetry and music fraternise with each other with the effect of a sudden conspiracy. The poets sometimes seem to write for the musicians; yet, still more often, the musical settings flow into the poems so precisely that they seem born to offer their lyricism and ardour ... and just as *Mignon* inspired Schumann, Franz Liszt, and Hugo Wolf, certain poems of Verlaine solicited equally the music of Debussy and Fauré. This privileged conjunction has come about twice in the history of music: first during the German Romantic era, and then in France after 1870.[16]

Arriving during a period of poetic revolution from which such authors as Stéphane Mallarmé, Comte de Lautréamont, and Arthur Rimbaud emerged, Verlaine appeared at the point at which the conception of poetry was being renewed in a form amenable to music. Debussy, who chased every avant-garde poetic movement, admittedly chose one of the least radical of Mallarmé's poems in his youth ('Apparition'). The poet's work had to await 1913 before inspiring two masterpieces by Debussy and Maurice Ravel with the same title (*Trois poèmes de Stéphane Mallarmé*), then triumphed during the post-World War II avant-garde with Pierre Boulez (*Pli selon pli*, composed 1957–62 and revised until 1990). Rimbaud also proved a belated inspiration for composers: Benjamin Britten, *Les illuminations* (1939); Jean Barraqué, 'L'époux infernal' (*Trois mélodies*, 1950); Gilbert Amy, *Une saison en enfer* (1980). Verlaine's works, in dialogue with the poet's contemporaries and friends, present less audible and visible ruptures. The author of *Ariettes oubliées* was concerned with creating a poetry that could seek, through the failures of language, to register the impermanence of the psyche, as well as the fragile relationship between a fluid consciousness and an equally unstable world. Verlainian song opts for whisperings, little voices, a minor aesthetic, all nuance, which can trace the subtle changes of the heart. With *Fêtes galantes* (1869), *La bonne chanson* (1870), and *Romances sans paroles* (1874), music discovered in poetry not only a sympathy with an expressivity based in rhythm and timbre (and certainly, the fluidity that Verlaine sought meshes ideally with the musical syntax), but also the way in which an art can free itself from its own shackles. With Verlaine, Fauré, and Debussy, poetry rethought itself through music, which helped emancipate it from a linguistic regime that, as Nietzsche wrote, constitutes an alienating edifice of beliefs and ideological systems – just as music reinvented itself differently, freed from the dual constraint of being a pseudomorph of language and a formal rhetoric bound to a syntactic structure (regular phrasing with respect to prosody, and, more generally, the system of tonality). Verlaine imposed an ironic aesthetic of offsetting, of failure, signifying a different human truth, open, hesitant: this little music, cunningly lame, cleverly risky, creates the idea of an art based in sensory experience and realised through its own limitations – the forms to which it shrinks, the inconstant and equivocal nature of the sensations that realise it, the restlessness of consciousness wavering in its pursuit of wholeness. With Verlaine, Fauré and Debussy made the *mélodie* a site for aesthetic reflection, which through the concentration of musical material (economy of instrumental means, rarefaction of effects through an understatement that verges on silence) seeks to free music from everything that shackled it to rhetorical craft. To Verlaine's poems, which say little, as little as possible, or whisper in the silence that enfolds and calls forth poetry, the *mélodies* add the sonorous 'mystère de l'instant':[17] the work embodies the encounter of language with the concreteness of experience – acoustic, vocal – that only touches on a theme (literary, musical) at the very moment when it reveals itself in vanishing.

This theoretical discussion bears directly on performance. Composers from Fauré to Poulenc tirelessly demanded a literal execution of their compositions. The *mélodie* does not ask singers to explain the text by underlining its sense, nor does it need dramatic effects (nothing could be more absurd than to transform the *Histoires naturelles* of Jules Renard and Maurice Ravel into a zoo or barnyard, nor could anything be more tasteless than to hoot at the 'women with large breasts' in 'La grenouillère' by Guillaume Apollinaire and Francis Poulenc).

Twentieth Century: Dissemination

During the first decades of the twentieth century, the *mélodie* became a fullfledged, established genre. As it escaped the bourgeois salon, it became a serious genre that drew educated audiences and, concurrently, became an art for professional performers. As Jean-Paul Sartre noted, post-Romantic authors like Gustave Flaubert and Leconte de Lisle no longer belonged to a generation that wrote for everyone (like Hugo or George Sand), but for fellow members of the world of letters. The same was true of composers from 1870 onwards. Debussy's *Cinq poèmes de Baudelaire* and Ernest Chausson's *Serres chaudes* (on poems by Maurice Maeterlinck), like Fauré's *La bonne chanson*, inspired by Verlaine's eponymous collection, flaunt their status as an elitist art. Written somewhat later, the seemingly simpler *mélodies* of Poulenc remain within the bounds of erudite music, intended for a specialised amateur audience that enjoyed Maurice Delage's *Trois chants de la jungle* (1935) and still had the extra-tonal adventures of Ravel's *Trois poèmes de Stéphane Mallarmé* in their ears. The *mélodie* thus followed the impulse of French poetry, which under Mallarmé's growing influence had fashioned itself according to the aristocratic image of an erudite and, above all, metapoetic stance – which is to say, it was enshrined within a critical tradition. Leaving the salon behind, the *mélodie* like every other form proved susceptible to growing formal experimentation, leading to the generic indeterminacy that overtook it following the Second World War.

After the First World War, French poetry presented a complex situation. The second half of the nineteenth century, so rich in great authors and major poetic works, had permitted the coexistence of Romanticism with its unavoidable figure of Hugo (who died in 1885), the Parnassian movement (a motley assemblage), and the Symbolist currents that combined two opposing movements – a Symbolism that prolonged the mystic tendencies of Romanticism and its quest to recover the echoes between the deep self and the depths of transcendence, and a Symbolism that sought to devise a language responding to the originality and irregularity of the idiosyncratic. The turn of the century and pre-war decades thus appear divided between a return to spirituality (Francis Jammes, Paul Claudel) and a decadentist movement. After the war of 1914–18, Dada and Surrealism burst upon the intellectual, political, and aesthetic terrain of French poetry. Apollinaire (who inspired a goodly number of composers from Poulenc to Claude Ballif, with a detour through Shostakovich's Fourteenth Symphony) forged a new path and 'New Spirit' for French poetry: appearing in 1913, *Alcools* opened with the verse 'À la fin tu es las de ce monde ancien' (In the end, you are weary of this old world). Free verse, emancipation of punctuation, openness to science and technological discoveries, liberation from figural logic (that announces Surrealism) – here was truly invention on the march, which continues with *Calligrammes* (1918), advancing with new formal experiments, typographic layouts, collages, simultaneous processes. After Apollinaire, Surrealism takes centre stage until the Second World War, with an interdisciplinary and international reach. Automatic writing, collective or not, throws into question the notion of the author. The 'stupéfiant image' (Louis Aragon), liberated by techniques aimed at the unconscious, plunges into an experience of the real without bounds or depth, in which representation of the self and world dissolves. Beginning from Surrealism but taking separate paths, daunting personalities such as Antonin Artaud or Georges Bataille unveiled a new experience of poetry as its own deformation. In this lush landscape, it was not André Breton, leader of the Surrealists, who interested composers, but Robert Desnos and, above all, Paul Éluard who inspired them (from Francis Poulenc to Costin Miereanu). Undoubtedly, this was because Éluard, like Apollinaire, preserved amid his formal renovation of poetry echoes of a melancholy sensibility, of a *planctus* through which French poetry and music could together represent the fractures in the individual through the restless quality of a poetry evading what it says.

This fragmented landscape without boundaries, seeking to dissolve its own borders, indeed constituted French poetry and compositional practice. The breach, which would widen over the course of the century, resulted in a growing spectrum of poetic choices and, at the same time, a new formal treatment of poetry. The choice of old poets was not new (Darius Milhaud's settings of Claude Ronsard, André Bon's of Louise Labé), but it intensified. Yet the appeal of foreign authors, whether set in the original language (James Joyce by Albert Roussel, Sumerian texts by François-Bernard Mâche) or in translation (Chinese poems of Li-Ho and Chang-Chi by Roussel, Rabindranath Tagore by Milhaud, Federico García Lorca by Charles Chaynes), like the appeal of political subjects (such as the anti-colonialist *Chansons madécasses* of Évariste de Parny, set by Maurice Ravel), eventually overflowed the banks containing the *mélodie* during the previous century. This eclectic character, incidentally, would become a feature of twentieth-century *mélodies*, poetic-musical works that no longer chose to identify with a genre so strongly connected historically to the salon and bourgeoisie.

Endgame?

On 4 June 1958, in his *Journal de mes mélodies*, Francis Poulenc reported that the *mélodie* had run its course: 'I flip through this journal with a certain melancholy. The time has passed for writing *mélodies* (at least for me).'[18]

Roland Barthes, who theorised the genre in two memorable articles, pronounced quite similarly in 1972: 'The French *mélodie* has disappeared ... because the French abandoned their language ... as a space for pleasure, for delight (*jouissance*)'.[19] Is this to say that after the generation of Les Six (Poulenc, Milhaud, Auric, Honegger, Tailleferre, Durey) and La Jeune France (Daniel-Lesur, Olivier Messiaen, André Jolivet), the genre no longer interested composers? Judging by the titles and generic designations of their works, we would have to conclude that the *mélodie* did tend to disappear. But looking more broadly at musical settings of poetry, it seems clear that this activity persevered and even enjoyed a certain resurgence at the end of the 1970s, after years in which music was entangled in the logic of serialism. Searching for new ways to free themselves from the constraints imposed by poetic material, music undoubtedly chose this moment to free itself from poetry and establish its own syntax. During the last three decades of the twentieth century, however, music built a new rapport with a poem 'between centre and absence', in Pierre Boulez's felicitous phrase: a poem pulverised, reconstituted, dislocated ... This was music in the learned tradition, striving alongside the other arts for a general deconstruction of the rules and genres that had governed the organisation of the aesthetic sphere, a meeting of experimental poetic experience that called into question everything that could define it (verse, typographic configuration, syntactic organisation). From the disfiguration of many reconfigurations, French poetry – whether *bruitiste, faciale, littérale, objectiviste, oulipienne, sonore,* or *visuelle* – ceaselessly reinvents itself in a dissemination that defies the logic of genre. Thus, poetry and music pursue their dialogue according to ever new modalities, and the *mélodie* is heard once again, from afar and growing ever fainter, but always a bit audible.[20]

Translated by Stephen Rumph

Notes

1. 'For my part, here is how I would define the French *mélodie*: it is the festival ground (or song) of the cultured French language.' Roland Barthes, 'La Musique, la voix, la langue', in *L'obvie et l'obtus: Essais critiques III* (Paris: Éditions du Seuil, 1982), 249.
2. Michel Faure and Vincent Vivès, *Histoire et poétique de la mélodie française* (Paris: CNRS Éditions, 2000), 50.
3. Barthes, 'Le grain de la voix', in *L'obvie et l'obtus: Essais critiques III* (Paris: Éditions du Seuil, 1982), 242.

4. Françoise Escal, 'Entretien avec André Boucourechliev', *Revue des sciences humaines. Musique et literature*, 205 (January–March 1987), 133–4.
5. Marcel Proust, *Le côté de Guermantes: À la recherche du temps perdu* (Paris: Gallimard, Quarto, 1999), 1062.
6. Pierre Bernac, *Francis Poulenc et ses mélodies* (Paris: Éditions Buchet-Chastel, 1978), 35.
7. Quicherat's ideas were propagated in Wilhelm Ténint's *Prosodie de l'école moderne* (1844) and Louis Becq de Fouquières' *Traité général de versification française* (1879). For further reading, see Jean-Claude Milner and François Regnaut, *Dire le vers* (Paris: Éditions du Seuil, 1987).
8. Immanuel Kant, *Critique of Judgment*, trans. Werner Pluhar (Indianapolis: Hackett, 1987), 106 (original italics).
9. As Hélène Cao noted in her preface to her *Anthologie du Lied* (Paris: Buchet-Chastel, 2010), Friedrich Nietzsche railed against the cultural heritage of his German contemporaries in *Twilight of the Idols* (1889): 'The German even imagines God as singing songs'. See *Twilight of the Idols or How to Philosophize with the Hammer*, trans. Richard Polt (Indianapolis: Hackett, 1997), 10.
10. Jean-Marie Gleize, *Poésie et figuration* (Paris: Éditions du Seuil, 1983), 19–20.
11. Preface to her edition of the *Méditations poétiques* (Paris: Le Livre de Poche, 2006), 14–15 and 20.
12. Lamartine, *Cours familier de littérature*, 28, *entretien* 163 (Paris: Chez L'Auteur, 1869).
13. Introduction to Louis Alfred Niedermeyer, *Vie d'un compositeur moderne (1802–1861)* (Paris: Fischenbacher, 1893), vii–viii.
14. Gabriel Fauré, 'Souvenirs', *La revue musicale*, 4, no. 11 (October 1922).
15. Theodor Adorno, *Aesthetic Theory*, trans. Robert Hullot-Kentor (London and New York: Continuum, 1997), 151.
16. Vladimir Jankélévitch, *Fauré et l'inexprimable* (Paris: Plon, 2019), 17.
17. See Vladimir Jankélévitch, *Debussy et le mystère de l'instant* (Paris: Plon, 1976).
18. Poulenc, *Journal de mes mélodies*, ed. Renaud Machart (Paris: Cicero éditeurs/ Éditions Salabert, 1993), 61.
19. Barthes, 'Le grain de la voix', 243.
20. See, for example, the *Improvisation-lieder* by Christophe Tarkos and Thierry Aué (1994).

2 | French Versification and Song: Interconnected Worlds

DAVID HUNTER

An extraordinary feature of the *mélodie*'s history is the extent to which the worlds of music and poetry intertwine. Musicians and poets mingled in salons and other artistic gatherings, sometimes developing close friendships. Composers routinely set contemporary verse, at times working from unpublished manuscripts. They were present at discussions of poetic practice and heard their poets' voices. Some, such as Claude Debussy, published (and set) their own poetry, while others, such as Gabriel Fauré, won prizes at school for verse composition. The composers of the *mélodie* therefore encountered the conventions that broadly governed French poetic practice from the late sixteenth century until the mid-nineteenth century not as abstract concepts but as part of a living tradition.

Poets send interpretative messages through their choice of metre, rhyme patterns, and so on. A knowledge of French prosody and versification techniques offers us an insight into how composers used their understanding of contemporary poetic practice to 'read' the poems they set and to inform (or not) their musical responses. The value of such knowledge is underlined in advice from distinguished singing teachers – the famed baritone Pierre Bernac wrote that 'the literary text deserves the same care, the same scrupulous accuracy, in short, the same respect that is demanded by the musical text'[1] – and by modern approaches to the *mélodie* (see for instance Helen Abbott's *Baudelaire in Song*).[2]

This chapter sets out the basics of classical French versification, ending with a brief discussion of free verse and poetic prose.[3] I distinguish French practice from English verse traditions and highlight how that practice was increasingly challenged as the nineteenth century progressed. The transformation of poetry into song remains mysterious and magical, but I hope to offer an aid to analysis and interpretation. All my examples are taken from poetry set by the composers of the *mélodie* and both the original texts and English translations can be found in Graham Johnson and Richard Stokes' *A French Song Companion*.[4]

French vs English Versification

Amid the continuing and at times heated scholarly debates about the nature of French verse, there are some broad areas of agreement. While languages such as English have retained defined points of accentuation within individual words – 'de**bates**', '**na**ture', 'a**gree**ment' in the previous sentence – in French, accentuation within words has become much attenuated over the centuries. Instead, stress typically falls on the last accentuable syllable in any word group – 'un joli ma**tin**', but 'un matin brum**eux**'.

This has important implications for the two verse traditions. The concept of metre implies recurrence, and the classic English iambic pentameter (five-foot, ten-syllable metre) is built on repeated patterns of stressed and unstressed syllables, as in Alfred, Lord Tennyson's 'The Kraken', set by Benjamin Britten (where / represents a metrically stressed syllable):

His ancient, dreamless, uninvaded sleep
 x / x   /   x   / x / x   /

The repetition of such a pattern would become monotonous, so English poets typically introduce rhythmic variations. For instance, 'uninvaded' in the line above might in practice be scanned x x / x. Nevertheless, the metre retains a sense of underlying pulse.

The classic French alexandrine line is constructed very differently. In its traditional form, it has twelve syllables, divided into two equal six-syllable sections known as *hemistiches* by a juncture or 'caesura'. There are fixed metrical stresses on the sixth and twelfth syllables. In principle, additional stresses may occur in any other position in the line; in practice, a four-segment structure is relatively common (the *alexandrin tétramètre*), as in the following line from Paul Verlaine's poem 'Green', set by both Debussy and Fauré. Stressed syllables are in **bold**, while the caesura is indicated by // and divisions between other word groups by /:

Que le **vent** / du ma-**tin** // vient gla-**cer** / à mon **front**
   1 2 3   4 5 6   7   8 9 10 11   12

This line can be said to have a 3–3–3–3 rhythmic structure. But note that other lines in the same poem may have a different structure, for example the 4–2–4–2 of

Et qu'à vos **yeux** / si **beaux** // l'hum-ble pré-**sent** / soit **doux**
1   2 3   4   5   6   7   8   9 10   11   12

Unlike in English verse, therefore, the stress pattern of one French line does not predict the next, and the way in which the poet disposes his or her syntax and word order influences the shape of the line to a greater degree.

Moreover, while in principle the English iambic pentameter has ten syllables, in practice the variations introduced by the poet may reduce or increase the syllable count without the ear being unduly troubled. The underlying metre carries the poem along. French verse, in contrast, with its lack of a regular rhythmic pulse, has traditionally relied on a precise syllable count, as well as features such as end rhyme discussed later, both to highlight its status as poetry and to distinguish different metres. A key question in French versification is therefore 'What counts as a syllable and when?'

Counting Syllables: The 'Mute E'

The main difficulty revolves around how to treat syllables involving 'e', 'ent', and 'es', which have been estimated to end around 25 percent of French words. The following lines by Théophile Gautier, set by Hector Berlioz in 'Au cimetière', contain three such syllables:

Connaissez-vous la blan**che** tom**be**
Où flot**te** avec un son plaintif

These endings – often designated by the term 'mute e' – have traditionally been considered to add a mellifluousness to French verse. Although typically unvoiced or barely perceptible in ordinary speech, they may be pronounced in verse performances and are traditionally given note values in song settings. The basic rules for counting them in poetry are:

- A mute e at the end of a line is not included in the syllable count. So 'tomb(e)' only counts as one syllable (whereas the final 'e' will be enunciated in musical settings).
- In contrast, a mute e within the line does count. So 'blanche' counts as two syllables.
- However, where a word within the line ending in 'e' is immediately followed by another word that starts with a vowel or unaspirated 'h', the mute e is suppressed or 'elided', as in 'flott(e)'. This does not apply to the endings 'ent' or 'es' whose final consonants prevent any elision.

Gautier's lines are therefore in an eight-syllable or octosyllabic metre:

Con-nais-sez-vous la blan-che tomb(e)
 1   2   3   4   5   6   7   8

Où flott(e) a-vec un son plain-tif
1 2   3 4 5 6   7   8

Note that in traditional verse practice, the mute e was considered too weak to bear metrical stress and therefore could not be positioned, for instance, on the sixth syllable of an alexandrine. It was also considered bad practice to begin the second hemistich of an alexandrine with such a syllable. If poets wished to place a word such as 'flotte' at the caesura, they had to ensure the mute e in the word could be elided. The following line by Francis Jammes, from Lili Boulanger's cycle *Clairières dans le ciel*, illustrates this practice, as well as the general approach to syllable counting:

de plan-tes dont la tig(e) // aim(e) à pous-ser dans l'eau
1   2   3   4   5 6   7   8 9 10 11 12

Another issue for syllable counting is whether to count the contiguous vowels in words such as 'suave' as one syllable or two. The rules are complicated and often involve some poetic licence. A practical approach is for the reader to count the syllables in other lines and work backwards. For instance, Ernest Chausson's 'Sérénade italienne', a setting of a Paul Bourget poem, is in an octosyllabic metre, suggesting that in the line 'Le vieux pêcheur italien' the poet is counting 'vieux' as one syllable and 'italien' as four.

Scanning the Mute E

Syllable count matters. The twelve-syllable alexandrine and the ten-syllable decasyllable, for instance, are fundamentally different lines with their own history and structure. Lines with an odd number of syllables also convey significant meanings. Being able to distinguish between the different metres is an aid to interpreting a poet's intentions.

The treatment of the mute e in scansion is also important. Since the metrical stresses in a French line typically fall on the last accentuable syllable of a word group and the mute e is not considered suitable to bear stress, in scansion the syllable is normally counted as part of the following word group, even if this appears to divide a word in two. The following line from Alphonse de Lamartine's poem 'Le vallon', set by Charles Gounod, would be scanned thus:

Un a-si/le d'un jour // pour at-ten/dre la mort
 1 2 3 4   5   6   7   8 9   10 11 12

The pattern 3–3–3–3 in this example may help to contribute to a sense of evenness and lassitude that reflects the poet's exhausted emotional state.

There is one major exception to this practice, typically found in invocations, where the word ending in a mute e is deemed separate enough from the words that follow, by dint of punctuation, syntax, or meaning, to justify being isolated in scansion. The second line of Guillaume Apollinaire's poem 'La carpe', for instance, set by Francis Poulenc, might be scanned 2–4–2 to emphasise the sense of wonderment at the fish's longevity:

Car-pes, / que vous vi-vez long-temps!
  1   2   3   4 5 6   7   8

The Common French Metres

An initial distinction among French metres is between *vers composés* (lines of nine syllables or more) and *vers simples* (lines of eight syllables or less), the longer lines having a more complex structure and being considered more weighty or noble. One theory is that the ear cannot discern recurring patterns of greater than eight syllables, hence the need for caesuras in the longer lines.

The Alexandrine

The alexandrine dates back to the twelfth century. From the seventeenth century onwards, and indeed into the twentieth century, the alexandrine remained the ideal against which French verse was measured. Such is its impact that the line has been seen to promote a particular way of apprehending the world, its central caesura encouraging relationships of symmetry or antithesis between its two *hemistiches*. A line such as

Jean de La Ville de Mirmont's 'La mer est infini(e) // et mes rêves sont fous', set by Fauré, seems to suggest an identity between the boundless sea and the free-ranging nature of the poet's dreams. In contrast, the structure of the line 'Mais, hélas, l'air t'emport(e) // et la terre m'enchaîn(e)' from Fauré's 'Le papillon et la fleur', a setting of Victor Hugo, emphasises the difference between the butterfly in flight and the earthbound flower.

Both of the lines above might be taken to illustrate another idea about the alexandrine – that there is a distinct curve to the line, with the first hemistich characterised by rising intonation and a forward momentum, whereas the second hemistich displays a falling intonation and appears more inward-looking. While these ideas are thought-provoking, it is important also to recognise the alexandrine's flexibility. For instance, the line 'J'étais tris/t(e) et pensif // quand je t'ai rencontré(e)' from Fauré's 'Rencontre', a setting of Charles Grandmougin, could be scanned 3-3-6 to contrast the poet's flat, depressed state with the sudden rush of excitement at his new encounter.

The Decasyllable

The ten-syllable or decasyllabic line was found as early as the eleventh century. It was used in epics such as the *Chanson de Roland* and was the preferred line for lyric verse in medieval times. By the seventeenth century it had been dethroned by the alexandrine, but it re-emerged in the lyric verse of nineteenth-century poets such as Théophile Gautier and Charles Marie René Leconte de Lisle.

The classic shape is 4-6 with a caesura after the fourth syllable and a tri-accentual stress pattern. Clément Marot's 'Chanson XIII', set by George Enescu as 'Languir me fais', is an example:

Mais je me **plains** // de l'en-**nui** que j'ac-**quiers**
 1   2   3   4   5 6 7 8 9   10

A rapid first section is therefore followed by a more measured and reflective second section.

A less common 6-4 form of the decasyllable is also found, but more significant for the *mélodie* is the 5-5 structure with a central caesura. This form of the line was employed in medieval times for song texts and popular poems before reappearing in the lyric poetry of the nineteenth century. Leconte de Lisle's 'Le colibri', set by Chausson, is an example:

Le vert co-li-bri // le roi des col-lin(es)
1   2   3 4 5   6 7 8 9 10

This form raises questions about whether to attempt a traditional three-stress scansion in line with the 4-6 decasyllable or to consider a four-stress reading to reflect the syllabic equality of the two hemistichs. In the line above, for instance, the stresses on coli**bri**, **roi** and col**lin**(es) are unexceptional. But what of 'vert'? Do we pass quickly by, seeing it as an insignificant attribute of the bird? Or do we place stress on the word (as Chausson's rhythmic pattern does) as a symbol of youth and freshness that makes the bird's eventual poetic death that much more affecting?

The Octosyllable

The French octosyllable, or eight-syllable line, has a long history. During the sixteenth and seventeenth centuries it was mainly associated with minor genres, but it re-emerged as one of the most frequently used metres of the nineteenth and early twentieth centuries.

The octosyllable, as the longest *vers simple*, has no caesura, and only one fixed metrical stress on its eighth syllable. The resulting flexibility potentially offers the reader greater scope to discern different stress patterns in scansion than is possible in more formally structured metres such as the alexandrine. For example, in Jacques Ibert's 'Chanson à Dulcinée', a setting of Alexandre Arnoux, the line 'Toujours proch(e) et toujours lointain(e)' could be scanned 3-5 but a 3-3-2 reading might better capture the poet's frustration at not seeing his beloved.

The metre's flexibility also brings it closest to the normal speech patterns of French and may underpin its traditional connections with song.

Shorter Lines

The student of the *mélodie* will come across many shorter lines. Poulenc's 'C'est ainsi que tu es' sets six-syllable lines by Louise de Vilmorin, while both Fauré and Reynaldo Hahn set Verlaine's four-syllable 'La lune blanche', in the latter case as 'L'heure exquise'. However, the most common use of such shorter lines, particularly those comprising four syllables or less, is as a complement to a longer line, often serving as a refrain, echo, or burlesque.

The vers impair

Metres with odd numbers of syllables (*vers impairs*) feature in the history of French verse but were generally associated with lighter verse, including popular song. 'Au clair de la lune', for instance, is in a five-syllable metre (although the mute e at the end of the line is enunciated when sung). Later in the nineteenth century, poets such as Verlaine promoted the use of the *impair* in a programmatic way to create a fluid, musical, and anti-rhetorical form of poetry in contrast to the even-numbered metres traditionally favoured by French poets. His 'Art poétique', which begins 'De la musiqu(e) avant toute chos(e)', explicitly extols the virtues of the *impair* and is not surprisingly composed of nine-syllable lines.

Stanzaic Forms

Traditionally, poets structure their poems internally, typically by using blank spaces and recurring rhymes. They do so to help the reader or listener perceive the structure of the poem; to offer moments of drama, pause, or reflection; and to create force-fields of similarity and contrast that stimulate meaning. The discussion that follows uses a standard notation where a small *a* designates the first rhyme in a poem, a small *b* the second, and so on.

The Couplet

The most basic pattern, which dates back many hundreds of years in French verse, is the couplet or pair of rhyming lines. Fauré's 'Le don silencieux', a setting of Jean Dominique (pen name of Marie Closset), is an example:

Je mettrai mes doux mains sur ma bouche, pour taire   *a*
Ce que je voudrais tant vous dire, âme bien chère   *a*

In traditional usage, pairs of lines followed each other without a break, creating a pattern *aabbccdd* and so on, as in Gounod's 'O ma belle rebelle', a setting of Jean Antoine de Baïf. However, by the nineteenth century, some poets had begun to insert blank space between the pairs of rhyming lines, forming isolated couplets that can be annotated *aa bb cc*, etc. Fauré's 'Quand tu plonges tes yeux dans mes yeux' a setting of Charles Van Lerberghe, follows this pattern.

The notable feature of the couplet is the rapid return of the rhyme, the second line immediately responding to the first. In some cases, this can convey a sense of narrative assurance, as in Verlaine's poem 'La dure épreuve va finir', set by Hahn as 'La bonne chanson'. However, in others the couplet may contribute to a sense of enclosure and disquiet. One celebrated example is Debussy's setting of Verlaine's 'Colloque sentimental', where the couplet form, combined with the poet's careful use of blank space and punctuation, surrounds each fragmented statement and response with silence, highlighting the painful embrace in which the characters are locked:

- Qu'il était bleu, le ciel, et grand, l'espoir!   *a*
- L'espoir a fui, vaincu, vers le ciel noir.   *a*

The Quatrain

The quatrain, or four-line stanza, is commonly found in the poetry of the *mélodie*. It comes in two main forms. First, an *abab* rhyme scheme – known technically as *rimes croisées* – where the strongest punctuation is often placed at the end of the second and fourth lines. Henri Duparc's 'Chanson triste', a setting of Jean Lahor (pen name of Henri Cazalis), is an example:

Dans ton cœur dort un clair de lune,   *a*
Un doux clair de lune d'été,   *b*
Et pour fuir la vie importune,   *a*
Je me noierai dans ta clarté.   *b*

Some literary critics have suggested this stanzaic structure gives *rimes croisées* the appearance of a sequence of cinematic 'shots' and a forward narrative momentum.

The other main pattern is *abba*, known as *rimes embrassées*. Here the return of the *a* rhyme is suspended, and the *b* lines can seem as if in parentheses. The second half of the stanza is also a mirror image of the first half. Tristan l'Hermite uses this form of quatrain in his poem 'Le promenoir des deux amants', set by Debussy, to suggest the sense of enclosure in the dark grotto and to complement the references to Narcissus later in the poem:

Auprès de cette grotte sombre   *a*
Où l'on respire un air si doux,   *b*
L'onde lutte avec les cailloux,   *b*
Et la lumière avecque l'ombre.   *a*

Other Forms of Stanza

Many other stanzaic variations can be found in the *mélodie*, including *sixain* (six-line), *huitain* (eight-line), and *dizain* (ten-line) forms. It is always worth considering why the poet has chosen a particular form and what it adds to the poem. For instance, Jean Passerat's 'Ode du premier jour de mai', set by Gounod, begins with a forward-moving quatrain in *rimes croisées*, followed by a couplet that suspends movement and acts as a fulcrum for the poem, and ends on a more inward-looking quatrain in *rimes embrassées*. An energetic wake-up call is therefore followed by a pause that explains the poet's joy (spring has arrived) and then a more serious reflection on the passing of time and the need to seize the day.

Stanzas with an odd number of lines are less common in the *mélodie*. Apollinaire's '1904', set by Poulenc, uses a *quintil* (or *quinzain*), a five-line form, structured *ababa*, which can be likened to a quatrain in *rimes croisées* thrown forward one more line, ending the stanza in a deliberately awkward way that reflects the new arrival's disorientation.

Three-line stanzas (*tercets*) are also uncommon. Verlaine's poem 'J'allais par des chemins perfides', set by Fauré, is a rare example of a *mélodie* based on the *terza rima* made famous in Dante's *Divine Comedy*, where the middle rhyme of the first stanza becomes the rhyme for lines one and three of the following stanza and so on, giving the poem a powerful forward movement. A *tercet monorime*, where the same rhyme is repeated throughout the stanza, is also found, particularly among Symbolist poets of the late nineteenth century, who exploited its incantatory qualities to suggest states of spiritual impotence and ennui. Charles Cros' 'Nocturne', set by Chausson as *Chanson perpétuelle*, is a famous example:

Puisque je n'ai plus mon ami,   *a*
Je mourrai dans l'étang, parmi   *a*
Les fleurs, sous le flot endormi.   *a*

Other Stanzaic Features

Poets can of course exploit other features, such as punctuation and typographical layout, to enhance the expressive effects of their stanzaic choices. In Verlaine's 'La lune blanche', set by both Fauré and Hahn, the final line of each *sixain* is separated from the rest of the stanza by dots and a blank line:

La lune blanche	a
Luit dans les bois;	b
De chaque branche	a
Part une voix	b
Sous la ramée …	c
Ô bien-aimée.	c

The structure helps suggest the poet's leap into amorous reverie, while at the same time the return of the *c* rhyme as part of a couplet highlights the close link between this reverie and the poet's ecstatic appreciation of nature.

Another poem by Verlaine, 'Spleen', set by Debussy, creates a different effect, the division of what would normally be quatrains into isolated two-line segments underlining the poet's own spiritual dislocation:

Les roses étaient toutes rouges,	a
Et les lierres étaient tout noirs.	b
Chère, pour peu que tu te bouges,	a
Renaissent tous mes désespoirs.	b

Fixed Forms

French poets can draw on a range of traditional verse templates. The nineteenth century saw a renewed interest in these forms as poets sought new expressive opportunities. In this section, I examine two of the most popular 'fixed forms' – the sonnet and the rondel.

The Sonnet

The sonnet made its first appearance in French verse in the sixteenth century. After falling out of favour in the eighteenth century, it was revived in the following century by major poets such as Charles Baudelaire, Leconte de Lisle, Verlaine, and Stéphane Mallarmé.

The French sonnet shows the influence of its Italian origins. Its fourteen lines traditionally have a rhyme scheme *abba abba ccd ede*, although *ccd eed* is also a common pattern for the final six lines. The form therefore combines a pair of quatrains based on only two rhymes, organised in *rimes embrassées*, with a pair of tercets using three rhymes. Unlike the English sonnet, the four stanzas are traditionally separated typographically. Mallarmé's poem 'Surgi de la croupe et du bond', set by Maurice Ravel, is an example of the classic form.

Surgi de la croupe et du bond	*a*
D'une verrerie éphémère	*b*
Sans fleurir la veillée amère	*b*
Le col ignoré s'interrompt.	*a*
Je crois bien que deux bouches n'ont	*a*
Bu, ni son amant ni ma mère,	*b*
Jamais à la même Chimère,	*b*
Moi, sylphe de ce froid plafond!	*a*
Le pur vase d'aucun breuvage	*c*
Que l'inexhaustible veuvage	*c*
Agonise mais ne consent,	*d*
Naïf baiser des plus funèbres!	*e*
À rien expirer annonçant	*d*
Une rose dans les ténèbres.	*e*

However, variants to these traditional forms are legion. For instance, Baudelaire's 'La vie antérieure', set by Duparc, retains the pattern of *rimes embrassées* in the quatrains but switches the rhymes to create an *abba baab* scheme, while deploying an unusual *cdd cee* pattern in the tercets.

A key moment in the structure of the French sonnet is the move from the quatrains, with their two solid enclosed rhymes, to the freer tercets, each of which is structurally incomplete. This transition, commonly called the *volta*, or 'turn', typically sees the poem move from description to analysis, or experience to emotion, as the poet reveals the true significance of what has gone before.[5] Both Duparc's setting of 'La vie antérieure' and Fauré's setting of Leconte de Lisle's 'Le parfum impérissable' give dramatic musical expression to this 'turn'. However, the *volta* does not invariably appear at line nine. For instance, Gautier's 'La caravane', set by Chausson, delays the exploration of the poem's core image (humanity travelling across Time's desert) until the second tercet. The *volta* therefore occurs at the twelfth line.

The Rondel

The rondel is one of a range of forms originally associated with dance. Théodore de Banville was a particularly active exponent of the form in the latter half of the nineteenth century. The basic shape of the rondel is *ABba abAB abbaA*, where the letters as usual identify the rhyme scheme and the capitals indicate repeated lines. Debussy's 'Rondel: Pour ce que Plaisance est morte', a setting of Charles d'Orléans, is an example.

Pour ce que Plaisance est morte	A
Ce may, suis vestu de noir;	B
C'est grand pitié de véoir	b
Mon cœur qui s'en desconforte.	a
Je m'abille de la sorte	a
Que doy, pour faire devoir;	b
Pour ce que Plaisance est morte	A
Ce may, suis vestu de noir.	B
Le temps ces nouvelles porte	a
Qui ne veut déduit avoir;	b
Mais par force du plouvoir	b
Fais des champs clore la porte,	a
Pour ce que Plaisance est morte.	A

The form makes significant technical demands on the poet, who needs to find five *a* and five *b* rhymes. The repeated lines should also add something new to the poem each time they recur, infusing the text of the poem above with a haunting insistence. Meanwhile, there is often a change of tone after the second stanza, rather like the *volta* in the sonnet, while the disappearance of the second part of the *AB* refrain in the final stanza focusses attention on the last line, leaving the reader in a state of unfulfilled expectation that may prompt a wider reflection on the poem's meaning.

Rhyme

For many centuries, rhyme was considered a fundamental part of French lyric poetry. As the author of a popular nineteenth-century treatise on verse, Louis Quicherat, wrote, 'la rime est le fondement et la condition de notre poésie' (rhyme is the foundation and very condition of our poetry).[6] Given the relative weakness of accent in French and the importance of syllable count in distinguishing different metres, rhyme was seen as essential in differentiating poetry from prose. It was also a key element in the music of verse. The poets of the late nineteenth century went even further, viewing the correspondences created by rhyme, particularly 'rich rhymes', as a source of new and surprising meanings.

The core of any rhyme in regular French verse is the vowel, the minimum condition being that the stressed or 'tonic' vowel in the rhyme words should be identical phonetically – for example attendu/bu. Like English, French versification distinguishes between rhyme and assonance. Where consonants sounded after the tonic vowel are identical phonetically, rhyme is formed, for example enseigne/craigne; otherwise assonance obtains, as in astre/quatre. Assonance is found extensively in early French poetry and reappeared in free verse, discussed later.

Rhyme Degree

By the nineteenth century, verse theorists had developed an elaborate classification of rhyme by degree. The categories were:

- *rime pauvre* (or *faible*) where only the tonic vowel rhymes – vie/folie
- *rime suffisante* where the tonic vowel and any following consonant(s) rhyme – belle/immortelle
- *rime riche* where the tonic vowel, any following consonant(s), and any immediately preceding consonant(s) rhyme – passe/espace
- *rime léonine* where the tonic vowel, any following consonant(s), any immediately preceding consonant(s), and any immediately preceding vowel(s) rhyme – breuvage/veuvage

These rules had some inconsistencies. For instance, vent/souvent would be classified as *riche* while ombre/sombre would be merely *suffisante* despite its denser concentration of sounds. So, later a simpler classification based on the number of identical elements in the rhyme words was adopted.

However, being able to identify rhyme degree under the traditional system remains a valuable tool for analysing a poet's expressive intent. *Rimes pauvres* or *suffisantes* may suggest the prosaic or weary, as if the narrator in a poem lacks energy or will. The rhymes in Verlaine's 'Le ciel est, par-dessus le toit', set by Fauré and Hahn, are predominantly of this type. *Rimes riches*, on the other hand, may be used to suggest colour or drama and to highlight the poet's own dexterity, as in Debussy's 'Pierrot', a setting of Banville.

Changes in rhyme degree may also be used structurally to draw the reader's or listener's attention to moments of special significance within a poem.

Leconte de Lisle, for instance, deploys *rimes léonines* in the final lines of his poem 'Phidylé', set by Duparc, to underline the ecstatic erotic climax.

Rhyme Gender and Alternation

French versification makes a distinction between 'masculine' and 'feminine' rhymes. Masculine rhymes occur when the main stress falls on the final syllable, such as horizons/gazons. In feminine rhymes, the syllable bearing the main stress is followed by a mute e, for instance, nocturne/taciturne. Rhyme gender is distinct from grammatical gender – a word such as 'mer' is a feminine noun but forms a masculine rhyme.

Rhyme gender is a topic of real significance in traditional French verse. The presence of a mute e on feminine rhymes, even if not articulated, has traditionally been thought to prolong the tonic vowel and any following consonants, making such rhymes softer and more evanescent, in contrast to the more abrupt and unyielding masculine rhymes. Meanwhile, by the end of the sixteenth century, it had become widely accepted practice for masculine and feminine rhymes to alternate within a French poem, the rhyme gender changing at each change of rhyme, as in the following quatrain from Berlioz's 'L'île inconnue', a setting of Gautier:

Dites, la jeune belle (feminine)
Où voulez-vous aller? (masculine)
La voile ouvre son aile (feminine)
La brise va souffler! (masculine)

The concept of rhyme gender and its alternation therefore helps poets create variations in sound patterns and tone within their texts (especially if one accepts that rhymes of different genders have different qualities). And where the poets of the *mélodie* break these rules, for instance by using only rhymes of one gender, one is prompted to ask what expressive effect they are trying to achieve. Do the insistent masculine rhymes in Verlaine's 'En sourdine', set by Fauré, Debussy, and Hahn, hint that the speaker is much more demanding and impatient than his words might initially suggest? Or does the unbroken sequence of feminine rhymes in Catulle Mendès' 'Dans la forêt de septembre', set by Fauré, help to evoke an autumnal hush?

Final Thoughts

A short chapter cannot do justice to the complexities of French rhyming practice. Classical verse theorists, for instance, proscribed certain practices, such as rhyming singulars with plurals (berceau/tombeaux) or mixing masculine and feminine rhymes (folie/lit). As the nineteenth century progressed, and in their search for new means of expression, poets committed deliberate transgressions of these rules, harking back to early French verse where these practices had been common. They also became bolder in their use of techniques such as internal rhyme.

Free Verse, Prose Poems, and Prose

Early Innovations

Between the end of the sixteenth and beginning of the nineteenth centuries, poets were under pressure from verse theorists, their peers, and their audiences to adopt the metrical constraints and other conventions outlined earlier in this chapter and to shape their poems accordingly, typically by aligning content and syntax with hemistichs, line endings, and stanzas. Nevertheless, many found ways of introducing greater flexibility into their work, although primarily in minor genres such as comic verse. La Fontaine, for instance, mixes lines of different metre in the same poem to vary the tempo of his narrative and suggest different tones of voice, while still following the traditional rules around placing caesuras, syllable counting, and alternating masculine and feminine rhymes.

By the early nineteenth century, poets such as André Chenier and Hugo had begun to weaken the central caesura of the alexandrine, so crucial to classical versification, to create what is often referred to as the *alexandrin trimètre*. The following line from Franz Liszt's 'Enfant, si j'étais roi', a setting of Hugo, would seem to fall naturally into a 4-4-4 pattern:

Si j'étais Dieu / la terr(e) et l'air / avec les ond(es)

Later poets such as Verlaine, Arthur Rimbaud, and Mallarmé took further liberties with what were considered the rules of good verse, creating what was known as the 'vers libéré'. Their innovations included stanzas or poems written entirely in masculine or feminine rhymes, more extensive use of metres with odd-numbered syllables, and increasingly bold displacements of the caesura in longer lines. In some cases, such as Mallarmé's line 'Monte, comme dans un jardin mélancolique', from the poem 'Soupir' set by both Debussy and Ravel, the central caesura of the alexandrine was effectively effaced. However, Verlaine and Mallarmé both generally persevered with broadly traditional approaches to counting syllables and using rhyme to delineate line endings and stanzas.

Free Verse

The stage was set then for the free verse, or *vers libre*, poems that began to appear in France from the late 1880s onwards and continued the move from traditional poetic eloquence and rhetoric towards a more conversational approach. The *vers libre* had many different origins, from pre-classical verse and popular song to the influence of translations of the Bible and poets such as Walt Whitman. Any element of a poem could be varied. Line lengths might range from the very long to the very short; regular rhyming might be abandoned in favour of mixed rhyme, assonance, alliteration, rhymelessness, or enhanced internal sound patterning; the layout of the poem on the page might be subject to radical experimentation (Apollinaire's 'Bleuet', set by Poulenc, is a good example) or its punctuation suppressed; and syllable count became much more problematic through the irregular or ambiguous treatment of the mute e and contiguous vowels.

In Poulenc's 'Rayons des yeux et des soleils', a setting of Paul Éluard, for example, the first eight lines of the poem seem to establish an octosyllabic metre following traditional rules of syllable counting. But the following two lines have nine syllables and the remainder of the poem mixes two octosyllables with one four- and one nine-syllable line. There is no consistent rhyme scheme, but the poet repeats some syntactic structures and words.

Two points are important here. First, just as free verse allowed its poets to establish a personal rhythm and flexible means of expression, no longer constrained by externally imposed rules around line lengths or rhyme schemes, so it pushed many decisions on how to read a particular poem back onto the individual reader, whose decisions on how to segment the text, what sound patterns to emphasise, or how to handle the mute e within the poem can make a difference to how the poem is approached and interpreted.

Second, at the same time, the *vers libre* did not spell the end of regular verse. Poets such as Apollinaire were steeped in the French verse tradition and continued to produce poems with standard syllable counts and rhymes alongside or even mixed in with their free verse output. The advent of free verse did mean, however, that the use of traditional metres and rhyme schemes could now be interpreted as a positive choice of the poet, even a device to locate their work within a particular French tradition. Louis Aragon's wartime poem 'C', memorably set by Poulenc, with its eight-syllable metre and single repeated rhyme reminiscent of the sequences of assonances found in medieval French verse, might be interpreted as a subtle act of resistance to Nazi occupation through its very form.

The Prose Poem

The status of the prose poem has been much debated. From the point of view of this chapter, the interest lies in how traditional approaches to versification can be used for analysis. As Katherine Bergeron has pointed out, the opening part of Pierre Louÿs' 'La flûte de Pan', one of Debussy's *Trois Chansons de Bilitis*, could be scanned as a series of octosyllables:[7]

Pour le jour des Hy-a-cin-thies
 1   2 3   4   5 6 7   8

Il m'a don-né u-ne sy-rinx
1 2   3   4 5 6 7 8

   Meanwhile, a phrase such as 'si doucement que je l'entends à peine' from later in the same piece has the shape of a traditional decasyllable with a caesura after the fourth syllable. Louÿs himself argued that a long training in poetry was required to produce such rhythmic prose. One might conclude that such is the influence of traditional versification that its resonances lie behind such works of poetic prose and continue to provide valuable tools for analysis beyond the realm of regular verse.

Notes

1. Pierre Bernac, *The Interpretation of French Art Song* (New York: Norton, 1978), 3.
2. Helen Abbott, *Baudelaire in Song: 1880–1930* (Oxford: Oxford University Press, 2017).
3. For a more detailed discussion of the contents of this chapter, see my *Understanding French Verse: A Guide for Singers* (New York: Oxford University Press, 2005).
4. Graham Johnson and Richard Stokes, *A French Song Companion* (New York: Oxford University Press, 2000). Lieder.net and oxfordlieder.co.uk are also invaluable sources of texts and translations.
5. See Roy Howat's chapter in this volume.
6. Louis-Marie Quicherat, *Petit traité de versification française*, 8th ed. (Paris: Librairie Hachette, 1882), 33–4.
7. Katherine Bergeron, *Voice Lessons: French Mélodie in the Belle Époque* (New York: Oxford University Press, 2010), 163–4.

3 | *Romance* to *mélodie*? The Trajectory of Berlioz's Songs

JULIAN RUSHTON

The route 'from *romance* to *mélodie*', as if from a simple to a more sophisticated type of song, has been assumed to run in one direction.[1] This evolutionary route relegates the simple *romance* to being no more than a forerunner of the high-art *mélodie*. True, songs generally classified as *romances* were often strophic and direct in sentiment, with singable tunes and simple piano parts; many such songs were aimed at a mass market. *Mélodies*, like German *Lieder*, might be more complex vocally, and in form and sentiment; the independent piano part conveys atmosphere and enhances expression. But if there is a distinction between these types of song, it was apparent in the eighteenth century long before the word 'mélodie' was in general use; terminology remained 'blurry at best, particularly in the 1840s'.[2] Songs of many types and varying degrees of musical richness coexisted for decades; in advertising and concert programmes they could also be identified by titles or subtitles such as *ariette, aubade, chanson, ballade, nocturne, rêverie,* or *lament*.

Songs that were widely distributed in print and published in a format that minimised complicated music-setting were readily classified as 'romances', even when their origin lay in opera. The poem is underlaid for the first stanza, with the remaining stanzas either written at the end on their own or with the vocal line rewritten with adjustments to ensure proper word-accentuation. This format was convenient for periodicals, as the song could be published on two pages for a single opening; more elaborate forms needed more space and cost more for the printer and purchaser.

Yet 'mélodie' cannot be disentangled from 'romance' solely on the basis of form. Some songs designated 'romance' by composers or publishers are through-composed. Forms characteristic of the *romance* (strophic, or ternary 'Lied form') often also sufficed for composers (once the word had been adopted) of 'mélodies'. If it were necessary to distinguish the genres, other musical parameters would have to be considered. Appealing tunes are not confined to *romances*, but *Lied* or *mélodie* suits songs with developments such as repeating a major-mode tune in the minor or otherwise varying it; having contrasted material; and perhaps including some recitative-like declamation. They are also less likely to be governed by symmetrical phrasing. As an example, Schubert's 'Der Lindenbaum' (*Winterreise*) first offers a folk-like major-key tune; in stanza 2 it is replayed in the minor; stanza 3 is declamatory; and stanza 4 returns to the original tune, differently accompanied. Most songs identified as *romances* offer less sophistication than this in harmony, rhythm, phrasing, or accompaniment, or as much complexity of feeling. Yet such distinctions are never absolute, leading Frits Noske to coin the pleonastic phrase 'romantic *romance*'.[3]

Another approach to distinguishing genres is by marketing and social context. If songs advertised as *romances* appealed to amateurs, and might be heard in salons or theatres, *mélodies* might be aimed at professional performance. But many fine 'mélodies' are accessible for competent amateurs, and songs called 'romance' were performed by opera singers in intimate surroundings; Annegret Fauser has referred to a 'promiscuity of genres'.[4] I would prefer to put it this way: within the single genre 'song' there exists a rich variety of types.

Appeal to a mass-market admittedly confined composers' imaginations to restricted vocal ranges and undemanding accompaniments, and the majority of what are perceived as *romances* have proved ephemeral. Yet this type endured well after 1830, France's 'year of Romanticism' and revolution. For example, Pauline Duchambge (1778–1858) composed about 400 *romances* between 1816 and 1840; she sought out poems by Marceline Desbordes-Valmore and other women poets, commissioned verses from Alphonse de Lamartine, and set Victor Hugo as early as 1819. Other composers were equally prolific, but most, unless also known like Adolphe Adam for their stage works, have been largely forgotten. *Romances* poured off the presses in their thousands and were unkindly compared to epidemics of cholera, pianists, and (still more unfairly) women composers.[5]

This chapter focusses on Hector Berlioz (1803–69), who might seem to have progressed in a linear fashion from *romance* to *mélodie*.[6] There are indeed stylistic changes within his relatively small output of songs, including revision for later editions. His work is symptomatic of changing taste in songwriting, anticipating the richness of later nineteenth-century French song (hence the title of Noske's pioneering study). Berlioz's earliest published works can be classified as *romances*; but his songs published in 1830 were titled *Neuf mélodies irlandaises*, although some could well have been described as *romances*.

Example 3.1. Jean-Paul Égide Martini, 'Plaisir d'amour', refrain

Ancestry

The *romance* developed from popular traditions that included the *pont-neuf*, topical songs set to existing tunes.⁷ Opéra comique evolved from forms in which new words were fitted to familiar tunes (*timbres*) until composers began to supply new music, adopting varied formal types for 'airs' including through-composition and *da capo* form. Some of these airs took on a life of their own outside the theatre, forming part of the popular 'romance' repertory. The word *mélodie* was later applied to songs that are *romances* in form and spirit, for their topic is usually *l'amour*, happy, unhappy, or mischievous. That the word 'mélodie' appeared in the title of Berlioz's 1830 collection and was picked up in Richault's 1833 publication of Schubert songs with French texts is a sign of the times rather than of a sudden shift in public taste.⁸ Arguably, indeed, assuming *romance* and *mélodie* could realistically be distinguished, they had coexisted well before 1800. In 1777–8, Mozart composed 'ariettes' for a young professional singer in Mannheim; 'Dans un bois solitaire' (K308) is a *mélodie avant la lettre* which, had it been in German, would be considered a true *Lied*, forerunner of Beethoven and Schubert. Yet it shares a sentiment common to many *romances*: the poem alludes to the mischievous love god.

Another composer not of French origin, Jean-Paul Égide Martini, composed his celebrated 'Romance du chevrier' ('Plaisir d'amour') a few years later (c. 1784).⁹ It continued in circulation for decades and was orchestrated by Berlioz as late as 1859. The poem by Jean-Pierre Claris de Florian is the complaint of a goatherd crossed in love, but Martini's setting is no simple strophic *romance* (see Example 3.1). The tune responds to the text, contrasting pleasure and 'chagrin'; both are set to stepwise ascents, but 'plaisir' rises firmly to the mediant while 'chagrin' is set lower, to an expressive arabesque. In what way, one might ask, is this not a 'mélodie'? The independent introduction and coda have melodic and rhythmic traits not used in the vocal sections. The song is a rondo with episodes, the second in the parallel minor, explaining the cause of the lover's despair: Sylvie, after protestations of love, has changed her mind.

Independent songs and airs from opéra comique that were distributed as sheet music formed part of the cultural climate that shaped Berlioz's musical language. In a home with no piano, he learned the guitar as a teenager; the earliest music in his hand consists of guitar arrangements of piano parts (the so-called *Receuil de romances*, H8).[10] Some of these songs are by well-known opera composers (Boieldieu, Dalayrac); some of the poetry is by Florian, poet of 'Plaisir d'amour' and some of Berlioz's own early songs. Another composer excerpted for the sheet-music market was André Grétry. His *Richard Cœur-de-Lion* (1784) was revived in the nineteenth century; at least two airs entered the salon. Laurette's 'Je crains de lui parler la nuit' speaks of her beating heart (she is in love); it is 'remembered' by the countess in Tchaikovksy's 1890 opera *Pikovaya dama*. The minstrel Blondel's *romance* ('Une fièvre brûlante') plays a role in the king's rescue; the music is intended to evoke a medieval style and was used for piano variations by Beethoven (WoO 72).[11] The distant past and exotic locations are both prominent in poetry popular with composers; they combine in Hugo's 'La captive' (*Les orientales*, 1829) where the singer is a Spanish prisoner in an Ottoman harem.

In the evolutionary story of song genres, Louis Niedermeyer (1802–61) is credited with leading the *romance* on the road to *mélodie*. Camille Saint-Saëns thought he had reached that hypothetical goal: Niedermeyer 'broke the mould of the tired old French *romance* and, inspired by the beautiful poems of Lamartine and Victor Hugo, created a new genre, a superior art analogous to the German *Lied*'.[12] His most celebrated song, 'Le lac', sets Alphonse de Lamartine. It was composed in 1821 and published with a fine title page showing a lone figure looking pensively at a lake; the overhanging branch is bare of leaves and a solitary bird flies by. 'Le lac' exemplifies the romantic attraction to untamed nature. Noske acknowledged Saint-Saëns' more generous interpretation but still considered Niedermeyer's songs to be *romances*, despite features he associated with the *mélodie*: fine poetry, a close word-music relationship, and elaborate accompaniments reflecting the words (including what Noske unkindly calls a 'rather heavy description' of waves). But 'Le lac', too, is a *mélodie avant la lettre*.[13]

The other composer Noske singled out for his 'romantic *romances*' is Hippolyte Monpou (1804–41), born a month after Berlioz and associated with him by Théophile Gautier.[14] Monpou set translations of poems favoured by composers of *Lieder* and well-known French authors who also interested Berlioz (Victor Hugo, Pierre Jean de Béranger, Théophile Gautier). However, the earliest in the roughly eighty Monpou songs listed by Noske appeared in

1830, too late to have affected Berlioz. Noske's classification of Monpou's songs as *romances* reflects a perceived decline of the *romance* type in earlier criticism, without regard to its continuing popularity after the adoption of the word 'mélodie'. A premature obituary of the *romance* by Ernest Legouvé appeared in *La Revue et Gazette musicale* (1837), yet the composer Antoine Romagnesi thought it worthwhile to theorise the genre as late as 1846; *romances* continued to be published and sold in quantity.[15] In 1852, reviewing Berlioz's songs, Joseph d'Ortigue responded to an imaginary query: 'M. Berlioz has indeed composed *mélodies*, even *romances*.'[16] This deprecatory attitude persisted; Evelyn Reuter describes the *romance* as 'a sickly salon form with its tedious couplets, its thin accompaniments, its predictable phrasing'.[17] Far from dead, however, its influence can still be felt in songs generally classified as *mélodies*, including some by Berlioz, and Fauré applied the term 'romance' to his early song 'S'il est un charmant gazon' (published as 'Rêve d'amour').[18]

Berlioz's Early Songs

In 1863, Berlioz published a *Collection de 32 Mélodies*, which was reprinted in 1864 with one addition (hence, *Collection de 33 Mélodies*, H139).[19] Fauser suggests that the selection had its own rationale, but it does not include songs composed before 1830.[20]

In chapter 4 of his *Memoirs*, Berlioz stated: 'My attempts at composition during my adolescence are stamped with a deep melancholy. Nearly all my *mélodies* were in the minor mode'.[21] Yet those that survive are all in major keys, as are all but one in the *Recueil de romances*. They are all strophic; Berlioz used strophic-related forms in other genres throughout his career. Only one is in the minor mode, a song of *chagrin d'amour* from *Blaise et Babet* by Nicolas Dezède (1783). The only hint of an original minor-mode song is the lost setting of Florian ('Je vais donc quitter pour jamais') that Berlioz remembered and used in *Symphonie fantastique*; some of the poem can be fitted to the tune.[22]

Following publication of 'Le dépit de la bergère' (H7), possibly as early as 1819, Berlioz, still in his teens, published six more songs in 1822–3 (H9–11 and 14–16). There are a few existing autographs, but most of these songs survive only thanks to the legal deposit of publications. Three are duets and one with solo voice has a choral refrain. All have piano accompaniment, although one offers harp as an alternative. Some of Berlioz's piano accompaniments can be adapted as hypothetical guitar originals. A later song, 'La captive' (1831, H60A), was improvised by

Example 3.2. Hector Berlioz, 'Le dépit de la bergère', comparison of first and last stanzas

Berlioz, guitar in hand, in the hills near Rome; he then notated a piano accompaniment (the first of several versions) for amateur performance in the Villa Medici.

'Le dépit de la bergère' is a *romance* of *chagrin d'amour* (the poet, 'Mme***', is unidentified). It varies the strophic pattern more than anything in the contemporaneous *Receuil de romances* (see Example 3.2). After three identical stanzas (8 + 8 bars, and 4-bar coda), the fourth diverges at m. 9, reaching an intermediate cadence on the supertonic (E minor). Resolving this expands the second 8-bar phrase to eleven bars, with five in the new coda.[23]

The closest of Berlioz's early songs to the spirit of the *Recueil* is 'Toi qui l'aimas, verse des pleurs' (H16, published 1823), yet it is dedicated to Caroline Branchu, an opera singer and exponent of Berlioz's first musical hero Gluck.[24] The main extension of strophic form in these early songs is the duet 'Le montagnard exilé' (H15; poem by a friend, Albert du Boys), subtitled 'Chant élégiaque'. Its 248 bars comprise two tempi, with sections in the parallel mode (E♭ minor).[25] Stanzas 2 and 7 vary stanza 1, in 4/4; stanzas 3–6 are in 6/8, with 'canons and imitations' (as the score proclaims); there is a melancholy piano coda. Berlioz notates more dynamics than were usual in popular *romances*: the singers are told in stanza 6 to sing *à voix sourde* (in a muted voice), and in stanza 7 *éteignez presque entièrement la voix* (extinguish the voice almost entirely). Perhaps already Berlioz's ambition to write expressive music – eventually operas, like Niedermeyer and Monpou – motivated his stretching of the 'romance' genre: 'Le montagnard' is a through-composed *mélodie* for two voices.

Berlioz either rejected or forgot these early songs, and for most of his student years in Paris he concentrated on sacred and dramatic music. His next songs appeared in published collections. The first (1829) contains settings of lyrics by Johann Wolfgang von Goethe, translated by Gérard de Nerval: *Huit scènes de Faust* (H33) was designated Op. 1, but soon withdrawn, the music being revised for *La Damnation de Faust* (1846). The work was not aimed at salon performance, and only Mephistopheles' Serenade (no. 8), accompanied by guitar, could readily be used on stage; the other movements are orchestrated. Besides a sextet and three choruses, the set contains five solos, two with choral acclamations and one with a chorus tacked on at the end (so Berlioz actually set nine of Goethe's lyrics).

Marguerite's ballad 'Le roi de Thulé' (subtitled 'Chanson gothique') was composed late in 1828 with piano accompaniment; only the orchestral version has a viola solo. By 'Chanson gothique', Berlioz probably intended to encourage a certain naïveté in performance, although he could have been alluding to the raised fourth at the opening (B♮ in F major, immediately neutralised). As in the popular repertoire, the second and third stanzas ('couplets') are underlaid with the voice part on its own; in the printed *Huit scènes*, this layout is also used for Brander's 'Rat' song and the Serenade. Mephistopheles' satirical 'Flea' song uses strophic variations, the orchestral accompaniment developing along with the tale (the insects become livelier in each stanza).

Marguerite's two solos cover the entire stylistic range of the set. The first version of 'Le roi de Thulé' includes a touching piano coda, with fragments of the tune and a deep sigh, carefully notated. At the other extreme is 'Une amoureuse flamme' (no. 7), a translation of the Goethe poem set by Schubert as 'Gretchen am Spinnrade' (the version in *La Damnation de Faust* begins 'D'amour l'ardente flamme'). Berlioz offers no hint of the spinning wheel, instead composing a quasi-operatic aria in rondo form with a melancholy refrain sometimes confided to a solo cor anglais rather than the voice. The second episode, in 9/8, has a flowing melody; the third, back in 3/4, reaches a climax of longing at 'O caresses de flamme'. This is hardly the brand of love typical of the *romance* genre, but Berlioz titled it 'Romance de Marguerite'.

In 1830 Berlioz published *Neuf mélodies irlandaises imitées de l'anglais* (Op. 2, H38), with piano accompaniment (hereafter referred to as *Irlande*, the title of the revised third edition, 1849). Three were later orchestrated. Besides a duet (the strophic ballad 'Hélène') and three choruses, the collection contains five solos, all but the last strophic; the only one of these to be orchestrated was no. 4.

No. 1 'Le Coucher du soleil' (H39), subtitled 'Rêverie' [sic]
No. 4 'La belle Voyageuse' (H42), subtitled 'Légende irlandaise'
No. 7 'L'Origine de la Harpe' (H45), subtitled 'Ballade'
No. 8 'Adieu Bessy' (H46), subtitled 'Romance'
No. 9 'Élégie en prose' (H47)

Except for no. 9, the verses by Thomas Gounet are based on Louise Swanton Belloc's prose translation of Thomas Moore's *Irish Melodies*. Gounet himself composed another setting, 'Les souhaits', strophic, square in phrasing, and with a short, somewhat cryptic piano coda that might suggest the influence of his friend Berlioz, but his song has nothing like the rhythmic or harmonic interest of Berlioz's.

The choice of title for the 1830 collection may have contributed to establishing the term 'mélodie' for songs less popular in style; Noske points to Moore's influence.[26] In the first edition, three songs have the first stanza underlaid with accompaniment and later stanzas with the voice on its own. One exception is no. 4, where only the words appear. In no. 7 Berlioz adjusted the opening of each stanza and made more alterations later. For no. 8 he set the 'original anglais' as well as Gounet's 'Imitation française', using two vocal staves. The English accentuation is risible, starting with second-syllable stress for 'Bessy', corrected in the 1849 edition.

Berlioz specified voice-types in the first edition, which was somewhat outside the norms for the mass-market *romance* (it could limit a song's appeal to amateurs). Nos. 1, 8, and 9 are for tenor, no. 7 for soprano or tenor. The voice for 'La belle Voyageuse' is identified as 'Jeune paysan' which, as with 'Le roi de Thulé', was no doubt intended to encourage artlessness in performing this carefully crafted song. Juvenile male roles in opera were normally taken by female singers, and Berlioz's eventual second wife, the mezzo-soprano Marie Recio, sang 'La belle Voyageuse' (orchestrated) in 1842.

While nos. 4, 5, and 8 could have been sold as 'romances', the atmosphere of the first and last songs lies somewhat outside that genre as usually conceived. 'Le Coucher du soleil', a *Larghetto* in two strophes, has a chromatic introduction closing on the dominant of F minor; a simple cadence establishes the tonic A♭.[27] Harmony and tessitura suggest that Berlioz could have had in mind operatic tenors such as Adolphe Nourrit, or Alexis Dupont who sang two of Berlioz's Prix de Rome cantatas. The voice reaches high A♭ almost at once, but this is used locally as a Neapolitan, leading to an intermediate cadence on G (at first major). Chromatic steps within the piano chords resolve this, and the voice's F_5 initiates a melodic sequence, B♭ minor then the recovered tonic A♭ major, which is not seriously threatened thereafter. The vocal range covers nearly two octaves (C_3–$B\flat_4$). The lowest notes are an analogue for the sun sinking into the sea, chiming with the poet's tender memories and, in stanza 2, thoughts of the afterlife. By way of closure, Berlioz moves through third-related major chords: E♭ to C (not V of F minor in this context) to A♭, imitating the harp by directing the piano to use the 'Grande Pédale'.

Harmonic adventures also characterise 'Le roi de Thulé' and 'La belle Voyageuse'; and the introduction of 'L'Origine de la Harpe' (repeated as coda) boldly moves from G to E♭, taking in a G-minor chord before settling into imitation of the eponymous instrument (see Example 3.3 online). When the melody breaks out of 4/4 for three bars of 3/4, it still flows naturally and Berlioz strengthened the piano cadence for the final stanza. Monpou sometimes used metrical changes, for instance in 'L'Andalouse', but such things are rare at this time. As to form, in the 1849 edition 'La belle Voyageuse' is written out in full, cutting the piano coda from two stanzas and adding the voice (to 'La la') at the close, with a touch of imitation.[28] 'Adieu Bessy', originally strophic, became a through-composed song (a *mélodie*) transposed down from A♭ to G with an elaborated piano part ending with a high-register tremolo.

Example 3.3. [online only] Berlioz, 'L'Origine de la Harpe' (*Neuf mélodies irlandaises*), introduction and comparison of stanzas 1 and 4. To view this example please visit www.cambridge.org/9781316514474 and navigate to the Resources tab

Irlande is a remarkable collection. Fauser makes a good case for its coherence, as against the complete editions (old and new) that print its choral and solo numbers in separate volumes.[29] The last song, 'Élégie', stands apart from the rest: in prose not poetry, and through-composed in two large sections marked by a mid-point cadence (m. 32). Throughout *Irlande* the piano offers more than mere support, but here it aspires to powerful effects; persistent tremolo invites the orchestration Berlioz never undertook, although in 1860 he orchestrated the no less demanding piano part of Schubert's 'Erlkönig'. He had composed 'Élégie' in an access of love and despair associated with the Irish actress Harriet Smithson; such was the strength of his feelings that Berlioz could not abide hearing it sung. For the 1849 edition he added a second vocal staff with English underlay, though still with errors such as three pitches for 'a-do-res'. He added a lengthy explanation of the text, replacing a covert dedication to Smithson with one to the memory of the Irish patriot Robert Emmet, whose speech prior to his execution had inspired Moore's poem.[30]

Berlioz after 1830

Thanks to the publisher Richault and the advocacy of Nourrit, Schubert's songs became known in French in the 1830s, but Berlioz had already reached maturity in the collections just discussed. He distanced himself from any comparison, writing in 1852 to Joseph d'Ortigue that his own songs 'have nothing in common with the form or style of Schubert's'. D'Ortigue echoed this in his review: 'There is nothing in common between Berlioz's songs and those of Rossini or Schubert'.[31]

After *Irlande*, Berlioz's songwriting could be considered to have retrenched a little, as the next few songs, readily classifiable as *romances*, were published on their own. The most successful was 'La captive' (H60), originally (1831) in four identical strophes. Composed a little earlier, 'Le pêcheur' (subtitled 'Ballade imitée de Goethe') was incorporated into *Lélio, ou le retour à la vie* (H55), the sequel to *Symphonie fantastique*; it is accompanied by piano, although the other pieces in *Lélio* are orchestral. In this song, each stanza starts alike and changes from minor to major at mid-point, but after two almost identical stanzas the accompaniment becomes increasingly agitated as the fisherman is lured to his watery doom (see Example 3.4). The third stanza introduces an operatic tessitura (reaching $C\sharp_5$ in head voice), and the fourth graphically illustrates the fisherman's disappearance, omitting five bars. The details of tempo variation and

Example 3.4. Berlioz, 'Le pêcheur', comparison of stanzas, beginning at m. 11

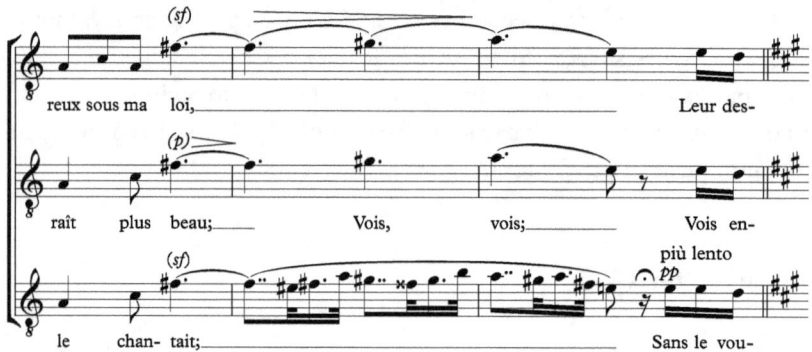

dynamics further distance the song from the norms of the *romance*. 'Le pêcheur' was performed professionally, in *Lélio* by Dupont (1832) and on its own by Boulanger in the Hôtel de *L'Europe littéraire* (1833).

When Berlioz revisited the pastoral topic late in 1833, he may have known that Ricour would shortly publish the first issue of a new periodical, *La Romance* (1 January 1834). 'Le jeune pâtre breton' (H65, also known as 'Le paysan breton') was perhaps intended for Ricour, but it was 'Les champs' (H67, poem by Béranger) that appeared in *La Romance* in 1834.

Example 3.4. *(cont.)*

The six-stanza love-song 'Je crois en vous' (also 1834; H70, poem by Guérin) was subtitled 'Romance' and published in *La Protée* the same year.[32] Berlioz was apparently in demand despite his reputation as a difficult modernist. Duplessis, editor of *La Protée*, seems to have asked for another Guérin setting, but on 10 October 1834 Berlioz turned down the invitation:

I've tried and failed to find something passable for the pretty Romance by M. Guérin, but can think of nothing that isn't ordinary or shapeless. Each stanza has a character suited to different music, which would make the piece too lengthy for your journal's publication format ... Such pieces should be, as it were, improvised, and if one doesn't succeed at the first attempt, it is better simply to give up.[33]

This may have been a polite way to reject an unappealing poem, given that 'Je crois en vous' had been carefully sketched.[34] But Berlioz never revised it as he did other songs; instead, he used the tune in *Benvenuto Cellini* in the overture and the Carnival scene where, headed 'ariette', it is played by a cor anglais.

'La captive' soon attracted professionals and was subjected to the greatest elaboration of any Berlioz song. The version published in 1833 has an optional cello part; it was sung in the Hôtel de *L'Europe littéraire* by Mme Kunze-Boulanger. Berlioz was not the only composer to use more than a piano, and a solo horn was added to 'Le jeune pâtre breton'.[35] When orchestrated, 'Le jeune pâtre' and 'La captive' were sung by Cornélie Falcon of the Opéra (November 1834). An orchestral version of 'La captive' was sung by Pauline Viardot in London (1848), apparently in E major, the song's original key, but the score published by Richault as Op. 12 (1848, H60 F) is in D, perhaps transposed to suit the contralto Émilie Widemann who sang it in Paris; nevertheless, it was advertised as 'chantée par Madame Viardot'. The subtitle 'Orientale' is replaced by 'Rêverie', and this elaborate version was rearranged for voice and piano, a simple *romance* that had evolved into a through-composed *mélodie*. In this version, the voice part is sometimes declamatory, with the tune played instrumentally; one stanza adopts the rhythm of a bolero.[36] Monpou may have influenced this example of the French attraction to Spanish idiom; his setting of 'La captive' appears feeble in comparison to Berlioz's, but a bolero rhythm appears in 'L'andalouse' (1830, poem by Alfred de Musset), which created a minor scandal gleefully reported by Gautier.[37]

Berlioz took advantage of publication opportunities to turn choral works with orchestra into songs with piano. These include another of Hugo's *Orientales*, 'Sara la baigneuse' (H69; the definitive version has three choral groups); another Béranger setting, 'Le cinq mai' (H74), originally a bass solo with chorus; and the 1846 cantata *Chant des chemins de fer* (H110), which has two solo 'couplets' between the refrains, like the choruses in *Irlande*. But although these appeared in his final collection (*33 Mélodies*), they are not songs in the normal sense, and the piano versions are reductions of works conceived orchestrally.

Les Nuits d'été

For his closest-knit song collection, Berlioz took six poems from Théophile Gautier's *La Comédie de la mort* (1838). It is the only group of songs in which Berlioz set poems by one author in the original language. Some of the same poems were set by others, no. 3 by Monpou, for whom the poem may have been written, and later by Félicien David, Charles Gounod (who also set no. 6), and Fauré. No. 4 was set by Bizet and no. 5 by Duparc. *Les Nuits d'été* (Op. 7, H81) was published for voice and piano in 1841, dedicated to a fellow-composer, Louise Bertin. Gautier's titles, if different, are in parentheses:

No. 1 'Villanelle' (H81; 'Villanelle rhythmique'); A major
No. 2 'Le Spectre de la rose' (H83); D major, orchestrated in B
No. 3 'Sur les Lagunes' (H84, 'Lamento'); G minor, orchestrated in F
No. 4 'Absence' (H85, orchestrated 1843); F♯ major
No. 5 'Au Cimetière' subtitled 'Clair de lune' (H86; 'Lamento'); D major
No. 6 'L'île inconnue' (H87; 'Barcarolle'); F major

The title and nature of *Les Nuits d'été* (Summer Nights) have been puzzled over. The only explicitly seasonal song is no. 1, anticipating the coming of spring; the others are at least compatible with summer (in no. 2 the window is open and nos. 3–5 suggest outdoor settings). The set arguably forms a short cycle, with a hidden narrative. Interpretation in relation to Berlioz's love-life is speculative, but by 1840 his marriage to Harriet Smithson was in difficulties and he was probably starting his affair with the mezzo-soprano Marie Recio.[38] The songs proceed from love in spring and the summer season of balls (nos. 1–2), by songs of love lost through absence and death (nos. 3–5), to an exuberant conclusion suggesting new love. The set is cyclic in that both versions, piano and orchestral, have striking but coherent key-schemes; there are several motivic connections, most apparent between nos. 3 and 6, reanimating motifs of lament to suit the more cheerful context of the last song.[39] 'Absence' was orchestrated in 1843 with a dedication to Recio, but the rest were orchestrated later and published by Rieter-Biedermann (Winterthur) in 1856, with each song dedicated to a professional singer with whom Berlioz had worked in Germany; these were of different voice-types. So it is problematic for one singer, rather than three or four, to sing the orchestral version in the published keys, although transposition poses risks for some of Berlioz's sensitive instrumentation.

By any criteria – formal, melodic, harmonic, word-setting, embodied emotion – *Les Nuits d'été* constitutes Berlioz's supreme achievement in this *mélodie* genre. The songs are all through-composed, reinterpreting established formal patterns in various ways. The autograph of 'Villanelle' shows him notating a strictly strophic song, then deciding on strophic variations. He subtly altered the melody and harmony of the second and third stanzas, preceding the latter by a short interlude and changing its intermediate cadence from C♯ minor to C major (the tonic being A); a 6/4 chord (m. 102) secures the new modulation and initiates a fresh bass imitation.

The four songs of absence or loss are all slow but strikingly varied in character. 'Le Spectre de la rose' is an elaborate strophic variation. The introduction (a later addition) and each stanza begin alike, but only the

Example 3.5. Berlioz, 'Sur les Lagunes' (*Les Nuits d'été*)

a) Opening

third stanza ends in the tonic. In the original version, in D, stanza 1 closes a semitone below on D♭. Stanza 2 ('O toi, qui de ma mort fut cause') diverges as early as its third bar, ending with a glorious climax in the dominant (A major) as the ghostly rose tells the sleeping listener not to fear; it comes from paradise and needs no requiem mass or 'De profundis'. Stanza 3 matches the first for five bars, but with piano tremolo, and it has an

b) Refrain

intermediate cadence in the relative minor. Its final bars are punctuated by silences. 'Sur les Lagunes' is no less wide-ranging in tonality but is in ternary form. The voice soon ranges beyond notes of the tonic scale (G minor) and the insistent opening motif is cunningly reharmonised in B♭ and B minor (see Example 3.5a). A refrain ('Ah, sans amour s'en aller sur la mer') sweeps down over an octave and a half (see Example 3.5b).

'Absence' is the only one of these songs for which Berlioz altered Gautier's verse-form. He set only three out of eight stanzas, with the first ('Reviens, reviens, ma bien-aimée') twice repeated as a refrain, resulting in a simple rondo form. The other stanzas form two episodes, variations of each other. 'Au Cimetière' is a ternary form with two stanzas to each section. It is especially restless in harmony; from D major, enharmonic shifts in stanza 2 reach as far as A♭ (mm. 29–33). Stanza 4, when cooing doves remind the poet of the dead lover's voice, starts with a chromatic bass ascent towards an ecstatic phrase in C major ('Sur les ailes de la musique')

Example 3.6. Berlioz, 'L'île inconnue' (*Les Nuits d'été*), mm. 93–111 (voice only)

[Musical notation: Allegro spiritoso ♩. = 96, with text: "Cet-te ri-ve ma, chè-re, On ne la conn-aît guè-re, Cet-te ri-ve, ma chè-re, On ne la conn-aît guè-re Au pa-ys des a-mours. On ne la con-naît guè-re, on ne la con-naît guère Au pa-ys des a-mours." Poco ritenuto marking.]

but returns to D and fades to softly grinding dissonances. The third section (stanzas 5–6) reprises the first stanza; stanza 6 starts like stanza 2 but avoids its highest notes and ends by recalling the dissonances – clarinet on B♭ against the strings' A – from stanza 4.

'L'île inconnue' rounds off the set with refreshing ebullience, its opening on a 6/4 chord recurring to punctuate the freest form in *Les Nuits d'été*. The lovers are together; a ship is ready; but *her* choice of destination is not from the exotic places *he* offers. She wants to go where love endures; he says that place is unknown. Departures from the tonic are picturesque rather than troubling; for the dialogue, she has ten bars in the dominant (C major), and his response is in an ironic minor mode, F with flattened G (not quite an orthodox 'Neapolitan') (see Example 3.6). The accompaniment chatters mockingly (mm. 92 and 94), then breaks into semiquavers (a pair of gurgling clarinets in the orchestral version). In further touches of irony, Berlioz sets 'On ne la connaît guère' to a motif from 'Sur les Lagunes' (compare the bracketed notes in Examples 3.5b and 3.6). Finally, *he* repeats the question ('Où voulez-vous aller?').

After *Les Nuits d'été*

Berlioz's later song composition was sporadic, although Stephen Rodgers argues persuasively for its continued importance to his life and work.[40] The *32 (33) Mélodies* incorporate two collections of short vocal works published with picturesque titles in 1850, *Fleurs des landes* (Op. 13, H124) and

Feuillets d'album (Op. 19, H121). The latter contains three songs, one of them the *aubade* 'Les champs', not as published in *La Romance* but, like 'Adieu Bessy' and 'La captive', transformed as a through-composed *mélodie*. After two stanzas in their original form, Berlioz omitted two and recomposed the last two, so what is now stanza 3 begins in the subdominant, regaining the tonic (E♭) for the refrain ('Viens aux champs'). The last stanza begins dramatically with a touch of C minor ('C'en est fait! Adieu, vains spectacles! Adieu, Paris') to climax over tremolo, before recovering the mood of the first stanza.

Three late songs were orchestrated. The *ballade* 'La mort d'Ophélie' (H92) is Berlioz's loveliest song after *Les Nuits d'été* (the orchestral version is for female chorus).[41] 'Le chasseur danois' (H104) is simpler; only the fourth stanza is varied as the singer realises that the huntsman, his father, is not sleeping but dead (yet it ends with the same rousing chorus). 'Zaide' (H107, subtitled 'Boléro', with castanets) is a touching example of intra-European exoticism. The singer laments her exile from Granada in the minor-key episodes of a rondo form. A song where the piano writing invites the orchestration Berlioz never undertook is 'La belle Isabeau' (H94), subtitled 'Conte pendant l'orage', the thunderstorm reminiscent of Niedermeyer's lake. The title illustration implies a warning of the dangers of elopement from a mature woman (contralto) to young girls (chorus).

Berlioz's last songs are a curiosity. *Fleurs des landes* comprises 'Le jeune pâtre breton', a duet, a chorus, and two settings (with different titles) of the same text by Adolphe de Bouclon: 'Le matin' in D major (H125, subtitled 'Romance') and 'Petit oiseau' in F minor (H126, subtitled 'Chanson de paysan'). 'Le matin' is through-composed as strophic variations, stanza 3 introducing a new melodic shape (as with 'Les champs') and stanza 4 starting like stanza 1 but ending differently (with stylised birdsong: piano trills). 'Petit oiseau' is straightforwardly strophic apart from the rearranged underlay of later stanzas. In this dual setting, Berlioz demonstrates less the separation of *romance* from *mélodie* than of the salon from the 'chanson gothique'. Placing 'Petit oiseau' after 'Le matin' might suggest that, settled in Paris with a mistress, he still hankered after scenes of his youth and his first love Estelle Dubœuf, with whom he had recently tried to make contact.

His lyrical impulse found a further outlet, with a similar contrast between sophistication and folklore, in two diegetic songs for tenor in his grand opera *Les Troyens*: the courtly 'Chant d'Iopas' (Act 4), for which he abandoned a strophic plan evident in sketches for a rondo-like form with virtuosic variations, and 'Chanson d'Hylas' (Act 5), strophic but fading into fragments and silence as the sailor lad, longing for the home he will never see again, falls asleep.

After Berlioz

Berlioz's most distinguished French near-contemporary, Louise Farrenc, wrote little for voices. Others composed *romances* in quantity; some produced more complex songs. Among younger colleagues, Gounod and Bizet, whom he praised in reviews, took a lead, at least in part, from him. He praised Louise Bertin's *Six ballades* (published 1842), which largely conform to the *romance* prototype, like some of his own songs. When Bertin's own poems were set by Casimir Gide in 1851, Berlioz wondered why she had not composed them herself.[42]

The repertoire on the borderline between *romance* and *mélodie* was enriched by foreign composers. Liszt and Wagner wrote French as well as German songs; Rossini and Donizetti produced French songs alongside many in Italian; British composers turned to poets such as Lamartine, Hugo, Gautier, and Verlaine. Extracts from operas converted to *romances* for the salon included selections from Meyerbeer who also published song collections; Berlioz praised the latter in 1835, finding in one of them a certain 'naïveté gothique' suited to its quasi-medieval topic.[43]

In conclusion, I return to my opening thoughts. The path from *romance* to *mélodie* is not a direct 'progress'. Songs from around 1800 and earlier hint at musical elements later associated with the 'romantic *romance*' and romantic cultivation of the *Lied* (in translation) and *mélodie*. French developments ran parallel to those in other countries with an art song tradition, like Germany and Britain (where the native tradition was strengthened by Haydn's *English Canzonets*). In short, *romance* and *mélodie* coexisted from the later eighteenth century through the nineteenth and are in many cases indistinguishable. But while Legouvé's obituary for the popular *romance* was premature, it is not surprising, in view of musical developments in this and other genres from about 1830, that a way of composing which privileged a gentle simplicity or (in heroic *romances*) a sturdy diatonicism, and in which a passage in the parallel minor was often the furthest exploration of the tonal palette so richly developed in other genres, should date more quickly than songs that are more complex emotionally and employ richer musical resources – harmonic, melodic, rhythmic, pianistic. Perhaps something of the character of earlier 'popular' genres resurfaced later in beautifully crafted works that enrich the language of song by melding older styles with modern idioms, daringly applied by composers such as Reynaldo Hahn and Francis Poulenc.[44]

Notes

1. Chapter 7 in David Tunley, *Salons, Singers and Songs: A Background to Romantic French Song, 1830–1870* (Burlington, VT: Ashgate, 2002) is headed 'Romance into Mélodie'. Chapter 5 of Jean-Michel Nectoux, *Gabriel Fauré: A Musical Life*, trans. Roger Nichols (Cambridge: Cambridge University Press, 1991) is subtitled 'From Romance to Mélodie'.
2. Stephen Rodgers, 'Miniatures of a Monumentalist: Berlioz's *Romances*, 1842–1850', *Nineteenth-Century Music Review*, 10, no. 1 (2013), 121.
3. Frits Noske, *French Song from Berlioz to Duparc*, 2nd (revised) ed., trans. Rita Benton (New York: Dover, 1970), 12–22.
4. Annegret Fauser, 'The Songs', in *The Cambridge Companion to Berlioz*, ed. Peter Bloom (Cambridge: Cambridge University Press, 2000), 111. See also Tunley, *Salons, Singers and Songs*, Chapters 1 and 2.
5. See William Cheng, 'The French Romance and the Sexual Traffic of Musical Mimicry', *19th-Century Music*, 35, no. 1 (Summer 2011), 34–71.
6. Julian Rushton, 'Berlioz and *Irlande*: From Romance to Mélodie', in *Irish Musical Studies: The Maynooth International Musicological Conference 1995*, Part Two, ed. Patrick F. Devine and Harry White (Dublin: Four Courts Press, 1996), 224–40.
7. Claude Duneton, *Histoire de la chanson française*, vol. 1 (Paris: Seuil, 1998), 409–11.
8. *Six mélodies célèbres avec paroles françaises par M. Bélanger de Fr. Schubert*; Noske, *French Song*, 26, 413.
9. Born in Switzerland to German parents, Martini (also known as Schwarzendorf) Italianised his birth-name (Martin) but spent much of his career in France.
10. H. numbers from D. Kern Holoman, *Catalogue of the Works of Hector Berlioz* (New Berlioz Edition, vol. 25, Kassel: Bärenreiter, 1987). *Recueil de romances* is in Berlioz (ed. Ian Rumbold), *Arrangements of Works by Other Composers II*, New Berlioz Edition, vol. 22 (Kassel: Bärenreiter, 2004).
11. David Charlton, *Grétry and the Growth of Opéra-Comique* (Cambridge: Cambridge University Press, 1986), 230–2, 237–40. There are variations on 'Je crains de lui parler' by G. F. Pinto. Cheng lists piano pieces, not all by French composers, based on *romances* by Louise Puget in 'The French Romance', 58.
12. Camille Saint-Saëns, introduction to Louis Alfred Niedermeyer, *Vie d'un compositeur moderne (1802–1861)* (Paris: Fischenbacher, 1893), pp. vii–viii.
13. Noske, *French Song*, 12–15; the cover is illustrated opposite p. 13.
14. Ibid., 299–303.
15. Antoine Romagnesi, *L'Art de chanter les romances, les chansonnettes et les nocturnes et généralement toute la musique du salon* (Paris: Chez l'Auteur,

1846). Noske, *French Song*, 1–12; Tunley, *Salons, Singers and Songs*, 89–101; Cheng, *The French Romance*, 39.
16. Joseph d'Ortigue, 'Revue musicale', *Le Journal des débats* (1 July 1852). Translation by Julian Rushton, *Berlioz Society Bulletin*, 214 (January 2022), 34–40.
17. Evelyn Reuter, 'Berlioz mélodiste', *Hector Berlioz 1803–1869* (*La revue musicale*, special issue 233, 1956), 31.
18. Gabriel Fauré, *Correspondance suivie de Lettres à Madame H.*, ed. Jean-Michel Nectoux (Paris: Fayard, 2015), 29.
19. Berlioz, *Songs with Piano* (ed. Ian Rumbold), New Berlioz Edition, vol. 15 (Kassel: Bärenreiter, 2005). Each Berlioz song is entered alphabetically in Julian Rushton (ed.), *The Cambridge Berlioz Encyclopedia* (Cambridge: Cambridge University Press, 2017).
20. Fauser, 'The Songs', 121–4.
21. *Mémoires d'Hector Berlioz de 1803 à 1865*, ed. Peter Bloom (Paris: Vrin, 2019), 145. *The Memoirs of Hector Berlioz*, trans. and ed. David Cairns, 2nd revised ed. (New York and London: Everyman's Library, 2002), 15.
22. Words were fitted to the tune by Julien Tiersot, whose version is reproduced in Noske, *French Song*, 97.
23. Facsimile of the first page in Berlioz, *Songs with Piano*, 295. Partial transcription for guitar by Barry Gibson in Julian Rushton, *The Musical Language of Berlioz* (Cambridge: Cambridge University Press, 1983), 61–3.
24. On 'Toi qui l'aimas', see Julian Rushton, *The Music of Berlioz* (Oxford: Oxford University Press, 2001), 169–71.
25. Published 1823, the title identifying Berlioz as 'Élève du Chevalier [Jean-François] Lesueur'.
26. Berlioz's role in establishing the word *mélodie* is assumed by Jorge Arandas, 'Mélodies, Ballades, romances et autres chansons', in *Hector Berlioz, Cahier dirigé par Christian Wasselin & Pierre-René Serna* (Paris: Éditions de l'Herne, 2003), 105–9.
27. Rushton, *The Music of Berlioz*, 176–8. Reuter singles out this song as 'by far the best' in *Irlande*; 'Berlioz mélodiste', 32.
28. The rhythm and harmony of 'La belle Voyageuse' are particularly striking; Rushton, *The Musical Language*, 63–6.
29. Fauser, *The Songs*, 113–18.
30. In the 1830 edition 'THS' (possibly 'FHS') above the title is assumed to mean 'To' or 'For' Harriet Smithson. Berlioz, *Mémoires*, 226–7; *Memoirs*, 71–2. Rushton, *The Musical Language*, 95–7.
31. Berlioz, letter of 5 May 1852, *Correspondance générale IV. 1851–1855*, ed. Pierre Citron, Yves Gérard, and Hugh Macdonald (Paris: Flammarion, 1983), 150–1. D'Ortigue, 'Revue musicale'. This view is supported by Reuter, 'Berlioz mélodiste', 36.
32. Berlioz, *Songs with Piano*, xii–xv.

33. Berlioz, *Correspondance générale, II. 1832–1842*, ed. Frédéric Robert (Paris: Flammarion, 1975), 203; an earlier letter accepting the commission, ibid., 201.
34. D. Kern Holoman, 'The Berlioz Sketchbook Recovered', *19th-Century Music*, 7 (1984), 282–317.
35. Tunley mentions Auguste Panseron (1795–1859), who composed around 500 romances, some with an additional instrument, in *Salons, Singers and Songs*, 61.
36. The orchestral version has been called a sort of symphonic poem; Tom S. Wotton, *Hector Berlioz* (London: Oxford University Press, 1935), 82. See also Wotton, *Berlioz. Four Works. The Musical Pilgrim* (London: Oxford University Press, 1929), 40–4.
37. The two forms of 'La captive' are compared by Tunley, who also quotes the first page of 'L'andalouse', in *Salons, Singers and Songs*, 75, 80–8. Cheng discusses 'L'andalouse' with an illustration of the title page in 'The French Romance', 45–7.
38. Peter Bloom suggests that Recio was part of the inspiration for love-songs composed for mezzo-soprano, although the original edition is for 'mezzo-soprano or tenor'. *Les Mémoires d'Hector Berlioz*, ed. Bloom, 473–4.
39. For a full analysis of the keys and motifs, see Julian Rushton, '*Les Nuits d'été*: Cycle or Collection?', in *Berlioz Studies*, ed. Peter Bloom (Cambridge: Cambridge University Press, 1992), 112–35.
40. Stephen Rodgers, 'Miniatures of a Monumentalist', 123–4.
41. See ibid., 127–37.
42. Berlioz, *Critique musicale*, vol. 3, 498–505 and vol. 7, 440.
43. Berlioz, *Critique musicale*, vol. 2, 337.
44. My thanks to David Charlton who kindly looked over an early draft of this chapter and made valuable suggestions.

4 | The *Mélodie* Comes of Age (Gounod, Saint-Saëns, Bizet, Massenet)

STEVEN HUEBNER

Mélodie and *romance*

Writing to his friend Louis-Désiré Besozzi in 1842, Charles Gounod bemoaned the 'brutish influence' of the *romance* à la Loïsa Puget on the French musical scene, an 'epidemic' that killed the taste of listeners.[1] The *Neue Zeitschrift für Musik* opined that half the goods emerging from Parisian musical presses seemed to be *romances*.[2] Business figures from the same year were impressive: 500 *romances* published as sheet music in Paris, each selling roughly 500 copies at an average of two francs a piece.[3] Complete piano-vocal arrangements of operas with several hundred pages went for between 10 and 20 francs, so the price for two-page *romances* suggests high demand indeed. Payment to composers for a single *romance* was often in the range of 500 francs. In 1859, with two works premièred at the Opéra under his belt, Gounod earned 6,666 francs from the sale of the entire *Faust* score, a mere thirteen times more than a single *romance* payment for what was surely several hundred times the amount of work. Once again, the price differential speaks to demand. There was a distinct whiff of commodity production. Fétis once observed that sheer volume was key to the success of composers in the genre.[4]

The heyday of the salon *romance* was the second quarter of the century, just when Gounod was cutting his teeth in his craft. Composers and performers ranged from dilettantes to professionals. Capsule definitions, then and now, have referred to a web of aesthetic attributes related to simplicity, accessibility, sentimentality, and sweetness. And, on a more technical level, to uncomplicated harmonies, limited vocal ranges, and unambitious piano parts. The form was almost always strophic. In a small treatise on the *romance* from 1846, Antoine-Joseph Romagnesi surveyed a more detailed subgeneric landscape with an implicitly wider aesthetic palette: sentimental *romances*, serious and dreamy *romances*, heroic and rhythmic *romances*, passionate and dramatic *romances*, and *chansonettes*. Different topical associations crisscrossed their way through the repertoire: *barcarolles*, *pastorales*, *tyroliennes*.[5] Some writers suggested a nationalist genealogy with generic roots back to the eighteenth-century *air tendre* or to the eponymous opéra-comique aria type, or beyond that even to medieval troubadours. The critic Paul Scudo described it as 'une forme essentielle de notre esprit national'.[6] As William Cheng has demonstrated, the *romance* was also feminised at every level: in discourse about it as a cultural object, in its putatively easy listening demands, in the nature of its subjectivity, and in its intended performance venue.[7] Cheng's reformulation of an anonymous nineteenth-century critic's description of the genre makes the point, where the question 'How do we take a liking to the *romance* which presents itself in a manner so simple, modest, and without pretension?' suggests as a subtext 'How do we take a liking to a woman who presents herself in a manner so simple, modest, and without pretension?'[8]

Gounod's complaint about the *romance* betrays alarm at unhealthy aesthetic values. His concern rhymes with conventional histories of French song where he himself came to be seen as a pivotal figure in the displacement of the lightweight *romance* by the sophisticated *mélodie*. 'The real initiator of "*mélodie*" in France was Charles Gounod', wrote Maurice Ravel in an important survey of the art songs of Fauré.[9] Gounod's initiative did not emerge out of nowhere. Composers active before him in the 1830s such as Berlioz and Giacomo Meyerbeer have also been identified as progenitors of an aesthetically weighty version of the French art song.[10] For all of them, the circulation of Schubert's *Lieder* in France during the second half of the 1830s proved inspirational, especially through the advocacy of the tenor Adolphe Nourrit.[11] Critical discourse at the time marked the Schubertian *Lied* as distinct, almost a binary opposite to the *romance*. In an encomium published in 1841, the critic Henri Panofka wrote of how 'like all true German artists, Schubert gave himself over to *rêverie*, a precious quality to which we owe inspiration and real depth; it is *rêverie* that draws us away from vulgar daily life and allows us to create our own world ... *rêverie* contributes to the moral development of the artist'.[12] Of course, this was a masculine dreamer. The gendered aspect of Panofka's remarks is difficult to avoid, coming as it does after descriptions of Schubert's supportive male coterie. One can scarcely imagine anyone writing about the French *romance* in this way. If the *romance* was an art of the surface, the implication was that the *Lied* was one engaged with depth. And although surface need not be understood in a pejorative way – especially when attached to constructs of naturalness, simplicity, and the feminine – that is how critics coloured it then and now, casting the *Lied* as a multidimensional object with sophisticated harmonies and piano parts in contrast to the flatness of the *romance*. But the *Lied* was German and the way lay open to create a supposedly analogous French genre.

Such perceptions of aesthetic influence were only one way that *romance* and *mélodie* were understood as genres in the middle third of the nineteenth century. Criteria for generic attribution were multivalent. As Kitti Messina has shown, generalisations about musical characteristics of each, such as we have already noted, yield many exceptions.[13] *Romances* could come in more-or-less musically ambitious forms, *mélodies* in more-or-less modest guises. Frits Noske considered Louis Niedermeyer's 'Le lac' (1820), to a poem from Lamartine's *Méditations poétiques*, a *romance* – a 'romantic *romance*' to be exact – drawing attention to its declaimed dramatic introduction analogous to an operatic *scène*.[14] On the other hand, for Saint-Saëns (writing in the preface to a short biography by Niedermeyer's son) the piece followed a path *away* from the romance that was more like a *Lied*.[15] Here, as always, discursive use shapes genre. Saint-Saëns had worked at Niedermeyer's school early in his career and was keen to demonstrate that his senior colleague had been grossly underestimated. Niedermeyer set poems by Hugo whom Saint-Saëns venerated and would certainly have judged too good for the faded *romance*. In short, generic association of Niedermeyer's salon vocal works with the *Lied*, and the *mélodie* beyond, served Saint-Saëns' purpose well. But on an empirical level, perception of poetic quality is not a very stable generic marker. There are plenty of pieces called *romance* in print with poetry by Hugo. Whereas Saint-Saëns wrote of Niedermeyer 'breaking the mould of the old and faded *romance*', Noske, a mid-twentieth-century musicologist, argued that the *romance* could itself evolve without losing its generic integrity. To flip the coin, twenty years after 'Le lac', a collection of pieces by Loïsa Puget that one could say fit 'the mould of the old and faded *romance*' bore the generic designation *Mélodies* (in large letters) *ou chansonettes* (in small script) on its title page. Perhaps this was merely a generic use of the word along the lines of how we use 'melody' in English, and/or an attempt to recuperate prestige in the face of criticisms of Puget such as Gounod's. In his treatise, Romagnesi sometimes refers to the same piece as a *mélodie* in one place and a *romance* in another.

Reflections on genre feed the questions: was the *mélodie* an outgrowth of the *romance*? Or a strong reaction against the *romance*? Or even a separate generic strain that coexisted happily with it? A bit of all three, with the answer depending on discursive context as well as social and critical frames at play. Whatever the perspective, the *romance* proved resilient as a generic indication in French musical scores and musical criticism even after 1850, and its entwinement with the *mélodie* could be further illustrated. But as argued persuasively by Katherine Bergeron, the construct of genre here has its limitations.[16] This might be cast (in English) as emphasising the use of the word *mélodie* alone, without an article. For Bergeron writes of *mélodie* as an expressive value by describing qualities of authenticity, memorability, and evocation in a conjoining of the *melos* of poetry with that of music. Ravel's remarks about Gounod as initiator of French *mélodie* lean in the same direction. After noting that French art song had no real analogue to the *Volkstümlichkeit* of the *Lied*, Ravel observes the 'composer of [the song] "Venise", of the [opéra comique] *Philémon et Baucis*, and the [aria] shepherd's song in *Sapho* rediscovered a secret harmonic sensuality lost since the French *clavecinistes* of the seventeenth and eighteenth centuries'.[17] There is much to unpack here, not least the nationalist orientation of the remarks: Ravel implicitly seeks to separate *mélodie* from *Lied* by counterbalancing the idea of *Volkstümlichkeit* with the refined and sensitive harmonies of *ancien régime* French composers. By citing examples from different vocal genres, he also implies that the aesthetic values of *mélodie* travelled beyond art song. Just a few years later, the respected critic Georges Servières situated the qualities of Gounod's *mélodies* in the 'elegance of his forms' and 'flexibility of his melodic arc'.[18] In an extended posthumous survey of Gounod's art, Saint-Saëns remarked that from a young age Gounod went against the headwinds of a musical culture where 'mélodie' meant accessibility and working 'with a motif that implanted itself effortlessly in memory'.[19]

Charles Gounod

A relatively little-known Gounod *mélodie* titled 'Ce que je suis sans toi' (Louis de Peyre) gives a taste of the writing that Ravel, Servières, and Saint-Saëns had in mind when they described a fresh voice distinct from purveyors of the *romance* – even though it is strictly strophic. It is as close to 'typical' of Gounod's style as one might imagine, with the proviso that his output is less uniform than sometimes made out. The abandoned lover compares his isolation to ivy cut from the supportive elm tree:

Ce qu'est le lierre sans l'ormeau
Qui fut l'appui de son enfance,
Lui donnant dans chaque rameau
Un échelon pour sa croissance:
Voilà ce que je suis sans toi;
Par pitié, garde-moi ta foi!

Example 4.1. Charles Gounod, 'Ce que je suis sans toi', mm. 1–9

[Musical score: Vocal line with text "Ce qu'est le lier-re sans l'ormeau Qui fut l'appui de son enfan-ce, Lui don-nant dans cha-que ra-meau Un éche-lon pour sa crois-san-ce," with piano accompaniment]

Just like ivy without the elm
That supported it in childhood,
Providing to each bough
A scaffold for its growth:
So too am I without you;
For pity's sake, continue to trust me!

Varied placement of accents within a grid of four-measure phrases is key to the style (see Example 4.1). Gounod reads the first distich of eight-syllable lines to create continuity between the noun 'l'ormeau' and its relative subordinate clause, as in 'Ce qu'est le lierre / sans l'ormeau Qui fut l'appui de son enfance' (Just as the ivy / without the elm that was its support since childhood). The vocal line mirrors this by articulating the line ending 'l'**ormeau**' on the

Example 4.1. *(cont.)*

weak second beat of m. 3, thus pushing momentum forward to m. 4 and a stretched-out setting of 'enfance' on the third and fourth beats to outweigh the mute e on the strong beat of m. 5. The next distich begins on the third beat of m. 5 with a new rhythmic figure that leads to the first line ending on a strong beat ('rameau') and then to the rhythmic equivalence of the rhymes 'croissance' and the earlier 'enfance'. Measure 10 brings the refrain and yet another rhythmic configuration: the speaker addresses the lover directly with local-level syncopation on the downbeat. In this way, the voice takes up the fervent rhythmic figure of the accompaniment as if rhetorically to emphasise the demonstrative quality of 'Voilà'. The bass in m. 11 then initiates a descending tetrachord from the minor tonic with side-slipping common-tone shifts in the harmony. The poetic line acquires greater intensity the second time through because of the B♭ harmony in m. 12. An unexpected shift to a lush ninth chord on the third beat of m. 13 for the pitch E projects the entreaty 'Par pitié', the vocal climax and expressive centre of the excerpt. Such attentiveness to prosody within a flexible approach to symmetrical phrase structure is matched by elegantly controlled register across the entire strophe around this moment: from the beginning, the vocal line repeatedly tests high D, then breaks through to E and descends wave-like from there (with text repetition) through an evaded cadence in F major to the final cadence on low D (now, Schubert-like, back in the tonic major). Gounod achieves notable flexibility and attentiveness to prosody within symmetrical phrase structure.

'Ce que je suis sans toi' is a mid-career piece dedicated to the opera tenor Victor Capoul and written in 1868, a year after the premiere of *Roméo et Juliette* when Gounod was at the highwater mark of his reputation. He well knew that *mélodies* sung by opera stars of the day were one tool to maintain visibility in Parisian salons frequented by influential opera patrons. Gounod wrote art songs his entire career, with a particularly intense period of activity during his sojourn in England from 1871–4, following the Franco-Prussian War. He published one hundred in French, in addition to over fifty in English and twelve in Italian for the cycle *Biondina*, also written in London. Gounod's first pieces in the genre date from the late 1830s, well before he wrote his first complete opera *Sapho* (1851), and they became an important vehicle for the development of a personal sound inflected with influences from Mozart, Schubert, and particularly Mendelssohn. Many of his earliest songs already show the hallmarks of his mature style and include some of his best known today, pieces such as 'Le vallon' (1840; Lamartine), 'Le soir' (1840; Lamartine), and 'Lamento – Chanson du pêcheur' (1841; Gautier). Gounod composed the first two within a few days of arriving at the Villa Médicis following his Prix de Rome win.[20] Through the work of Gounod one can also make the case that the *mélodie* was a breeding ground for a style that transformed French opera. In 'Le vallon', an ageing wanderer returns to the valley of his youth, something of a romantic cliché. Gounod begins by mimicking Schubert's 'Der Doppelgänger' with stark declamation over the very same chromatic motif in long note values. Schubert, however, builds to a bitter cry of anguish, ironic considering Heine's poetry that seems to mock the speaker. Gounod (for whom both irony and bitterness seem to have been inimical) changes the tense mood of the opening to quiet resignation in the relative major. 'L'amour seul est resté' ('Only love remains'): the wanderer then sings to a rising sequence of syncopated octaves in the piano, like the orchestral activity for Faust's declarations in his love duet with

Marguerite. Voice and piano then bring the *mélodie* strophe to a close in fluid counterpoint that the piano leads, a texture characteristic of *Faust* and Gounod's style more generally.

The bridge between *mélodie* and opera is particularly clear with 'Le soir' and the 'Chanson du pêcheur' because Gounod added both to *Sapho* as arias for the prima donna Pauline Viardot. Because he worked on the opera in close contact with her it seems likely that encouragement to include these *mélodies* came from Viardot herself. That *mélodies* were deemed appropriate for moments of high drama, especially the 'Chanson du pêcheur' (marshalled as 'O ma lyre immortelle' for Sapho's suicidal leap), speaks to the genre's growing aesthetic prestige, as well as to a quest for greater lyrical intimacy in opera. Both 'Le soir' and the 'Chanson du pêcheur' were still unpublished when *Sapho* was written. The 'Chanson du pêcheur' would remain so until two years after Gounod's death and 'Le soir' was incorporated into the first volume of *Vingt mélodies* published in 1864. (Anthologising vocal music was common at the time and another bridge between *mélodie* and opera because material cut from stage performance – not the case with 'Le soir' – made its way into such collections.) For 'Le soir', Gounod selected only six of the thirteen quatrains in Lamartine's eponymous poem, thereby undermining its sense. The *mélodie* focusses on evening as a metaphysical moment and the speaker's questioning of a ray of light from Venus, but it eliminates the solace derived from an association made between the beam and the speaker's ancestors by Lamartine. Adhering to a ground plan that he frequently used, Gounod arranges the stanzas of the poem into two groups of three so that the music only repeats once. The initial piano passage serves later to separate the two musical strophes and also bring the *mélodie* to a close.

The *mélodie* achieves an exquisite sense of stasis by beginning with repeated notes on a non-functional $I^{6/4}$ chord (see Example 4.2). In place of dominant harmony, the bass slips down to the third degree of the scale in m. 3 and then to the root of a I^7 chord in m. 5. Voice exchange between the soprano and bass, much as in Schubert's 'Der Wegweiser', finally leads to a tonic cadence and the entry of the voice, *pianissimo*, and also on $I^{6/4}$ harmony. Reference to Venus in the heavens above brings a slight rise in tessitura and a flatward turn that settles on the minor subdominant, another Schubertian moment now deeply evocative of the luminescent mystery. For the final phrase of the strophe (not shown), the vocal line moves to its registral highpoint and then undulates downward for the final low cadence to text repetition, much like 'Ce que je suis sans toi'.

Example 4.2. Gounod, 'Le soir', mm. 1–16

Gounod wrote a strictly strophic setting of Gautier's 'Lamento – Chanson du pêcheur' in 1841, the same year that Berlioz composed his more varied version to incorporate in *Les Nuits d'été*. Much later in 1886, Pauline Viardot herself set the same text, doubtless remembering her association as a performer with Gounod's *mélodie* many years before. And when the young Gabriel Fauré took it up, he dedicated it to Pauline Viardot for its publication in 1877. Gautier reserves special treatment for the refrain distich, 'Que mon sort est amer / Ah! sans amour s'en aller sur

Example 4.2. (cont.)

la mer' (How bitter is my fate, / Ah! to set out to sea without love) by repeating the last syllable of both lines, as if to draw bitterness into the vast expanse of the sea. Gounod evocatively blends the two elements with a wave-like descent through Neapolitan harmony from the high vocal dominant to the low dominant on the final vocal cadence. The Neapolitan produces a morbid colour, as it often does in Schubert as well, and drifts into a sense of maritime openness suggested by the final vocal pitch on the fifth scale degree stretched across four downbeats. Doubtless because the song (at least with Gautier's poem) remained unpublished in Gounod's lifetime, he returned to it in 1872 during his London sojourn with the title 'Ma belle amie est morte'. Reflective of a move away from strophic settings in his later career (though these by no means completely disappeared), Gounod set only the first stanza of Gautier's poem. A barcarolle accompaniment in 12/8 with left hand fifths and fourths replaces the swelling semiquaver accompaniment in 3/4 of the early version. As so often with Gounod, register is carefully controlled on the macro-level: it builds with increasing and calculated intensity to the vocal climax of 'Ah sans amour s'en aller sur la mer' set to $V^{6/4}$, which eventually makes its way to a perfect cadence through (once again) the Neapolitan. The effect of a linear descent through an octave is redolent of the Berlioz setting. Gounod then brings the song to a close by repeating the first two lines of the poem several times ('Ma belle amie est morte / Je pleurerai toujours') in a passage that sounds initially as if it might be the return to A in an ABA ground plan, but functions more like a coda, a persistent afterthought of sadness that drifts away on a single *pianissimo* pitch.

Although he had been writing *mélodies* for a long time, it was the publication of the collection *Six mélodies* in 1855, four years before the premiere of *Faust*, that put Gounod on the map as a master of art song and that has remained popular with performers to the present day. The literary range is broad: two sixteenth-century poets, Jean Antoine de Baïf and Jean Passerat, Alfred de Musset (two poems), Hugo, and one text by an unknown poet, possibly Gounod himself. The sixteenth-century settings participate in nostalgia for the French Renaissance that was later nourished by Saint-Saëns, Debussy, and Ravel. Gounod brushes archaic colour lightly. 'O ma belle rebelle' (Baïf) does no more in this respect than play up mediant and submediant harmony, as in the first vocal phrase, and introduce a syncopated figure and ornament in the final vocal cadence reminiscent of sixteenth-century chanson. Except for a final vocal flourish at the end of each stanza, 'Le premier jour de mai' (Passerat) deals more in pastoral topics than in archaic colour. The Musset poem 'Le Lever', where the lover beseeches his beloved to join him on a hunt, was already a famous *romance* set by Hippolyte Monpou. One measure of the distance between *romance* and *mélodie* is Gounod's virtuosic and sonorous piano part filled with hunting horn figures. The well-known 'Venise' is the other Musset setting, an evocation of the languid mystery of Venice at night, an atmosphere propitious for amorous assignation. The harmonies seem to speak of a site of eternal desire. In the last quatrain they float indecisively between tonic major and minor: just before the final cadence the chords tilt flatward to A♭ in the G-minor context in m. 7 (see Example 4.3). Then, the end of the strophe settles on a tonic major chord that at first sounds like a dominant half-close cadence because it is achieved through augmented-sixth harmony (mm. 10–11). The sense of G major as final tonic emerges through emphasis and reiteration in a non-functional alternation with B-major harmony, a magical melding of cadential closure with endless yearning.

Gounod turned his attention to great romantic poets such as Lamartine (six poems), Hugo (three), Gautier (three), Musset (two), and Banville (two) mainly in the first half of his career. But considered within his entire œuvre they represent only a small part of his total output. He also showed little interest in setting more modern poetry after 1850. Many of his poets came from his own milieu, amateurs and friends, most conspicuously the Catholic writer Anatole de Ségur (four poems) and operatic collaborators

Example 4.3. Gounod, 'Venise', mm. 31–46

such as Emile Augier (five) and especially Jules Barbier (seventeen). A substantial minority of the songs are to sacred texts: Gounod was a man of deep faith and a prolific composer of religious music. Some of the sacred songs were anthologised together with secular pieces, for example the inclusion of 'Jésus de Nazareth' (Adolphe Porte) in the first collection of *Vingt mélodies*, as well as in his own anthology of Latin liturgical music (*Œuvres religieuses de Charles Gounod*, Choudens, 1895).

Gounod has conventionally not been seen at his most imaginative here, but it should be recognised that his music played an important role in practices of domestic piety in both France and England. In generic terminology, one might prefer the term *cantique* over *mélodie* for pieces with sacred texts. 'Jésus de Nazareth' is called a *chant évangélique*. 'Prière du soir' (Charles Ligny) is called a *mélodie*. Here the generic cross-over might be motivated by the subject matter: the speaker beseeches God not with pious thoughts but rather to insure the fidelity of the beloved. Rubbing shoulders of secular and sacred informs Gounod's most famous piece, the Ave Maria descant on the first prelude of Bach's *Well-Tempered Clavier*. It started its life as a purely instrumental chamber composition to which Gounod then added grandiloquent words from a Lamartine poem, 'Le livre de la vie est le livre suprême', in 1853. The Ave Maria text followed six years later.[21]

On a culturally contrasting pole, Gounod set relatively few poems with exotic subject matter and he applied *couleur locale* sparingly. The most famous of these is 'Medjé' (Jules Barbier), styled a 'chanson arabe' in publication but with a musical setting that might have served for a gypsy song just as well. 'Boléro' (Barbier), perhaps with a nod to the Spanish family origins of its dedicatee Pauline Viardot, draws more extensively on Spanish idiom, a rare example in Gounod's œuvre. A tangential connection to Viardot also exists in the posthumously published late song 'À une jeune grecque' because of its source text by the ancient Greek poetess Sappho, whom she had impersonated in Gounod's first opera. Exceptionally, *couleur locale* was a major concern here, but as Gounod imagined was appropriate for a culture from which few musical traces survive. This makes for something of an experimental setting, with a threadbare and static piano part dominated by open fifths and syntactically unusual seventh chords that accompany a recitative-like vocal line.

Camille Saint-Saëns

The kind of inventiveness that Gounod applied to the texture of 'À une jeune grecque' was more characteristic of his younger colleague Camille Saint-Saëns (1835–1921). A child prodigy, Saint-Saëns was already composing accomplished art songs, as well as many other genres, at the age of sixteen. He wrote *mélodies* continuously until the last year of his long life, which saw the composition and publication of his remarkable cycle *Cinq poèmes de Ronsard*. Born twenty-seven years before Claude Debussy, Saint-Saëns outlived him by three. He remained unremittingly hostile to the music of

Debussy and modern syntax more generally, especially the dissolution of tonal grammar. Though a mentor and friend to Gabriel Fauré, he became mystified by the direction of his musical language as well. Writing to the operetta composer Charles Lecoq in 1913 about the musical language of Fauré's opera *Pénélope*, he complained: 'I am making a superhuman effort to come to terms with *Pénélope*. I simply cannot get used to never settling down in any key, to consecutive fifths and sevenths, and to chords demanding a resolution that never comes'.[22] Over the course of his career, Saint-Saëns' reputation shifted from one of a progressive – and by progressive in the 1860s and '70s one should include attachment to the work of Schumann, admiration for Berlioz, and respect for Wagner – to that of an antediluvian figure. In historical narratives emphasising stylistic progress, including narratives about the development of the *mélodie*, the temptation has been to position him before Fauré and Debussy, indeed, on a road that leads to them. Yet his activity in the *mélodie* – 115 solo songs and four cycles – makes other claims for our attention even when it seems stylistically conservative, claims related to sheer prosodic craft, virtuosity, character, and ingenuity.

As early as 1885, Saint-Saëns identified Gounod as a major figure in the orientation of French composers to more sensitive prosody, describing his work as a reaction against the poor text-setting of the early nineteenth century and a return to the scrupulous attention to prosody of composers such as Lully and Gluck, though without claiming stylistic similarity to them.[23] Some of Saint-Saëns' earliest songs show the rhythmic elasticity characteristic of Gounod. In 'Guitare' (Hugo), written in 1851, Saint-Saëns distributes each of four five-syllable lines in the stanza differently:

Comment, disaient-ils,
Avec nos nacelles
Fuir les alguazils?
Ramez, disaient elles!

How, they said,
With our boats
Can we escape the guards?
Row, they said!

The first line launches with a syncopation and no vocal downbeat; the first four syllables of the second line sound like a big arpeggiated upbeat to the downbeat on the last syllable; the rising arpeggio of the third line begins on the downbeat; and the fourth line is stretched out across three downbeats with text repetition (see Example 4.4 online). Gounod himself had published very little secular music by this point, so his influence on the young Saint-Saëns might

Example 4.4. [online only] Camille Saint-Saëns, 'Guitare', mm. 4–13. To view this example please visit www.cambridge.org/9781316514474 and navigate to the Resources tab

have taken place in the informal setting of salon culture where unpublished songs were performed, or through other private contact.

Saint-Saëns' first major anthology, *Vingt mélodies et duos* (published in 1878), gives a good sense of the range of his style in the first part of his career. Like the dramatic ballad identified as a narrative subgenre in the German art song (of which of course Schubert's 'Erlkönig' is the most famous example), Saint-Saëns designated the two pieces in the anthology with an extended narrative as *ballades*: 'Les pas d'armes du Roi Jean' (Hugo) and 'La mort d'Ophélie' (Ernest Legouvé, after Shakespeare). In the first, the speaker tells of a provincial nobleman in the Middle Ages who attends a joust in Paris with his brother: the trip to the capital, the tumultuous excitement, the young women and matrons in the stalls, the death of a page boy in the arena, and the return to a boring life in their château. Hugo's archaic vocabulary and the rapid-fire rhymes generated by trisyllabic lines find apt treatment in the folksy initial melody of this through-composed setting. Adhering to tradition in the *ballade* subgenre, Saint-Saëns spins a picturesque piano part with trumpet calls, sweeping arpeggios for the beautiful Yseult, church-like music to mourn the page, and a humorous whispered *pianissimo* conclusion that takes up the initial melody. 'La mort d'Ophélie' tells of how Ophelia, after slipping into a stream, is momentarily kept from sinking by her billowing dress. The texture is now less variegated, but nonetheless picturesque in its depiction of the torrent by a haze of semiquavers turning around themselves. In a way of writing that was new for its time, Saint-Saëns often doubles the bass line in octaves with the voice part, while the aquatic figuration runs in the middle of the texture.

Saint-Saëns shows similar inventiveness in figuration and texture in the *mélodies* of the 1878 anthology. 'Le lever de la lune' begins austerely with a bare whole-note scale in the piano that the voice follows with slightly more active declamation. The key is therefore unclear for thirteen measures, the music as mysterious as the enigma drawn around the moon in the poetry. Settling into warmer music in B major, the moon then becomes the 'fille aimable du ciel' (the friendly daughter of the heavens). At fourteen settings, Victor Hugo was the poet whom Saint-Saëns set the most, though mainly early in his career. In addition to 'Les pas d'armes du Roi Jean', several other Hugo poems are represented in the 1878 anthology. In 'La cloche', a tolling bell sounds periodically in the depths of the piano. The speaker compares the gloomy resonance of the bell to unhappy love, a metaphor that Saint-Saëns encapsulates by beginning with *religioso* music above the bell and finishing with an operatic melody reaching up to high A♭ as the bass ringing accelerates. In 'L'attente', the speaker urges the squirrel, stork, eagle, and lark to perch on a high lookout to keep watch for the return of her beloved. Rather than track each image, the piano, tremolo throughout, captures the anxious and anticipatory *état d'âme* of the speaker. Saint-Saëns realised Hugo's 'Puisque j'ai mis mes lèvres à ta coupe encor pleine' (published as 'Extase') around 1860, a few years before the young Fauré set the same poem. The two- and four-measure phrase structural predictability of Fauré's piece sets the flexibility of Saint-Saëns' in relief. 'Extase' starts with two three-measure phrases, followed by a four-measure phrase (that fragments two plus plus), and then another three-measure phrase launched by a strong downbeat instead of the expressive syncopation at the beginning of the first two three-measure phrases on the word 'Puisque' (see Example 4.5a). Later in the song, faintly anticipating the Debussy sound, Saint-Saëns arpeggiates the voice along half-diminished harmony, with expressive metrical displacement of the principal verbal accents (see Example 4.5b).

'Le matin' is about the slow crescendo of sounds in early morning. The register slowly opens towards the bass while a descending arabesque from the upper reaches of the keyboard suggests rays of light. The piano creates a wide registral gulf to capture the quality of the early morning sonic environment. The whole has a transcendental feel appropriate to Hugo's Romanticism: in the alternation between F♯ major and D major, a *pianissimo* E♮ in the bass in m. 5 is associated with the latter key and then adjusted upward to E♯. These sounds are at once otherworldly and troubling, and on a strictly syntactical level not something one would see in Gounod. Fauré set the same text as 'L'aurore' to three-part counterpoint and an unassuming vocal part of limited ambitus that may serve as a foil to highlight Saint-Saëns' exploration of piano figuration and sonority, as well as his more dramatic vocal lines. Another fine Hugo setting, this one written somewhat later in 1870 and not included in the 1878 anthology, is 'Si vous n'avez rien à me dire'. It illustrates intersections between the *mélodie* and Robert Schumann's style. Schumann's influence makes itself felt in the dreamy arpeggiated piano accompaniment, piquant dissonances, and the extension of the piece with a piano postlude. The voice part begins on the dominant and does not finally settle on the A-major tonic until the end of each stanza, rather like beginnings over the dominant in the first song of *Dichterliebe* or 'Mondnacht' from the Eichendorff *Liederkreis*, Op. 39. In the manner of *mélodie*, predominantly even note values allow the vocalist to shape the lines expressively around the natural shape of each line.

Example 4.5a. Saint-Saëns, 'Extase', mm. 1–15

Saint-Saëns' settings of Hugo were certainly highlights of the *mélodie* repertory of the 1860s and 1870s, and they were matched in inspiration by a continuous stream of pieces throughout his career (except for a marked decrease in activity in the late 1870s and 1880s). A landmark in this output was the ambitious cycle of six *mélodies* called *Mélodies persanes* (1872) to poetry by Armand Renaud from an eponymous collection published in 1870.[24] Renaud is commonly grouped with the Parnassian poets, a literary

Example 4.5b. Saint-Saëns, 'Extase', mm. 52–5

movement between the Romantics and later Symbolists. Now aesthetic values had shifted to emotional restraint, objectivity, and the cultivation of formal beauty for its own sake. Saint-Saëns himself has often been described as a cool classicist with a relatively impersonal sound and objective orientation, and therefore naturally allied with the Parnassian movement whose best-known poets were Charles Marie René Leconte de Lisle, Théodore de Banville, and François Coppée. In an extended preface to his collection, Renaud argued (with noteworthy cultural sensitivity for his time) that all too often different cultures of the Middle and Far East had been lumped together without respect for their profound differences.[25] His own interest was Persian poetry, which he admired for its beauty of form and emotional detachment. Questioned as to why he did not include more actual Persian terms and expressions in his poetry, he explained that his intent was to create the *effect* of Persian poetry using the French language. Subject matter turns around sumptuous oriental palaces, warriors, enclosed women, and drug-induced dreams, but all spun out through images that avoid cliché. That Saint-Saëns' settings apply orientalising *couleur locale* modestly, less than in a work such as *Samson et Dalila* written around the same time, mirrors Renaud's approach. The first poem selected

Example 4.6. Saint-Saëns, 'Sabre en main', mm. 1–8

by Saint-Saëns, called 'La brise', has the most conventionally orientalist flavour: the piece begins with E sounding as tonic but with two sharps in the key signature to reflect a modal (Dorian) flavour. The bass consists of open fifths in a habanera-like rhythm. Renaud writes a *ghazel* – a strict Persian form consisting of couplets wherein the same rhyme occurs in all even numbered verses – and Saint-Saëns underlines the effect with a minim on each rhyme. 'Au cimetière' creates a sense of stasis with an extended, reiterated A in the bass that grounds delicate chromatic play between F♯ and F♮ above. Modal melismas occasionally slip into the texture in the second song, 'La splendeur vide', and especially in the fourth, 'Sabre en main' (see Example 4.6). It begins with forcefully reiterated half-diminished chords where the functional quality of E♮ as a leading tone gets dissipated in the modal colour of the subsequent melisma. But most of the piano in this song is taken up with martial rhythms that would have served any Western European warrior as well, and a brash *fortissimo* and long piano postlude flirt with Western parade ground bombast. The speaker of 'La solitaire' yearns for her lover with a melody that could have been sung by a Parisian debutante in an opéra comique. And 'Tournoîment' describes the fantastic visions of an opium-derived dream with virtuosic twisting piano figuration that would not have been out of place in a concerto. As the speaker refers to visions of Jupiter and Saturn, the passagework races to the upper reaches of the keyboard for an ethereal conclusion to the cycle, another illustration of the scope of Saint-Saëns' pianistic imagination in his *mélodies*.

French composers after 1850 often took to folding pastiche of earlier styles into instrumental music, opera, and *mélodies*. Saint-Saëns was particularly adept. One thinks of the Baroque prelude style at the beginning of the Second Piano Concerto or the pavane in the opera *Henry VIII*, passages where it is difficult to discern more modern syntax. Strict pastiche is strict imitation, but usually in neo-classical music of the late nineteenth century, Saint-Saëns' included, one might speak of a sliding scale in the number of modern elements introduced. His setting of François Coppée's 'Marquise, vous souvenez-vous' (published as 'Menuet' in 1870) hews very closely to the eighteenth-century idiom of a composer like Jean-Philippe Rameau. The poem playfully evokes a dancer so caught up in the admiration triggered by her graceful minuet that she forgets to execute the last *révérence*. But a more modern style does peek through, ever so slightly: the register on the keyboard is much wider than it would have been in the eighteenth century, the chords sometimes thicker, and some of the left-hand figuration atypical. Saint-Saëns' most extended exploration of pre-Beethovenian idioms is the *Cinq poèmes de Ronsard* (1921). Here the sliding scale tilts more to recent idioms, and in several of the songs the archaic elements seem the exception. 'L'amour blessé' (titled 'Le petit enfant Amour' by Ronsard) tells a story about Cupid running to Venus after being stung by a bee. The music has a modern theatrical quality, especially to depict Cupid's pain with mock seriousness and the lush splendour of Venus' smile, but baroque style is felt in several extended melismas. The first *mélodie* in the cycle, 'L'amour oyseau', sounds throughout like a Bach three-part invention and the last, 'L'amour malheureux', has the easy interchange of motivic material between bass voice and soprano of a Bach minuet.

Georges Bizet

As his career unfolded, Saint-Saëns often enjoyed the support of Gounod, and when he himself became an influential figure on the French scene he returned the favour. Gounod's relationship with Bizet (1838–75), three years Saint-Saëns' junior, was more that of a paternalistic mentor. As a young man Bizet arranged several of Gounod's compositions. He described Gounod both as the leading light in French music and, more anxiously, as the principal influence to overcome while he sought to develop his own compositional voice.[26] That influence emerges in various forms throughout Bizet's career and is felt even in the music for Micaëla in *Carmen*, premiered shortly before he died at the age of thirty-six. But overcome it Bizet did, through a sure-footed sense of music theatre and a cultivation of a more colourful palette – rhythmic, harmonic, orchestral. Bizet's commitment to opera was even more sustained than the already considerable activity of Saint-Saëns and Gounod in the theatre. In one form of completion or another, he was involved with no fewer than thirty projects in his short life and, despite his manifest talent, repeatedly came up against obstacles until *Carmen*. The posthumous international triumph of a composer more celebrated in death than while alive makes for a poignant and Mozart-like story. Works previously ignored received new exposure, and this includes a body of around thirty *mélodies*, a genre to which he turned somewhat later than Saint-Saëns: the two principal collections are *Feuilles d'album* representing pieces up to 1866 and a *Vingt mélodies* anthology published in 1873 representing work since then. As with Saint-Saëns, the poets were mainly of the Romantic generation, with seven Hugo settings and six of Lamartine.

Saint-Saëns once remarked that whereas he and Bizet had many character traits in common, their aesthetics were fundamentally different: he contrasted his own search 'for stylistic purity and formal perfection' to Bizet's quest for 'passion and life'.[27] Something of the difference between them emerges in comparing the Bizet version of Victor Hugo's 'Guitare' (a rather popular text also set by Édouard Lalo, Louis Lacombe, and Jules Massenet) to the Saint-Saëns version already discussed. Where Saint-Saëns is concise, syntactically traditional, and observant of the sequence of words in the poem, Bizet provides a sumptuous setting that freely repeats the text, plays up local colour, and overflows with material (see Example 4.7). Over guitar-like strumming in the piano, the *mélodie* begins with an extended melisma that plays with the exotic augmented second. The harmonic shifts are idiomatically Spanish: C minor to G minor to E♭ major. The latter harmony ushers in the text of the poem, the sense of which becomes lost as a reprise of the melisma interrupts the first line of poetry. The first two lines are then repeated to a dance-like figure that makes for awkward text-setting, especially the *fortissimo* downbeat on the first unaccented syllables of 'Avec nos nacelles'. Here Bizet ostensibly sacrifices prosody for character. The mood changes entirely for the entreaty to the sailors to row away

Example 4.7. Georges Bizet, 'Guitare', mm. 5–16

('Ramez disaient-elles'), a brighter F-major chord to B♭ major, marked *con grazia*, that then gets abruptly snapped back with virtuosic brio to the C-minor tonic. The text has become an excuse for a rhythmically varied setting replete with theatrical character and clever musical touches, for example, the mimicking of the dance-like voice figure on 'Comment disaient-ils' later in the piano grace note figure of m. 14 or the exchange of the melismatic figure between piano bass line and voice.

Several of Bizet's best-known *mélodies* share this virtuosic, extroverted, and dramatic character. Rather than Gounod's injection of intimacy from the *mélodie* into opera discussed earlier, the direction is now reversed with absorption of theatrical elements into the *mélodie*. To stay briefly with exotic subject matter, Hugo's 'Adieux de l'hôtesse arabe' about the sorrow

Example 4.7. *(cont.)*

of the exotic lover at the departure of the Western male – this became something of an orientalist cliché – called forth a magnificent setting filled with operatic performance indications in Italian such as *con dolore, con slancio,* and *con dolcezza.* Bizet chose the bipartite form favoured by Gounod: four stanzas are grouped two 2 + 2 with substantially the same music in each half, but also with subtle variation because of the different text. Each part builds to a vocal apex followed by a chromatic descent through a tenth (marked *con disperazione*). Bizet reserves a set of histrionic vocal sighs for the conclusion, followed by a smooth semiquaver melisma that melts away into a terminal *pianissimo* trill and silence – no mean vocal feat. Alfred de Musset's 'Adieux à Suzon' also provided Bizet occasion for a sprawling *mélodie.* Driven by restless desire to continue exploring the world, the speaker leaves his beloved Suzon after only eight days. The poem is laid out as five stanzas, each punctuated with a refrain underlining the speaker's impatience to travel 'bien loin, bien vite'. The changing part of each strophe draws attention to the emotions of the lovers during their week together. Bizet succeeded in combining the frenzied character of the peripatetic speaker with more amorous sentiment. The piece is superficially like Schubert's 'Erlkönig' because contrasting affects are set against a kinetic accompaniment in perpetual motion: the triplets of a galloping figure at the beginning animate the entire *mélodie*. As early as the first strophe the key shifts from D major to darker B♭ major with a slight *ritenuto*, *pianissimo* dynamics, and a more lyrical line for the protagonist to express regret as he heads into the unknown. The buoyant mood of the opening returns at the refrain. The second strophe sustains the rhythmic energy, but now the turn is to F♮ minor and a hushed *sotto voce* confession that his heart still palpitates for her. Here and beyond, the harmonies extend beyond Gounod's palette.

The delightful and distinguished 'La coccinelle' (Hugo) has a narrator and two speaking parts, the beloved and a ladybird. In the story, the speaker is distracted from noticing that his love has puckered up for a kiss by a ladybird on her neck. His fascination causes the kiss metaphorically to fly off and brings a punning moral from the ladybird: 'Les bêtes sont au bon Dieu! / Mais la bêtise est à l'homme' (Animals belong to God, foolishness to humankind). This highly sectional *mélodie* starts with recitative that alternates with piano passages, as might occur in the interaction between voice and orchestra before an opera aria. The set piece proper, triggered by the first reference to the 'petit insecte rose', is a light-hearted waltz where the piano leads and the voice superimposes its part above, once again as might occur in a stage work. Illustrative of Bizet's fine dramatic instinct, the text spools out in fragmented form to reflect the narrator's shyness and hesitation. The ladybird's moralising words are set to a change of tempo and texture, and the waltz gives way to an arpeggiated accompaniment marked Andante – with a shift to a *scherzando* indication to underline humankind's foolishness. In a coda, Bizet superimposes the main motif of the waltz over the arpeggiated figure, a technique of tying materials together with a foot in the world of instrumental music composition as much as in opera. The descending line against tonic pedal in the bass reminds one of Gounod's style. Bizet repeats words profusely here (again operatically, as in the coda of an aria), reaching back to the second strophe (of five) for 'J'aurais dû' (I should have) and to the fourth strophe for 'Hélas', a free distribution of text that seems once again calculated for dramatic effect.

More conventionally introspective lyrical utterances in Bizet's œuvre are also vocally ambitious. Aquillon, Zephyr, and Cupid figure in 'Rose d'amour' to a text by Charles Millevoye, a transitional figure between eighteenth-century letters (witness the mythological references in this poem) and Romantic poetry. In this parable about reawakened love, a rose in a valley withers until Cupid arranges its marriage to a gentle breeze. The first two strophes (of three) begin the same way – softly, introverted, declamatory, and low in the tessitura – but then evolve to different conclusions as the voice widens its range and lyrical valence. The third strophe, depicting the marriage, takes on a somewhat grandiose flavour in the manner of the operatic Gounod with pulsing triplets in the piano and, later, shimmering (orchestral) right-hand tremolos. 'Douce mer' shows Bizet in a more restrained posture, but one no less evocative. Lamartine's speaker compares floating on the sea in an oarless boat to the beloved's embrace. The generic reference is barcarolle, with a sense of stasis created by extended bass pedals. The most kinetic bass line is saved for a complete cadential progression at the end as the speaker surrenders to the waves. Some of the harmonies recall the chromaticism in Gounod's 'Venise', but now the voice dwells considerably on the tonic and fifth scale degree, giving an open effect suggestive of the maritime ambience.

Jules Massenet

Born in 1842, Jules Massenet was four years Bizet's junior and only seven years younger than Saint-Saëns. Although Massenet's personal relationship with Gounod was more distant than either of his colleagues, he too followed in his musical footsteps. Like Bizet, his creative energy was mainly directed toward opera. Bizet's tragic and untimely death after the premiere of *Carmen* in 1875 left the way open for the young Massenet to become the dominant figure in French opera composition at the fin de siècle. The important premiere of *Le roi de Lahore* in 1877 at the Opéra produced the kind of visibility for him that Bizet never achieved in his short life, and he went on to write nearly thirty operas after this, including chestnuts of the repertory *Manon* (1884) and *Werther* (1893).

Like Gounod and Saint-Saëns, Massenet began his career perceived as a progressive composer and ended it derided by a younger generation. The critique of Massenet in some quarters was particularly virulent because it was tainted with thinly veiled attacks on his character. He was said to be a charmer, hyper-sensitive to criticism, and overly concerned with pandering to the market. A veneer of conservative accessibility softened the more modern elements of his style, which included a loosening of phrase structure and up-to-date post-Wagnerian chromaticism. Unchallenging meant lightweight. Because of this, and often in very blatant ways, his music was unrelentingly characterised by critics of the day as feminine. Debussy, for example, famously wrote, 'We know how much this music is animated by frissons, outbursts, and embraces that seem to want to go on forever. The harmonies resemble arms, the melodies, napes of the neck'.[28] The overwhelmingly male critical establishment judged that Massenet was particularly adept at projecting feminine psychology in his operas. Such perceptions blended easily with the idea that his main market was female listeners who saw themselves in his music. And his personal popularity with women was legendary. The writer Léon Daudet once recalled how adoring female admirers immediately surrounded the composer when he appeared at a salon: regardless of their age, Massenet, master of the compliment as well as the piano, treated them all as if they were twenty.[29]

Though little written about, Massenet's output of over 250 *mélodies* from the mid 1860s to his death in 1912 at some level must have also played into such critical appraisals, many of which will strike the modern reader as an awkward blend of naïveté and presumptuousness. Regardless of such rhetoric, it should be recognised that one of Massenet's great strengths was the development of a personal sound – more individuated than that of Saint-Saëns or even of Bizet – that travelled freely from opera to *mélodie*. Massenet often favoured a fluid outpouring of quavers with rapid registral displacements in compound metre. The beginning of 'Septembre' (1891), to a poem by the Franco-Romanian writer Elena Varescu, illustrates this aspect of his style:

L'ombre des feuilles danse et tremble
Sur l'herbe qu'elles vont couvrir;
La nature veut, ce me semble,
Être plus belle avant de mourir.

The shadow of the leaves dances and trembles
On the grass that they will cover;
It seems that nature wants
To become more beautiful before dying.

The 12/8 line moves up to E♭ on the weak beat of the measure and then cascades down an octave (see Example 4.8a online). The rhythms push gently forward to create a musical enjambment between the first two lines of text. Massenet varies metrical placement of the vocal phrases over the 12/8

Example 4.8. Jules Massenet, 'Septembre'
a) [online only] Mm. 3–11. To view this example please visit www.cambridge.org/9781316514474 and navigate to the Resources tab
b) Mm. 19–26

metrical grid – sometimes beginning with an upbeat and elsewhere further back in the measure to produce smooth elasticity in the line. He often shifts quickly between lyrical flight and single-pitch declamation as in later in this *mélodie* (see Example 4.8b). Here, vocal reiteration of tonic E♭ prepares the lyrical emphasis on the punch line (relating to nature's final burst before winter) before the poem becomes preoccupied with the soul of the speaker. The voice shifts upwards from the repeated E♭s to rotate briefly around B♭

and then repeat A♭ several times for the aside 'ce me semble'. In a post-Wagnerian harmonic move, the A♭ respells to G♯ to accommodate the semitone shift of key from E♭ major to E major. Typically for Massenet, the voice then suddenly becomes more mobile, moving up to the registral apex of the song and then down an octave for the cadence.

'Enchantement' (1889) to poetry by the minor writer Jules Ruelle, to whom Massenet turned on eight other occasions, provides another example of his personal and very accessible salon style. The speaker sings praises of an unknown woman with whom he has fallen in love but who remains merely a vision that he does not approach, a superficial object of his imagination celebrated in sentimental poetry that is long on conventional yearning but short on sophisticated figurative language – 'Qui donc es-tu? / Je n'en sais rien, mais je t'adore!' (Who then are you? I don't know, but I adore you!). The initial melody arches upwards gradually in three segments that articulate the same rhyme on successive downbeats (*luit, nuit, séduit*) and then cascades down at the cadence, all in quavers with rapid articulation of syllables (see Example 4.9a). Massenet carefully marks the expressive emphasis with *tenuto* indications including, most characteristically, on each note at the cadence. From the beginning performers must negotiate between the *tenuto* directives and the implicit expressive emphasis produced by the lilting dotted rhythm on the fourth beat of each of mm. 2–4. This rhythm provides a pervasive motivic stamp somewhat different than the way 'Septembre' is written. After the D♭ tonic slips down to C major for a few measures (not shown), the vocal line becomes even more impassioned (see Example 4.9b online). Chromaticism has given way to a bass line that rises diatonically by step from tonic D♭ to dominant harmony and a cadence, and the piano right hand doubles the voice to lend further expressive – some might say garish – weight. Rapid shifting between registers fuels the breathless desire of the speaker as does a *stringendo* to *più mosso* and further *tenuto* markings.

'Septembre' dates from 1891, 'Enchantement' from 1889: Debussy had composed his Baudelaire songs by this time and his *Prose lyriques* were soon to follow, as were Fauré's Verlaine cycles *Cinq mélodies 'de Venise'* and *La bonne chanson*. With the challenging musical language of his colleagues on one side, and the cabaret and music hall repertory on the other, to say that Massenet's *mélodie*s in the 1880s and 1890s occupy a middlebrow space is an aesthetic judgement that can be made in gender-neutral terms without denigrating his obvious compositional gifts. Indeed, it might credibly be argued that, taking into account the generic context of the *mélodie* and his own reputation, the Massenet of 'Septembre' and

Example 4.9. Massenet, 'Enchantement'
a) Mm. 1–6
b) [online only] Mm. 14–22. To view this example please visit www.cambridge.org/
9781316514474 and navigate to the Resources tab

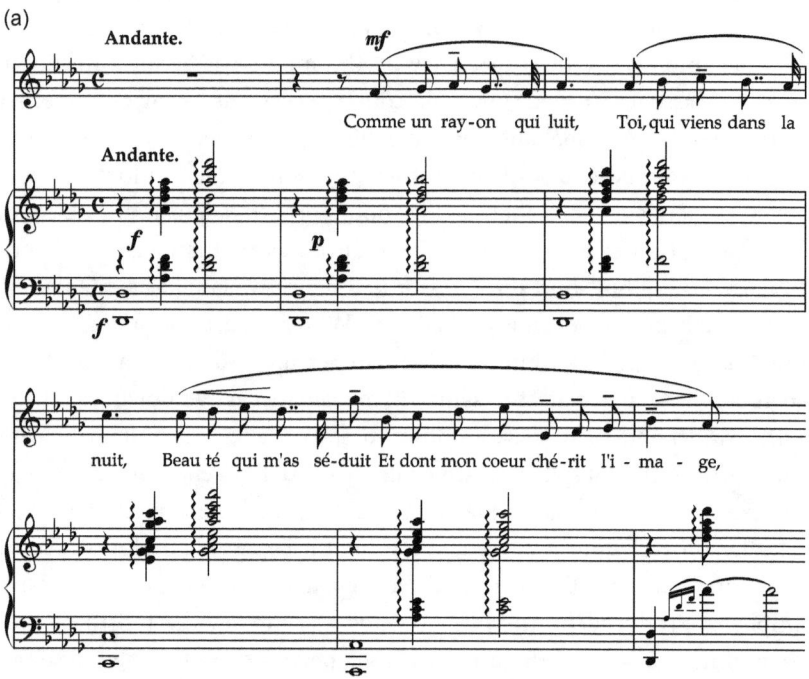

'Enchantement' represents the quintessence of what it meant to be middlebrow at the fin de siècle.

It is also worth remembering that he did begin writing *mélodies* in the mid-1860s, and shifting focus to an earlier period draws attention to a context where Massenet was seen as a modern and fresh voice on the French musical scene, as we have already observed. This is particularly true with respect to his cultivation of song cycles in the 1860s, little explored before that time by French composers. One of the works that put Massenet on the map as a young star was his cycle *Poème d'avril* (1866) to poetry by Armand Silvestre, usually thought of as a minor Parnassian and the poet whom Massenet would set the most frequently, including in two subsequent cycles *Poème du souvenir* (c. 1878) and *Poème d'hiver* (1882). *Poème d'avril*, drawn from Silvestre's collection *Rimes neuves et vieilles* (1866), tells of a short springtime romance with an imaginative blend of spoken recitation interspersed with short piano interventions, recitative, and song. Silvestre identifies this section of his book as 'Vers pour être chantés', which suggests a lighter kind of poetry. He was to go on to work with Massenet in the theatre, but the paradox in the case of this song cycle is that not all its words are meant to be sung. The collection is truly cyclic because the first piece announces the incipits of subsequent songs between passages of recitation. It begins with arpeggiated chords, evoking the strings of a lyre struck before poetic declamation, and it ends with the same strummed texture. The lyre figure also returns in the left hand of the fourth song 'Le printemps a bu'. Massenet shows a remarkable affective range: Schumannian lyricism in the second song, a coquettish declaimed poem 'Riez-vous? Ne riez vous pas' followed by a light *scherzando* piano solo piece that takes up its mood, and an austere accompaniment and limited vocal ambitus for reflections on the brevity of love in 'Que l'heure est donc brève'. The last song, 'Je pars', brings the latent drama to the fore as it assumes the form of a simulated dialogue for the lovers at their point of rupture over an *agitato* accompaniment. The cycle ends on a bitter note. Nostalgia over affairs of the heart is left to the next Silvestre cycle, *Poème du souvenir*. The technique of blending recitation with song was to reappear in *Expressions lyriques* (various poets, composed early 1900s) using the texture of melodrama and unmarked pitches, distantly related to Schoenberg's *Pierrot lunaire* composed the year before, but on a different scale of experimentation. Consonant with the critical paradigm of his feminisation, Massenet's steps forward were timid. To say this recalls critical perspectives towards the *romance* thirty years before. Despite its claim to greater aesthetic legitimacy than the *romance*, the *mélodie* could thus also invite similar feminine type-casting. Even the repertory by ostensibly more progressive composers after 1870 was not immune from this perspective, one much harder to pin on the *Lied* as the century went on.

Notes

1. Loïsa Puget (1810–89) was a prolific composer of *romances*. Cited by Gérard Condé, *Charles Gounod* (Paris: Fayard, 2009), 627.
2. Joachim Fels, as cited by Rainer Gstreine, *Die vokale Romanze in der Zeit von 1750 bis 1850* (Innsbruck: Edition Helbling, 1989), 30.
3. Jacques-Auguste Delaire, *Histoire de la romance* (Paris: Printed by De Ducessois, 1845), 1.
4. As cited by Gstreine, *Die vokale Romanze*, 30.
5. David Tunley, *Salons, Singers and Songs: A Background to Romantic French Song 1830–1870* (repr. Oxford and New York: Routledge, 2016), 59.
6. Scudo, *Esquisse d'une histoire de la romance* (Paris, 1842) cited by Gstreine, *Die vokale Romanze*, 15.

7. William Cheng, 'The French Romance and the Sexual Traffic of Musical Mimicry', *19th-Century Music*, 35 (2011), 34–71.
8. Cheng, 'The French Romance', 42.
9. Maurice Ravel, 'Les Mélodies de Gabriel Fauré', in Maurice Ravel, *Lettres, écrits, entretiens* (Paris: Flammarion, 1989), 322.
10. This position is taken by Frits Noske, *French Song from Berlioz to Duparc*, 91–125. See also the last instalment of A. Thurner, 'Étude comparé sur la chanson, la romance et le lied', *Revue et gazette musicale de Paris* (13 October 1867).
11. For a very thorough survey see J. G. Prod'homme and Frederick H. Martens, 'Schubert's Works in France', *The Musical Quarterly*, 14 (1928), 495–514.
12. Henri Panofka, 'Biographie: François Schubert', *Revue et gazette musicale de Paris* (14 October 1841).
13. Kitti Messina, 'Mélodie et romance au milieu du XIXe siècle: Points communs et divergences', *Revue de musicology*, 94 (2008), 59–90.
14. Noske, *French Song*, 12.
15. Camille Saint-Saëns, preface to Louis Alfred Niedermeyer, *Vie d'un compositeur modern (1802–1861)* (Paris: Fischenbacher, 1893), in *Écrits sur la musique et les musiciens 1870–1921*, ed. Marie-Gabrielle Soret (Paris: Vrin, 2012), 477–9.
16. Katherine Bergeron, *Voice Lessons: French Mélodie in the Belle Époque* (Oxford: Oxford University Press, 2010), 6.
17. Ravel, 'Les Mélodies de Gabriel Fauré', 322–3.
18. Georges Servières, 'Charles Gounod, compositeur de melodies', *Le Ménestrel* (15 April 1938).
19. Camille Saint-Saëns, 'Charles Gounod', in *Écrits sur la musique*, 507.
20. Charles Gounod, *Mémoires d'un artiste* (Paris: Calmann-Lévy, 1896), 85.
21. Condé, *Charles Gounod*, 710.
22. Cited in Jean-Michel Nectoux, *Gabriel Fauré: A Musical Life*, trans. Roger Nichols (Cambridge: Cambridge University Press, 1991), 335.
23. Saint-Saëns, 'La Poésie et la musique', in *Écrits*, 346.
24. For additional insight into this work, and Saint-Saëns' *mélodies* more generally, see Annegret Fauser, 'What's in a Song? Camille Saint-Saëns's *Mélodies*', in *Camille Saint-Saëns and His World*, ed. Jann Pasler (Princeton: Princeton University Press, 2012), 210–29.
25. Armand Renaud, *Nuits persanes* (Paris: Alphonse Lemerre, 1870), 6–7.
26. For an extended study of the relationship between these two figures see Michel Poupet, 'Gounod et Bizet', *L'Avant-Scène Opéra: Roméo et Juliette*, 41 (1982), 106–17.
27. Saint-Saëns, 'Causerie musicale: Georges Bizet', in *Écrits*, 344.
28. Claude Debussy, 'D'Ève à Grisélidis', in *Monsieur Croche et autres écrits*, revised ed., ed. François Lesure (Paris: Gallimard, 1987), 60.
29. Léon Daudet, *Souvenirs littéraires* (Paris: Grasset, 1968), 34.

5 Fauré's Individual Songs and Collections

ROY HOWAT

Affectuosa memoria David Tunley.

Fauré's songs, covering six pivotal decades from 1861 to 1921, include 101 surviving solo songs, three duo songs, one for SATB, two solo *cantiques* to French religious texts, plus one solo song left incomplete, one (possibly two) lost, and forty-five accompanied vocalises recently published *in toto* for the first time.[1] Discounting his librettists and traditional texts, Fauré set at least thirty-two poets, the ones he set most being Charles Van Lerberghe (eighteen settings in two cycles, 1905–14), Paul Verlaine (seventeen settings including two cycles, 1887–94), Armand Silvestre (twelve settings, 1878–1902), Victor Hugo (ten settings including a cantata, 1862–75), and Charles Marie René Leconte de Lisle (five settings, c. 1870–97).

Forty-three of Fauré's solo songs comprise his seven defined song cycles, involving five poets; these are dealt with in Chapter 9. The remainder form the focus of this chapter.[2] Of them, most of the solo songs up to 1904 (along with two cycles, *Poème d'un jour* and the *Cinq mélodies 'de Venise'*, Op. 58) make up the three established collections of *Vingt mélodies*; compiled between 1879 and 1908, they are still in print. External to these are four songs for more than one voice, along with eight solo songs from between 1862 and 1919 that are discussed below. Besides issues of how Fauré's song cycles relate to his other songs, central threads in this chapter are the poets Fauré chose, how he related compositionally to them, and his lifelong activity as pianist in his songs.[3]

Fauré and His Poets

Fauré's approach to poets has long been clouded by confused ordering in the three *Vingt mélodies* collections: the first volume in particular ordered its contents without discernible logic, conveying a false impression of a young Fauré hopping randomly from poet to poet. (The opus numbers 1–8 long associated with the First Collection, along with the opus number 10 for two vocal duets, were added years later for non-musical reasons and observe no chronological order.) As it is, exact chronological order is impossible to establish for most of his first twenty songs (this is why they appear in slightly variant order in the 2010 Hamelle-Leduc and 2014 Peters critical editions). What we can ascertain, however, points to Fauré methodically selecting particular poets in turn. His first six songs – possibly seven – were certainly settings of Victor Hugo. He then turned to Charles Baudelaire (three settings, probably around 1870) and Leconte de Lisle (a special case, of whom more below), then Théophile Gautier (four settings, early 1870s). His presence from around then in the social circle of Pauline Viardot brought some lighter verse (Louis Pomey, Marc Monnier, and two Tuscan texts adapted in French by his friend Romain Bussine), along with the more substantial Sully Prudhomme ('Ici-bas!' and 'Au bord de l'eau', followed a few years later by 'Les berceaux'). Traversing Charles Grandmougin for *Poème d'un jour* in 1878, Fauré then took a literal prompt from the *Vers pour être chantés* of Silvestre, whose poems form the backbone of his song output between 1879 and 1884 (prior to a final pair in 1904). Two settings of Auguste Villiers de L'Isle-Adam followed in 1886–7, and two of Jean Richepin in 1888, intersecting with seven years of concentration on Paul Verlaine (1887–94) that resulted in three single songs and two cycles. Four ensuing settings of Albert Samain, from 1894 to 1902, preceded two of Catulle Mendès in 1902. Incidental theatre music had meanwhile yielded four songs between 1889 and 1898 ('Chanson' and 'Madrigal' for Edmond Haraucourt's *Shylock*, 'Sérénade' for Molière's *Le Bourgeois gentilhomme*, and 'Mélisande's Song' for Maurice Maeterlinck's *Pelléas et Mélisande* in Jack Mackail's translation, Fauré's only setting of English). The remaining songs involve a few poets he set only once and the four cycles of his last two decades. Fauré personally knew at least half the poets he set.

That basic chronology immediately supports some long-obscured pairing – notably the early Sully Prudhomme pair, and 'Sérénade toscane' with 'Après un rêve' in either their original Tuscan or Bussine's French adaptations – plus two implicit cycles. One of them can be found in Fauré's three Baudelaire songs, whose choice of poems suggests a Baudelairean trilogy of love ('Hymne'), reason ('La rançon'), and mortality ('Chant d'automne'). They also comprise his first through-composed forms (in 'Hymne' alone the final strophe recapitulates the opening one, underlining their reciprocity in Baudelaire's poem), exploring techniques seen nowhere else in his output. The virtually monothematic 'Hymne' is based on a rising chromatic motive treated in contrapuntal imitation and rhythmic augmentation, which returns at strategic moments in 'La rançon' (in inversion) and

Example 5.1. Gabriel Fauré, 'Chant d'automne', mm. 56–9

'Chant d'automne'.[4] A resulting sense of leitmotif, together with the fluid forms, conveys an impression of Fauré wrapping Baudelaire's verse in musical procedures redolent of Baudelaire's hero Wagner. (Almost two decades later Debussy would do the same, clothing his *Cinq poèmes de Charles Baudelaire* in the most overtly Wagnerian music he ever concocted.)

Fauré's turn to Baudelaire may have been in collusion with Duparc and Chabrier who both set 'L'invitation au voyage' in 1870, a tumultuous year in which French art was being urgently rethought.[5] The qualities of Fauré's Baudelaire settings are best sensed through the poems' dramatic urgency – a crucial context for reading Fauré's rather laconic tempo headings *Allegretto vivo* and *Andante* (of which more later). In 'Chant d'automne' a defining marker of tempo is the transition into the closing strophe, where the piano semiquavers in mm. 57 take over the motion and sounding tempo of the preceding quavers, the voice's new quavers in rhythmic augmentation of what went before (see Example 5.1). To enable that relationship along with a viable tempo from m. 57, the song needs to be launched at a lively clip (the *Andante* heading relating to the longer notes of the vocal line rather than the piano's quavers). However they were conceived, these three songs, performed alertly, make a highly dramatic cycle that exudes, for the first time in Fauré's output, the urgent intensity that would return later that decade in his Violin Sonata in A Major, Op. 13, and Piano Quartet in C Minor, Op. 15.

Looking earlier again, Stephen Rumph has made a compelling case for reading what appear to be Fauré's first four songs – 'Le papillon et la fleur', 'Puisque j'ai mis ma lèvre', 'Mai', and 'S'il est un charmant gazon' – as an Anacreontic cycle on Hugo's *Les chants du crépuscule*.[6] Much of Rumph's case rests on Fauré's response to the poems' structural, syntactic, and rhetorical characteristics, starting with how the piano's opening flutter in 'Le papillon' marks out a 12 + 3-note sequence that mimics the poem's line structure (alexandrines alternating with trisyllables); the piano introductions in 'Puisque j'ai mis' and 'S'il est un charmant gazon' then harmonically mimic the hypotactic syntax that characterises those two poems. Rumph also notes that manuscript versions of 'Puisque j'ai mis', 'Mai', and 'S'il est un charmant gazon' are linked by a pentatonic descent in the piano that introduces or rounds off strophes.

It may have been just the lack of a publisher in Fauré's early years that dispersed those Hugo and Baudelaire sets. Only from 1869 did his early songs start to appear in print, one by one, with the exception of a 'sampler' volume published in 1871 by Georges Hartmann that juxtaposes four songs by different poets ('Lydia', 'Hymne', 'Mai', and 'Seule!'): we can well imagine that the composer would not have passed up that early chance of a collected volume, even if it involved extracting at least two songs from larger groups.

From 1878, Fauré's access to a regular publisher (Hamelle) coincides intriguingly with a new pattern that ran until 1902: his non-cyclic opus groups from Op. 18 onward not only mix poets but sometimes split a single-author pair over different groups. The separation of Fauré's two meditative Villiers de L'Isle-Adam settings ('Nocturne' and 'Les présents') across Opp. 43 and 46 may have been a matter of their very affinity: in performance 'Les présents' makes a more effective pair with the Verlaine setting 'Clair de lune', as Op. 46. Fauré's similarly contemplative settings of Albert Samain appear in different opus groups by simple dint of their eight-year compositional spread: 'Soir' appeared with the Verlaine setting 'Prison' as Op. 68,[7] 'Arpège' with the Leconte de Lisle 'Le parfum impérissable' as Op. 76, and 'Accompagnement' rounds off Op. 85 after Fauré's two dramatically contrasted settings of Catulle Mendès.

Leconte de Lisle, by contrast, marks a sort of compositional ritornello in Fauré's song output, with just a single song appearing at intervals of several years: 'Lydia' around 1870, 'Nell' in 1878, 'Les roses d'Ispahan' in 1884, 'La rose' in 1890, 'Le parfum impérissable' in 1897, and finally an abandoned stab at 'Dans le ciel clair' in 1902.[8] The five completed settings home in on Leconte de Lisle's penchant for the exotic, yielding from Fauré a vein of such sensuous harmonic richness as to risk indigestion (or inebriation, like Leconte de Lisle's 'Le colibri') if taken more than one at a time. Might they nonetheless be viewed as a sort of socially distanced cycle? Their sequence is strikingly cogent, from the mythical Greco-Roman 'Lydia', through the real 'Nell' from Ayrshire in Scotland, to two mid-Asian evocations that straddle an Anacreontic salute to Greek Antiquity.[9]

Their musical characteristics add intrigue. 'Lydia' accommodates the poem's four quatrains in a compact two-strophe form, whose four-part piano texture doubles voice throughout. (The pianist has to know how to let the piano's doubling shadow the vocal line unobtrusively.) 'Nell', by contrast, avoids textural doubling, its rippling piano part marking out counterpoint against the voice, the poem's four quatrains nested in a partly strophic AA'BA" sequence. In 'Les roses d'Ispahan' the voice circles almost amorously around a more static piano part, in a stricter AABA song form, the third quatrain rising dramatically as the poem moves from description to direct address. 'La rose' opens with a dialogue of phrases between voice and piano, the texture then literally upended by the interrupted cadence at the song's exact mid-point, after twenty-eight of its fifty-six bars – a precision redolent of the poem's Parnassian sculpting. In 'Le parfum impérissable', a four-part piano texture mostly shadows the voice but sometimes overarches it with descants, in a compressed through-composed structure again articulated at its exact mid-point (midway through m. 17), this time by the surge of passion as we cross the *volta* of Leconte de Lisle's sonnet, shifting once again from description to direct address. (We may note that the exact midway divisions occur in the two songs whose structures are neither musically strophic nor poetically symmetrical: in 'La rose' it comes after thirteen of the poem's nineteen lines, entailing considerably more spacious syllabification of the final six.)

'Nell' and 'Les roses d'Ispahan' can be sensed as added spice in the Op. 18 and 39 groups otherwise based on Silvestre. 'La rose' was added more incidentally to the otherwise sombre Richepin–Verlaine triptych of 1888 that originally comprised Op. 51, but which Hamelle (to Fauré's annoyance) had still not published by 1890. Even in its original triptych form, Op. 51 had ended with something of a wild card in the form of Fauré's second Verlaine setting, 'Spleen', whose fluidity dissipates the declamatory drama of 'Larmes' and 'Au cimetière'. (Its poem is 'Il pleure dans mon cœur'; Fauré carried the title 'Spleen' over from another poem in Verlaine's *Romances sans paroles*, 'Les roses étaient toutes rouges'. Both poems, incidentally, figure in Debussy's *Ariettes*, published in 1888 and revised in 1903 as *Ariettes oubliées*.)

Verlaine stands alone among Fauré's poets in providing text for both single songs and cycles. Fauré's first Verlaine setting, 'Clair de lune' of 1887, marks a new departure in the way its text, in Graham Johnson's words, forms 'a vocal obbligato' over virtually autonomous instrumental music, voice and piano coalescing at focal moments 'as if by chance'.[10] Fauré had been introduced to Verlaine's poetry by the eccentric Count Robert de Montesquiou (the inspiration for Des Esseintes in J. K. Huysmans' novel *À rebours* and for Marcel Proust's Baron de Charlus). Shortly after completing 'Clair de lune', Fauré requested from Montesquiou an *ad libitum* text that could be sung through, or over, his recently completed *Pavane*. Affinity with 'Clair de lune' is clear, each piece opening with an introductory paragraph from the piano or orchestra, the vocal element then entering almost haphazardly. Although the male-female dialogue format of Montesquiou's *Pavane* text is based on Silvestre (as we shall see), the lines themselves spoof Verlaine's *Fêtes galantes*, most obviously 'Clair de lune' and 'Mandoline'. (Two of Montesquiou's phrases, 'Observez la mesure!' and 'La cadence est moins lente!', might also be read as a sly dig at Fauré's known distaste for sluggish rhythm or tempi.) Fauré in turn subtitled 'Clair de lune' 'Menuet' (the only such subtitle he marked on a song), a natural companion for a *Pavane*: premiered together in April 1888 in orchestral form, they manifest the same adroit blend of frivolity, melancholy, dance, and irony that epitomises the *fête galante*. Revealingly, the conductor Sir Adrian Boult recalled hearing Fauré in the early 1900s give impromptu after-dinner piano performances of the *Pavane*, sometimes with a singer or two or a flautist reading over his shoulder, 'never slower than crotchet = 100'.[11]

As early as 1870 Fauré's vocal lines can be seen exploring varied relationships with their accompaniments, from the imitative polyphony of 'Hymne' through the more punctuating voice-piano dialogue that highlights Gautier's declamatory lines in 'Chanson du pêcheur'. By the mid 1870s Sully Prudhomme's poetry was prompting a more sinuous dialogue of voice and piano, featuring either imitation or sharing of the line (see Example 5.2).

By the later 1870s and early 1880s, crisscrossing Paris to give lessons, Fauré must have smiled at Armand Silvestre's 'La fée aux chansons', the plaint of a fairy obliged to teach singing to recalcitrantly obtuse birds. Silvestre's quicksilver virtuosity of allusion, rhyme, and assonance, well suited to Fauré's rhythmic and harmonic agility, encompasses an ability to

Example 5.2. Voice-piano dialogue in Fauré's Sully Prudhomme settings
a) 'Ici-bas', mm. 21–4
b) 'Au bord de l'eau', mm. 2–6

spring sudden intensity, as in 'Le secret' (a favourite of Ravel's), the vehement 'Fleur jetée', or the austere 'Le voyageur' and 'Automne' that round off Op. 18. The Cherubino-like 'Notre amour' (from Op. 23) and 'Chanson d'amour' (from Op. 27) are neatly countered in the four-voice *Madrigal* Op. 35 that Fauré wrote for the wedding of his friend André Messager in 1883. Its text, from Silvestre's *Madrigaux dans le goût ancien*, features a teasing boys-girls dialogue that Fauré impishly set to the theme of Bach's cantata *Aus tiefer Not schrei' ich zu dir*.[12]

Two striking songs of 1906 remain little known, having missed inclusion in the three Hamelle 'Collections'. 'Le don silencieux', in Fauré's words, 'bears no resemblance to any of my previous works or to anything else I know ... with no principal theme, it gives expression to the words as and when they occur, it begins, unfolds, and ends, nothing more, and yet it is one'.[13] 'Chanson' (Op. 94), his only setting of Henri de Régnier, is again unlike any other: close in texture to the Op. 98 cello *Sérénade* that Fauré wrote for Pablo Casals, it forms a more overtly twentieth-century companion to the preceding song pair that comprised Op. 87, the two lightly dancing Silvestre 'Madrigals' 'Le plus doux chemin' and 'Le ramier'.

Adventures in Syllabification

In an article of 1922 devoted to Fauré's songs, Maurice Ravel declared that Fauré's 'declamation, combining aptness with exquisite grace ... succeeds in capturing the elusive music of the French language'.[14] From one who could be fierce about prosodic faults, such praise prompts a look at aspects of Fauré's prosody that have attracted both criticism and defence.[15] Nowhere better illustrates this than the first vocal entry of his output, in 'Le papillon et la fleur', where the weakest syllables of the poem's first two alexandrines coincide with the half-bar metrical stresses (see Example 5.3).

A pivotal element here is the rhythmic variety within Hugo's alexandrines (in which the only compulsory stresses are on the sixth and twelfth syllables). The iambic flow of the opening 'La **pau**-vre **fleur** di-**sait** | au **pa**-pil-**lon** cé-**leste**' in practice articulates 3/4 hemiolas against the piano, reflecting Fauré's lifelong penchant for cross-rhythms. (Similar 3/4 melodic lines over an accompaniment in 6/8 feature in the central part of his first piano barcarolle, and in the opening vocal entry of his later song 'Notre amour'; see also Examples 5.1 and 5.2b.) The ensuing alexandrines continue to run independently of the 6/8 metre (see mm. 14–15 in Example 5.3, where the differentiation neatly matches the poem's 'destins différents'), until mm. 30–31, where the poem finally synchronises smoothly with the piano, in the anapaests of 'Mais hé-**las**, l'air t'em-**porte** | et la **ter**-re m'en-**chaîne**'. That brief relaxation neatly sets the stage for disruption in mm. 38–39, where the emphatic 'Mais **non**, tu vas trop **loin** | parmi les **fleurs** sans **nombre**' cuts across the piano in broader augmented binary patterns. Fauré's innocently waltzing strophic setting for this song quietly achieves several ends at once, letting the poem's strategically differentiated rhythmic patterns literally speak for themselves (singers just have to know to follow the prosody without marking the metre), while neatly locating all the poem's formal stresses on main beats.

Quietly farther-reaching is the way 'Le papillon et la fleur' consistently launches its lines from the second quaver of the bar (see Example 5.3). (The one exception, for immediate reasons of prosody, is the on-beat start of 'Tu fuis' at m. 50.) 'Puisque j'ai mis ma lèvre', probably the next song Fauré composed, conversely launches all its alexandrines from the last quaver of the bar, counterintuitively stretching the repeated line-starter 'Puisque' over the barline at each occurrence (see Example 5.4a). His next song, 'Mai', despite opening with the same word 'Puisque', instead launches its lines consistently from the first beat of the bar (see

Example 5.3. Fauré, 'Le papillon et la fleur' (first published key), mm. 10–17

Example 5.4b). So does the ensuing 'S'il est un charmant gazon' (as shown in Example 5.4c), whose poem mostly alternates heptasyllabic and pentasyllabic lines. (The song's 1864 manuscript version observes this vocal rhythm throughout; the 1875 first edition shifted just the opening of the last strophe a beat forward.) One further effective option remains – that of launching lines as long up-beats from mid-bar – and it duly occurs in 'L'aurore', Fauré's remaining song from Hugo's *Les chants du crépuscule* (see Example 5.4d).

Coming from a teenager who won literature prizes at school, this boldly systematic differentiation (artificial in the full sense) has all the appearance of a compositional 'conceit' or dare. It is also musically seductive, for example in the way 'Puisque j'ai mis' offers singers a sophisticated treatment of 'long' syllable upbeats to underline the poem's pervading hypotaxis. Given the contrasting underlay for the same opening 'Puisque' in 'Mai', we may laugh at the almost appalling ease with which the opening alexandrine of Example 5.3 could fit the music of Example 5.4a – or various such permutations over Examples 5.3 and 5.4a–b – resulting each time in a bland comfort zone that Fauré's music habitually avoids like the plague. Each apparent 'misfit' is in fact carefully tailored to its song, in a manner that strikingly matches a Baudelairean credo of 1856 (though printed only decades later): 'Anything that is not slightly distorted lacks life; from which it follows that irregularity – that is, the unexpected, surprise, astonishment – are an essential part and the characteristic of beauty.'[16]

Example 5.4. Rhythmically differentiated line starts in Fauré's early Hugo settings
a) 'Puisque j'ai mis ma lèvre' (final manuscript key), mm. 8–13
b) 'Mai' (manuscript key), mm. 3–6
c) 'S'il est un charmant gazon' (1864 autograph version), mm. 9–12
d) 'L'aurore', mm. 1–3

Manuscript and Printed Versions

Only three of the five Hugo settings above reached print in Fauré's lifetime, eight to ten years after their composition. Among various retouches, the published versions show a few debatable changes. Publisher pressure may have pushed 'Le papillon et la fleur' into C major from its manuscript key of D♭ major – ironically, for the manuscript key lies much more easily under the hand, and highlights how closely the opening of the song shadows Chopin's lepidopteran Valse Op. 64 no. 1, in the same key of D♭. The published version of 'Mai' tightens the intermission between the song's two strophes from two bars to one, but thereby loses the pentatonic 'sign-off' after each musical strophe that linked the song's manuscript version to 'Puisque j'ai mis' and 'S'il est un charmant gazon'; it also leaves 'Mai' with a blander printed ending, and with only one bar of vocal respite in the course of the song.

'S'il est un charmant gazon' suffered most in its 1875 first edition, crassly titled 'Rêve d'amour' (to Fauré's disgust) by the publisher Choudens. Fauré may not have helped by replacing the manuscript's *Animé* heading and semi-staccato piano bass (see Example 5.4c) with *Allegretto* and a legato bass line. A longstanding view of that song as stickily sentimental can be countered by its fresher 1864 presentation (the Peters edition prints both versions), including a perkily crisp four-bar piano ending that necessitates a snappy tempo (around crotchet = 152). There possibly lies the nub, for the manuscript ending falls flat if taken under tempo. The first edition ends instead with a reiteration of the song's eight-bar piano introduction and ritornello: perhaps a safer compromise, it ironically loses a vital pointer to the song's energy and humour. (It may be that when Fauré gave away his early presentation copies of 'Mai' and 'S'il est', he retained only rougher drafts that later required reconstruction when publication became possible; surviving early rough copies of 'Le papillon' and 'Mai' omit to notate an ending.)

Why did 'Puisque j'ai mis' and 'L'aurore', along with 'Tristesse d'Olympio' (c. 1865), remain unpublished? While one factor may have been the lack of a publisher, Fauré may later have quailed at allowing the high-risk syllabification of 'Puisque j'ai mis' into print. He might also have been inhibited by the song's uncanny resemblance to the second of Liszt's *Consolations* for piano: they have almost the same main theme (in a not dissimilar texture), a theme that then features in each middle section in the piano's tenor register. (Unlike Chopin, Liszt was then very much alive; he and Fauré eventually met in the late 1870s.) A broader textual issue is that

'L'aurore' and 'Tristesse d'Olympio' set less than a quarter of their respective poems; in the process 'L'aurore' derives an attractively short, lighter-hearted song from Hugo's much longer rumination.

Might these factors have underlain Fauré's dissatisfaction, later in life, with his early settings of Hugo? (In 1911 he opined that he had never succeeded in setting Victor Hugo, and only rarely Leconte de Lisle, to his satisfaction: 'their poetry is too full, too rich, too self-sufficient for the music to adapt to it successfully'.[17]) The sophisticated compositional wit with which he meets Hugo's allusions and structures rules out technical or literary unawareness. Given Fauré's tendency to personal diffidence, he may have been nagged later by the thought that he had borrowed from some of the poems what he most wanted, filtering out elements of preaching or soul-searching extrinsic to his nature.

That cannot be said of Fauré's last solo setting of Hugo, 'L'absent', whose autograph manuscript bears the date 3 April 1871, one of the bloodiest days of the Paris Commune. An unlikely day for composing, the date may have served to flag what Hugo's poem had foretold in 1853, the violent endgame of Louis-Napoleon's seizure of power in 1851. (The poem comes from Hugo's *Les châtiments*, written in protest at Louis-Napoléon's power seizure.)[18] 'L'absent' thus marks a sombre sequel to Fauré's early *Chants du crépuscule* group, whose poems had celebrated the promise of the July 1830 revolution.

Prosody and Word-Painting

'L'absent' already embodies the more speech-like prosody characteristic of Fauré's later years. In 'Au cimetière', 'Prison', or 'Le parfum impérissable' (and in parts of his later cycles), Fauré's chord-per-beat accompaniments let the prosody speak compactly but fluidly around the piano's effective metronome. Even the slow-to-moderate tempo headings of 'Le parfum impérissable', 'Accompagnement', or 'Le don silencieux' necessitate deceptively rapid vocal delivery and vigorous enunciation, within the songs' intimate ambit. On that topic Fauré wrote to the pianist Robert Lortat that 'Le don silencieux' was 'above all to be spoken [*surtout à dire*], with its marvellous art of word-colouring'.[19] (The verbs *dire* or *déclamer* were habitually used of *mélodie* performance, together with the more occasional *soupirer*, *susurrer*, even a facetious *gueler* in a letter from d'Indy to Chabrier.[20])

In lighter contexts, Fauré's prosodic idiosyncrasy sometimes masks a ruse. In 'C'est la paix' of 1919 (a text he loathed but was institutionally obliged to set), Fauré was determined to replace the word 'poilus' (the French equivalent of 'Tommies') by 'soldats', in the teeth of the poet's resistance. His successful strategy can be gleaned from the score, where the second syllable of 'sol-dats' is spread over two tied minims on a top E_5 (mm. 18–19), scotching any chance of reinstating the 'u' vowel.

Not surprisingly, the stylised line launches seen in Examples 5.3 and 5.4 give way in later songs to more speech-like variation. That is also not without pattern, as can be seen in 'Prison', whose three-bar vocal phrases set an initial pattern of each phrase starting a beat later, relative to the metre, than the previous one (respectively midway through m. 1 beat 3, m. 5 beat 1, and m. 8 beat 2), a sequence then partly reiterated across mm. 14 and 18. Dovetailing these, the double-semiquaver vocal entries in mm. 11 and 21 feel like rhythmically agitated reiterations of the preceding entry, as if shaking the prison-like bars of the piano's unyielding crotchet chords. In a song whose explosive intensity is unmatched in Fauré's entire output, these tolling chords literally tick away the seconds (according to Fauré's metronome marking of crotchet = 60) up to and through the devastating final line, 'Qu'as-tu fait de ta jeunesse?' (What have you done with your youth?). A *raison d'être* for this song – Fauré's last Verlaine setting, completed late in 1894, almost a year after *La bonne chanson* – might be extrapolated from Claire Croiza's advice to singers in *La bonne chanson*: 'The descent', she observes, 'will come, but ... Fauré has not put it into the music.'[21] It duly found its music in 'Prison', whose poem was prompted by Verlaine's incarceration for wounding Arthur Rimbaud in a drunken quarrel (some months after he had abandoned his young wife Mathilde Mauté, for whom he had written the poems of *La bonne chanson*). The sombre sequel that 'Prison' forms to *La bonne chanson* uncannily matches the way 'L'absent', twenty-three years earlier, capped Fauré's early settings of Hugo.

Unlike Debussy's penchant for close text-tracking, Fauré's word-painting often hides in plain sight. We recognise it in the bell-chimes of 'Prison', the lute-, guitar-, or mandolin-like figurations of 'Puisque j'ai mis', 'S'il est un charmant gazon', 'Mandoline' (from the *Cinq mélodies 'de Venise'*), the 'Sérénade' from *Le bourgeois gentilhomme,* and the Op. 94 'Chanson'; or the pattering rain of 'Spleen', the tanpura evocation in the drone bass of 'Les roses d'Ispahan', the perfume-like swirls of piano descant in 'Le parfum impérissable', the flecks of spray from the piano's right hand on the last page of 'Les berceaux', and the piano descant evoking the poet's flute in 'Arpège'. A defining factor – as with the programmatic metronome marking of 'Prison' – is often one key phrase of a poem. The minor key of 'Clair de lune' takes a cue from Verlaine's line 'Tout en chantant sur le mode mineur'

Example 5.5. Fauré, 'Les berceaux', mm. 19–20

– but sidesteps the obvious by slipping into major mode for that particular line (as Ravel noted with delight).[22] The major mode that ends 'Chant d'automne' may be unexpected, but is harmonically undermined from so many angles as to convey more unease than a minor ending would; it also comes on the heels of one of Fauré's most literal pieces of word-painting, the pounding left-hand chords in mm. 39–47 that underline Baudelaire's hammering of nails into an imagined coffin.

Localised word-painting emerges more quietly from the *poco rall.* that stretches out 'l'horizon immense' in 'Mai', the contrapuntal perpetuation of rising chromatics prompted by 'immortalité' in 'Hymne', or the tolling funeral bell that ends 'L'absent'; the list easily goes on. None of them is more ingenious than the combination that focusses the climax of 'Les berceaux': as the voice's falling end-syllable is swamped by the rising wave of the piano's *Rheingold*-like bass, the latter breaks with an unmistakable 'Tristan' chord, in an aurally graphic metaphor for the poem's blend of cradle, sea, love, and danger (see Example 5.5).

A vital aesthetic underlying these emerges from Fauré's answers to a journal's questionnaire posed in 1911, 'What should be set to music?' Of 'Spleen' he responded, 'The sound of the raindrops is only incidental . . . the loving and anxious lamentation is the essential thing', adding that in both 'Spleen' and 'Green' (from Op. 58) 'the accompaniment must aim at *underlining* the intense feeling which the words merely *sketch*'.[23]

Singers

In 1868, 'Le papillon et la fleur' received its concert premiere from the celebrated Caroline Miolan-Carvalho, for whom Fauré had stepped in at short notice as accompanist (an event that probably helped him find a publisher). Otherwise, his earlier songs were mostly heard first in domestic or salon circles, with Fauré at the piano accompanying some reputable singers associated with cultured salons or teaching practices, like Félix Levy, Marie Trélat, Julie Lalo, or Henriette Fuchs. From 1871, the Société nationale became a regular professional-level platform, whose altruistic basis made it an allowable venue for several skilled singers whose social background vetoed commercial careers, as well as for young talent that included Jane Huré, aged just seventeen when she premiered two songs including 'Les berceaux' in 1882.

From the late 1880s, as Fauré's reputation spread, the tenor Maurice Bagès de Trigny became his concert singer of preference, often touring abroad with him. The high C-major version of 'Nocturne' was probably devised for him; 'Larmes' and 'Au cimetière' of autumn 1888 immediately suggest his supple high range (he and Fauré had been part of a group visiting Bayreuth that summer); and it was explicitly for Bagès that Fauré wrote 'La rose' in 1890 – whose vertiginously high, quiet ending had to be recomposed for the 1908 Third Collection, at some musical cost, after it became apparent that few singers could manage the 1890 ending.[24] (Both versions appear in volume 2 of the Peters edition.)

Social conventions prevented Emma Bardac (Fauré's muse for *La bonne chanson*) from performing in public; the same would have gone for Émilie (Mimi) Girette, whose voice, musicality, and intelligence captivated Fauré around the turn of the century. In 1902 she delightedly noted that 'When [Fauré] is accompanying me we are one person, he follows me and yet I sense everything that he wishes'.[25] For her he composed 'Accompagnement' in 1902, and he subsequently dedicated 'Le plus doux chemin' to her on her marriage to the pianist Édouard Risler. Jane Bathori, Jeanne Raunay, Claire Croiza, Madeleine Grey, and Charles Panzéra played more public roles in presenting Fauré's subsequent songs; all but Panzéra were accompanied by Fauré in concert. (His last documented platform appearance was in 1919, performing *La chanson d'Ève* with Madeleine Grey.)

Fauré's Songs in Performance

A physical sense of Fauré at the instrument comes through his piano parts. Repeated triads are a favoured opening gambit ('Après un rêve', 'Au cimetière', 'Prison'), opening out in contrary motion (the shared opening progression of 'Après un rêve' and 'Prison' is anticipated verbatim in the central part of 'L'aurore'). Another opening progression involving contrary motion is shared by the otherwise different textures of 'Nell' and 'Mandoline'. Fauré's known ambidextrousness goes with his insistence on strong bass lines: supporting the sonority from the bass and attenuating the right hand often solves or averts balance problems in songs like 'Fleur jetée'.

The mezzo-soprano Claire Croiza, for whom Fauré wrote *Le jardin clos*, counselled that singers should learn thoroughly the poem of any Fauré song, even before mastering the music 'as a vocalise'.[26] The latter aspect was addressed in an initiative almost certainly prompted by Fauré, a multi-volume, multi-composer collection of accompanied wordless vocalises compiled by the Conservatoire voice professor Amédée-Louis Hettich and published by Editions Leduc from 1907 onwards; the series opens with Fauré's own *Vocalise-étude* of 1906. These can now be supplemented by the numerous accompanied vocalises Fauré composed between 1906 and 1916 as Conservatoire sight-reading tests (now published in a Peters edition). Their particular value lies in training exactly the elements they were designed to test, usually starting by pitching exposed triads, then other varied intervals, before adding progressive rhythmic variety and tonal modulation, sometimes making the singer sustain a note or an enharmonic renotation over a disconcerting tonal swerve in the accompaniment.[27] Several of them make beautiful concert pieces that already figure on commercial CDs.

The performance of Fauré's songs has long been dogged by questions of transposition. His chosen keys sometimes follow obvious logic (as in the Lydian-inflected F major of 'Lydia'), and he had some intuitive preferences, such as E♭ or F♯ major for night songs ('Nocturne' of 1886, plus four songs from later cycles: 'En sourdine', 'La lune blanche', 'Jardin nocturne', and 'Diane, Séléné'). There is no evidence, however, that he was opposed to pragmatic transposition. For some songs, an original key can no longer be ascertained; several songs survive in more than one autograph key; and copious documentation attests to Fauré performing his songs in transposed keys, sometimes for important premieres. 'Clair de lune' is a graphic case: some of its surviving sketches are in G minor, others in B♭ minor, though the song itself was premiered in C minor (with orchestra), sung by Maurice Bagès reading off a manuscript copy in B♭ minor![28] Nearly all Fauré's songs up to 1904 were printed in at least two keys; the appearance of his post-1905 songs in only medium or low keys may have been partly a matter of their limited sales, and there is now no viable reason to hamper their availability to higher (or lower) voices of the kind Fauré regularly worked with, within the bounds of taste and clarity discernible in the transpositions he authorised.

What kind of voice Fauré envisaged might sometimes be intuited from details of vocal writing or texture. Although 'Ici-bas!' was premiered in 1874 by the soprano Marguerite Baron, we might deduce from Example 5.2a that Fauré wrote the song with a male voice in mind, given the appoggiaturas that ostensibly sound simultaneously with their resolutions in mm. 22 and 23 (and again in m. 26): sung an octave lower they correctly become sevenths or ninths. (In practice, the timbral difference between voice and piano helps mitigate any audible problem.) 'Nocturne' (Op. 43 no. 2) is a rarer case, defined (uniquely for Fauré) on its original printed title page as a contralto song in E♭. Early manuscript or printed transpositions took it up variously to F♯, G, A♭, and C – in the last two cases shifting the piano part downwards to meet the voice an octave lower (on paper, for performance with male voice maintains the original pitch relationship). Of these options, the Third Collection of 1908 retained only the original E♭ and the C-major transposition (vocally a major sixth apart, by far the farthest transposition of any of his songs), suggesting Fauré grappling with the challenge of a song conceived in a particular tessitural colour.

Claire Croiza also emphasised an essential quality of 'allant' (moving on) in Fauré's music, and summed up: 'for Fauré more than anyone else the expression has to be found within a framework of keeping in time'.[29] The pianist Vlado Perlemuter, who worked with Fauré in his last years, put it more bluntly, dubbing Fauré 'the terror of singers', as he 'wanted the *mélodie* to be played quite in measure, no rubato'.[30] Fauré's usage of tempo headings is individual, and he admitted to difficulty in deciding them: in a letter of July 1888, he confessed to being regarded by his colleagues as 'devoid of common sense when it comes to indicating a tempo'.[31] His frequent tinkering with these before or after publication left many songs with variant tempo headings that often make best sense when read in mutual context. As an extreme example, different editions of 'Ici-bas!' since 1879 have variously been headed *Andantino* or *Adagio*; given the poem's wistful (not tragic) mood, *andantino* (the original manuscript indication) can be read against the semiquaver flow (see Example 5.2a), and *adagio* against the broad two-in-the-bar, in the literal sense of 'not hurried'. (Fauré's early cantata *Super flumina Babylonis* bears the revealing heading *adagio con moto*. A manuscript of 'Ici-bas!' also shows a variant texture necessitating a flowing tempo, as printed in an appendix to the Peters edition.) For Fauré, *allegretto* is characteristically lighter than *allegro* but not necessarily slower, his *andante* sometimes matching the word's French transliteration 'allant' (as per Croiza's observation). *Quasi adagio* appears more often than *adagio*, literally signifying 'almost at ease' – or even 'not quite at ease', aptly enough when it appears above the unnervingly implacable 'Prison'. A degree of breathlessness is also central to some amorous poems like 'Hymne' or 'Chanson d'amour' (where Fauré's breathing commas create the effect), a quality Fauré specified in his Op. 58 'Venetian' cycle: 'For "Green" I can't overemphasize not to sing *slowly*: its pace is lively, passionate, almost *out of breath!*'[32] Broader dynamic outlines also allow some plasticity: the first prints of 'Aurore' (Op. 39 no. 1) and 'Larmes' (Op. 51 no. 1) show the last line of the former, and the main reprise of the latter, each marking the culmination of a crescendo rather than the drop to *p* printed in subsequent editions. Analogous variants of dynamic shaping can be found in manuscript sources of 'Mandoline' and 'En sourdine' (from Op. 58).

A natural musical tempo often emerges from the spoken poem (pointing us back to Croiza's first dictum), as can quickly be sensed from the opening vocal rhythms in 'Mai' or 'Lydia'. Another pointer to tempo can be Fauré's idiosyncratic way of placing 'le' or 'la' on strong beats (anywhere but the comfort zone of upbeats), as in 'Lydia' ('**Le** jour qui luit est **le** meilleur'), 'Seule!' ('**Le** vent du soir'), or 'L'absent' (launching m. 34 with a dotted minim at '**La** maison est vide'). In each case a flowing tempo is of the essence to avoid the prosody 'grounding': the basic minim tread of 'Seule!' and 'L'absent' is also defined by their original ¢ time signatures (which post-1877 editions corrupted to a four-in-the-bar C). Spoken pacing also helps remedy a few metronome markings that implausibly contradict poetic and musical sense, notably in 'Nell', 'Notre amour', and 'Chanson d'amour'.

Fauré's songs throughout his career show frequent reworking to suit varied circumstances, sometimes over different printed versions, sometimes in early manuscript versions that are less refined but closer to the compositional process. Performing options shown in the Peters edition include variant endings for at least nine songs, the longer manuscript central intermission in 'Mai', the complete early manuscript version of 'S'il est un charmant gazon', four different tessitural realisations of 'Nocturne', an encore verse for the *Shylock* 'Chanson' that was a touch too risqué to print even at that time, numerous variants of dynamic shading or shaping, and many variant syllabifications, some of which suggest intrinsic tempi, convey added vigour, or make better sense of a poetic enjambment (notably at the end of 'La rançon'), even if some of them entail higher risk in performance.

As this chapter has demonstrated, Fauré's songs spring from immensely skilled and practical musicianship, flexible enough to adapt to circumstances but underpinned by great rigour and compositional wit. Complementing Perlemuter's strictures, the violinist Hélène Jourdan-Morhange pinpointed not just Fauré's insistence on unyielding musical forward motion, but his balancing street-urchin sense of fun that she termed 'l'esprit gavroche'.[33] Blanche Fauré-Fremiet, the composer's daughter-in-law, remembered him as 'a southerner, with a great sense of gaiety and prone to joking', and Fauré's younger son Philippe equally recalled his father's lifelong penchant for pranks and parody.[34] Close observation repeatedly shows that element subtly operating as compositional wit, often just under the music's surface. To see all these indicators of Fauré's compositional process and practical working life in combination can now usefully encourage the informedly confident performance that these songs demand and deserve.

Notes

1. *Gabriel Fauré, 45 Vocalises*, ed. Roy Howat and Emily Kilpatrick (Peters Edition, 2013: EP 11385). See Jean-Michel Nectoux, *Gabriel Fauré: A Musical Life*, trans. Roger Nichols (Cambridge: Cambridge University Press, 1991), 459–60 regarding the loss in 1924 of what would have been Fauré's last song, 'Ronsard à son âme'.
2. For song-by-song commentary, see the Peters critical edition (*Gabriel Fauré, Complete Songs*, ed. Roy Howat and Emily Kilpatrick, 4 vols (high and medium voice), EP 11391–4 (Leipzig, London, and New York, 2014–22)) or Graham Johnson, *Gabriel Fauré, The Songs and Their Poets* (Aldershot: Ashgate, 2009).
3. See Roy Howat, 'Fauré the Practical Interpreter', in *Fauré Studies*, ed. Carlo Caballero and Stephen Rumph (Cambridge: Cambridge University Press, 2021), 170–91.
4. See Roy Howat and Emily Kilpatrick, 'Wagnérisme de Fauré: *Pénélope* (1913) et les mélodies', in *Wagner, 1913–2013, Ruptures et Continuité*, ed. Marie-Cécile Leblanc and Danièle Pistone (Paris: Presses de la Sorbonne-Nouvelle, 2015), 25–38.
5. See Chapter 1 of Emily Kilpatrick, *French Art Song: History of a New Music, 1870–1914* (Rochester: University of Rochester Press, 2022).
6. Stephen Rumph, *The Fauré Song Cycles: Poetry and Music, 1861–1921* (Oakland: University of California Press, 2020), 3–30.
7. Renumbered Op. 83 in the Hamelle Third Collection; see the critical commentary to vol. 2 of the Peters edition.
8. See the appendix to vol. 2 of the Peters edition.
9. The title comes from Robert Burns, 'Ode to Handsome Nell' (Burns' teenage crush Nellie Kilpatrick).
10. Graham Johnson and Richard Stokes, *A French Song Companion* (New York: Oxford University Press, 2002), 165.
11. See the preface to Peters Edition EP 7526 (Gabriel Fauré, *Pavane* Op. 50, ed. and arr. Roy Howat for 2 voices, flute, and piano), designed as a reconstruction of what Boult would have heard.
12. First noted by Charles Koechlin, this allusion is amplified in Nectoux, *Gabriel Fauré: A Musical Life*, 108.

13. Letter of 22 August 1906 from Fauré to his wife, in Nectoux (ed.), *Gabriel Fauré: His Life through His Letters*, trans. J. A. Underwood (London: Marion Boyars Publishers, 1984), 345.
14. Maurice Ravel, 'Les Mélodies de Gabriel Fauré', *La revue musicale* (special issue, *Hommage à Gabriel Fauré*, October 1922), 26.
15. See Roy Howat and Emily Kilpatrick, 'Editorial Challenges in the Early Songs of Gabriel Fauré', *Notes*, 68, no. 2 (December 2011), 263–4.
16. Charles Baudelaire, *Journaux intimes; Fusées; Mon Cœur mis à nu*, ed. Ad. van Bever (Paris: Crès et Cie, 1920), 16.
17. 'Sous la Musique que faut-il mettre?', *Musica*, 101 (February 1911), 38.
18. For discussion of this particular poem's importance in 1871, see Chapter 2 of Kilpatrick, *French Art Song*.
19. Jean-Michel Nectoux (ed.), *Gabriel Fauré, Correspondance, suivie de Lettres à Madame H.* (Paris: Fayard, 2015), 469
20. See Georges Servières, *Gabriel Fauré* (Paris, 1930), 26 and his review of Fauré's 1897 Second Collection in *Le Guide musical*, 44, no. 4 (23 January 1898), 71–4; the d'Indy letter is quoted in *Emmanuel Chabrier: Correspondance*, ed. Roger Delage, Frans Durif, and Thierry Bodin (Paris: Klincksieck, 1994), 387n.
21. Betty Bannerman (ed. and trans.), *The Singer as Interpreter: Claire Croiza's Master Classes* (London: Gollancz, 1989), 90.
22. Ravel, 'Les Mélodies de Gabriel Fauré', 24–5.
23. 'Sous la Musique que faut-il mettre?', 38.
24. See Kilpatrick, *French Art Song*, 122–5 and 171–84.
25. Diary entry of 12 January 1902, quoted in Jean-Michel Nectoux, 'Deux interprètes de Fauré: Émilie et Édouard Risler', *Études fauréennes*, 18 (1981), 11.
26. Bannerman, *The Singer as Interpreter*, 80.
27. See Roy Howat and Emily Kilpatrick, 'Gabriel Fauré, the Paris Conservatoire and His Collected Vocalises', *Singing* (AOTOS journal), 64 (Spring 2013), 9–13.
28. See Howat and Kilpatrick, 'Editorial Challenges in the Early Songs of Gabriel Fauré' , 268–74, and 'Fauré's Middle-Period Songs', 312–13.
29. Bannerman, *The Singer as Interpreter*, 79–80 and 92.
30. Transcript of a conversation in the 1970s between Vlado Perlemuter and Roger Nichols, kindly communicated by Roger Nichols; see also Howat, 'Fauré the Practical Interpreter', 179–81.
31. Nectoux, *Gabriel Fauré: His Life through His Letters*, 141.
32. Letter from Fauré to Marguerite Baugnies, quoted in Philippe Fauré-Fremiet, *Gabriel Fauré* (Paris: Albin Michel, 1957), 71–2.
33. Hélène Jourdan-Morhange, *Mes amis musiciens* (Paris: Les Éditeurs français réunis, 1955), 24.
34. 'Brève rencontre avec Blanche Fauré-Fremiet', *Journal de Vichy* (28 June 1958); Fauré-Fremiet, *Gabriel Fauré*, 54.

6 | Debussy's Early Songs: Finding His Compositional Voice

MARIE ROLF

Introduction: Context and Scope

Debussy's path toward artistic maturity is best traced through his early songs.[1] More than any other genre, the *mélodie* exposed him to multiple aesthetic influences and provided him with ready-made formal structures, offering a laboratory in which he could refine his prosody, develop his notion of melodic arabesque, expand his harmonic and contrapuntal techniques, and experiment with rhythmic subtlety and suppleness. It would be a mistake, however, to infer that his compositional maturation progressed in a straight line. Instead, Debussy explored numerous eclectic directions, working out ideas in a combination of traditional and revolutionary ways, and in the process of self-editing over a period of about fifteen years, found his unique compositional voice.

Debussy began setting songs while he was a teenage student at the Conservatoire. These compositions reflect his budding fascination with literature, the people with whom he associated, and influences from his travels as well as from growing up in the cosmopolitan city of Paris. While the young composer never attended a lycée, his literary interests were nurtured by classmates at the Conservatoire and other, primarily well-heeled, individuals who befriended or employed him. Raymond Bonheur remembered bonding quickly with Debussy (known as Achille at the time) when he spotted a volume by Théodore de Banville in the hands of his fellow student, and he recalled hearing Debussy play some of his early songs, at first mostly on poems by Paul Bourget but subsequently on the poetry of Paul Verlaine.[2] Remarking on the fact that Achille was an avid reader in spite of his paltry education, Bonheur also noted that, in addition to his aesthetic attraction to the work of Banville and Verlaine, Debussy was inspired by Charles Baudelaire, Edgar Allan Poe, Stéphane Mallarmé, and Jules Laforgue.[3] Similarly, Paul Vidal recalled hearing the young composer play two of his earliest songs, 'Madrid' and the 'Ballade à la lune', both on poems by Alfred de Musset; while the latter *mélodie* has not been traced, the manuscript of 'Madrid' was dedicated to Vidal and fellow classmate Henri Passerieu.[4] Paul and Achille were residents together at the Villa Médici as winners of the Prix de Rome, and there Vidal reported that everyone 'adored' hearing Debussy's Verlaine songs 'Chevaux de bois', 'Mandoline', and 'Fantoches'.[5] He also remembered Achille's predilection for the poetry of Banville, Bourget, and Verlaine, at a time when the latter was known to only a select few.[6] Moreover, Vidal had in his personal collection the manuscript of at least one early song by Debussy, based on Banville's 'Aimons-nous et dormons'.

Prior to their time together in Rome, Vidal helped his friend secure two part-time jobs. He recommended that Achille succeed him as accompanist for the Concordia choral society, where he was exposed to masterpieces by Bach, Handel, and Gounod, among other repertoire; but first and foremost was an accompanying job in the voice studio of one Madame Moreau-Sainti, where Achille met the woman who would inspire no fewer than twenty-nine of his songs: Madame Marie Vasnier. The young bachelor was smitten with this older married woman, and their relationship quickly transitioned from studio accompanist to personal composer to clandestine lover. His early songs were designed to feature Marie's high and agile voice, and they were based on poetry that not only was readily available in the Vasnier family library but that vicariously conveyed his amorous feelings for his muse. Soon Achille was spending long hours at the Vasnier home, and he and Marie even gave the occasional public performance, as on 12 May 1882 when they premiered two of his songs, 'Fête galante' and 'Les roses'.

In addition, Achille's summer jobs exposed him to the literary works of Gustave Flaubert and Richard Wagner (while in the employ of Madame Marguerite Wilson Pelouze in her château at Chenonceaux during the summer of 1879) as well as to text-based works of Tchaikovsky and other Russian composers (while working for Madame Nadezhda von Meck during the summers of 1880–82). With the latter he travelled to Moscow, Vienna, Venice, Florence, and Rome, absorbing the sights and sounds of these diverse locales and cultures. It was on one of these journeys that Achille dedicated the manuscript of 'Rondeau' to Nadezhda's son Alexander von Meck; two other manuscripts – for 'Souhait' and 'Triolet à Philis', both from 1881 – were composed in Florence and Rome, respectively. Thus, despite the modest circumstances in which Debussy was born and his severely limited general education, his intellectual growth was fostered by personal associations and life experiences such as these. Access to the libraries of the Vasniers and Mesdames Wilson Pelouze and von Meck, not to mention those of the Popelin family and Count Giuseppe Primoli (with whom he became close in Rome during 1885–7), fed Achille's insatiable curiosity, and these resources were augmented by the rich musical and literary friendships and experiences he enjoyed.

Our knowledge of other early influences and sources of Debussy's literary education, especially during the formative years of 1879–83, is ever expanding. Ten years ago, Denis Herlin brought to light the composer's relationship with Henry Kunkelmann (also known as Henry Kerval), eight years Achille's senior, who himself was a composer and organist as well as a disciple of César Franck and an ardent Wagnerian. While few details about the Debussy-Kunkelmann connection are known, we have ten manuscripts of songs that Achille dedicated to Henry, six of which are copies of works he had initially composed for Marie Vasnier and four of which are known only from the Kunkelmann source; the latter group involves poetry by Charles Cros, Maurice Bouchor, and Charles Marie René Leconte de Lisle.[7]

Just as his literary development was self-motivated, so were his early songs virtually independent from his formal composition lessons at the Conservatoire, which began with Ernest Guiraud in December 1880. By then, the eighteen-year-old had already written several songs. His studies with Guiraud focussed on larger choral works and other genres required by the Conservatoire for the annual examinations, repertoire that was often dramatic in nature and thus quite different from the intimate *mélodie*. Only one song, a 'Romance', appears in the Conservatoire records, from 31 January 1881, just one month after Achille had begun studying with Guiraud.

This chapter focusses on Debussy's early efforts in the genre of the *mélodie* and involves fifty-seven songs, roughly two-thirds of Debussy's total output in this genre. Figure 6.1 (available online) identifies the songs investigated, listed by the poets who inspired them, beginning with those to whom Debussy turned most often. Individual songs are listed alphabetically rather than chronologically under each poet, as the dates of many of them still need to be confirmed.[8] The table shows that half of Achille's early song settings were based on poems by Verlaine (seventeen) and Banville (twelve), followed by nine settings of Bourget poems, three each on the poetry of Théophile Gautier, Leconte de Lisle, and Musset, two Bouchor settings, and one each on poems by others.

The songs in this list were composed during the thirteen-year span between 1879 and 1892, from Debussy's youthful attempts at age seventeen to his attainment of artistic maturity around age thirty. By 1892, he was already working on his *Prélude à l'après-midi d'un faune*, the masterpiece that, in the famous words of Pierre Boulez, 'awakened' modern

Figure 6.1. [online only] Songs and poetic texts studied. To view this figure please visit www.cambridge.org/9781316514474 and navigate to the Resources tab.

music.[9] In the process, he had found his unique compositional voice, primarily by responding to literary prompts from Parnassian and Symbolist poets. The following discussion will highlight songs that demonstrate Debussy's evolving poetic choices and aesthetic preferences, his increasingly sophisticated approach to form and prosody, and several idiosyncratic stylistic features that he developed in the process.[10]

Texts: Poets, Aesthetics, Subjects, Influences

Debussy chose to base his early song settings on poems written by his contemporaries, the sole exception being Alfred de Musset. This attraction to recent literature aligned with his propensity to push the boundaries of musical conventions. He even became personally acquainted with some of these poets, including Banville, Bourget, Bouchor, and Vincent Hyspa. By 1890, Debussy had met Mallarmé, not only participating in the poet's 'mardis' but soon responding musically to his eclogue, 'L'après-midi d'un faune'. It seems plausible that he may have met Paul Verlaine, as Achille was studying piano with the poet's mother-in-law, Madame Mauté, even during the period when Arthur Rimbaud entered Verlaine's life. And he may have known Cros through the Mauté family or through his classmate Bonheur. After 1894, the year in which Debussy's *Faune* launched modern music on its path, he set the *Chansons de Bilitis* by his close friend Pierre Louÿs. It was not until much later that he moved away from the work of contemporary writers, turning to the texts of Renaissance poet François Villon and medieval poets Charles d'Orléans and Tristan L'Hermite, although he eventually returned to Mallarmé for his final song settings.

Debussy found his compositional voice through the lens of Symbolist writers such as Verlaine, Mallarmé, and Maeterlinck, but one might trace the origins of his artistic exploration through other literary sources, primarily the poetry of several Parnassians. The Parnassian ideals of restraint, precision, and clarity of form were influenced by Gautier's doctrine of 'art for art's sake', and their subjects often dwelt on exotic or past civilisations, mythology, and epic sagas. Their mouthpiece was *Le Parnasse contemporain* (three volumes were published, in 1866, 1869, and 1876), a reference to Mount Parnassus, the home of the Greek gods. While the Symbolists shared with the Parnassians a joy in the sheer sound and musicality of their verse, they focussed on other qualities, such as spiritualism, dreams, mysticism, and the power of a symbol to suggest, rather than to precisely describe, an idea. The boundaries between these two philosophical approaches were porous, as demonstrated by the inclusion of poems by Mallarmé and Verlaine in *Le Parnasse contemporain* alongside poems by Gautier, Leconte de Lisle, and Banville. Indeed, David Evans points out that 'Banville's poetry blends elements of Romantic idealism with Parnassian formalism and the musical suggestion of the Symbolists'.[11]

One could argue that Banville's work provided the fulcrum on which Debussy's aesthetic sensibilities would pivot. Aware that the texts he chose could covertly express his affection for Marie Vasnier, Achille initially gravitated toward love poems. In his settings from 1880–1, themes of melancholic love or love-death, à la *Tristan*, permeate songs such as 'Caprice', 'Les baisers', and 'Souhait', as well as Gautier's 'Coquetterie posthume', and the image of Zephyr (god of the west wind who accompanied Cupid) features in Banville's 'Rêverie' and 'Triolet à Philis' (published as 'Zéphyr' in 1932 by Schott) as well as in Gautier's 'Les papillons'. The Banville dramatic works to which Achille was drawn – in particular, *Hymnis*, *Diane au bois*, and *Florisse* – centred on Greek subjects, a Parnassian ideal that resonated with the Hellenistic interests of Marie's husband Henri Vasnier, who was a member of the Association des études grecques. It is quite possible that the young composer would have encountered these texts, or those such as *Hélène* or the 'Eglogue' by Leconte de Lisle that also dealt with Greek subjects, in the Vasnier library.

Banville songs that Achille subsequently tackled in 1882, including 'Sérénade', 'Pierrot', and 'Fête galante', are harbingers of the *commedia dell'arte* characters and *fêtes galantes* subjects that we associate primarily with Verlaine. The musical depiction of a guitar in Banville's 'Sérénade' is echoed by the mandolin that accompanies the serenaders in Verlaine's 'Mandoline', and Achille opened these songs in identical fashion, with the tuning of each instrument: a series of perfect fourths, starting on E for the guitar, and rolled open fifths, based on G, for the mandolin. The dreamy Pierrot and newlywed Arlequin of Banville's 'Pierrot' reappear in Verlaine's 'Pantomime', now joined by the characters of Cassandre and Columbine, and Achille's settings of these poems share several traits. Both are cast in E major and in a 2/4 metre, and they exude the playful qualities of the *commedia dell'arte* with trills and chromatic juxtapositions. Both melodies open with the perfect-fourth interval of B_4–E_5, and they quote the popular folk tune 'Au clair de la lune'.[12] All four of these songs – 'Sérénade', 'Mandoline', 'Pierrot', and 'Pantomime' – as well as 'Fête galante' end with fanciful vocalises, written especially for Marie Vasnier. Furthermore, Achille recycled his elegant tune from 'Fête galante' as the 'Menuet' in his

Example 6.1. Figural variation in Claude Debussy, 'Nuit d'étoiles'
a) First refrain
b) Second refrain
c) Third refrain

Petite Suite for piano, four hands – an example of his utilising song settings as a laboratory for his instrumental works.

In addition to his identification with Banville's subject matter, Achille grew increasingly attentive to the structural properties of his poems. He often favoured texts that carried refrains, as they afforded ample opportunity for repetition and variation in his *mélodies*. His first published song, on Banville's 'Nuit d'étoiles', included refrains that feature figural variety in the piano (Example 6.1).

All three songs set to Leconte de Lisle's poems contain refrains that helped Achille structure his compositions; they range from verbatim repeated vocalises in 'La fille aux cheveux de lin' to reharmonised returns and registral changes in 'Jane' to lengthy and elaborate refrains in the epic 'Les elfes'. Incidentally, in the first refrain of 'Jane' Achille substituted the word 'blessé' (wounded) for 'brisé' (broken); such textual licence appears throughout Debussy's early songs, sometimes on purpose and sometimes because he was working from memory. Extensive vocalises in 'Les elfes' are echoed in the refrains of Gautier's 'Chanson espagnole' and his 'Séguidille', which provided an opportunity for Achille to show off Marie's coloratura. The exoticism of 'Séguidille', a song that channelled Bizet's *Carmen* (a composition that Achille clearly knew), is surpassed only by his setting of the work of another Parnassian poet: Armand Renaud's 'Flots, palmes, sables', a 'mélodie persane' that features wildly elaborate arabesques throughout the vocal part but most memorably in its three refrains (see Example 6.2).

Achille's explorations in exoticism were not limited to Spain and Persia; he experimented with a Far Eastern subject in his song on Marius Dillard's 'Rondel chinois'. This time the returning lines of text were embedded within the poetic form of a rondel: *ABba abAB abbaA(B)*; yet, Achille respected only the three strophes, casting them in a large-scale ABA ternary design, and did not literally repeat the music for the poem's invariant *A* and *B* lines:

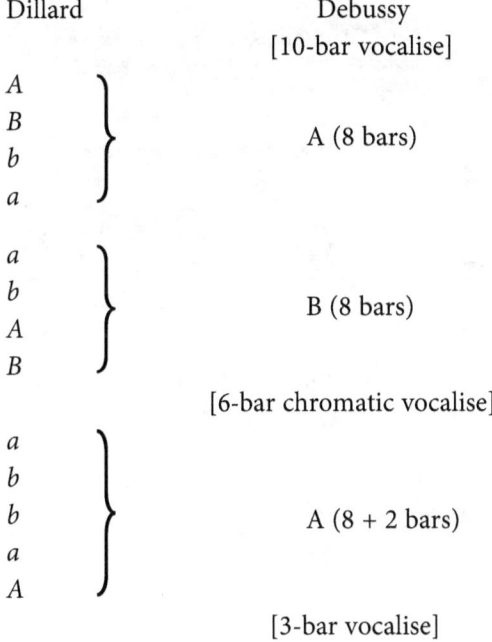

Example 6.2. Debussy, refrain of 'Flots, palmes, sables'

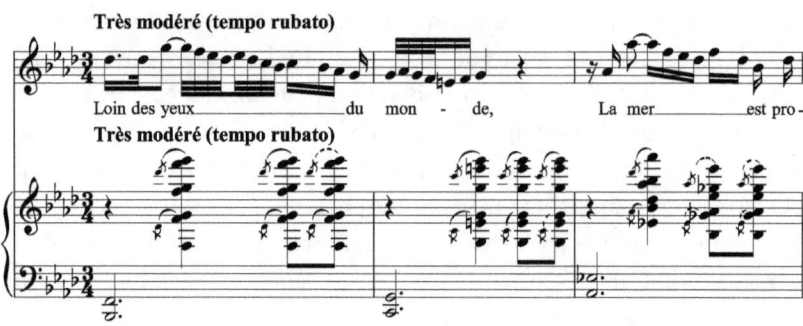

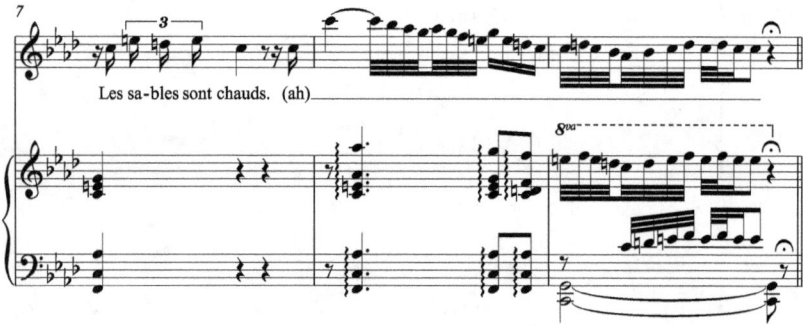

In contrast, he followed the *A* and *B* returns in the *triolet* form more closely in his setting of 'Zéphyr': *ABaA abAB*.

Banville	Debussy
	[2-bar breeze motive]
A ⎫ B ⎭	A (4 bars)
a ⎫ A ⎭	B (4 bars)

```
           [1-bar breeze motive]
a  ⎫
b  ⎭        B (4 bars)
A  ⎫
B  ⎭        A (4 bars)
           [2-bar breeze motive]
```

In addition to relying on poetic structures often employed by Parnassian writers, such as refrains and rondel and *triolet* forms with their embedded returns, Achille set five of Banville's *dizains*, 'à la manière de Clément Marot', a Renaissance poet who favoured this symmetrical construct that pivots on a central axis, between lines 5 and 6: *ababbccdcd*. (Debussy would return to this ancient poetic form in his 'Ballade que Villon fait à la requeste de sa mère pour prier Nostre Dame' of 1910.) While Achille's choices of Banville texts explored many different forms – in addition to the five *dizains*, they include three sestets, a septet, an octet, a *triolet*, and a sonnet – it is notable that there is not a single quatrain among them. He would rely on the latter form in setting poetry by others, such as Gautier, Léon Valade, Leconte de Lisle, Bouchor, and Verlaine. In Debussy's earliest Banville essays, he clearly was intrigued by less conventional poetic constructs, including heterometric poems such as 'Aimons-nous et dormons' and 'Nuit d'étoiles'.[13] These irregular lines invited greater musical flexibility and foreshadowed his interest in free verse, developed in works such as his self-authored *Proses lyriques* and in Louÿs' *Chansons de Bilitis*.

Achille's trajectory from Banville to Verlaine was by no means direct. Along the way, as we have seen, he sampled poems from other Parnassians such as Gautier, Leconte de Lisle, and Valade, and he explored the Symbolist leanings of writers such as Renaud, Cros, and Bouchor. From fall 1883 until 1885, he concentrated on poems by Bourget that replace Banvillian themes of tormented love with languishing sentiments that dwell on past love (such as 'Paysage sentimental' or 'Regret') and earlier depictions of sweet romance experienced in Nature with languorous feelings borne in silence (as in 'Silence ineffable' and 'Musique'). Even songs that feature arabesque melodies and sprightly characters end with ambivalent feelings (as in 'Voici que le printemps' or 'La romance d'Ariel'). It is tempting to read these poetic choices through an autobiographical lens, as during this period Achille was confronting the consequences that his departure for Rome would have on his relationship with Marie. A similar progression can be observed in the Verlaine texts to which the composer was drawn. His initial encounters with the poet's fanciful and elegant *Fêtes galantes* (1869) soon turn inward and move toward states of ennui and bleak despondency in the *Ariettes* (as in

'C'est l'extase', 'Il pleure dans mon cœur', 'L'ombre des arbres', and 'Spleen'). As Achille absorbed the Symbolist ideals of understatement and suggestion as well as the power of a symbol to evoke an idea, he gravitated towards poems like 'En sourdine' (literally, 'muted'), the opening song in *Fêtes galantes I*, going so far as to connect it with 'Colloque sentimental', the last song in Debussy's *Fêtes galantes II*, by a shared arabesque-like motive (symbol) that evokes the plaintive nightingale. And the Symbolists' privileging of dreams and mystical elements finds voice in songs like his setting of Mallarmé's 'Apparition'.[14]

While Debussy's response to these poetic and personal influences is unquestionable, his compositional development was not isolated from the work of other composers and the musical trends of the time. For example, his forays into exotic idioms, such as in 'Madrid', 'Rondel chinois', 'Les elfes', 'Flots, palmes, sables', 'Séguidille', and 'Chanson espagnole', reflect the cultural mix permeating Paris in the nineteenth century. Numerous French composers were writing songs tinged with exoticism, and some even dealt with the same poems prior to Debussy's compositions, perhaps serving as direct models for him. For instance, Gautier's 'Séguidille' was set by his harmony teacher Émile Durand as well as by Jules Philipot in 1874, by Émile Bourgeois in 1875, and by Manuel Giro, a Spanish composer who had moved to Paris that same year, all well before Achille tackled it in 1883. Similarly, Musset's text for Debussy's 'Chanson espagnole' had been set by Conservatoire professor Léo Delibes in 1874 under the well-known title 'Les filles de Cadix', as well as by Manuel Giro in 1879. The venerable Camille Saint-Saëns composed his *Mélodies persanes* in 1870, based on poetry by Armand Renaud, whose 'Flots, palmes, sables' Debussy set a dozen years later in 1882. These and many other parallel settings and associations demonstrate that Debussy was keenly aware of and responsive to both the literary and musical works of his contemporaries.[15]

The following analyses will demonstrate that Debussy's deep identification with Symbolist values shaped his compositional development and informed his unique compositional voice. I will focus on three songs – from 'Caprice', Achille's early Banville *mélodie* from 1880, to his setting of Verlaine's 'Clair de lune' from 1882 and its revision in 1891, to his subtle and sophisticated response to Verlaine's 'Spleen', published first in 1888 by Veuve Girod and then in a revised version in 1903 by Fromont. My goal is to show how the composer's approach to text-setting changed over time, especially as Achille encountered Verlaine's work. Along the way, I will point out compositional procedures in these representative settings that recur in other early songs. My hope is that these emblematic works will inform readers' and performers' understanding and interpretation, serving as models whose characteristic features may be observed in other Debussy songs they might be studying or performing.

'Caprice' (1880)

Achille's first known song on a Banville poem, 'Caprice', was composed for Marie Vasnier. He clearly identified personally with the text, which portrays a passionate lover whose beloved, after initially seeming to spurn him, invites him to kneel at her feet and fulfil his destiny to 'adore her until death'. Any doubt about an autobiographical connection is laid to rest by the dedication that has been enigmatically crossed out on the manuscript: 'These songs, conceived as it were with you in mind, can belong only to you, as does their author'. Moreover, the tempo is marked *Molto Allegro = mais avec un Sentiment passionné*. This is only the first of at least half a dozen other dedications to Marie that are similarly intimate in nature.[16]

Achille chose to cast 'Caprice' in F♯ major, apparently his signature key for Marie, as nearly a third of his songs for her were written in F♯, or G♭. It must have suited her high tessitura (evidently topping out on a high C♯$_6$) in addition to fitting well under the pianist's (that is, his own) hands. Achille turned to this key in many of his early Banville songs, including 'Les baisers', 'Rêverie', 'Aimons-nous et dormons', and 'Les roses', not to mention songs based on the poetry of others that he wrote for Marie, including 'Tragédie' (Valade), 'La fille aux cheveux de lin' (Leconte de Lisle), 'Les papillons' (Gautier), the 1882 setting of 'Clair de lune' (Verlaine), and 'Apparition' (Mallarmé).

Banville's 'Caprice' consists of two octosyllabic sestets that each carry the rhyme scheme of *ababcc*; while the sestets divide into 4 + 2 lines with respect to rhyme, they divide into 2 + 4 with respect to the poetic discourse, in which the lover's expressive gesture in the first two lines is followed by a response from the beloved in the next four lines:

Quand je baise, pale de fièvre,	a	When, pale with fever, I kiss
Ta lèvre où court une chanson,	b	Your lips from which a song bursts forth,
Tu détournes les yeux, ta lèvre	a	You avert your eyes, your lips
Reste froide comme un glaçon,	b	Remain cold as ice,
Et, me repoussant de tes bras,	c	And, pushing me back from your arms,
Tu dis que je ne t'aime pas.	c	You say that I do not love you.

Mais si je dis : Ce long martyre	d	But if I say: this long martyrdom
M'a brisé, je romps mon lien !	e	Has shattered me, I'm severing ties!
Tu réponds avec un sourire :	d	You reply with a smile:
Viens à mes pieds ! tu le sais bien,	e	Kneel at my feet! You know very well,
Ma chère âme, que c'est ton sort	f	Dear soul, that you are destined
De m'adorer jusqu'à la mort.	f	To adore me until death.

Achille chose to follow the latter scheme in setting 'Caprice', cadencing in tonic at the end of line 2 of the poem, and inserting interludes after the first sestet (line 6), and after the lover's entreaty in lines 7–8. In addition, the piano figuration changes for each section of the text, at m. 9 (after the first *b* line), m. 13 (at the first *c*), m. 16 (after the second *c*), and m. 27 (after the first *e*). Figure 6.2 juxtaposes the poetic structure with the musical form as they are reinforced by the harmonic motion of the song. Achille casts Banville's first sestet as a musical AB, in F♯ and B♭, respectively; he often favoured third relations, and many other early songs also feature enharmonic reinterpretation. His middle section (C) hovers between B♭ and F♯, reflecting the lover's unresolved anguish. A dominant prolongation eventually leads to the return of tonic in m. 33, along with a truncated variant of A and B. The AB C A'B' is thus a large-scale ternary form, consisting of sixteen bars, sixteen bars, and eleven bars, respectively. As John Clevenger has observed, 'the vast majority of Debussy's early compositions involve ternary designs'.[17]

Figure 6.2 also illustrates Debussy's habitual preference for off-tonic openings; both the F♯ and B♭ tonal centres are approached via traditional ii-V-I progressions, and their resolutions occur at the ends of

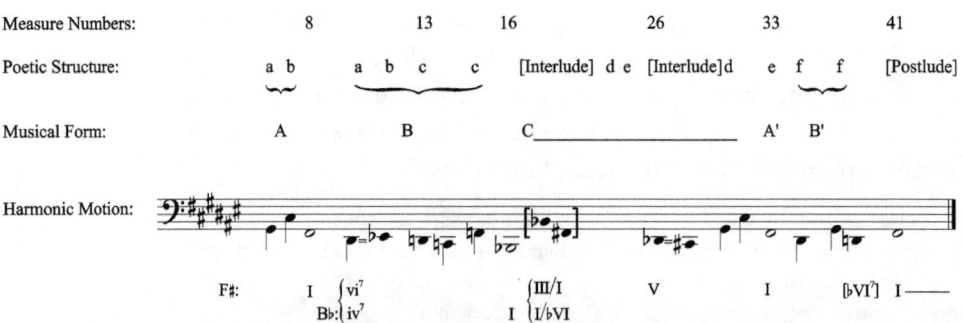

Figure 6.2. Poetic and musical structure of Debussy, 'Caprice'

Example 6.3. Debussy, 'Caprice', mm. 20–34

poetic lines. The only time in this song when the poetic and musical structures coincide with a strong tonal resolution is at m. 33, on the dramatic climax – 'Viens à mes pieds' – when the beloved finally relents to the lover's fervent entreaties. This moment has great impact, especially since it follows a passage of uncertainty, characterised by harmonic oscillation as well as non-synchronous parsing of the poetic lines and the piano (marked by brackets above the voice and piano in Example 6.3).

Unlike most Debussy songs, 'Caprice' has no piano introduction (see Example 6.4). On the other hand, like many early Debussy songs, it exhibits a regular two- and four-bar phraseology. This self-imposed musical constraint often necessitated a manipulation of the text. For example, the first line of the poem is delivered by a leisurely four-bar antecedent phrase; but the second line of text is covered in only two bars, compelling Achille to repeat that poetic line in order to balance the musical antecedent phrase with a four-bar consequent phrase. Similarly, at the end of the poem, Achille's melodic phraseology forced him to repeat the words 'de

Example 6.4. Debussy, 'Caprice', mm. 1–8

m'adorer'. This is a common phenomenon in his early songs, where musical considerations often prevail over the text. By 1888, with his *Ariettes*, and thereafter, Debussy avoided textual repetitions altogether.

In addition, his prosody improved dramatically over time. In 'Caprice', successful moments, such as on the words, 'Mais si je dis: Ce long martyre m'a brisé', which follow the natural speech declamation and poetic enjambment, contrast with awkward ones. This appears in the emphasis on the second syllable of 'pâ-*le*' in m. 3, due both to its occurrence on a beat as well as the rise in pitch, or the similar emphasis on the second syllable of 'u-*ne*' in m. 5. Another especially clumsy passage occurs on the last line of text, with a rise in pitch for the last syllable of 'a-do-*rer*' and metric emphasis on the last syllable of 'jus-*qu'à*'.

Along with such awkward prosody, Achille's early melodies are filled with melismas, either simple ones such as those in mm. 1 and 3 of 'Caprice' or more florid ones such as those that occur especially in the exotic text-settings, like the passage shown in Example 6.2. By 1890, he shows a far greater sensitivity to prosody and he eschews melismatic treatment, favouring instead the syllabic declamation that would permeate *Pelléas et Mélisande*.

'Caprice' is typical of Debussy's songs in that the piano is equally, and often largely, responsible for delivering the melodic content. From the outset, the voice and piano are doubled in octaves, continuing in subsequent passages, such as for the lines 'Ce long martyre' and 'je romps mon lien' (Example 6.3). Following the vocal outburst in mm. 25–6, it is the piano that carries the climactic moment on the downbeat of m. 27 with the highest note of the song, $C\flat_6$, sustained over a fraught dominant-eleventh chord in the following bars, and precisely at the Golden Section.[18] Vocal lines are often relegated to triadic outlines and conjunct motion over the piano's harmony, and they often end on the third or fifth of the chord, rarely on the root (as in m. 8 in Example 6.4, m. 26 in Example 6.3, and also the final note of the song). Debussy's predilection for averting full closure in this way lends a suspensive quality to his music that has often been described as wistful or dreamy. Contributing to that elusiveness is his use of harmony, delaying the tonic or weakening the resolution to the tonic. The final cadence of 'Caprice' features a bass motion from $\flat\hat{6}$ to $\hat{1}$, where a D^7 acts as a German augmented-sixth chord, resolving to F♯ (though in root position rather than resolving first to a $^6_4$). Harmonic clichés based on motions from $\flat$VI to I were prevalent in songs and piano music of the 1880s and 1890s.[19]

'Clair de lune' (1882 and 1891)

As far as we know, Debussy reset the same poem in only three instances, all of them involving Verlaine poems: 'En sourdine', 'Clair de lune', and 'Colloque sentimental'. A comparative analysis of his two versions of 'Clair de lune' reveals much about his compositional growth.[20] Shortly before his departure for Rome, Debussy gave a manuscript of his 1882 setting to Marie in what is now known as the *Recueil Vasnier*.[21] Back in Paris and nearly a decade later, in 1891, Debussy returned to this poem, composing what appears at least superficially to be an entirely new setting, which he eventually published with Fromont in 1903 as the third of *Fêtes galantes I*. The new version may have been influenced by Fauré's setting, composed in 1887 and published by Hamelle in 1888.[22] While Debussy's sprightly 1882 rendition depicts Watteau-like bergamaskers dancing in the moonlight amongst ecstatic fountains through two motives in the piano, it does not match the elegance of Fauré's hemiola-laced *menuet*, in which the piano delivers the primary melody in a minor key as the voice elaborates around it.[23] Debussy responded with a revision in 1891 that was deeply attuned to the melancholic overtones of Verlaine's poem. Following a brief examination of this text, we will compare Debussy's two versions, noting features they have in common as well as their distinct qualities.

The first poem in Verlaine's collection of *Fêtes galantes*, 'Clair de lune', is cast in three quatrains, which Debussy followed in his ternary (ABA) setting. Verlaine utilised the decasyllabic lines that were often employed by Gautier and Leconte de Lisle (as opposed to the octosyllabic metre, which was commonly used during the nineteenth century, seen in Banville's 'Caprice'). In this poem, he deviated from the classic division of 4 + 6 syllables in the first and third strophes (caesuras are marked by vertical strokes).

Votre âme | est un paysage choisi	a	Your soul is a chosen landscape
Que vont charmant | masques et bergamasques	b	Bewitched by maskers and bergamaskers,
Jouant du luth | et dansant | et quasi	a	Playing the lute and dancing and almost
Tris- | -tes sous leur déguisements fantasques.	b	Sad under their fanciful disguises.
Tout en chantant | sur le mode mineur	c	While singing in the minor mode
L'amour vainqueur | et la vie opportune,	d	Of victorious love and the good life,
Ils n'ont pas l'air | de croire à leur bonheur	c	They don't seem to believe in their happiness
Et leur chanson | se mêle au clair de lune,	d	And their song mingles with the moonlight,

Au calme clair de lu- | -ne triste et beau,	e	With the calm moonlight, sad and beautiful,
Qui fait rêver | les oiseaux dans les arbres	f	That sets the birds in the trees dreaming
Et sangloter d'exta- | -se les jets d'eau,	e	And the fountains sobbing with ecstasy,
Les grands jets d'eau svel- | -tes parmi les marbres.	f	The tall, svelte fountains among the marble statues.

The prosody in Debussy's 1882 setting of 'Clair de lune' is already far improved over that in 'Caprice', and it reflects Verlaine's caesuras in lines 1, 3–6, and 9–11, as shown by the brackets below the text in Example 6.5. In fact, it is so well done that there is little left to improve upon in the 1891 version; the only passages that follow Verlaine's caesuras more closely are in lines 7–8 and 12, where the words 'l'air', 'chan-*son*', and '*svel*-tes' receive longer durations than in the 1882 song. Debussy's metric treatment is remarkably synchronous in the two settings; the ticks above each line in Example 6.5 designate points where their bar lines coincide, and the circled text illustrates many phrases where the same note values (or similar durations, given the different metres) are employed.

Phrases in the 1882 song group traditionally into four-bar units but are occasionally extended by two bars, as illustrated in the piano introduction (see the ticks in Example 6.6). This opening presents the two motives that permeate Debussy's song: descending chords in semiquavers that depict streams of moonlight, and ascending chordal bursts in quavers that represent the fountains. It also introduces the motions of $\flat\hat{6}$-$\hat{5}$ and $\flat\hat{2}$-$\hat{1}$ to colour the poignant dichotomies in Verlaine's text, which exude 'triste' yet 'beau' qualities and where the characters do not trust in their happiness, as they sing of 'victorious love and the good life' but 'in the minor mode'. The opening ten bars prolong the dominant of F♯ major (Marie's key, as we saw in 'Caprice'), leading to the structural downbeat of the song in m. 11.

Achille found ways to enhance Verlaine's ambivalent images and his poetic structure with his harmonies. For example, the second quatrain (the B section of Debussy's ternary form) begins in the third-related key area of D♯ minor (vi), to underscore the text about 'singing in the minor mode'. Similarly, in the first quatrain, the word 'Tristes' is enhanced by a shift to a minor seventh in lieu of the previous dominant-seventh chord, and it is immediately followed by an unstable diminished sonority in the voice and piano for the reference to the 'déguisements' (disguises) of the maskers and bergamaskers (see

128 MARIE ROLF

Example 6.5. Prosody in Debussy, 'Clair de lune' (1882 and 1891 versions)

Example 6.6. Debussy, 'Clair de lune' (1882), mm. 1–11

Example 6.7. Debussy, 'Clair de lune' (1882), mm. 24–9

Example 6.7). In addition, the struggle between ♭6̂ and 5̂ and between ♭2̂ and 1̂ plays out in mm. 25–29.

In the second quatrain, when the poet's singers question the veracity of their happiness (line 7), Achille employed a harmonic sleight of hand, treating a whole-tone dominant sonority as a French augmented sixth (the bass C♯ acts as a D♭), and resolving it to an F $^6_4$ chord. While effectively enhancing the text, this harmonic surprise leaves us in a distant key from the tonic (where we expect to be for the return of A). Achille extricated himself from this tonal dilemma in the way he typically did in his early songs, by sequence,

Example 6.8. Debussy, 'Clair de lune' (1882), mm. 39–53

moving in this case from the bass C_2 to E_2–E_4 and then down a third to $C\sharp_4$, the dominant of $F\sharp$, to prepare the return of A in m. 54 (see Example 6.8). Though effective harmonically, this device necessitated a repetition of line 8, beginning in m. 47 – not unlike the textual repetitions observed in 'Caprice'.

One other repetition of text occurs at the end of the song, where Achille inserted an 'Ah' for two bars, followed by a four-bar reiteration of the opening line of the third quatrain, 'Au calme clair de lune triste et beau', recalling the ambiguous effect of $\flat\hat{6}$-$\hat{5}$ and $\flat\hat{2}$-$\hat{1}$ (see Example 6.9). Note, as observed in 'Caprice', the composer's characteristic melodic cadence on the third or fifth of the chord, rather than the root, weakening the sense of closure.

Example 6.9. Debussy, 'Clair de lune' (1882), mm. 75–84

Such textual reiteration is completely absent from the 1891 setting, in which the music becomes the unequivocal servant of the poem. The voice, now in a distinctly lower tessitura and more limited range, declaims the text around the piano part, which delivers the melodic-harmonic structure of the piece. As Debussy was no longer writing specifically for Marie Vasnier, he no longer felt compelled to compose a high $A\sharp_5$ for her; the 1891 setting attains only an $F\sharp_5$, allowing the text to be delivered in understated, Symbolist fashion. Melismas occur only on the words 'bonheur' and 'marbres', at the ends of lines 7 and 12, as opposed to the frequent two-note melismas of the 1882 song. The result is a melody that is less memorable than the lilting 1882 song, but one that is more closely intertwined with the piano part in its assimilation of Verlaine's Symbolist aesthetic.

Debussy now reveals the deeper, hidden, 'chosen' landscape of the soul rather than the superficial charm of the masked characters on which he focussed in 1882. His 1891 setting exudes utter quietude, opening with the piano's slow unveiling of a suspended landscape in a tranquil atmosphere that is created through a 'very moderate' 9/8 metre, mesmerising two-bar groupings, and an incantatory, arabesque-like pentatonic motive. While this pendulous sonic universe may initially appear to be light years away from the gaiety of Debussy's 1882 song, nascent connections exist between the two settings. For example, the F♯ tonic of the early version now becomes the progenitor of the later version's pentatonic collection, and a rhythmic motive from the 1882 song is recycled: compare the bracketed rhythmic motives in mm. 77–9 of the piano in Example 6.9 with those that open the 1891 song in Example 6.10. In addition, the structural function of this piano introduction is similar to that of the 1882 setting: as an extended upbeat that resolves in this case not to F♯ major but to the darker mode of G♯ minor, approached now by its minor dominant with its ♭$\hat{7}$ scale degree.[24]

Indeed, many other compositional features of the 1891 version are latent in the 1882 song and reappear in adaptation. The piano still carries the primary melodic-harmonic material, including motives that serve to unify each setting. However, in lieu of the traditional text-painting of the moonlight and fountains, Debussy now relies on more abstract rhythmic pulsations, derived from his earlier version, which saturate his 1891 setting. Example 6.11 illustrates how this rhythmic motive is juxtaposed and intertwined within various textures and harmonies in a process of continual variation, a compositional procedure that features in mature works like the *Prélude à l'après-midi d'un faune*.

Examples 6.11c and 6.11e show the offbeat accompaniment generated by rhythmic pulsations, which lends a sense of underlying anxiety or tension throughout the song. As in the 1882 setting, Debussy's 1891 version still underscores the words 'Tristes' (quatrain 1) and 'Ils n'ont pas l'air de croire à leur bonheur' (quatrain 2), but this time with whole-tone and half-diminished sonorities, respectively. And he still makes effective use of respelled augmented-sixth chords, first between quatrains 2 and 3 (Examples 6.11d–e), and then within the latter to enhance the words 'sangloter d'extase' (see Example 6.12).

Furthermore, Debussy continued to express the bittersweet qualities of the poem in his use of half-step motions around a tonal scale degree; in lieu of the ♭$\hat{6}$-$\hat{5}$ and ♭$\hat{2}$-$\hat{1}$ motions from 1882, he now employs ♯$\hat{4}$-$\hat{5}$ and $\hat{6}$ (which is flatted in a minor key)-$\hat{5}$ (see mm. 5–6 in Example 6.10). While doubling the opening vocal line, he artfully covers it in an inner voice of the piano, and these doubled lines often subsequently diverge (see beat 4 of m. 6 in Example 6.10), generating a linear bifurcation to which performers

Example 6.10. Debussy, 'Clair de lune' (*Fêtes galantes I*, 1891), mm. 1–6

should be attuned. The second quatrain of the 1891 song opens with a repeat of the opening emblematic tune and harmony, now in the piano only and down an octave; the vocal part's entry on E_4 emanates from the piano's E_3, but now the notion of a single-note bifurcation within a doubled line is expanded into a full-blown two-part counterpoint between the voice and the primary melody in the piano.

While the emblematic tune is no longer present at the opening of the third quatrain, the distinctive ♭$\hat{6}$–$\hat{5}$ lingers, and the tonic of G♯ minor is still projected (though mingled with B major, the resolution of the previous augmented-sixth chord, shown in Example 6.11d–e), suggesting a tripartite form that features variation of a single idea (AA'A") rather than the

Example 6.11. Motivic juxtapositions in Debussy, 'Clair de lune' (1891)
a) Introduction, m. 1
b) Quatrain 1, mm. 9–10
c) Quatrain 2, m. 16
d) Quatrain 2, mm. 19–20
e) Quatrain 3, mm. 21–22

contrasting middle section that we heard in the 1882 song (ABA). Now each of the sections begins in G♯ minor (albeit clouded in the third quatrain) and moves elsewhere in its own way, with the voice diverging

Example 6.12. Debussy, 'Clair de lune' (1891), mm. 25–6

Example 6.13. Debussy, 'Clair de lune' (1891), mm. 27–32

and converging with the piano, while variations of the rhythmic motive unify the entire song.

A final important element that permeates the 1891 version involves a pentatonic set – (025) in pitch-class set notation – that is overlaid on the basic tonal framework. This pitch collection lends a static, numbing quality (the 'calme clair de lune') to the song and appears both melodically and harmonically throughout the work. Its melodic introduction in the piano (see the circled sets in Example 6.10) is echoed in the concluding vocal line and harmonic motion (see the circled sets in mm. 29–30 of Example 6.13).[25]

The ambiguity of Verlaine's poem is thus reflected in the form and melodic-harmonic motions of Debussy's song; poetic images can be ambiguous, and so can musical structure and tonality. Debussy accordingly found a way to interpret and transpose the Symbolist qualities of Verlaine's poem within his music, and in the process he was forging his own compositional voice.

Verlaine's 'Clair de lune' would continue to influence Debussy over several decades, inspiring what is arguably his best-known piano piece – 'Clair de lune', the third movement of his *Suite bergamasque* from 1890, published by Fromont in 1905. One could posit that, given its 9/8 metre in the key of D♭, its arabesque-like melody, and its pentatonic inflections, as well as its ♭$\hat{6}$–$\hat{5}$ motions, this piano piece has much in common with the 1891 song, hence its shared title. The *commedia dell'arte* characters in Verlaine's poem figure in the title of another work for piano, *Masques*, published in 1904 by Durand.[26] And as late as 1909–10 Debussy was contemplating a ballet set in eighteenth-century Venice, *Masques et bergamasques*, for Sergei Diaghilev's Ballets Russes.[27]

'Spleen' (published 1888)

Even though considerable scholarly attention has already been given to Debussy's masterful *Ariettes*, we would be remiss to ignore them completely. Composed between 1885 and 1887 and published individually by Veuve Girod in 1888, the six *Ariettes* were revised and published collectively as the *Ariettes oubliées* by Fromont in 1903, a year after the successful launch of *Pelléas et Mélisande*. While a full analysis of 'Spleen' is beyond the scope of this study, I will merely highlight several compositional seeds discernible in the 1888 song that blossom fully in Debussy's future vocal and instrumental works.

Verlaine cast his octosyllabic poem in couplets that group further into three quatrains in *rimes croisées* (*abab, cdcd,* and *efef*):

Les roses étaient toutes rouges	a	The roses were all red	
Et les lierres étaient tout noirs.	b	And the ivy was all black.	
Chère, pour peu que tu te bouges,	a	Dear, you need only move	
Renaissent tous mes désespoirs.	b	To rekindle all my despair.	
Le ciel était trop bleu, trop tendre,	c	The sky was too blue, too tender,	
La mer trop verte et l'air trop doux.	d	The sea too green and the air too mild.	
Je crains toujours – ce qu'est d'attendre!	c	I always fear – it is to be expected!	
Quelque fuite atroce de vous.	d	Some horrible escape from you.	
Du houx à la feuille vernie	e	Of the holly with burnished leaves	
Et du luisant buis je suis las,	f	And of the shiny boxwood, I am weary,	
Et de la campagne infinie	e	And of the infinite countryside	
Et de tout, fors de vous, hélas!	f	And of everything, alas, except for you!	

Couplets 1 and 3, written in the imperfect tense, describe the environment, though with greater intensity in couplet 3: the roses and ivy were *all* ('tout') red and black, but the sky and sea were *too* ('trop') blue/tender and green/mild. Couplets 2 and 4, on the other hand, are written in the present tense, and they describe the poet's personal emotions, which similarly progress to greater intensity in couplet 4. Verlaine punctuates each of these four couplets with a full stop, as opposed to the comma that connects couplets 5 and 6. The alternation between description of the landscape and the poet's feelings accelerates in these last two couplets, so much so that, in the final line, the three syllables of description – 'Et de tout' – merge with the rhymed three syllables of emotion – 'fors de vous'. This climactic moment of the poem ends in the only way it can, with the ultimate expression of ennui and dejection: 'hélas!'

Debussy conveyed Verlaine's single-minded despondency by structuring his *mélodie* around the piano's initial single-line motto – one of his characteristic monophonic openings – which he repeated seven times throughout the thirty-four-bar song.[28] This motto recurs relentlessly on the same pitch, B♭, for five of those iterations (four of which are even in the same register), although its harmonic and contrapuntal context varies (see Example 6.14). The only exception is in couplet 5 (Example 6.14d–e), where the motto begins on D and where Verlaine's – and Debussy's – acceleration begins; Roy Howat has pointed out that this moment occurs at the Golden Section.[29]

Debussy emulates Verlaine's alternation between objective and personal elements in couplets 1–4 through changes in texture and with rests in the

Example 6.14. Appearances of the motto in Debussy, 'Spleen' (*Ariettes*)
a) Introduction, mm. 1–4
b) Couplet 1, mm. 9–10
c) Couplet 4, mm. 18–19
d) Couplet 5, mm. 22–3
e) Couplet 5, mm. 24–5
f) Couplet 6, mm. 28–9

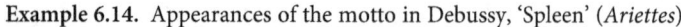

Example 6.14. *(cont.)*
g) Couplet 6, mm. 30–1

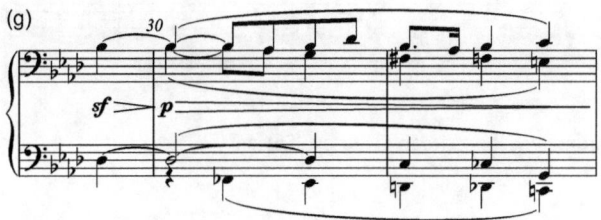

voice after each couplet. He expresses the poet's mounting anxiety through increased rhythmic motion, transforming the descending, dotted-quaver-semiquaver motive of the motto into an ascending figure (performed *poco stringendo*) in couplet 2. He increases the tension even further with an ascending figure (now *stringendo*) in couplet 4. Verlaine's poetic acceleration in couplets 5 and 6 is mirrored in Debussy's music by a passage – *poco a poco animato*, with no vocal rest between the couplets – that attains the dynamic and registral extremes of the song.

Woven into the tight motivic structure of the piano part, where virtually every note emanates from the opening motto, the vocal declamation is treated with maximum flexibility. It opens with a listless recitative on a single pitch, whose rhythms, mirroring the text, convey no regular metre (Example 6.15). The vocal entry in couplet 2 similarly obfuscates our metric sense, as it begins on beat 3 with a long-held F♭$_5$ and then cascades down an octave in a rhythm that still simulates the metric freedom of a recitative (Example 6.16a).

Nor is the listener grounded tonally at this point. The piano's opening motto is not harmonised until m. 4, when we hear chords a tritone apart, G♭ and C (Example 6.14a). These two sonorities linger in the listener's ear until the beginning of couplet 5 (Example 6.14d), when Debussy finally moves to a B♭ chord that we ultimately understand is the subdominant in the key of F minor, the tonic that is not reached until the final bar of the song. Thus, in retrospect, we understand the opening G♭-C motion to be a Neapolitan-dominant progression, more progressive than the traditional ii-V-I motions that established the tonal centres in 'Caprice' (refer to Figure 6.2).

Thus, for the first eight bars of this song, the listener remains in suspense, with no idea what metre or key we are in. By m. 9 (Example 6.14b), we could conceivably hear a triple metre, though it is clouded by the triplets in the right hand against the duple subdivisions in the left. The nebulous vocal sigh

Example 6.15. Debussy, 'Spleen', mm. 4–8

Example 6.16. Enharmonic vocal entries in Debussy, 'Spleen'
a) Couplet 2, mm. 9–11
b) Couplet 3, mm. 14–15

in mm. 9–11 (Example 6.16a) offers no rhythmic or tonal clarity. The song finally settles into a regular metric feeling at the beginning of couplet 3 in m. 14, when this sigh reappears on the same pitch (notated enharmonically), now in heterophony with the piano (Example 6.16b) and in counterpoint with the dotted quaver-semiquaver from the tail of the motto. Here Debussy is applying to the vocal line the same principle that he used for the motto in the piano: repeating a gesture that remains invariant while altering its harmonic and contrapuntal environment.

Debussy transferred virtually all of these compositional techniques – a monophonic opening which is pregnant with harmonic and contrapuntal possibilities that are worked out in the course of the piece, tonal and metric ambiguity, delay of tonal resolution, and variation processes – to his orchestral masterpiece, the *Prélude à l'après-midi d'un faune*, and even earlier to *Printemps*, one of his submissions to the Académie des Beaux-Arts as a Prix de Rome winner. And his completely syllabic text-setting, pared down to the point of unaccompanied recitative, is fundamental to his vocal writing in *Pelléas*. The expressive use of silence, so intentional in his opera, can be observed in 'Spleen' with the expectant fermata in m. 4 before the vocal entry (Example 6.14a) as well as the piano's hesitant rest on the downbeat of m. 32, before finally moving to the cadence.[30] And the specific juxtaposition of F♯ and C harmonies (notated as G♭ and C in 'Spleen') runs throughout *Pelléas et Mélisande*, especially during Act 4, Scene 4, where these tonal centres reflect the ambiguities in Maeterlinck's Symbolist play.[31] Virtually all of these compositional procedures were developed by Debussy through his songs as musical analogues to the understated, suggestive, equivocal qualities inherent in the works of the Symbolist writers.

Conclusion

Debussy's early songs provided fertile ground for his compositional exploits, which were keenly attuned and responsive to the aesthetics of his contemporary poets. His friend Paul Dukas perceptively observed that 'the greatest influence on Debussy was that of writers, not of musicians'.[32] As his interest shifted from the work of the Parnassians to the Symbolists, and from topics of love, nature, and the *fêtes galantes* to world-weary subjects replete with ambiguity, he moved away from traditional word-painting, as seen in his 1882 setting of 'Clair de lune', towards a response to poetic constructs, as seen in 'Spleen'. This increasing interest in abstract formal structures may be found in many of his mature songs, such as his musical setting of the 'Harmonie du soir' pantoum from the *Cinq poèmes de Baudelaire*.

In selecting his texts, Debussy experimented with a variety of poetic forms, including quatrains, sestets, *dizains*, *triolets*, rondels, and sonnets. Of the fifty-four poems we have considered, more than half involve octosyllabic metre (35 percent) or heterometric verse (20 percent); Debussy chose decasyllabic poems and those that feature *vers impairs* (odd-numbered syllables per line, Verlaine's ideal) 15 percent of the time, and alexandrines 13 percent.[33] Despite this vast assortment of poetic structures, and the fact that 35 percent of the time Debussy gravitated toward irregular constructs, presumably attracted by the flexibility they would afford in his musical settings, his early songs rely most often on traditional ternary forms and two- and four-bar phraseology.

The composer typically entrusted the essential melodic-harmonic content to the piano, weaving the vocal line around it. In the earliest songs, he was often appending the text to a pre-conceived melody, resulting in awkward prosody, melismatic passages, and textual repetitions as a consequence of the tune's phraseology. In addition, most of these songs feature a high tessitura because they were composed explicitly for Marie Vasnier. Gradually, over a period of five or six years, Debussy shunned this approach, opting for rigorous syllabic treatment of the text, lowering the tessitura, and limiting the range of the vocal part, in response to the understated qualities of Symbolist poetry. As his sensitivity toward prosody became more subtle and refined, his rhythmic treatment became more flexible, combining triple with duple subdivisions of the beat, and even moving toward a recitative-like style of declamation, as seen in 'Spleen'. Ultimately, his mastery of rhythm, metre, and silence grew in sophistication, enabling him to create that unique Debussyan sense of mystery as he suspended time for the listener – again, a Symbolist notion, one that we experience in the *Faune* and *Pelléas*, as well as the *Nocturnes* and other works.

Debussy's approach to tonality is equally elusive. The earliest songs typically exhibit traditional harmonies, with a predilection for third relations and the occasional 'surprise' chord of a diminished seventh or respelled augmented sixth, as seen in 'Caprice'. But many of them also reveal the composer's penchant for off-tonic openings, a technique that he kept in his mature arsenal. It is only in later songs – such as 'L'ombre des arbres', 'Spleen', or the 1892 setting of 'En sourdine' – that he delayed a resolution to tonic until the final bar of the piece. In addition to this artful evasion, he obscured normative harmonic expectations by overlaying pentatonic or whole-tone material atop what is basically a tonal framework; we observed, for example, a whole-tone colouring of the word 'Tristes' in the 1891 setting of 'Clair de lune', which is also rife with pentatonicism.

As Debussy developed confidence, he was increasingly prone to favour slow harmonic rhythms, even to the point of relying on ostinato passages to govern large sections of his songs, as in 'Regret', from 1884; even more obvious are the bell ostinatos that permeate 'Les cloches' and 'Les angélus' from 1886 and 1891, respectively. Static harmonies, in combination with metric instability (created by duple/triple juxtapositions, occluded downbeats, and the like), provided a receptive environment to develop his notion of the melodic arabesque, featured in so many of his songs, piano pieces, and other instrumental works.[34]

At the same time, perhaps ironically (and often overlooked by scholars), Debussy's contrapuntal prowess developed exponentially. The sophisticated interweaving of motivic material in 'Spleen' is a far cry from the homophonic setting of 'Caprice', where the voice and piano often cautiously double each other. And his process of continually altering the context around an invariant motto, so seminal to his compositional technique, is clearly developed in the songs. We observed this procedure in 'Spleen', but it is also present in many other songs, such as 'Romance' ('L'âme évaporée'), 'Le son du cor', and 'L'échelonnement des haies'.

Our glimpse into Debussy's compositional laboratory has revealed that he expanded his vocabulary and techniques, developing his unique 'chimie musicale' (musical chemistry) in vocal settings as he searched to find musical analogues for Symbolist ideals.[35] As he confessed to his teacher Ernest Guiraud, he sought the poet who, 'in saying things half-way [by implying or suggesting rather than by stating], would allow me to graft my dream onto his'.[36] He ultimately found those poets in Verlaine, Mallarmé, and Maeterlinck, whose works served as catalysts for his stylistic evolution and led him to artistic maturity.

Notes

1. I am grateful to David Grayson and Stephen Rumph for their invaluable editorial comments and to Noah Kahrs for preparing the musical examples.
2. Raymond Bonheur, 'Souvenirs et impressions d'un compagnon de jeunesse', *La revue musicale* (1 May 1926), 3–4 (99–100).
3. Ibid., 8 (104).
4. Paul Vidal, 'Souvenirs d'Achille Debussy', *La revue musicale* (1 May 1926), 12–13 (108–9).
5. Ibid., 15 (111).
6. Ibid., 15–16 (111–12). Among the seven extant letters sent from Rome by Achille to Émile Baron, his cherished bookseller in Paris, is one (probably from September 1886) in which the young composer requests 'anything' by Verlaine; see Claude Debussy, *Correspondance (1872–1918)*, ed. François Lesure and Denis Herlin (Paris: Gallimard, 2005), 52.
7. Claude Debussy, *Quatre nouvelles mélodies*, ed. Denis Herlin (Paris: Durand, 2012).
8. Volume 1 of the forthcoming critical edition of Debussy *mélodies* (Paris: Durand), co-edited by Denis Herlin and Marie Rolf, will posit a chronology, based on a thorough study of the manuscripts – paper type, handwriting, dedications – as well as poetic choices and historical context.
9. Pierre Boulez, *Relevés d'apprenti* (Paris: Éditions du Seuil, 1966), 336, and *Notes from an Apprenticeship*, trans. Herbert Weinstock (New York: Alfred A. Knopf, 1968), 345.

10. For a brief discussion of each of Debussy's songs, see Denis Herlin's liner notes for *Claude Debussy: Intégrale des mélodies*, Jean-Louis Hagenauer et al., Ligia LIDI 02201285-14, 2014, 4 compact discs.
11. David Evans, *Théodore de Banville: Constructing Poetic Value in Nineteenth-Century France* (London: Legenda, 2014), 253.
12. The refrain in 'La belle au bois dormant' (1890) also features a French folk song, 'Nous n'irons plus au bois'.
13. Other examples from the early songs include Musset's 'Rondeau' and 'Chanson espagnole', Bouchor's 'On entend un chant', Renaud's 'Flots, palmes, sables', Gautier's 'Séguidille', Bourget's 'Regret', 'Beau soir', and 'Les cloches', and Verlaine's 'L'ombre des arbres'.
14. Other early songs that engage with magical elements in the context of legends include 'L'archet' by Cros, 'Les elfes' by Leconte de Lisle, and 'La belle au bois dormant' by Hyspa.
15. Particularly noteworthy are the dozens of settings of Gautier's 'Les papillons', including one by Conservatoire professor Louis-Albert Bourgault-Ducoudray in 1880, that surely influenced Achille.
16. Debussy's dedications on the manuscripts of his songs are reproduced in Margaret G. Cobb (ed.), *The Poetic Debussy*, 2nd ed. (Rochester: University of Rochester Press, 1994); they are also available in the catalogue at the end of François Lesure, *Claude Debussy: Biographie critique* (Paris: Fayard, 2003).
17. John Clevenger, 'The Origins of Debussy's Style', PhD dissertation, University of Rochester, 2002, 1312.
18. Many of Debussy's works conform, consciously or not, to the proportions of the Golden Section, a classical ratio that has been traced in architecture, art works, and biological growth patterns.
19. See especially pp. 293-9 in Alexandra Kieffer, 'Reverie, Schmalz, and the Modernist Imagination', *Journal of the American Musicological Society*, 74, no. 2 (Summer 2021), 289-363.
20. See also Roger Nichols, 'Debussy's Two Settings of "Clair de lune"', *Music and Letters*, 48 (1967), 229-35, and Douglass Green, '"Clair de lune": An Analytical Study of Various Versions', paper delivered at the annual meeting of the American Musicological Society in Vancouver, 1985. For other comparative studies, see my 'Debussy's Settings of Verlaine's "En sourdine"' in *Perspectives on Music*, ed. Dave Oliphant and Thomas Zigal (Austin: Humanities Research Center, The University of Texas at Austin, 1985), 205-33, and my essay on 'La première ébauche de "Colloque sentimental"', in *Regards sur Debussy*, ed. Myriam Chimènes and Alexandra Laederich (Paris: Fayard, 2013), 193-210.
21. A facsimile reproduction of the Recueil Vasnier was published in 2011 by the Centre de documentation Claude Debussy in Paris. It includes four other songs from Verlaine's *Fêtes galantes*, six Bourget songs, and one each based on Gautier and Musset poems.
22. See Emily Kilpatrick, *French Art Song: History of a New Music, 1870-1914* (Rochester: University of Rochester Press, 2022), 123-5.

23. On the Watteau–Verlaine–Debussy connections, see Gurminder Kaur Bhogal, *Claude Debussy's 'Clair de lune'* (Oxford: Oxford University Press, 2018), 70–8.
24. This suspensive, four-bar introduction was not part of Debussy's original compositional plan, as it is absent from two early manuscript sources for this song, now in the Arthur Honegger (private collection in France) and Robert Owen Lehman collections (on deposit at The Morgan Library & Museum in New York City).
25. The rhythmic motive in the left hand (M.G.) in mm. 30 and 31 is notably absent from the Honegger as well as the Lehman manuscripts.
26. On the connection between Verlaine's maskers and bergamaskers in his 'Clair de lune' and Debussy's various piano pieces, see Roy Howat, 'Debussy's *Masques*, *L'Isle Joyeuse* and a Lost Sarabande', *Journal of the Musicological Society of Australia*, 10 (1987), 16–30.
27. Gabriel Fauré would confect just such a stage work, *Masques et bergamasques*, in 1919 for the Opéra de Monte-Carlo. His orchestrated version of 'Clair de lune', for tenor, constituted the sixth movement of this eight-movement pastiche.
28. See James Hepokowski, 'Formulaic Openings in Debussy', *19th-Century Music*, 8, no. 1 (Summer 1984), 45–7.
29. Roy Howat, *Debussy in Proportion: A Musical Analysis* (Cambridge: Cambridge University Press, 1983), 34–6.
30. In a letter to Ernest Chausson from 2 October 1893, Debussy reported that while working on *Pelléas* he found himself using 'quite spontaneously at that, a means of expression that seems rather unusual, namely silence (don't laugh!), and perhaps the only way to assert the emotion of a phrase'. Debussy, *Correspondance*, 161.
31. See especially pp. 143–7 in Marie Rolf, 'Symbolism as Compositional Agent in Act IV, Scene 4 of Debussy's *Pelléas et Mélisande*', in *Berlioz and Debussy: Sources, Contexts and Legacies*, ed. Barbara L. Kelly and Kerry Murphy (Aldershot: Ashgate, 2007), 117–48.
32. Cited in Robert Brussel, 'Claude Debussy et Paul Dukas', *La revue musicale* (1 May 1926), 101 (197).
33. Five songs have seven syllables per line, including Verlaine's 'Mandoline', 'En sourdine', 'C'est l'extase', and 'L'échelonnement des haies', as well as Girod's 'Fleur de blés'. Verlaine's 'Chevaux de bois' and LeRoy's 'Les angélus' have nine syllables, and Verlaine's 'La mer est plus belle' has five.
34. For recent discussions of the arabesque, see Gurminder Kaur Bhogal, *Details of Consequence: Ornament, Music, and Art in Paris* (Oxford: Oxford University Press, 2013) and Stephanie Venturino and Jonathan Dunsby, 'The Evolution of Claude Debussy's Arabesque Idea', in *Debussy Studies 2*, ed. Barbara Kelly and David Code (Cambridge: Cambridge University Press, 2025).
35. Beginning with a letter to Chausson from 2 October 1893 (Debussy, *Correspondance*, 160) and in other correspondence thereafter, Debussy habitually referred to his compositional experiments in these terms.
36. Maurice Emmanuel, *Pelléas et Mélisande de Claude Debussy: Étude historique et critique; Analyse Musicale* (Paris: P. Mellottée, 1926), 35.

7 The Franckist-Wagnerian Strain (Duparc, Chausson, Chabrier)

ANDREW PAU

On 17 November 1871, a piano trio by the Belgian-born César Franck (1818–90) was chosen to open the inaugural concert of the Société nationale de musique, a society formed in the aftermath of the Franco-Prussian War to promote French music. Franck was already in his fifties and still relatively unknown as a composer. The winter of 1871–2, however, was to mark a significant change in his reputation and renown. In February 1872, Franck assumed the organ professorship at the Paris Conservatoire, where he developed a reputation for 'teaching composition in place of the instrument over which he had been asked to preside'.[1] Building on his associations with the Société nationale and the Conservatoire, Franck became an influential mentor to a group of younger composers. Two members of this *bande à Franck* in particular, Henri Duparc (1848–1933) and Ernest Chausson (1855–99), would make notable contributions to the French art song repertoire.[2]

Besides Franck, the other major formative influence on the composers of Duparc and Chausson's generation was Richard Wagner. Duparc travelled to Munich in 1869 with Vincent d'Indy to hear *Tristan und Isolde* and *Das Rheingold* and returned in 1870 for the first run of *Die Walküre*. Chausson, for his part, went to Munich in 1879, the same year that he became Franck's student, and wrote of Wagner that '[t]o understand an art in a completely new way ... strikes me as the doing of a great genius'.[3] Wagner also had a life-changing impact on Emmanuel Chabrier (1841–94), who gave up a position at the Ministry of the Interior to become a full-time composer after attending a performance of *Tristan* at Munich in 1880.

Wagner's impact on cultural life in late nineteenth-century France extended beyond music to literary and intellectual circles. Charles Baudelaire wrote in 1861 of the strong sense of pleasure (*volupté*) that *Tannhäuser* had engendered in him, arguing that 'no musician excels like Wagner does in *painting* space and depth, material and spiritual'.[4] More than two decades later, the *Revue wagnérienne*, a journal whose contributors included Paul Verlaine and Stéphane Mallarmé, found in Wagner's aesthetics and philosophy an inspiration for Symbolism.[5] Friedrich

Example 7.1. César Franck, 'Lied', mm. 1–11

Nietzsche predicted around the same time that 'the more French music learns to shape itself according to the real needs of the *âme moderne*, the more it will "Wagnerise"'.[6]

Late Nineteenth-Century Harmonic Practices

The songs of the *bande à Franck* reflect the differing ways in which their mentor and Wagner used the chromatic language characteristic of late nineteenth-century harmony. Laurence Davies has argued that while 'Franck's chromatic leanings were always aimed at making modulation easier', Wagner 'was inclined to prefer static (or at best slow-changing) harmony, using chromatic movement to give a sense of inflection'.[7] Franck's 'Lied' (1873), for instance, begins with a chromatic sequence, with the local tonic shifting quickly from F♯ minor to A minor to C♯ major in the course of a mere eight bars, suggesting a sense of emotional restlessness and exemplifying Franck's mature style of 'obstinate and incessant modulation' (see Example 7.1).[8] By contrast, the entire sixteen-bar introduction to Wagner's 'Traüme' from *Wesendonck Lieder* (1857–8), the model for the love duet in *Tristan und Isolde*, is supported by a tonic pedal

Example 7.2. Contrasting chromatic practice in Wagner and Duparc
a) Richard Wagner, 'Träume' (*Wesendonck Lieder*), mm. 1–12
b) Henri Duparc, 'Phidylé', mm. 46–9

that imparts an overall sense of tranquillity even as the shifting chromatic chords above suggest deeper emotional shadings (see Example 7.2a).

Viewed in this light, many of the songs of Duparc, Chausson, and their contemporaries can be thought of as reflecting the combined influence of Franck and Wagner. Duparc's 'Phidylé' (1882), for example, begins and ends with long passages of 'Wagnerian' static harmony that reflect the pastoralism of the text, contrasting with a 'Franckian' central section that changes key signature four times in the space of nineteen bars. The passage shown in Example 7.2b arguably represents a fusion of these impulses, with a slow-moving transition from tonic to dominant combined with quick-changing chromatic harmonies.

Examples 7.1 and 7.2 also illustrate the nineteenth-century harmonic practice based on common-tone relations that David Kopp has called 'common-tone tonality'.[9] In Example 7.1, the secondary key areas of A minor and C♯ major are both linked to the F♯-minor tonic triad through one common tone. In Example 7.2, both excerpts juxtapose common-tone-related triads in close succession: A♭ major, F minor, F♭ augmented, and A♭

minor in mm. 1–4 of Example 7.2a are linked by the common tone A♭, while A major, F♯ major, and B♭ minor in the second and third bars of Example 7.2b are linked by the common tone C♯/D♭. These harmonic transformations are often accompanied by chromatic voice leading, giving the music a sensuous quality that consorts well with late nineteenth-century French poetry.

Another harmonic trait associated with the composers of the Franckist-Wagnerian school is the use of plagal progressions in place of authentic progressions. Example 7.1 begins with a plagal expansion of the F♯-minor tonic, with the subdominant harmony (B minor) supplemented by an added sixth (G♯), a characteristic dissonance that resolves upward by step. (The conception of the added sixth as a characteristic dissonance in subdominant harmonies can be traced back to the theories of Jean-Philippe Rameau.[10]) Plagal progressions, which preserve the tonic scale degree as a common tone, are often described as having a 'static' quality, compared to authentic progressions, which are more directional or goal-oriented. While Example 7.1 represents a fairly superficial use of a plagal expansion, many composers in the generation succeeding Franck would elevate the plagal harmonic system to a higher level of structural significance. Chausson was especially fond of plagal sonorities and many of his songs end with a structural plagal cadence: 'Le charme', 'Amour d'antan', 'Apaisement', 'Les morts', and 'Les heures', to name a few examples.

Finally, the boxed portions of Examples 7.1 and 7.2 all reflect different voicings and resolutions of the half-diminished-seventh chord, famously known as the '*Tristan* chord' from its use at the opening of the prelude to Wagner's opera. This sonority is ubiquitous in the songs of Duparc and Chausson, with Ralph Scott Grover noting that the *Tristan* chord appears in twenty-seven of Chausson's thirty-five published songs.[11] It is important to note, however, the many different ways in which the chord can be resolved. In Example 7.1, the chord functions as a subdominant added-sixth chord in a plagal progression in the minor mode (the prelude to Act 3 of *Tristan und Isolde* starts with a similar plagal progression). In Example 7.2a, one note of the chord shifts downward to create a dominant-seventh chord. Only in Example 7.2b does the chord follow the specific resolution in the *Tristan* prelude, albeit in a different voicing.

Franck

Franck was not a prolific song composer, producing only around twenty songs in a compositional career that spanned almost fifty years. His earliest songs reflect a variety of Romantic tropes, from a mildly exotic serenade ('L'émir de Bengador') to a ballad in the style of Walter Scott ('Robin Gray'). Franck's melodic style tends toward squareness, with rhythms often repeated exactly despite variations in accentual patterns in the text, bringing his songs 'closer in spirit and style to the *romance* than to the *mélodie*'.[12]

From a harmonic perspective, Franck often uses contrasting key areas to delineate different sections of the text. In 'Souvenance' (1842–3), whose five stanzas trace the memories of a person in enforced exile, the first two stanzas are in F♯, the third in B♭, and the final two in G, in each case alternating between parallel minor and major. A similar use of contrasting key areas to delineate discrete sections of text can be found in songs by Duparc ('Chanson triste', 'Soupir', 'Phidylé', 'Testament', 'La vie antérieure') and Chausson ('L'aveu', 'La caravane', *Chanson perpétuelle*).

Many of Franck's songs combine restatements of the same melodic material with increasingly active variations in the accompaniment that ratchet up the emotional intensity over the course of a song. Examples of this technique include 'Aimer' (1849), 'La vase brisé' (1879), and 'Nocturne' (1884), in which the accompaniment for the same melody moves from quavers to triplets to semiquavers over successive strophes.[13] This technique was similarly adopted by Duparc in 'Au pays où se fait la guerre', 'L'invitation au voyage', and 'Élégie', and by Chausson in 'Printemps triste' and 'La cigale'.

Franck's last two songs were written in the final years of his life and carry a more religious cast. 'Les cloches du soir' (1888) begins and ends with a chorale-like accompaniment, with the tolling of the evening bells likened to a song from heaven. 'La procession' (1889) was first performed with orchestral accompaniment and depicts a religious procession in the countryside. The opening prelude features some effective antiphonal writing for low strings and woodwind choir and contrapuntal devices such as imitation and pedal point. The song has an overall cyclic quality, with the first line of the text and the contrapuntal textures in the accompaniment returning at the end. The seriousness and grandeur of the work provide a fitting close to Franck's song-writing career.

Duparc

Duparc is perhaps the quintessential composer of French art song in that his entire compositional output was defined by the genre. Indeed, his only composition of note outside of the songs is the symphonic poem *Lénore* (1875). Duparc first became Franck's student at the Jesuit College of Vaugirard in Paris in the late 1860s and wrote sixteen songs and one duet between 1868 and 1884, with half of these compositions completed by 1871. Suffering from severe self-doubt and health problems that were vaguely defined as 'neurasthenia', Duparc stopped composing in his mid-thirties, even though he would live for almost fifty more years.

Duparc's first five songs were published in 1870, but he would later attempt to suppress three of them, saving his approval only for 'Chanson triste' and 'Soupir'. In 'Chanson triste' (1868–9), the dream-like quality of Jean Lahor's poem is reflected in the incessant semiquaver pattern in the accompaniment and a wandering vocal melody that never manages to settle on the tonic scale degree, with three of the four quatrains ending on a scale fragment ascending into the dominant (F-G-A♭-B♭). The interplay in the song of flat- and sharp-side keys, with their conventional associations with darkness and brightness, further brings out the emotional shadings of Lahor's poem. 'Soupir' (1869) follows a similar harmonic trajectory but has a more explicitly ternary form. Duparc reflects the melancholic longing of Sully Prudhomme's text with long dominant pedals and repeated syncopated sigh figures in the accompaniment.

The three songs suppressed by Duparc were ultimately preserved despite his wishes. In 'Romance de Mignon' (1869), Duparc's setting of 'Là-bas' with block tonic chords played over a low dominant pedal is virtually identical to the setting of the words 'C'est là' in 'La vie antérieure' fifteen years later. 'Sérénade' (1869) resembles 'Chanson triste' in its constantly pulsating accompaniment but is more conventionally sentimental in character. 'Le galop' (1869) is a dramatic portrayal of a ride on a galloping horse, with a repeated-note accompaniment in G minor that surely owes no small debt to Schubert's 'Erlkönig'. A similarly breathless piano accompaniment provides the backdrop to the duet 'La fuite' (1871), which depicts the flight of two lovers across a desert to a dramatic text by Théophile Gautier.

'Au pays où se fait la guerre' (1869–70), which sets another dramatic scenario by Gautier, is a soliloquy of a noble lady pining in her tower for her beloved to return from war. The distant historical setting is suggested by the modal piano introduction, with its use of the subtonic scale degree in place of the leading tone. The first vocal phrase, which recurs as a refrain throughout, is harmonised using a plagal progression, with the minor dominant in m. 8 moving to an inverted subdominant chord in m. 9 before returning to the tonic in m. 10.[14] As in 'Soupir', Duparc uses long dominant pedals to convey a sense of yearning and unfulfilled expectation. The

Example 7.3. Duparc, 'L'invitation au voyage', mm. 3–10

accompaniment becomes more rhythmically active throughout the song, reflecting the protagonist's growing impatience, and builds up to an impassioned statement of the refrain with *fortissimo* tremolos in the piano. In a cyclic touch, the modal introduction returns to round off the song, initiating a new cycle of waiting.

'L'invitation au voyage' (1870) sets Charles Baudelaire's poem from *Les fleurs du mal*, in which the poet invites his beloved on a journey into an idealised landscape. Duparc's song begins with a pastoral drone bass and oscillating arpeggiated chords (see Example 7.3). The cadence at the end of the example is a modally mixed plagal cadence, with an inverted minor subdominant harmony (F minor with D as an added sixth) resolving into the major tonic (C major). This plagal cadence, which is repeated in mm. 29–30, preserves the tonic pitch C as a common tone. Indeed, even if one discounts the drone bass, C is present in the harmony in all but five of the thirty-nine bars that comprise the first stanza and provides the first pitch for the monotone declamation of the refrain ('Là, tout n'est qu'ordre est beauté'). The constant presence of this common tone imparts a serene and static quality to the music that complements Baudelaire's poetry.[15] An authentic cadence in the key of the dominant finally appears at mm. 56–7, accompanying a description of ships arriving from the ends of the earth. However, the return to the tonic is marked once again by a plagal cadence in mm. 70–71. Duparc's song thus turns traditional harmonic syntax on its head by subordinating authentic progressions to plagal progressions at every level of the harmonic structure, suggesting perhaps that Baudelaire's invitation is to a fantasy voyage that takes place through the looking-glass, as it were.[16]

'La vague et la cloche' (1871) describes a phantasmagorical dream in which the narrator is first battered by waves in a boat, then overwhelmed by clanging bells in a belfry. Duparc's setting is a fairly straightforward depiction of this scenario, with the turbulent waves represented by rumbling arpeggios in the bass register and the bells by an insistent ostinato. The song was originally conceived for voice and orchestra, and the piano part is a reduction that does not lie idiomatically in the hands. The poem ends with a rather unconvincing moral, where the waves and the bells are interpreted as metaphors for the 'useless work and eternal noise' of life.

The two songs composed by Duparc in 1874, 'Élégie' and 'Extase', are both reminiscent in their own ways of Wagner's 'Träume' (see Example 7.2a).[17] 'Élégie' draws heavily on a sighing lament figure in both the melody and accompaniment. The lament figure provides a unifying element when the accompaniment shifts from block chords to arpeggios, marking a hopeful turn in the text, at the beginning of the second stanza. Both the lament figure and the arpeggio figuration are fully incorporated into the texture when the opening melody returns at the end of the song, in a moving depiction of reconciliation and acceptance in the grieving process.

A descending sigh figure is also prominent in the introduction to 'Extase', this time combined with a chromatic line that floats above a slow-moving bass, reflecting the sensual imagery of Lahor's text. According to the composer Pierre de Bréville, Duparc deliberately wrote 'Extase' 'in the style of *Tristan*', and Stephen Rumph has noted numerous musical references to both *Tristan* and the *Ring* cycle in the song's first sixteen bars.[18] The song starts on an unstable dominant harmony in second inversion and takes a slowly meandering chromatic route before it finally reaches the tonic in m. 18 on the words 'Mort exquise', marking the erotic fulfilment of a love that is 'sweeter than death'. After the voice reaches a climactic high A, the piano starts the introduction again and everything is repeated. This time, however, the voice trails off in blissful contentment and the piano is left to finish the song on its own.

'Le manoir de Rosemonde' (1878–9) asks the listener to follow the trail of the protagonist, who is metaphorically bleeding from a wound inflicted by love. Duparc's piano accompaniment, another homage to Schubert's 'Erlkönig', imitates the rhythm of galloping horses in the left hand and the sound of hunting horns in the right. The vocal line consists mostly of dramatic declamation. While much of the song stays close to the tonic key of D minor, the harmonies start to stray as the text describes the process of roaming along difficult paths, aptly reaching the very distant chord of F♭ minor at the end of the line 'Bien loin, bien loin', before snapping back to D minor for an abrupt close.

Duparc's first two songs from the 1880s both focus on the subject of sleep and repose. 'Sérénade florentine' is a gentle lullaby with a syncopated accompaniment and an insistent three-note motivic figure that begins on an E♭ that never gets reconciled with the F-major tonic harmony surrounding it. 'Phidylé' (1882) is a more substantial song to a poem by Charles Marie René Leconte de Lisle, the leader of the Parnassian poets, featuring bucolic images of nature amid which two lovers rest under the noonday sun. As in 'L'invitation au voyage', Duparc introduces the pastoral fantasy of 'Phidylé' with ten bars of chords that all contain the tonic pitch, ending the first phrase with a plagal cadence. The different sections of the song are defined by different key areas and changes in figuration in the accompaniment. After a return to the main key, the refrain is repeated above the shifting chromatic harmonies shown in Example 7.2b and the song ends with a grand apotheosis of the opening material.

The two songs of 1883 treat themes of death and loss. 'Lamento' sets the same text from Théophile Gautier's *La Comédie de la mort* as Berlioz's 'Au cimetière' from *Les Nuits d'été*. Unlike Berlioz, Duparc only sets three stanzas of the poem, casting them in an AAB bar form. The two-bar piano introduction, representing perhaps the cry of the solitary dove deprived of its mate, returns at the end of each stanza and is also echoed in the vocal line multiple times. The austere chordal accompaniment of the first two stanzas gives way to a more agitated texture and intense outpouring of emotion in the final section. 'Testament' recounts the bitter legacy of a failed love. The turbulent accompaniment features an obsessive three-note descending motive and twice quotes (in transposition) the famous progression from the opening of the *Tristan* prelude, on the words 'Les tortures de mon cœur' (mm. 10–11 and 55–56).

Duparc returned to Baudelaire's poetry for his last song, 'La vie antérieure' (1884), which was originally conceived for voice and orchestra. Baudelaire's sonnet describes the narrator's past life amid splendour and luxury, in spite of which they suffer a secret sadness. The opening quatrain, describing a setting with majestic pillars and stone grottos, is accompanied by a stately ostinato figure in E♭ major punctuated by trumpet flourishes. For the second quatrain, which describes a seascape and sunset, the accompaniment gets more active both rhythmically and harmonically, ending on a D dominant-seventh chord. This chord resolves unexpectedly to the brightness of C major on the words 'C'est là', but the music shifts to E♭ minor (a change in key signature from zero to six flats) upon the revelation of the narrator's 'secret douloureux' and the song ends with a long piano postlude that recasts the opening material in the parallel minor. While the various sections are distinguished by different keys and textures, they are unified by recurring motivic fragments. One particularly subtle example is the rising vocal line C-C♯-D-E♭ in the description of the nude slaves in mm. 38–41, which is a much-disguised restatement of the C-D♭-D motive played by the second violins (or left hand in the piano version) in mm. 1–14.

Duparc's two celebrated Baudelaire settings, 'L'invitation au voyage' and 'La vie antérieure', represent signal achievements in that Baudelaire 'has often been considered to be a poet whose work is particularly unamenable to music'.[19] Both songs strike a balance between formal clarity and emotional intensity that aptly illustrates Baudelaire's maxim about the sonnet: '[b]ecause the form is restrictive, the idea bursts forth more intensely'.[20] By contrast, Debussy's Wagner-influenced *Cinq poèmes de Baudelaire* (1890) aim for a more extravagant freedom of form that 'begin[s] to think and feel like free verse'.[21]

'La vie antérieure' was Duparc's last completed work. Almost a decade later in August 1893 he would write to Chausson that 'I have retired, I consider myself a dead man, and musically speaking, I only ask to be considered as such'.[22] It was a sad end to the career of a composer who, in the words of Julien Tiersot, 'gave to the French *mélodie* a scope, a fullness, and a power which none of our composers, except perhaps Berlioz, had ever realised before, and which no other, indeed, has since surpassed'.[23]

Chausson

Chausson entered the Conservatoire as a student of Jules Massenet following his first trip to Munich in 1879, attending Franck's organ class as an auditor. By late 1880 he had decided to study exclusively with Franck, concluding his formal studies in 1883.[24] Duparc would later opine that 'Chausson comes more directly from Franck than us all'.[25] Chausson's published output consists of thirty-five songs for voice and piano (two without opus number) and two works for solo voice and orchestra (*Poème de l'amour et de la mer* and *Chanson perpétuelle*).

The *Sept mélodies*, Op. 2 (1879–82), date from Chausson's student days and combine tuneful melodies with relatively conventional harmonic palettes and formal construction. The majority of these are in ternary form. In 'Nanny', a melancholic meditation on lost love, the outer sections feature chromatic melodic lines and shifting broken chords anchored by a stationary tonic bass pedal. 'Le colibri' uses the same techniques but in the central section over a dominant pedal, as the text describes a hummingbird slowly descending on a flower. 'Sérénade italienne', which depicts a boat trip out to sea, is perhaps the most harmonically adventurous song in the set, with a swiftly modulating middle section that ends in A♭ major and returns to the tonic key of B major through the common tone E♭/D♯. 'Hébé', a depiction of the Greek goddess of youth, is a modal composition that features chant-like declamation. The song's subtitle refers to the ancient Greek Phrygian mode, which is equivalent to the medieval and modern Dorian mode.

The *Quatre mélodies*, Op. 8 (1882–8), are settings of poems by Maurice Bouchor, a friend and exact contemporary of Chausson's. Bouchor's poetry falls squarely within what Laurence Davies has called 'a cult of erotic lassitude in literature and music ... a period of sighs and regrets' during which poets and musicians 'celebrate[d] the act of reminiscence' and adopted 'symbols ... which emphasised the motive of change and decay'.[26] In 'Nocturne' (1886), the memories of a distant summer night are refracted through a chordal accompaniment that through much of the song projects a 9/8 rhythm that clashes with the 4/4 time signature and the rhythm of the vocal melody. In 'Amour d'antan' (1882), which reflects on the joys of a past love, the descending chromatic motive, repeated-note quaver accompaniment, and slow harmonic rhythm in the outer sections combine to create a paradoxical and melancholy sensation of time passing while memories remain frozen. 'Printemps triste' portrays the tears and sorrow of the narrator through a thick accompaniment that contains an obsessively repeated sigh motive, consisting mostly of appoggiaturas resolving downward into seventh chords. The triplet groupings that characterised the opening of 'Nocturne' return at the end of 'Nos souvenirs' (1888), whose text appropriately muses on how incredible it is when the past reappears. The explicit connection between the first and last songs in Op. 8 suggest that the four songs, even though composed at different times, embody a single consciousness and that the group can be viewed as a unified cycle.

Chausson's remaining songs for voice and piano from the 1880s were published as Opp. 13, 14, and 17. 'Apaisement' (1885), the first song of *Quatre mélodies*, Op. 13, is the first of Chausson's three settings of poems by Paul Verlaine. The poem from *La bonne chanson* (1870), titled 'La lune blanche' by Fauré and 'L'heure exquise' by Reynaldo Hahn, was perhaps set more than any other *mélodie* text. The choice of the unusual time signature of 1/2 allows Chausson great flexibility in determining the length of phrases, creating a feeling of improvisatory whimsy in the declamation of the text. The accompaniment is dominated by an oscillating figure that is mostly anchored by a tonic pedal in the outer sections but moves enchantingly by semitone in the central section. The dreamy sensuality of 'Sérénade' (1887), to a poem by Jean Lahor, is bookended by another oscillating progression, this time alternating between the E-major tonic and chords that contain the subtonic D♮, eliminating the leading-tone and the forward momentum that it represents. The text of 'L'aveu' (1887), like those of Op. 8, deals with sorrow at the loss of the past. 'La cigale' (1887), on the other hand, appears to be closer in both mood and style to Op. 2, with a text that recalls 'Le colibri' and a modal character that recalls 'Hébé'.

'La caravane', Op. 14 (1887), sets a sonnet by Gautier that contains an elaborate metaphor comparing life to a trek across 'the Sahara of the world' and death to an oasis that provides rest. Chausson's setting features steady and gradually modulating organ-like chords in the accompaniment that reflect the influence of Franck and contribute to a sense of grand religiosity, while simultaneously reflecting the trudging quality of the journey through 'the desert of time'. The texts for *Chansons de Miarka*, Op. 17 (1888), are taken from the novel *Miarka, la fille à l'ourse* by Jean Richepin and purport to be Romani songs. 'Les morts' is a song of mourning marked by chromatic alterations in the melody that create a sense of folksong-like modality. 'La pluie' celebrates the fall of rain, as imitated in the brilliantly shimmering piano part.

Poème de l'amour et de la mer, Op. 19 (1893), is Chausson's most extended composition for solo voice and 'the first French song cycle to be composed expressly for orchestra'.[27] The work uses texts from six poems by Bouchor to trace the trajectory of a love affair that begins in ecstasy and ends in heartbreak, with images of the sea and seaside locations providing a Symbolist backdrop throughout. The six poems are divided equally among two large movements ('La fleur des eaux' and 'La mort de l'amour') separated by an orchestral interlude, with smaller interludes further separating the individual poems within movements. The poems are supplemented by additional text at the end of the first movement, starting from 'Je saigne en regardant ma vie'.

Among Chausson's compositions, *Poème* is perhaps the one that reflects most directly the influence of both Franck and Wagner. The work is unified through recurring motives, recalling both Franck's cyclic form and Wagner's leitmotifs. At the singer's first entrance, the vocal melody, which had already been introduced by the violins in m. 6, is accompanied by simultaneous statements of the same motive in the orchestra, creating a kind of heterophonic effect (see Example 7.4a). The motive is restated in various guises in the orchestral interludes within the first movement. It is also recapitulated in the orchestra at the first vocal entry in the second movement, woven again into the orchestral fabric at multiple contrapuntal and rhythmic levels (see Example 7.4b).

The other main recurring motive in *Poème* is introduced by the orchestra at m. 76 or Rehearsal 6, directly after the end of the first poem. This second motive provides the main melodic material for both the Interlude and the final poem ('Le temps des lilas'), which Chausson also published as a stand-alone song for voice and piano.

Example 7.4b also shows the influence of Franck in its rapid sequential modulations (compare Example 7.1), with the motive stated successively in E major, G major, and B major. Elsewhere, the orchestral writing in *Poème* recalls Wagner at numerous turns: *Tristan* in the orchestral interludes within the first movement and *Parsifal* in the funereal march that frames the middle poem ('Le vent roulait') in the second movement.[28]

Chausson followed *Poème* with another song cycle, *Serres chaudes* (Hothouses), Op. 24 (1893–6), which sets five poems from the eponymous collection by Maurice Maeterlinck, whose play *Pelléas et Mélisande* had just premiered in Paris. Maeterlinck's poems are suffused with '[t]he hothouse artifice of Decadence' and language of 'opulent sickliness'.[29] 'Serre chaude' contains a list of incongruous images, where 'nothing is in its right place'. This strange catalogue is declaimed in a rhythm that imitates the pattern of speech, often on a single pitch, anticipating the style of writing that Debussy would later use in *Pelléas et Mélisande*. The song ends with a chorale after the exclamation 'Mon Dieu!'. In 'Serre d'ennui', Chausson brings out the parallelism in the lines 'Immobilement comme un songe' and 'Monotonement comme un rêve' by setting them both using descending-fifth sequences that comprise extended dominant harmonies. 'Lassitude' projects the titular emotion with an accompaniment that

Example 7.4. Ernest Chausson, *Poème de l'amour et de la mer*
a) 'La fleur des eaux', mm. 19–22
b) 'La mort de l'amour', mm. 32–42

combines slow-moving pedal points with a syncopated figure doubled at the octave in the inner voices. Ralph Scott Grover sees in this accompaniment the influence of Modest Musorgsky, whose music was brought to Chausson's attention by Debussy in 1893.[30] In 'Fauves las', which describes a collection of beasts symbolising the poet's emotions, the word 'passions' is found in both the first and last line. Chausson sets both instances with the rising pitches C-D♭ over a C dominant-ninth chord, leaving the end of the song harmonically unresolved. The last song, 'Oraison', is an extended version of the chorale that appeared at the end of 'Serre chaude', creating a cyclic frame for the entire work.

Serres chaudes is a less unified cycle than *Poème de l'amour et de la mer*, due in large part to the aesthetic differences between the texts. While Bouchor's texts for *Poème* trace a clear narrative thread, Maeterlinck's poems reflect a more disjunct consciousness in which 'the images fragment and collide as the would-be unifying structures disintegrate'.[31] This distinction is reflected in Chausson's musical settings. *Poème* is saturated with motivic connections and the texts are connected by orchestral interludes. By contrast, the only motivic link in *Serres chaudes* is between the first and last songs (a unifying device Chausson had previously employed in Op. 8), and each of the five songs is given its own distinctive accompaniment pattern. What the five Maeterlinck texts do share is an attitude of fin-de-siècle weariness, evidenced by the recurrence of words like 'ennui', 'langueur', and 'lassitude' across different poems. Besides *Serres chaudes*, several of Chausson's other song collections (for example, Opp. 8, 27, and 28) can perhaps be thought of as looser cycles unified by author and affect even if they are not cycles in name.

Following the Maeterlinck cycle, Chausson chose texts by another Symbolist poet, Camille Mauclair, for *Trois lieder*, Op. 27 (1896). 'Les heures' paints a haunting image of the hours gathering at a moonlit lake to die. Chausson's setting is spare and austere, with the syncopated pitch A present in the piano part throughout. 'Ballade' tells of a vision of angels and ships lost at sea, while 'Les couronnes' features a mysterious Mélisande-like girl who weaves three garlands while waiting in vain for a 'beau chevalier'. Chausson responds to the simplicity of these texts with pared-down textures, gently shifting harmonies, and dynamic markings that never go beyond *mezzo forte*.

A similarly austere mood pervades *Chansons de Shakespeare*, Op. 28, in translations by Bouchor. 'Chanson de clown' (1890) is an adaptation of Feste's song 'Come away, come away, death' from *Twelfth Night*. It recalls Duparc's 'Lamento' in affect, texture, and harmony. 'Chanson d'amour' (1891), which is adapted from 'Take, o, take these lips away' from *Measure for Measure*, starts in a subdued manner, but builds up to an impassioned, almost operatic climax that seems at odds with the simplicity of the text. 'Chanson d'Ophélie' (1896) is based on 'He is dead and gone, lady' from *Hamlet*. The meditation on death is given a dark touch throughout by the flattened second scale degree (F♮ in E minor), imparting a dissonant modal quality to the final plagal cadence.[32]

Chausson returned to Verlaine's poetry for *Deux poèmes*, Op. 34 (1898). 'La chanson bien douce' has a restless accompaniment that never settles on a key and gives no hint of the tonic of E♭ major until the very last word of the text, which appropriately enough is 'claire'. 'Le chevalier malheur' tells the tale of a wounded heart cured by the icy touch of a horseman representing misfortune. The lead-up to the moment of touch is marked by an implacable triple-dotted figure in the accompaniment. After a more placid section as the narrator's heart is reborn, the ominous triple-dotted motive returns at the end, accompanying the horseman's warning that the cure is good only once. The *Deux mélodies*, Op. 36, were Chausson's final published compositions for voice and piano. 'Cantique à l'épouse' (1896) is a tribute to conjugal love that ends in a mood of profound contentment, as the song's earlier chromaticism gives way to mostly diatonic harmonies. In 'Dans la forêt du charme et de l'enchantement' (1898), the piano spins a gossamer web that sets the scene for the tale of an enchanted forest.

Chausson's last work for voice, *Chanson perpétuelle*, Op. 37 (1898), exists in versions for orchestra and piano quintet, with the quintet version recalling Fauré's transcription of his cycle *La bonne chanson* from the same year. The narrator is a woman who, having been abandoned by her lover, revisits happier days in her memory before resolving to drown herself. The harmonic progressions at the beginning, which incorporate both minor dominant and plagal harmonies, bear a close resemblance to the opening of Duparc's 'Au pays où se fait la guerre', another dramatic ballad narrated by a woman bemoaning an absent lover. Chausson skilfully knits together the disparate sections of the song through recurring motivic material, building to a climax that constitutes a kind of *Liebestod*. *Chanson perpétuelle* received its premiere in January 1899, five months before Chausson's death in a bicycle accident.

Chabrier

Although Chabrier was actively involved in the Société nationale de musique and moved easily within Franckist-Wagnerian circles, it is difficult to associate him with any school of composition: as a young man, his only ambition was to be a brilliant amateur, and he did not undergo formal training in music.[33] In contrast to the serious-mindedness of Franck and his students, many of Chabrier's songs exhibit a combination of vivacity, wit, and archness that nods toward the popular tradition of the *cafés-concerts* and points forward to the worlds of Maurice Ravel and

Francis Poulenc, both of whom acknowledged Chabrier as a formative influence.

Chabrier's nine earliest songs date from 1862, the year that he joined the civil service as an official in the Ministry of the Interior. These songs were unpublished in his lifetime. The remaining years of the 1860s would bring forth two settings of Victor Hugo ('Sérénade de Ruy Blas' and 'Les pas d'armes du Roi Jean') and 'Ivresses', a *grande valse* that was later adapted into the *Suite de valses* for piano (1872). 'Sérénade de Ruy Blas' features many of Chabrier's stylistic markers: the use of ninth chords, chromatic embellishments of chord tones, large melodic leaps, doubling of the piano and vocal line, and an overall breezy quality in the piano refrain and the first stanza of the melody. The piano postlude ends with a harmonic surprise: the dominant harmony leads not into the expected tonic but to the subdominant, from which the song closes with a plagal cadence.

In 1870 Chabrier wrote a setting of Baudelaire's 'L'invitation au voyage', at around the same time as Duparc's more celebrated setting discussed above. Chabrier's setting includes a bassoon obbligato and begins with a syncopated motivic figure in the piano that is prominent throughout. Chabrier's conception of Baudelaire's idealised landscape is more rugged or distorted than Duparc's. The piano figure begins with the downward leap of a seventh, the first of many wide melodic leaps in the song. Ninth chords are prominent in the harmonies, most notably in the transition to the refrain. Although the song is mostly strophic, the refrain is set differently in the two strophes. The first refrain smooths out the disjunct melody, leading to a monotone declamation of the words 'luxe' and 'calme' that is not dissimilar to Duparc's setting and fits the peaceful invocation in the text. The second refrain, on the other hand, doubles down on the wide melodic leaps (including a fortissimo downward leap of an octave and a half) in an incongruous cadenza-like passage that precedes the quiet ending.

Chabrier's next song, 'Sommation irrespectueuse', was composed in 1880, the year that he resigned from the civil service to become a full-time composer. The song creates a seven-part rondo form out of twenty-two short quatrains by Victor Hugo. The refrain to this rondo consists of the first two quatrains declaimed in an artificially rigid rhythm without regard to accentual patterns in the text. The refrain is immediately repeated and returns three more times after that, each time to the same rhythms. The first two contrasting episodes (or couplets in the rondo) are similarly rhythmically constrained. In the last episode, however, the declamatory rhythm starts to loosen as the baritone protagonist loses control over his emotions, lapsing into recitative-like outbursts at the words 'Vous riez? . . . Je ris aussi' (You laugh? . . . I laugh as well). The return to strict rhythms in the final refrain and piano postlude does little to resolve the emotional tension.

Chabrier spent the first half of the 1880s working on his Wagnerian opera *Gwendoline*. The same period saw the composition of his most explicitly Wagner-influenced song, 'Tes yeux bleus' (1883). As with Duparc's 'Elégie' and 'Extase' from almost a decade earlier, Chabrier's song features a triple-time signature, a constant quaver accompaniment in block chords, slow-moving harmonies, and a high degree of surface-level chromaticism that all recall Wagner's 'Träume' (see Example 7.2a). The song is in C major, but the entry of the vocal line introduces flat-side accidentals that remain prominent throughout, perhaps representing the shadows and melancholy (*spleen*) that are eventually dispelled by the beloved's blue eyes.

The remainder of Chabrier's late songs mostly have simple strophic constructions and are less harmonically adventurous, reflecting perhaps the influence of the salon or more popular genres. 'Credo d'amour', 'Lied', 'L'île heureuse', 'Toutes les fleurs', and 'Chanson pour Jeanne' are all in three strophes, with the last-named song distinguished by a final strophe that takes an unexpectedly dark turn into the parallel minor mode, reflecting the death of Jeanne in the text.

More memorably distinctive among the strophic late songs are Chabrier's four humorous depictions of country life and farm animals. 'Ballade des gros dindons' pokes gentle fun at the pompous gait of turkeys, with a measured rhythm in the accompaniment interacting with alternating triplet and duplet figures in the melody. At the conclusion of each strophe, the piano breaks into an incongruous waltz that quotes the mandolin solo from Don Giovanni's serenade. In 'Les cigales', the strummed high-register arpeggios in the piano imitates the drone of cicadas, with some semitonal dissonances thrown in for good measure. The charmingly tuneful refrain suggests that cicadas sing better than violins. 'Pastorale des cochons roses' depicts a day in the life of a group of piglets from dawn to sunset. Following an E-major piano introduction, the melody begins in the E Aeolian mode above a pastoral drone and, perhaps following the frolicking pigs, goes through a few deft harmonic swerves before finally reaching E major. The meandering quality of the melody is further emphasised by melismatic passages. Finally, 'Villanelle des petits canards' imagines a row of ducks proceeding in single file to the rhythm of a toy-soldier march in the tradition of the gamins' chorus from Bizet's

Carmen. The comic effect of the song is accentuated by the insertion of rests between 'Ils vont' and 'les petits canards' in the melody, with the silence punctuated each time by bare octaves in the accompaniment. These witty animal sketches are of a piece with Saint-Saëns' *Carnaval des animaux* and can be considered forerunners to Ravel's *Histoires naturelles* and Poulenc's *Le bestiaire*.[34]

Other Franckists

Vincent d'Indy (1851–1931), who was instrumental in securing Franck's compositional and pedagogical legacies, wrote fewer than twenty art songs. 'L'amour et la crâne', Op. 20 (1884), is a dramatic setting of Baudelaire that begins with a ferociously distorted version of the progression that opens Duparc's 'L'invitation au voyage'. 'Lied maritime', Op. 43 (1896), to d'Indy's own text, shifts fluidly between duple and triple metre. The two strophes present mirror images of the sea as it reflects the narrator's mood, the first calm and the second more turbulent.

Charles Bordes (1863–1909), a co-founder with d'Indy of the Schola Cantorum, wrote more than thirty songs, including seventeen to texts by Verlaine. The four-song cycle *Paysages tristes* (1886) features some finely judged and delicate writing for both voice and piano, with the last two songs especially responsive to the melancholy of Verlaine's landscapes. Elsewhere, Bordes brings a more robust sensibility to Verlaine's poetry than does Debussy or Fauré, for instance setting the last word of 'Spleen' ('hélas!') as a *fortissimo* leap into a high note where Debussy opts for a low and soft monotone in his setting in *Ariettes* (1888).

Guy Ropartz (1864–1955) spent most of his career in Nancy and Strasbourg and 'devoted [a] uniquely long life to the propagation of Franckist ideas'.[35] His *Quatre poèmes d'après l'Intermezzo de Heine* (1899), with a framing prelude and postlude, are unified by the cyclic repetition of a four-note motive consisting of a lower-neighbour figure and a descending fourth, first stated in the form A-G-A-E and subjected to transposition and transformation in the piano part throughout. The motive bears a passing resemblance to the incipit of the Dies irae, as well as the opening of Franck's 'La procession' and the bell motive from Wagner's *Parsifal*.[36] It proves quite versatile, fitting easily with the gentle rowing motion of the first song, the brooding intensity of the middle two, and the funereal darkness of the final one. Like Chausson in *Poème de l'amour et de la mer*, Ropartz develops his recurring motive primarily in instrumental sections, reflecting perhaps the origins of Franck's cyclic principle in instrumental music.[37] Ropartz followed the Heine cycle with *Veilles de départ* (1902), a non-narrative cycle of five songs that similarly treats the theme of parted lovers but does not feature recurring motivic material.

Guillaume Lekeu (1870–94), who became Franck's last pupil but survived the older composer by only a little more than three years, wrote his own texts for *Trois poèmes* (1892). 'Sur une tombe' is a lament in which the elegiac opening melody becomes a recurring motive, transformed touchingly into major when the narrator speaks of reliving memories with the deceased. 'Ronde' has a charming refrain that is a light-hearted invitation to the dance. 'Nocturne' is an ecstatic evocation of the beauty of nature at night that impressively uses the full resources of *fin-de-siècle* harmony.

Other notable song composers among the *bande à Franck* include Alexis de Castillon (1838–73), Augusta Holmès (1847–1903), Mel Bonis (1858–1937), Gabriel Pierné (1863–1937), and Pierre de Bréville (1861–1949), whose longevity and prolific output of more than eighty published songs carried the activities of the Franckist school well into the twentieth century.

Notes

1. Laurence Davies, *César Franck and His Circle* (Boston: Houghton Mifflin, 1970), 139.
2. Charles Oulmont suggests that Duparc and Chausson were the 'two "children" loved most tenderly' by Franck as a father figure. Charles Oulmont, *Musique de l'amour: Ernest Chausson et 'la bande à Franck' et Henri Duparc ou de 'l'Invitation au voyage à la vie éternelle'* (Paris: Éditions Desclée de Brouwer, 1935; reprint, Paris: Istra, 1969), 10.
3. Ernest Chausson, *Ecrits inédits: Journaux intimes, roman de jeunesse, correspondance*, ed. Jean Gallois and Isabelle Bretaudeau (Monaco: Éditions du Rocher, 1999), 124; quoted in Paul du Quenoy, *Wagner and the French Muse: Music, Society, and Nation in Modern France* (Palo Alto: Academica Press, 2011), 70.
4. Charles Baudelaire, 'Richard Wagner et *Tannhäuser* à Paris', in *L'art romantique* (Paris: Conard, 1925), 208.
5. See Edouard Dujardin, 'La revue wagnérienne', in *Wagner et la France*, special issue of *La revue musicale* (1 October 1923; reprint, New York: Da Capo Press, 1977), 149.
6. Friedrich Nietzsche, *Beyond Good and Evil*, trans. Adrian Del Caro (Stanford: Stanford University Press, 2014), 161.
7. Davies, *César Franck and His Circle*, 163.

8. Léon Vallas, *César Franck*, trans. Hubert Foss (London: Harrap, 1951; reprint, Westport, CT: Greenwood Press, 1973), 241. Vallas notes that Franck would cry 'Modulate, modulate!' to his organ pupils at the Conservatoire.
9. David Kopp, *Chromatic Transformations in Nineteenth-Century Music* (Cambridge: Cambridge University Press, 2002), 1–3.
10. See Jean-Philippe Rameau, *Treatise on Harmony*, trans. Philip Gossett (New York: Dover, 1971), 73–81.
11. Ralph Scott Grover, *Ernest Chausson: The Man and His Music* (Lewisburg, PA: Bucknell University Press, 1980), 80.
12. Grover, *Ernest Chausson*, 69.
13. Frits Noske, *French Song from Berlioz to Duparc*, trans. Rita Benton (New York: Dover, 1970), 248.
14. Andrew Pau, 'Plagal Systems in the Songs of Fauré and Duparc', *Theory and Practice*, 41 (2016), 90–1.
15. For a metrical analysis of Duparc's setting of the refrain, see Helen Abbott, 'Performing Poetry as Music: How Composers Accept Baudelaire's Invitation to Song', in *Words and Notes in the Long Nineteenth Century*, ed. Phyllis Weliver and Katharine Ellis (Woodbridge, Suffolk: Boydell Press, 2013), 191–5.
16. For a more extended discussion of the use of plagal effects in 'L'invitation au voyage', see Pau, 'Plagal Systems', 91–9.
17. Sydney Northcote, *The Songs of Henri Duparc* (London: Dobson, 1949), 96 and 99; Stricker, *Les mélodies de Duparc*, 78–82.
18. Pierre de Bréville, 'Henri Fouques-Duparc (1848–1933)', *La musique française: Revue de la Société internationale des amis de la musique française*, 2 (May 1933), 91; Stephen Rumph, *The Fauré Song Cycles: Poetry and Music, 1861–1921* (Oakland: University of California Press, 2020), 214. Besides noting the musical references to Wagner in 'Extase', Rumph also calls Lahor's poem 'a Decadent homage to the *Liebestod*' (ibid.).
19. Helen Abbott, *Baudelaire in Song: 1880–1930* (Oxford: Oxford University Press, 2017), 3.
20. Charles Baudelaire, *Correspondance*, vol. 1, ed. Claude Pichois (Paris: Gallimard, 1973), 676.
21. Katherine Bergeron, *Voice Lessons: French Mélodie in the Belle Époque* (Oxford: Oxford University Press, 2010), 156.
22. Henri Duparc, 'Lettres de Henri Duparc à Ernest Chausson (1883–1899)', ed. Yves Gérard, *Revue de musicologie*, 38 (December 1956), 144.
23. Julien Tiersot, *Un demi-siècle de musique française: Entre les deux guerres 1870–1917* (Paris: Félix Alcan, 1924), 158. The translation is from Northcote, *The Songs of Henri Duparc*, 15.
24. Grover, *Ernest Chausson*, 16.
25. Oulmont, *Musique de l'amour*, 27.
26. Davies, *César Franck and His Circle*, 185.

27. Rumph, *The Fauré Song Cycles*, 95.
28. Grover, *Ernest Chausson*, 98. Chausson saw *Tristan* in Munich in 1879 and 1880, and *Parsifal* in Bayreuth in 1882 and again in 1889. Ibid., 15–16 and 49.
29. Patrick McGuinness, *Maurice Maeterlinck and the Making of Modern Theatre* (Oxford: Oxford University Press, 2000), 33.
30. Grover, *Ernest Chausson*, 101–4.
31. McGuinness, *Maurice Maeterlinck and the Making of Modern Theatre*, 33.
32. Chausson's Op. 28 includes a fourth Shakespeare song, 'Chanson funèbre', for four-part women's chorus, based on 'Pardon, goddess of the night' from *Much Ado about Nothing*.
33. Tiersot, *Un demi-siècle*, 173.
34. Roy Howat, 'Modernization: From Chabrier and Fauré to Debussy and Ravel', in *French Music since Berlioz*, ed. Richard Langham Smith and Caroline Potter (Aldershot: Ashgate, 2017), 219.
35. Davies, *César Franck and His Circle*, 110.
36. The resemblance to the Dies irae is noted in Mathieu Ferey and Benoît Menut, *Joseph-Guy Ropartz ou Le pays inaccessible* (Geneva: Éditions Papillon, 2005), 60.
37. Rumph, *The Fauré Song Cycles*, 95. Rumph contrasts the motivic practice of Chausson and Ropartz with that of Fauré in his song cycles.

8 | Women and French Song

ANNEGRET FAUSER

French art song had an image problem: *mélodies* inhabited a musical world that was often gendered feminine. This aesthetic framework formed a somewhat tricky environment for women creators to negotiate. If the feminising of the *romance* offered composers such as Loïsa Puget (1810–89) a privileged position of creative expression, it simultaneously devalued the genre in hierarchical terms detrimental not only to women creators but also to men writing songs.[1] By the turn of the twentieth century, more than one French composer and critic went out of his way to compensate by emphasising the artistic weight of French song. For example, the critic Camille Mauclair, writing in 1908, characterised the *mélodie* as the true realisation of Wagnerian music drama because of its seamless fusion of poetry and music; and the composer Florent Schmitt claimed in 1913 that a perfect song was worth a symphony.[2] The entanglement of genre and gender in the theories and practice of French art song thus shaped the way in which both national and international creators and audiences engaged with *mélodies*. What was – and remained – at stake well into the twentieth century can be seen in a text written in 1943 by the soprano Marcelle Denya when she was in exile in the United States during World War II. She declared: 'The intrinsic beauty, the originality, the subtlety of expression, the harmonic inventions of the French school of *mélodies* have, since 1850, neither a parallel nor an equivalent in any other country, Germany included'.[3] Thus, French song needed to be established as a genre with aesthetic significance. Nevertheless, the presence of the *mélodie* in performance spaces that ranged from the boudoir to the concert hall provided both challenges and opportunities, especially for female musicians, patrons, and consumers. During the long nineteenth century and well into the twenty-first, women contributed to French song as singers and pianists, composers and poets, patrons and muses, publishers and educators. Some composers like Augusta Holmès (1847–1903) not only wrote their own poetry but also performed their *mélodies* in a variety of settings. A *her*story of French song therefore offers a unique access point to a genre at the interstices of multiple fields of musical practice that range across socio-economic classes, professional positions, urban spaces, and artistic activities.[4]

Composers

Women's creative contributions to French song extended well beyond those of male composers. Not only were they active as composers and poets, but their roles as performers, hostesses, singing teachers, and muses added to the creation of *mélodies* in myriad ways. Perhaps most obvious, however, is the artistic work of female composers. Simply listing a few of the better-known musicians might offer a first idea of the wealth of *mélodies* owed to women. The songs of Pauline Viardot (1821–1910) have become so well known in recent years that they now routinely grace recitals. Clémence de Granval (1828–1907) was one of several aristocratic women whose contributions to French song were hugely popular among their contemporaries. Cécile Chaminade (1857–1944) became such a celebrity in the United States in the early twentieth century that Chaminade Music Clubs sprang up all around the country. Lili Boulanger (1893–1918) was the first woman to win the Prix de Rome and the composer of a magnificent song cycle, *Clairières dans le ciel* (1914), a work that Emily Kilpatrick explores in more detail in her own chapter here on Maurice Ravel and his contemporaries. There is Marguerite Canal (1890–1978), a prolific composer of *mélodies* who would be the second woman to win the Prix de Rome seven years after Boulanger. She is also routinely mentioned as the first woman to conduct a major series of orchestral concerts between 1915 and 1917. These and so many other composers – from Hedwige Chrétien (1859–1944) and Jane Vieu (1871–1955) to Armande de Polignac (1876–1962), Claude Arrieu (1903–90), and Claire Delbos (1906–59) – contributed individual *mélodies* and song cycles to a vast woman-created repertoire full of musical gems.

In one sense, it is tempting simply to make lists, naming the creators and their songs so that they may at least be recognised for their rich contributions. Yet at their most basic, their *mélodies* are simply part and parcel of the overall genre, sharing their musical and aesthetic character with those written by men, albeit much less acknowledged by scholars and performers over the past century or so. Just like their male counterparts, women composers set poets from Pierre de Ronsard to Victor Hugo and Stéphane Mallarmé. They chose forms as simple as strophic song and as expansive as symphonic settings for voice and orchestra. Their creations were published and performed less frequently, but – on the other hand – some of these songs quickly became favourites among both amateur and professional singers. If not recuperative then, what kind of perspective might offer a more productive sonic *herstory* of *mélodies*? Does gender form part of the compositional strategy of these composers and of their reception? And – more specifically in the case of song – is the poetic voice shaped by the gender of the composer as well as that of the singer?

Viardot's *mélodies* offer significant insight into these questions. A cosmopolitan and multilingual artist, she was intimately familiar with the distinctiveness of musical idioms in different cultural contexts. Franz Liszt commented in 1859 that this cosmopolitanism enabled her to claim art itself as her true home country as opposed to any single nation. Indeed, Liszt concluded, 'Viardot is capable of comprehending each ideal and of assimilating the secret meaning of whatever she has the opportunity to research, handling and mastering its forms'.[5] In her songs she set not only French poems but also English, German, Italian, Russian, and Spanish ones, and she drew on the tradition of the *Lied* as much as on those of the *mélodie* and *romance*. This cross-cultural reach put Viardot in a category of her own at a time when nationalism seemed to reign supreme, one that was as much admired as it was seen as a gendered lack of artistic consistency.[6] Especially in the context of female creators, stylistic pluralism was (and is to this day) considered a weakness because it connotes the absence of a unique artistic voice – a concept steeped in the myth of the (male) genius. In the twentieth century, for example, the Russian artist Natalia Goncharova was relentlessly criticised for her artistic pluralism, which even her lifelong partner disparaged as 'everythingism' and one critic questioned in 1913: 'Where is the true Natalia Goncharova, where is her artistic self?'[7] What could be celebrated, in effect, as the achievement of a polymath instead is qualified as denoting lack of greatness. By contrast, emphasising the pronouncedly French aesthetic of Viardot's *mélodies* then could provide a gender-positive reframing of her transnational musical fluency as she crosses aesthetic and geographical borders.

A delightful short song offers an entry point into this perspective. In 1895 Viardot published 'Bonjour mon cœur', setting the first stanza of a text from Ronsard's *Second livre des amours* (1556):

Bonjour mon cœur, bonjour ma douce vie.
Bonjour mon œil, bonjour ma chère amie,
Hé! Bonjour ma toute belle,
Ma mignardise, bonjour,
Mes délices, mon amour.
Mon doux printemps, ma douce fleur nouvelle,
Mon doux printemps, ma douce colombelle,
Mon passereau, ma gente tourterelle,
Bonjour, ma douce rebelle.

Good morning, my heart, good morning, my sweet life.
Good morning, my eye, good morning, my dear friend,
Hey! Good morning, my beautiful,
my sweetness, good morning,
my delights, my love.
My sweet spring, my sweet new flower,
my sweet pleasure, my sweet little dove,
my sparrow, my gentle turtledove,
good morning, my sweet rebel.

Viardot's setting at first glance seems like a simple *romance*, but it is, in effect, a through-composed *mélodie*. Likewise, the straightforward E♭ major of the opening soon expands through F minor and G minor, adding harmonic depth to what is ostensibly just a celebration of love in spring. She has omitted the subsequent stanzas of Ronsard's poem, which take a turn for the amorous worse, although the tonal twists (and the pointed diminished-seventh arpeggio on 'tourterelle') suggest that she is aware of them. Nevertheless, the poetic and sonic voices create a joyful counterpoint: clearly, Ronsard's text about courtly love is addressed to a female-identified subject – 'ma chère amie'. Yet the vocal character of the setting so dazzlingly ensounds what we know of Viardot's voice that one might easily read this *mélodie* as celebrating her own vocality; the words most emphasised through pitch, melisma, and harmonic surprise are those naming birds: 'colombelle' (little dove) and 'tourterelle' (turtle-dove). Viardot playfully connects them with being a sweet sonic rebel, with a vocal flourish pushing the boundary of *mélodie* with its melismatic gesture.[8]

Viardot's choice of Ronsard was not entirely unusual: fellow French composers such as Georges Bizet, Charles Gounod, Jules Massenet, and Camille Saint-Saëns had also occasionally drawn on the Renaissance poet whose verses had returned to the world of French music through the revival of *chansons* by, among others, Clément Janequin and Jacques Arcadelt. Nor was she the only woman to set his verse. Both Granval (in 1857) and Chaminade (in 1894) set Ronsard's 'Mignonne', a poem that Viardot used as well (in 1886). What is remarkable, though, is the frequency with which Viardot turned to poets from the thirteenth to the seventeenth centuries in her French songs, whereas most of her English, German, and Russian sources date from the nineteenth century.[9] It connotes a familiarity with the aesthetic concerns of French vocal music and its ancestors that had started to become a point of discussion among musicians and intellectuals from the mid nineteenth century on, and with which Viardot – a distinguished intellectual in her own right – was closely involved, not least through her notable performances (in 1859) as Orphée in Gluck's opera.[10] In the mid-1880s, for example, she wrote at least a dozen *mélodies* based on fifteenth-century poetry, six of which were published in 1886 as *Six chansons du XVe siècle*.[11] Like her contemporaries from Saint-Saëns to Claude Debussy, she used fleeting modal progressions to give her scores a historic tint.

Viardot did not turn to female poets any more frequently in her songs than many of her male colleagues, though one poetic choice is truly remarkable: in September 1889, she set a poem by Christine de Pisan (1364–c. 1430) that would have had to be sourced in an 1886 collection of the medieval poet's works rather than one of the more familiar anthologies of early texts.[12] This deliberate act of drawing on a female ancestral voice led to a song that – despite its character of a lament – starts out with the defiant line, 'Alone I am, and alone I want to be':[13]

Seulette suis, et seulette veulx être,
Seulette m'a mon doux ami laissée.
Seulette suis, sans compagnon laissée,
Seulette suis, dolente et désolée,
Seulette suis, en langueur mésaisée,
Seulette suis, plus qu'une autre égarée,
Seulette suis, sans amy de mon rêve.

Seulette suis, partout et en tout être,
Seulette suis, où je voise, où je siée,
Seulette suis, plus qu'autre rien terrestre,
Seulette suis, de chacun délaissée,
Seulette suis, durement abaissée,
Seulette suis, souvent toute éplorée,
Seulette suis, sans amy demeuray![14]

Alone I am, and alone I want to be,
alone, my sweet friend has left me.
Alone I am, left without a companion,
alone I am, mournful and desolate,
alone I am, in uneasy languidness,
alone I am, more than any other lost,
alone I am, without the friend of my dream.

Alone I am, everywhere and in all my being,
alone I am, where I look, where I sit,
alone I am, more than anything else on earth,

alone I am, by everyone forsaken,
alone I am, harshly cast down,
alone I am, often all tearful,
alone I am, and without a friend remain!

As with many other songs, Viardot selected only the part of the poem that suited her expressive purpose, stanzas 1 and 3, and she also changed some lines. Yet despite the clear two-part construction of her song, the two stanzas have a significantly different musical character – moving from the modal touch of the opening minor (with lowered leading tones) to the much more chromatically charged music of the second half that clearly moves from simple narration into a more impassioned voicing of the character – abandoned and grieving – at which point the return to the opening motive at the end takes on a rather painful tone.

Though Viardot did indeed turn to a good number of medieval and Renaissance poets in her *mélodies*, the majority of her poetic and musical choices were more in keeping with broader trends at the time. There are songs using poetry by well-known writers, including 'Chanson d'autrefois' (Hugo), 'Chanson mélancolique' (Armand Silvestre), 'Lamento' (Théophile Gautier), 'Madrid' (Alfred de Musset), and 'Ici-bas tous les lilas meurent' (Sully Prudhomme). Like her contemporaries, she also set verses by lesser-known poets, from Xavier de Maistre – who wrote the text for the much performed 'Haï luli!' (1880) – to Auguste de Châtillon, author of a charming 'Berceuse' (1884). A number of her songs, especially 'Madrid' and 'Havanaise', play on her identity as a Spanish-born woman, also relating to the well-known French predilection for musical exoticism. These and her other *mélodies* are thus thoroughly embedded in the sonic world of French song for all that they are also a testament to Viardot's cosmopolitan musical acumen.

If Viardot was generally subtle about her gender and poetic voice, Augusta Holmès was far more direct. Though of Irish descent, Holmès was born and lived in France. A student of César Franck, she considered herself, and fought to be acknowledged as, a professional composer. The vast majority of her 130 or thereabouts *mélodies* were published, contrary to those by numerous other women composers, and many were successful abroad as well.[15] An ardent Wagnerian of the first degree, she embraced the role of the tone-poet as author of both text and music. Rarely did she set verse by others. Her works were her creations alone, and especially in her songs, the poetic self is often gendered feminine or else remains unspecified. Moreover, she encouraged through interviews and other mediated remarks the often autobiographical readings of her *mélodies*. Few of her songs have a clearly identified male poetic voice, save in the case of her ballad-like dialogues.

Three among her best-known songs are 'Berceuse' (1892), seemingly a lullaby yet addressed to her love lost in delicious dreams, 'Les griffes d'or' (1889), which evokes a painful relationship with one lover accusing the other of holding their heart in golden claws, and 'Noël' (1884), a song familiar also in its English-language version as 'Three Angels Come Tonight'. All three songs are distinguished by their clear formal structures (either strophic or ABA), their soaring melodic lines that often traverse the full tessitura of a mezzo-soprano – Holmès' own vocal register – and an accompaniment that draws on the full chromatic language of the late nineteenth century without straying too far from its tonal grounding.

One genre in which Holmès excelled was ballads, a highly popular form in the framework of the French *mélodie* adopted by composers from Saint-Saëns ('La fiancée du timbalier', 1887) to Chaminade ('Ballade à la lune', 1894). Ernest Chausson went so far as to title two *mélodies* as ballads – 'Ballade' (1896) and 'Ballade française' (1898) – even though their texts are short lyric poetry. While Holmès' ballads may use mimetic male voices, their poetic self tends to be explicitly gendered female. An excellent example is 'Le ruban rose' (1899), a tale of a marquise of old, her page, and his best friend. The poem, which evokes the sphere of courtly love, consists of nine quatrains full of witty twists.[16]

Celui que j'aime est si mignon
Que les femmes en sont maries;
Il n'a ni chasses ni prairies;
Pas même le moindre pignon!

Il est de très bonne noblesse,
Et plus brave que ses aïeux!
Il est jaloux, un rien le blesse!
Ses étoiles, ce sont mes yeux.

Et puis, c'est un charmant visage
Fier et tendre, bien à mon gré.
Il ressemble à l'Amour poudré!
C'est pourquoi j'en ai fait mon page!

J'étais en grand habit de Cour,
Fard et mouches, dentelle;
Celui pour qui je me fais belle
A mes genoux parlait d'amour.

Et mon collier de ruban rose,
Je ne sais comment, s'en vola!

Il fut cueilli comme une rose
Par le Prince qui passait là!

'Voici votre ruban, Madame;
Reprenez-le contre un baiser!
Gardez-vous bien de refuser:
En ce cas, votre amant rend l'âme'.

Mon jeune ami, plein de fureur,
Dit: 'Madame n'est point en cause!
Il m'appartient, ce ruban rose,
Et je vous tuerai, Monseigneur!'

Et je le vis, au clair de lune,
Si joli pendant le combat,
Qu'il fut choisi par la Fortune
Pour que le Prince succombât!

'Il faut me consoler, Marquise',
Dit mon page, triste à demi;
'J'ai tué mon meilleur ami!'
C'est pourquoi je lui fus exquise!

The one I love is so delightful
that women are entranced by him;
he owns neither hunting grounds nor meadows;
not even the smallest garret!

He is of very noble stock,
and braver than his forefathers!
He is jealous, a mere nothing wounds him!
My eyes serve as his stars.

Moreover, he has a charming face
proud and tender, just as I like them.
He looks like the powdered cupid!
That is why I made him my page!

I was in grand court dress,
with makeup and beauty spots, lace;
he for whom I make myself beautiful
spoke of love at my knees.

And my necklace of pink ribbon,
I know not how, flew away!
It was picked up like a rose
by the Prince who was passing by!

'Here is your ribbon, Madame;
have it back for a kiss!
Be careful not to refuse:
for if so, your lover will give up his soul'.

My young friend, full of fury,
says: 'Madame has nothing to do with this!
It belongs to me, this pink ribbon,
and I will kill you, my lord!'

And I saw him, in the moonlight,
so pretty during the fight,
that Fortune made the choice
for the Prince to succumb!

'You must console me, Marquise',
said my page, half sad;
'I have killed my best friend!'
That is why I treated him so sweetly.

The playful wit in the poem also pervades Holmès' setting. She treats each group of three quatrains as a single musical strophe, with recurring motives in both piano and voice welding together its AA′B structure. She conjures the distant past by playing with modal tinges, from the opening mixture of major and minor in the piano to the cadences with flattened leading tones. The end of each musical strophe is marked by an exaggeratedly stretched-out perfect cadence. If at first the melody appears like a ballad in the folk tone, it quickly becomes a melodious sweep that challenges the singer with a long-held melodic high point marked *pianissimo*. The almost facetious turns of the text find their echoes in the musical setting. This is a song written for an audience to be delighted and surprised.

Holmès also composed a number of song cycles, including *Les sept ivresses* (1882), *Paysages d'amour* (1889), and *Les heures* (1900). One particularly fascinating cycle is *Les chants de la Kythare*̀de (1888), as the three songs – 'Kypris', 'Erôtylôn', and 'Thrinōdia' – are cast as the musical utterances of a female bard (or female kithara player), blended with highly sensual expressions of erotic desire. As the composer wrote in an autobiographical sketch, Ancient Greece was not only a pastoral space of true passion and love but also the cradle of music and poetry – a Wagnerian credo that Holmès thoroughly embraced.[17] The first of the three poems, 'Kypris', is dedicated to Aphrodite and ensounds the goddess's lullaby for Eros, held in her arms and jealously guarded from any outside disturbance. In the second song, 'Erôtylôn', the lyric persona identifies herself as Aède (or Aoede), the muse of voice and song, who pours out her desire for a beautiful boatman from Mytilene – the capital of Lesbos. The final 'Thrinōdia' is a hymn to Apollo to whom the immortal female bard finds herself chained. Holmès' poetry here is steeped in the sensual gestures of the Parnassians. Relying on a familiar musical trope, her arpeggiated piano textures suggest the musical bard's lyre. Her harmonic language is overall rather restrained, though she fleetingly shifts into mediant and submediant relations. If the opening lullaby is strophic (with a refrain), the final song is through-composed, extending the melodic range line by line until its high point, Apollo's call to the immortal muse.

Poets

During Holmès' lifetime, *Les chants de la Kytharède* was rarely performed as a cycle, though 'Kypris' was programmed rather frequently on its own, and the song cycle was known in the world of Parisian art and music. Holmès' erotic world of Ancient Greece – though steeped in French Hellenism – was unequivocally heterosexual: her vision of Lesbos was one inhabited by the loves of Aphrodite and Eros, Aède and Apollo (the boatman does, however, add an unexpectedly earthy character in the middle). When the openly lesbian poetess, Renée Vivien (1877–1909) – the British Pauline Mary Tarn – turned her interest to the island of Lesbos and its *kytharèdes* in her eponymous collection of poems (1904), hers were Sapphic poems that celebrated a sensual gyno-erotic world. For much of the twentieth century her poetry was set exclusively by male composers.[18] This is hardly surprising, for Vivien's gynocentric poetic voice could easily be usurped by a male composer exploring the sensuality of her verse, but it would be riskier for a female one. In 1910, the French conductor and composer, René-Emmanuel Baton, known as Rhené-Baton (1879–1940), chose several of her poems from *Dans un coin de violettes* for a song cycle with the same title (1919). The evocative opening line of the second song, 'Pour le lys' – 'Ô toi, femme que j'aime' – does take on a different connotation, in effect, when set by a male composer. Louis Aubert, for his part, used two of Vivien's poems as luscious orchestral songs: 'Nuit mauresque' (1911) and 'Roses du soir' (1910). The latter was also set by Charles Koechlin. Vivien was not the only lesbian poet whose gynocentric poetry was co-opted by male composers for its erotically evocative language. Fauré's penultimate cycle, *Mirages* (1919), set poems by Renée de Brimont (1880–1943). Its last song, 'Danseuse,' in particular, offers a sensuous appreciation of the dancer's body and performance through the gaze of the lyric persona, a flute player, whose gender the musical setting renders neutral.

As is the case with women composers, once the spotlight is turned on French song's poets it reveals the noticeable presence of female writers. None has the prominence of poets like Charles Baudelaire, Victor Hugo, or Paul Verlaine, but there are many female authors whose poems were set as *mélodies*. For example, French composers drew on close to one hundred different poems by Marceline Desbordes-Valmore (1786–1859), one of the key poets of French Romanticism, and her poetry remained in fashion well into the twentieth century. Both Bizet and Marguerite Canal set 'Si l'enfant sommeille' (from her collection *Pauvres fleurs* of 1839), and 'Les cloches du soir' attracted Franck as well as Liszt. Indeed, Canal's song is part of her collection *Quatre berceuses* (1948), all four on texts by Desbordes-Valmore. Other composers who turned to her poetry include Georges Auric, Alfred Bruneau, Hedwige Chrétien, Alberic Magnard, Saint-Saëns, and Ambroise Thomas – a group as varied as it was distinguished.

Female poets generally were contemporaries of the composers who used their texts. The poetry of Louise de Vilmorin (1902–69) was set by Claude Arrieu, Francis Poulenc, and Darius Milhaud, among others. Another example is Anna, Comtesse de Noailles (1876–1933), whose verse was the basis for a song cycle by Louis Vierne, published in 1930 under the title *Quatre poèmes grecs*, Op. 60. Saint-Saëns, too, set two poems by her, including one of his most enchanting *mélodies*, 'Violons dans le soir' (1907, with violin *obbligato*).[19] The poem was uniquely suited for a song composition because – in its poetic evocation of the violin – it offers a musical metatext for the composer to ensound in his setting, giving audible agency to the power of the violin's bow to transform the strings, with the singer a commentator more than the protagonist of the song.

One particularly fascinating connection between a poetess and two composers was that of Cécile Sauvage (1883–1927) whose poetry was set both by her son Olivier Messiaen and by his wife Claire Delbos (1906–59), who composed two song cycles on Sauvage's texts soon after her marriage to Messiaen in 1932. The first one, *Primevère* (1935), can be read in autobiographical terms given her choice of poems, including the central three songs (out of five), 'J'ai peur d'être laide', 'Mais je suis belle d'être aimée', and 'Je suis née à l'amour'. This taut cycle (each song only lasts about a page) takes the listener quickly from a woman's potential self-doubt to a self-confident reversal. The great melismatic flourish, for example, at the end of 'Mais je suis belle d'être aimée' evokes laughter (as does the piano in its prior interlude) while it emphasises 'quand je passe' (as I walk past), ending with a solo-voice cadential gesture. Delbos' musical irony continues in the fourth song, 'Je suis née à l'amour', where she first invokes the *Tristan* chord, and then interrupts its resolution, under the word 'matin' (I am born for love / as a lily to the morning). She returns to the quotation at the end of the song, clearly relying on the witty counterpoint of Wagner's deadly ending as Sauvage's text evokes blossoming of the woman's heart in love. To top it off, Delbos set as the final song of the cycle a poem celebrating her dress, hat, and shoes ('Dans ma robe à bouquets bleus'). Although this cycle – just like Messiaen's own *Poèmes pour Mi* (1936), which he wrote the year after Delbos' *Primevère* – is situated at the *mélodie*'s unique aesthetic intersection of private and public, where the poetic Self might be blended with that of the composer, it also offers a feminist rebuff to a Germanic mainstay of the international song repertoire: Robert Schumann's *Frauenliebe und -leben* (1840) and its problematic ventriloquism. Together with Delbos' second cycle, *L'Âme en bourgeon* (1937), *Primevère* offers a self-confident gynocentric view of marriage and maternity that stands also in fascinating contrast to Messiaen's far more traditionally configured *Chants de Terre et de Ciel* (1938).[20]

Canal, Delbos, Holmès, and Viardot were not the only women composers to set poetry by female poets both of their time and from earlier periods. This kind of female kinship in song was firmly established early on in the genre by composers such as Pauline Duchambge (1778–1858), who set poems by her friend Desbordes-Valmore. Lili Boulanger turned to Berthe Galeron de Calone (1859–1936) for her final surviving song, 'Dans l'immense tristesse' (1916). Cécile Chaminade set verse by almost a dozen women, including multiple poems by Rosemonde Gérard (1866–1953). Exploring all these creative connections further would seem essential to expanding any *her*story of French song.

Singers and *Salonnières*

Women's contribution to French song proved significant also through their work as sonic co-creators and patrons. Their voices can be found inscribed into the very fabric of a *mélodie* – famously in the songs that Debussy wrote for the high soprano voice of Marie Vasnier (1848–1923) – and, like Winnaretta Singer, Princesse de Polignac (1865–1943), female patrons enabled composers to write key works in the repertoire not only by offering financial support but also by providing the space for their composition and opportunities for their performance. Gabriel Fauré, for example, wrote the first two of his *Cinq mélodies 'de Venise'* in 1891 during his sojourn at the Palazzino Wolkoff in Venice, where he stayed with the princess and several mutual friends. In her memoirs, she recalled with some amusement the mixed success of this arrangement: 'I carefully prepared a quiet room with a piano as a study for Fauré to work in, but I had forgotten how fond he was of cafés; and I am obliged to say that he wrote his *Cinq mélodies de Venise* at a little marble table at the Café Florian on the Piazza [San Marco], in the midst of the noise and turmoil of a busy Venetian crowd, rather than in the peaceful room I had arranged for him'.[21] Women's involvement in the creation of *mélodies* straddled the worlds of private and public music-making in manifold ways as they enabled, performed, and promoted these compositions.

It is well known that artistic salons were vital spaces for music-making in Paris. Not only did they challenge the binary of public and private through their interstitial position, but they also often provided a hospitable laboratory for new musical ideas.[22] In contrast to the generally male-dominated and frequently hidebound institutions of French officialdom, the salons where female patrons with significant financial and intellectual resources organised concerts and more informal gatherings offered an environment conducive to artistic exploration. Many of the women who dominated the world of musical salons were themselves gifted musicians, often trained by the same teachers as their professional colleagues. Here traditional ideas about ideal womanhood in the nineteenth century – according to which musical practice contributed to a welcoming home environment – and individual women's musical ambitions came together in a synergy of creative agency. A musical education was a matter of course for any accomplished young woman in nineteenth-century Europe, whether a middle-class daughter such as Marguerite de Saint-Marceaux (1850–1930) or an aristocratic one like Elisabeth, Comtesse Greffulhe (1860–1952). It is hard to imagine from a twenty-first-century perspective how profoundly suffused women's education and daily practice were with considerable musical mastery, especially in piano and vocal performance. Any caricature of amateur dilettantism would not do justice even to those nineteenth-century women who were playing and singing for their own enjoyment as well as to fulfil their social obligations, and for whom an entire market of song publications had sprung up. Musical supplements of journals such as *Je sais tout* or *L'Illustration*, and albums produced by fashionable music magazines such as *Musica*, found their way onto the music stands of many households in Paris and elsewhere in France. Nor did they necessarily focus just on 'easy' pieces. Women were keen consumers of these compilations. Moreover, they were also frequent contributors to them as outlets for their *romances* and *mélodies*.[23]

Within the wide spectrum of amateur performance in France, musicians such as the Princesse de Polignac, Saint-Marceaux, or Vasnier were active not only as accomplished performers but also as artistic interlocutors with the musicians who frequented their salons. Their technical abilities and their musicality – both of which could be developed free from the pressures of a life on the concert stage – allowed for in-depth engagement with the music they loved.[24] This provided a unique attraction for composers. As Fauré wrote in 1902 to the Comtesse Greffulhe about his three songs, Op. 85: 'I dream of making you hear them sung by perfect interpreters, and I know of none among the professionals. It is the amateurs who express me and understand me the best'.[25] One of these songs – 'Accompagnement', Op. 85 no. 3 – was written earlier that year for another accomplished amateur performer, Émilie Girette (1876–1917). In her diary, she not only recounted how much she loved to sing and how hard she worked on her craft but she also expressed what artistic joy she found being accompanied on the piano by the composer himself. As Fauré repeatedly told her, 'Accompagnement' was indeed composed with her voice and personality in mind.[26] Another amateur singer and artistic interlocutor who inspired Fauré was Emma Bardac (1862–1934), for whom he wrote his lyric magnum opus, *La bonne chanson* (1894), and whom he considered one of his greatest interpreters.

That composers wrote their works for specific interpreters and their musical strengths was part of a centuries-old musical practice. Even the compositional consideration of the sometimes more limited abilities of dilettantes has a long tradition, as when Johann Sebastian Bach accommodated the viola da gamba skills of his then employer Prince Leopold of Anhalt-Köthen in his Brandenburg Concerto no. 6, BWV 1051, or when Wolfgang Amadeus Mozart tailored the three piano parts of his concerto in F major, K. 242, to the varying capabilities of Countess Antonia Lodron and her two daughters Aloysia and Giuseppa. What distinguishes the role of musical amateurs in the *her*story of French song, however, is that many of these performers could easily have made their way in the professional musical world and sometimes moved between the salon and the concert platform, as did Girette, for example. But whether because of social norms or personal preference, they chose to centre their musical activities in their salons.

How powerfully a *salonnière's* voice and musicality could shape the composition of *mélodies* can be witnessed in the works of Debussy who created many a piece for a particular patron and friend. Between 1881 and 1885, he turned to song as a shared musical practice when he wrote well over twenty songs for Marie Vasnier, a singer with whom he was infatuated, in whose salon he was a regular presence, with whom he made music, and whose husband was supporting the young composer. Composed over the course of five years, the *mélodies* 'were conceived in some way with you in mind', as he wrote in an autograph dedication, 'and can only belong to you'.[27] When he collected them into an album before leaving for Rome in 1885 (the '*Recueil Vasnier*'), his inscription made it clear that these *mélodies* 'only lived through her' and that they 'will lose their charming grace if ever they no longer pass through her melodious fairy mouth'.[28] Besides the obvious connection of the songs with Vasnier – encapsulating her vocality in their vocal range of a high coloratura soprano and melodic gestures suited for her voice's agility – they also open up the space to think beyond the straightforward relationship between a singer's voice and the vocal part a composer wrote for and with her. It brings the actual presence, agency, and authority of a musician such as Vasnier into sharp focus, especially given the asymmetrical relationship between a self-assured, highly cultivated, and beautiful thirty-two-year-old woman and a young, somewhat uncouth, and inexperienced composer. In a recent discussion of these songs, Julian Johnson draws thoughtful connections between the 'economy of aesthetic desire' that the songs encapsulate and 'the specific and biographical version that runs in parallel'.[29] Despite acknowledging this biographical link, however, Johnson centres his perspective on Debussy and his musical choices. He could not have made his disregard for Vasnier's actual part in, and contributions to, these songs any clearer, transforming her from empowered agent into an object of male desire: 'But it is not Marie-Blanche Vasnier I am interested in here, so much as her body. Or to be more precise, the *idea* of her body that Debussy evoked in his music'.[30]

Vasnier's taste in poetry, her performative practice, and her musical preferences proved to be as crucial an ingredient for Debussy's collection of *mélodies* as did her voice and vocal prowess. If, indeed, the idea of song as embodiment were to be deployed in this context, it might be more fruitful to think about sonic echoes of alterity and, in the words of Holly Watkins and Melina Esse, 'singing as embodied action'.[31] I invoke alterity in the sense of the French philosopher Emmanuel Levinas, who demands a radical acknowledgement of an Other's right to resist totalising appropriation within a closed narrative.[32] Therefore, if Fauré or Debussy cast their *mélodies* as encapsulating both the vocality and the persona of their musical collaborators – as they both explicitly did in the case of Bardac and Vasnier – then a gynocentric epistemology must pay attention to their co-creative agency, acknowledging the very vibrational practice of their embodied music-making as resonating in these *mélodies*.[33] If singing is indeed embodied action, then song can be understood as ensounded presence.

Professional concert and opera singers are no less crucial to the *her*story of French song. It is hard to overstate the impact of two singers, in particular, on the creation and promotion of French song: Jane Bathori (1877–1970) and Claire Croiza (1882–1946). Not only did both singers premiere notable works of the repertoire, touring Europe and the Americas extensively with programmes dedicated to the *mélodie*, but they also served as key multipliers because of their recordings, radio programmes, and teaching. Through this dedication to the genre of French song, they came to be understood as the very personification of the *mélodie*. Indeed, Bathori's contemporary, Georges Jean-Aubry, put it in these terms in 1916: 'She incarnates modern French song'.[34] Two male younger singers, Charles Panzéra and Pierre Bernac, came later to share their prominent position within the genre as they emulated their trail-blazing strategies in their own performing and teaching careers. Neither Bathori nor Croiza performed and recorded French song exclusively; indeed, both had started out on the opera stage and returned there from time to time, including Parisian performances of Gluck and Monteverdi. They also sang in oratorios, comprising such modern works as Edward Elgar's *The Dream of Gerontius* (1900, Parisian premiere with Croiza in 1906). Yet their creative lives were increasingly dedicated to the *mélodie*.

In the years leading up to World War I, Bathori and Croiza grew to be an integral part of the Parisian avant-garde, gaining a reputation as the interpreters of choice for composers seeking the best possible start for their new *mélodies*. In January 1914, for example, Bathori premiered both Igor Stravinsky's *Three Japanese Lyrics* and Ravel's *Trois poèmes de Stéphane Mallarmé* at a concert of the Société musicale indépendante. She had become a favourite of Ravel in 1904 after she stepped in – on a few hours' notice – to sing his *Shéhérazade* in a concert after the original soloist had to bow out for reasons of illness. In 1906, he dedicated his new *Histoires naturelles* to Bathori, who premiered the cycle with the composer at the piano in January 1907; two decades later, in May 1926, she would sing the first performance of another set of Ravel songs, his *Chansons madécasses*, in its version for flute, cello, and piano. Ravel was only one among the many composers who relied on Bathori's flawless interpretation of their *mélodies*, all the more so as she would often accompany herself on the piano, thus presenting a uniquely cohesive staging of the repertoire. Her reputation as a singer with perfect diction, exquisite musical nuance, and sophisticated musical understanding of the *mélodie* stayed with her for decades to come. Reputation is a valuable distinction in the economy of the arts, and it lends itself to reinforcement over the long term, often in a feedback loop.[35] In the case of Bathori, her own reputation also gave credence to the music she chose to promote in her concerts and later recordings – often integrating new pieces into exquisitely constructed programmes that highlighted French song through its history or within new music.[36] In 1914, the critic Léon Vallas not only lauded her unparalleled accomplishments as an artist but also made it clear that without her 'certain pieces would never have been written'.[37]

Her reputation both as a brilliant performer and a champion of new music led in 1917 to her taking over the Théâtre du Vieux-Colombier for two seasons. Her programming offered performance opportunities to composers mobilised in the war as well as many still barely known creative artists, including all six composers who would eventually be known as Les Six.[38] In the interwar years, she expanded her presence on the concert platform through recordings and radio programmes. As Henry Prunières noted in his reviews, there was a learning curve involved with the new technology, but eventually her discs reflected her impeccable musicianship.[39] Many also record her idiosyncratic choice to accompany herself when a song's composer was unavailable. Over the following four decades, both Bathori's concert tours – especially those to Argentina – and her radio presentations centred on French song. After her retirement from the concert stage, she focussed on her masterclasses.[40]

In many ways, Croiza's career could be described in parallel terms to that of Bathori (and they sometimes shared a concert platform), although her operatic presence was both more extensive and more distinguished and her pedagogical work began decades before Bathori's. Croiza started teaching at the École normale de musique in June 1922 and would be appointed professor of voice at the Conservatoire in 1934. Her general emphasis as a recitalist remained on repertoire composed before World War I, especially songs by Chausson, Debussy, Duparc, Fauré, and Ravel, although she did programme new *mélodies* by Arthur Honegger – several of which she premiered – and by Poulenc, including his *Poèmes de Ronsard* (1925). Croiza's pedagogical impact on French song performance was significant, and she began early to theorise its specific characteristics, first to the students in her masterclasses – many of whom transcribed their lecture notes – and then also in the framework of public discussion. In 1937, for example, she presented a paper to the IIe Congrès international d'esthétique et de science de l'art with the title 'L'art lyrique et l'interprétation' where she reflected on the role of the singer as mediator of musical and poetic expression.[41] A careful reading of Croiza's comments on song performance again positions the singer in the role of co-creator who – together with the musician's score – gives voice to the poetic character of the *mélodie*. Indeed, poetry was the driving force guiding her conception of the *mélodie* as musical embodiment of French verse. This vision of French song was one that she imparted to her students, who included, among others, Janine Michaud and Gérard Souzay.

Composers and poets, singers and *salonnières*, concert organisers and pedagogues – these were but a few of the many roles through which women shaped French song. One might add to this list their presence in music publishing, either as women involved in the family business – as was the case with Madame E. Troupenas, to whom Viardot dedicated one of her *mélodies* brought out by the publishing house – or as publishers in their own right, as with Jane Vieu (also a composer and singer), who operated between 1907 and 1925 a publishing house with Maurice Vieu, presumed to be her husband. Vieu published not only some of her own works – though many of her songs came out with Enoch – but also those of other women composers such as Hélène Fleury (1876–1957) and Armande de Polignac.

Women's work in song also challenges the aesthetic boundaries of the *mélodie* as a genre.[42] In 1901, the famous *diseuse* Yvette Guilbert (1865–1944) began what is usually referred to as her second career, dedicated to bringing alive the song repertoire of ancient France and connecting it to the popular *chansons* for which she had become famous in Parisian café-concerts. This shift in repertoire raises the question of what it might mean, then, for a *her*story of the *mélodie* that the same pieces from medieval and Renaissance repertoire were performed by Guilbert, on the one hand, and, on the other, Bathori in concerts that combine modern *mélodies* with historic *chansons* – both singers laying claim to performing 'the grand and beautiful song literature of our old homeland!'[43] These two cases strongly suggest that the performance space, social class, and aesthetic context of women's music-making were, in effect, closely intertwined with the generic framing of the *mélodie*, both connected to, and distinct from, popular genres. Establishing ancestry through historic *chansons*, as well as through the *mélodie*'s claims of poetic privilege, connects back to the issue of validating the genre. The fact that women played so many different roles in such validation reveals the importance of recovering the genre's *her*stories to reveal the multifaceted contribution of women, not just to the *mélodie* but also to musical worlds writ large.

Notes

1. Annegret Fauser, 'The Songs', in *The Cambridge Companion to Berlioz*, ed. Peter Bloom (Cambridge: Cambridge University Press, 2000), 109–24.
2. Annegret Fauser, *Der Orchestergesang in Frankreich zwischen 1870 und 1920* (Laaber: Laaber Verlag, 1994), 70 (Mauclair) and 111 (Schmitt).
3. Marcelle Denya, 'La Musique française à l'étranger', *Pour la victoire* (16 January 1943), 7 (translation by the author).
4. For a thoughtful appreciation of this shift in perspective, see Kimberly Francis, 'Her-Storiography: Pierre Bourdieu, Cultural Capital, and Changing the Narrative Paradigm', *Women and Music*, 19 (2005), 169–77.
5. Liszt (1859), cited in Beatrix Borchard, 'Pauline Viardot', *Musik und Gender im Internet*, https://mugi.hfmt-hamburg.de/receive/mugi_person_00000848?lang=en (accessed 15 July 2022).
6. See Borchard, 'Pauline Viardot'.
7. Jane Ashton Sharp, *Russian Modernism between East and West: Natal'ia Goncharova and the Moscow Avant-Garde* (Cambridge: Cambridge University Press, 2006), 1. Y. A. Tugenhold, cited in Irina Vakar, 'Goncharova – "This Name Had the Ring of Victory"', *The Tretyakov Gallery Magazine* (2014), 42, www.tretyakovgallerymagazine.com/articles/1-2014-42/goncharova-name-had-ring-victory (accessed 10 April 2018).
8. On Viardot's voice, see Beatrix Borchard, *Pauline Viardot-Garcia: Fülle des Lebens* (Cologne, Weimar, and Vienna: Böhlau, 2016), 145–6.
9. Viardot does set a poem by Petrarch in Italian.
10. Borchard explores the intellectual world of Viardot throughout the biography, *Pauline Viardot-Garcia*.
11. Pauline Viardot, *Six chansons du XVe siècle* (Paris: Heugel, 1886). For in-depth information on Pauline Viardot's compositions, see Christin Heitmann, *Pauline Viardot. Systematisch-bibliographisches Werkverzeichnis (VWV)* (Hamburg: Hochschule für Musik und Theater, 2012–), www.pauline-viardot.de/Werkverzeichnis.htm (accessed 1 July 2022).
12. Christin Heitmann, 'Seulette', *VWV 1191*, www.pauline-viardot.de/9Werk.php?werk=433 (accessed 1 July 2022). The manuscript is dated September 1889. The source text is Christine de Pisan, *Œuvres poétiques*, edited by Maurice Roy, vol. 1 (Paris: Firmin Didot, 1886). Viardot's *Six chansons du XVe siècle* and other early texts were sourced in Gaston Paris' anthology, *Chansons du XVe siècle publiées d'après le manuscrit de la Bibliothèque Nationale de Paris* (with musical transcription by Auguste Gevaert) (Paris: Firmin Didot, 1875).

13. Viardot notated the song in two keys: C minor and E minor. Both manuscripts are in the 'Fonds Viardot-Duvernoy' at the Conservatoire national supérieur de musique et de danse, Médiathèque Hector Berlioz. They have been digitised and can be accessed under https://mediatheque.cnsmdp.fr/modules/custom/pdf_viewer/templates/viewer.html?file=/get-attachment/8f916d46-189b-46b0-8e92-b936a7fcd661 (C-minor version) and https://mediatheque.cnsmdp.fr/modules/custom/pdf_viewer/templates/viewer.html?file=/get-attachment/af69c7a4-3b09-4f8e-961b-4b5f209a3f63 (E-minor version).
14. Text transcribed from the manuscript of the C-minor version. Viardot changed some of Pisan's words for her setting. The E-minor version has further changes.
15. Florence Launay, *Les Compositrices en France au XIXe siècle* (Paris: Fayard, 2006), 191.
16. Augusta Holmès, *Le ruban rose* (Paris: L. Grus, 1899). The score is available digitally both on ILMSP and on Gallica. For a different interpretation of the song, see Brigitte Olivier, *Les Mélodies d'Augusta Holmes* (Arles: Actes Sud, 2003), 75–7.
17. On the role of Hellenism in French culture and music, see Samuel N. Dorf, *Performing Antiquity: Ancient Greek Music and Dance from Paris to Delphi, 1890-1930* (New York: Oxford University Press, 2019).
18. See Marius Flothuis, '... *exprimer l'inexprimable* ...': *Essai sur la mélodie française depuis Duparc en dix-neuf chapitres et huit digressions* (Amsterdam and Atlanta: Rodopi, 1996), 154.
19. Camille Saint-Saëns, *Violons dans le soir* (Paris: Durand, 1907). For a more general discussion of the composer's song compositions, see Annegret Fauser, 'What's in a Song? Camille Saint-Saëns's *Mélodies*', in *Saint-Saëns and His World*, ed. Jann Pasler (Princeton: Princeton University Press, 2012), 210–31.
20. Claire Delbos, *Primevère* (Paris: A. Leduc, 1935); ead., *L'âme en bourgeon* (Paris: Éditions Fortin, 2009).
21. Polignac, 'Memoirs', cited in Sylvia Kahan, *Music's Modern Muse: A Life of Winnaretta Singer, Princesse de Polignac* (Rochester: University of Rochester Press, 2003), 52.
22. Jeanice Brooks, 'Nadia Boulanger and the Salon of the Princesse de Polignac', *Journal of the American Musicological Society*, 46, no. 3 (1993), 415–68; Myriam Chimènes, *Mécènes et musiciens: Du salon au concert à Paris sous la IIIe République* (Paris: Fayard, 2004), 619–90; Louis K. Epstein, *The Creative Labor of Music Patronage in Interwar France* (Woodbridge: Boydell, 2022), 42–71.
23. Launay, *Les Compositrices en France*, 185.
24. Chimènes (*Mécènes et musiciens*, 43–7) offers a range of personal testimonies about the importance of, and love for, music among French *salonnières*.
25. Cited in Graham Johnson, *Gabriel Fauré: The Songs and Their Poets* (Farnham and Burlington, VT: Ashgate, 2009), 382.
26. Chimènes, *Mécènes et musiciens*, 139.

27. Cited in François Lesure, *Claude Debussy*, translated and revised by Marie Rolf (Rochester: University of Rochester Press, 2019), 36.
28. Quoted in Julian Johnson, 'Present Absence: Debussy, Song, and the Art of (Dis)appearing', *19th-Century Music*, 40, no. 3 (2017), 242.
29. Johnson, 'Present Absence', 242.
30. Ibid., 242.
31. Holly Watkins and Melina Esse, 'Down with Disembodiment; or, Musicology and the Material Turn', *Women and Music: A Journal of Gender and Culture*, 19 (2015), 165.
32. See 'Meaning and Sense' (1964), in Emmanuel Lévinas, *Basic Philosophical Writings*, ed. Adrian T. Peperzak, Simon Critchley, and Robert Bernasconi (Bloomington and Indianapolis: Indiana University Press, 1996), 38–42.
33. See Nina Sun Eidsheim, *Sensing Sound: Singing and Listening as Vibrational Practice* (Durham, NC: Duke University Press, 2015), 154–85.
34. Georges Jean-Aubry, *La Musique française d'aujourd'hui* (Paris: Perrin, 1916), 273 (translation by the author).
35. Pierre-Michel Menger, *The Economics of Creativity: Art and Achievement under Uncertainty* (Cambridge, MA, and London: Harvard University Press, 2014), 161–3.
36. For a discussion of Bathori's programming, see Catharine Mary Schwab, 'The *Mélodie française moderne*: An Expression of Music, Poetry, and Prosody in *fin-de-siècle* France, and Its Performance in the Recitals of Jane Bathori (1877–1970) and Claire Croiza (1882–1946)', PhD dissertation, University of Michigan, 1991, 151-62.
37. Cited in Linda Laurent, Andrée Tainsy, Sonia Lee, and Isabelle Vellay, 'Jane Bathori et le Théâtre du Vieux-Colombier 1917–1919', *Revue de musicologie*, 70, no. 2 (1984), 231.
38. Laurent, Tainsy, Lee, and Vellay, 'Jane Bathori', 252.
39. Several of these comments are extracted in English translation in Ronald Woodley, 'Performing Ravel: Style and Practice in the Early Recordings', in *The Cambridge Companion to Ravel*, ed. Deborah Mawer (Cambridge: Cambridge University Press, 2000), 232–3.
40. For more on Bathori's influence on composers and championing of the *mélodie*, see Kilpatrick, *French Art Song*, 274–80.
41. A short and relevant extract from the manuscript of the lecture is given in Jean-Michel Nectoux, *Hommage à Claire Croiza*, exhibition catalogue (Paris: Bibliothèque nationale de France, 1984), 38.
42. Jacqueline Waeber, 'Yvette Guilbert and the Revaluation of the *Chanson Populaire* and *Chanson Ancienne* during the Third Republic, 1889–1914', in *The Oxford Handbook of the New Cultural History of Music*, ed. Jane F. Fulcher (New York: Oxford University Press, 2011), 264–95.
43. Yvette Guilbert, *La Chanson de ma vie* (Paris: Bernard Castel, 1927), 194 (translation by the author).

9 | Fauré's Song Cycles

STEPHEN RUMPH

Gabriel Fauré composed over one hundred songs between 1861 and 1921, yet a curious line bisects his lyric output. Until 1890 he wrote individual *romances* and *mélodies*; thereafter, he turned almost exclusively to song cycles. (The lone outlier is *Poème d'un jour*, a triptych from 1878.) In part, this cyclic turn reflects the new prestige of the *mélodie*, which was outgrowing its salon origins and becoming a 'serious' concert genre: instead of purveying songs singly for the domestic market as in the heyday of the *romance*, composers increasingly published their work in weightier groupings. The new collections also mirrored the rising literary ambitions of the *mélodie*, evident in the titles themselves – Claude Debussy's *Cinq poèmes de Charles Baudelaire* (1890), Ernest Chausson's *Chansons de Shakespeare* (1897), Maurice Ravel's *Trois poèmes de Stéphane Mallarmé* (1913), or Camille Saint-Saëns' *Cinq poèmes de Ronsard* (1921).

Yet Fauré's song cycles have a more personal motivation, rooted in lifelong creative patterns. As Roy Howat has traced in Chapter 5, the composer moved systematically through individual poets in his early years, exhausting the possibilities of Victor Hugo, Charles Baudelaire, Théophile Gautier, Sully Prudhomme, and Armand Silvestre. Thus, when he laid aside other poets in 1891–4 and wrote two song cycles on Paul Verlaine's verse, the *Cinq mélodies 'de Venise'* and *La bonne chanson*, Fauré was following long habit. Likewise, in the years 1906–14 he dedicated himself wholly to the poetry of Charles Van Lerberghe, composing the cycles *La chanson d'Ève* and *Le jardin clos*. Fauré's style shifted markedly between these different poets as he reimagined his musical idiom. As he wrote to his wife Marie in 1906, comparing *La bonne chanson* and *La chanson d'Ève*: 'The difference in character between the two poems must entail a difference in the music, and from that point of view my project interests me'.[1]

Moreover, Fauré's song cycles are truly integrated works. Far more than Debussy, Chausson, Ravel, or Poulenc, he conceived the song cycle as a musical and narrative unity rather than a collection of related songs. Fauré's first cycle, *Poème d'un jour*, has a clear narrative and tonal plan, and he further knit together his next three cycles with both thematic recollections and leitmotifs, deployed with a truly Wagnerian rigour. While no material recurs in his last three cycles, they also show signs of tonal planning, and his valedictory *L'horizon chimérique* has a clear narrative thread.

Finally, there is Fauré's curious practice of writing song cycles in complementary pairs. The Verlaine cycles both explore music as a conduit between human and natural realms. The Van Lerberghe cycles have garden settings, feature an Old Testament heroine, and end with the death of a solitary woman. Finally, *Mirages* (1919) and *L'horizon chimérique* (1921) concern voyages and, as the titles advert, probe the line between reality and fantasy. As these pairings suggest, Fauré regarded the song cycle as a vehicle to explore broad human, artistic, and even metaphysical themes.

This chapter sketches the vision behind Fauré's seven cycles, surveying their musical and expressive design but also exploring the peculiar synthesis of poetry and music in each work. The portrait emerges of an astute reader who closely followed the changing currents of French literature and aesthetics. Fauré's response to this world of ideas, which marries beauty and reflection, imagination and intellect, secures his song cycles a unique place in the history of the *mélodie*.[2]

Poème d'un jour, Op. 21

Fauré's first song cycle reflects his involvement with the Parnassian movement, which dominated French poetry during the Second Empire and well into the 1880s. The Parnassians rejected the social commitment, enthusiasm, and autobiographical candour of Victor Hugo and the Romantics, embracing instead the formalism and aestheticism of their spiritual father Théophile Gautier. The leader of the Parnassians, Charles Marie René Leconte de Lisle, expressed their ideal of timeless, impassive beauty in 'Vénus de Milo' from his *Poèmes antiques* (1852):

Oh, captivating symbol of impassive bliss,
Calm as the serene sea,
No sob has burst from your immutable breast,
Never have human tears tarnished your beauty.

The Parnassians practiced an exacting poetic craftsmanship, reviving the sonnet and other strict forms, mixing short and long lines, and cultivating rich rhyme. Their eponymous journal *Le Parnasse contemporain* appeared in 1866 and Fauré quickly embraced the movement. Beginning around 1870, he set three poems by Leconte de Lisle, four by Gautier, three by the movement's quirky philosopher Sully Prudhomme, and ten by Armand Silvestre, cited in a notable 1882 essay as one of the four 'chefs d'école' of Parnassus.[3] And in his first song cycle of 1878, Fauré set forth a veritable manifesto of Parnassian aesthetics.

Poème d'un jour, to texts by the minor Parnassian poet Charles Grandmougin, traces a brief romance from infatuation ('Rencontre') to abandonment ('Toujours') to resigned acceptance ('Adieu'). While the source of these unpublished poems remains uncertain, they have a clear musical model. Jules Massenet had recently composed a series of 'poème' song cycles, sentimental tales of ephemeral love: *Poème d'avril* (1866), *Poème du souvenir* (1868), and *Poème d'octobre* (1877). Song cycles were virtually unknown in France during the 1860s and *Poème d'avril* was the first with a unified narrative and thematic recollections.[4] The autograph of *Poème d'un jour* also follows a logical tonal plan from D♭ major to F♯ minor to G♭ major (B major, E minor, and E major in the first edition). Yet *Poème d'un jour* departs from its Massenetian models in one crucial detail: the first song identifies the protagonist as an artist, an 'isolated poet'. This opens the possibility of reading Fauré's cycle as an aesthetic allegory, a coming-of-age poem in which the artist reaches maturity through trials.

Fauré himself had passed through an ordeal that certainly informed *Poème d'un jour*. In 1877, the youngest daughter of his patroness Pauline Viardot broke off their engagement after only three months, leaving the composer devastated. *Poème d'un jour* undoubtedly responded to that trauma, yet the work transcends autobiography. As the poet-protagonist passes from unbridled passion to philosophical resignation, he realises the Parnassian ideal of impassivity, transforming personal tragedy into an enduring artistic form.

The successive metres and styles of Grandmougin's poems reflect the poet's maturation. 'Rencontre' unfolds in alexandrines, Hugo's preferred vehicle, and abounds in Romantic clichés – isolated poet, ocean sunset, ideal dream. 'Toujours' shifts to leaner octosyllalbles, while 'Adieu' refines the prosody further with alternating eight- and two-syllable lines:

Comme tout meurt vite, la rose
    Déclose,
Et les frais manteaux diaprés

> Des prés;
> Les longs soupirs, les bienaimées,
> > Fumées! ...

How quickly all dies, the rose
> In bloom,
And the fresh iridescent mantles
> Of the meadows;
The longs sighs, the beloveds,
> Up in smoke! ...

'Adieu' is a paragon of Parnassian verse, with its chiselled form and rich rhymes ('diaprés'/'prés', 'grèves'/'rêves', 'charmes'/'larmes'). The confessional tone of the first two songs has vanished and the pronoun *je* occurs only once, replaced by the impersonal *on*. Emotion has receded into form, personal expression into detached reflection.

Musical form and style follow the same trajectory in *Poème d'un jour*. The cycle begins with the loose strophes of the *romance*, moves to a modified *da capo*, and ends with a strict *da capo* form. Fauré indulged an uncharacteristically operatic manner in the first two songs, ending both with a ringing high note. 'Toujours' is Fauré's most violently impassioned song to date, swerving through chromatic byways as the poet bemoans his fate. In 'Adieu', by contrast, Fauré reached back to the serene archaism of his first Parnassian masterpiece 'Lydia' (Leconte de Lisle), reviving its chorale texture, *portato* articulation, steady quarter notes, and even a Lydian fourth in the opening phrase. The Apollonian song ends on a floating *pianissimo* high note above soothing plagal cadences.

Like 'Rencontre', 'Adieu' begins with a descending scale from D♭ then outlines an ascending minor-seventh chord (see Example 9.1). Yet this motivic recollection between the outer songs belongs to a deeper harmonic argument spanning the cycle. 'Rencontre' drifts persistently into the relative minor and the first four phrases form a complete period in F minor. The second half of the strophe reaffirms the D♭ tonic, but third relations return more chaotically in 'Toujours'. The middle section, the most audacious harmonic passage in early Fauré, modulates through a full minor-third cycle, F♯-A-C-E♭-F♯ (mm. 11–24). Moreover, Fauré reached each key through a chromatic modulation known in Neo-Riemannian theory as a 'Weitzmann transformation', in which the augmented triad provides

Example 9.1. Motivic recollection in Gabriel Fauré, *Poème d'un jour*
a) 'Rencontre', mm. 2–4
b) 'Adieu', mm. 5–8

a pivot between major or minor triads.⁵ At the nadir of *Poème d'un jour*, as the poet sinks into despair, tonality itself comes undone.

'Adieu' stabilises the harmony with its sturdy modal hymnody. The D♭-C-B♭ line from 'Rencontre' returns, but it is ensconced within the Lydian mode. And since the opening line now begins on the fifth degree, it confirms the tonic. A sudden dip into E♭ major near the end reawakens memories of the abyss (mm. 29–30), but the final phrase lays them to rest. Echoes of 'Toujours' also haunt the middle of 'Adieu', which revisits the F♯-minor key and agitated triplets. The *da capo* restores calm, containing chaos within the symmetrical form, whose three parts suggest a microcosm of the whole cycle. The 'poète isolé' has attained serenity, sublimating his passions within the eternal forms of beauty.

Cinq mélodies 'de Venise', Op. 58

Fauré returned to the song cycle in 1891, inspired by the verse of Paul Verlaine. He had discovered Verlaine through Robert de Montesquiou, cousin of his patroness the Countess Greffuhle, and thus began one of the supreme collaborations in art song history. The collections Fauré chose came from early in Verlaine's career: *Fêtes galantes* (1869), inspired by Antoine Watteau's fantastic eighteenth-century landscapes; *La bonne chanson* (1870), celebrating Verlaine's ill-fated marriage to Mathilde Mauté de Fleurville; and *Romances sans paroles* (1874), written during his scandalous flight with fellow poet and lover Arthur Rimbaud. Fauré began his *Cinq mélodies* during a trip to Venice with his patroness Winnaretta Singer, setting two poems from *Fêtes galantes*; on his return to Paris, he composed the remaining songs, drawing also on *Romances sans paroles*. Fauré dedicated Op. 58 to the princess in lieu of an unrealised operatic project with Verlaine.

Fauré seems to have decided on a cycle midway through composing the *Cinq mélodies*, and no obvious key plan or narrative governs the set. Fauré recalled themes from 'En sourdine' and 'Green' in the final song, but the true novelty of Op. 58 is the three-note motive that he developed across the cycle like a quasi-leitmotif. Nevertheless, the cycle betrays its haphazard origins, as he would later acknowledge.⁶ The unity of Op. 58 lies instead in its remarkable focus on music itself, a central concern of Symbolist poetics. Symbolism had emerged as a vibrant school in the late 1880s, with the ailing Verlaine as a spiritual mentor. As the most abstract art, music served the Symbolists as a paragon of an evocative and elusive language, content with its own inner play. Fauré imbibed the new poetics from Count Montesquiou (a patron of the great Stéphane Mallarmé), who served as the composer's literary advisor. The Symbolist fascination with music received further stimulus from the Wagnerian wave that crashed over Paris in the late 1880s. *Lohengrin* was mounted in Paris in 1888 and Wagner's works soon dominated the Opéra; the previous year, Fauré had conducted the *Siegfried Idyll* at a private soirée and he travelled to Bayreuth the next summer to hear *Parsifal* and *Die Meistersinger*. Meanwhile, *La revue wagnérienne* (1885–88) entwined the German composer's music with Symbolist poetics and featured contributions by both Verlaine and Mallarmé.

Music becomes an object of representation and reflection in the *Cinq mélodies*. 'Mandoline' describes a moonlit serenade, 'En sourdine' culminates in the twilight song of the nightingale, 'C'est l'extase' celebrates the naturalistic 'choir of little voices' surrounding the lovers, and 'À Clymène' evokes the gondolier songs that inspired much of Fauré's piano music: 'Mystic barcarolles, / Songs without words'. This astonishing outburst of 'scenic' music began in Fauré's first Verlaine setting, 'Clair de lune' (1887), where an antique minuet runs throughout the song, overshadowing the singer's *parlando* declamation.

'Mandoline' (no. 1) introduces a primary theme of both Verlaine cycles: music's role in bridging human and natural realms. The mandolin, depicted with jaunty staccato chords, is the principal character in Verlaine's moonlit musicale. The Watteauian vignette begins with insipid conversation between the serenading gallants and their ladies, but it ends with the wordless instrument: 'And the mandolin chatters / In the shivering of the breeze'. The singer soars in a luxurious cantilena on 'ramures chanteuses' (singing boughs), but the piano commandeers the vocalise for the rest of the song, suggesting that a more universal song animates the scene. In the third stanza, as the human characters dissolve into spinning shadows, the voice descends to its deepest note and the melody shrinks to semitones. Yet as human song withdraws, the scales of the singing branches return at the end of each phrase, recalling the animistic voice of the trees.

The common motive of the *Cinq mélodies* consists of a falling third and rising second and appears most clearly in 'Green' (no. 3). It returns in 'À Clymène' (no. 4), spun into a sequence of interlocking thirds, and undergoes inversion during the third stanza of 'En sourdine' (no. 2). The 'Venice' motive may lack the semantic content of a leitmotif, but it produced an authentically Wagnerian revolution in Fauré's songwriting. In passages of the *Cinq mélodies* and throughout *La bonne chanson*, the piano creates a symphonic texture in which the vocal line is woven into the fabric of developing motives. Motivic development also liberated Fauré's text-setting, as the first two stanzas of 'En sourdine' demonstrate: as the 'Venice' motive evolves in the voice and piano, the singer stretches out single syllables, rushes through whole lines, and splinters the text into breathless fragments. This is a radical departure from Fauré's early text-setting, which had closely followed the measured flow of the prosody. It approaches Wagner's 'musical prose', in which the leitmotivic web takes over the structural role once played by poetic metre and symmetrical phrase structure.

'À Clymène' links music to another fascination of the Symbolists: synaesthesia, the fusion of the senses. Fauré's barcarolle theme accompanies a litany of synesthetic imagery: the beloved's voice is a strange vision, her scent the colour of swans, and her entire being a harmony of tones and perfumes. Verlaine's poem ends by citing the source text of Symbolist synaesthetics, Baudelaire's 'Correspondances' (*Les fleurs du mal*), which had depicted a cosmos suffused with trans-sensory analogies:

[Your whole being] Has, with beneficent cadences,
In their correspondences
Led away my refined soul,
So be it!

Fauré emphasised this Baudelairean idea on the earlier line 'Tons et parfums' (Tones and scents) where the gentle barcarolle bursts out *fortissimo* in the distant key of E♭ minor (mm. 49–52). Moreover, Fauré effected this startling modulation through another chromatic Weitzmann transformation, highlighting the uncanny blurring of the senses. In the final stanza, Fauré set the lines about *correspondances* with a pair of nearly identical two-bar phrases, yet the second phrase respells the first enharmonically, transforming flats into sharps. This inaudible musical effect, perceptible only to the eye, nods urbanely to Baudelaire's ideal.

The final song, 'C'est l'extase', consummates the fusion of human and natural music. The first-person *je* vanishes altogether, replaced by the impersonal *c'est* (it is), and human speech migrates into the 'rustling of the woods' and its 'choir of little voices'. Unlike Debussy's swooning setting in *Ariettes* (1888), Fauré's song vibrates with inner vitality – offbeat palpitations, rapid harmonic rhythm, surging piano arpeggios – evoking the humming energy of this animistic world. When the recollections of 'Green' and 'En sourdine' appear in the third stanza, they respond to a musical image, but it is no longer purely human music:

This soul that laments
And this slumbering plaint,
It is ours, isn't it?
Mine, tell me, and yours,
Which breathes the humble anthem
On this warm evening so softly?

Tellingly, Fauré recalled the music from the third stanza of 'En sourdine', where the lovers listen to a nightingale's song voiced by the piano. The recollection of the birdsong completes the work of 'Mandoline', absorbing music into the resounding cosmos.

La bonne chanson, Op. 61

If any song cycle deserves the name, it is surely *La bonne chanson*. Fauré reordered Verlaine's poems to fashion a clear narrative: the nine songs trace a dramatic arc from the awakening of love (nos. 1–3) through separation and anxiety (4–5) to the joyful nuptials and symbolic return of springtime (6–9). The last song recalls five previous numbers in the manner of the *Cinq mélodies*, but Fauré has wedded these recollections to the cycles of nature: the first three songs pass in review after the words, 'Let summer come! Let autumn and winter come again!' The composer forged careful links between the songs and, most originally, connected them through a network of six recurring motives.

La bonne chanson accentuates every novel feature of the *Cinq mélodies*. The harmony is bafflingly unpredictable, full of rapid modulations, elliptical progressions, and tonal non-sequiturs, as in the opening phrase of 'J'ai presque peur, en verité' (no. 5) or the final pages of 'Avant que tu ne t'en ailles' (no. 6). The motivic web has fully overgrown the piano accompaniment, entangling the vocal line in its polyphonic thickets. Indeed, musical prose is the norm in *La bonne chanson* where Fauré expanded, contracted, and fragmented Verlaine's verse to fit the motivic lines in the piano. The opening of the first song, 'Une Sainte en son auréole', epitomises this fluid interplay of text and motive; the most extreme example comes at the beginning of the last song, 'L'hiver a cessé', where Verlaine's opening line (but only the first hemistich!) arrives on the cadence of a long piano prelude spun out of prior motives.

These dizzying novelties unsettled contemporary listeners. The sympathetic Marcel Proust wrote in 1894, 'Did you know the younger composers are almost unanimous in disliking *La bonne chanson*?' And even Saint-Saëns reportedly advised his friend to burn the score, confiding that 'Fauré has gone completely out of his mind!'[7] Nevertheless, performers and listeners who have absorbed themselves in *La bonne chanson* can attest to the impeccable taste with which Fauré shaped its explosive energies. Each harmonic digression finds its way home with unfailing logic, each dazzling form enchains with the next in a single captivating flow. Ravel rightly praised the 'incomparable symphony whose nine parts are ordered and balanced so as to form one vast lyric poem, stirring and perfect'.[8]

Composed in the years 1892–4 during summer vacations, *La bonne chanson* bears the imprint of Fauré's lover Emma Bardac. Debussy's future wife, for whose daughter Fauré composed the *Dolly Suite*, served as artistic advisor and interpreter. The published order of the songs, unlike that of the *Cinq mélodies*, bears little relation to their compositional chronology and Fauré tinkered repeatedly with their arrangement. The leitmotivic design, however, clearly formed part of Fauré's original design, as two early songs from 1892 attest: the arabesque-like 'Mathilde' motive from 'Une Sainte en son aureole' (no. 1), associated with the beloved, returns at her mention in 'J'allais par des chemins perfides' (no. 4).

Only two of Fauré's motives have the mimetic stamp of Wagner's leitmotifs: the majestic 'Sun' motive with its falling octave and dotted rhythm, and the twittering pentatonic 'Birdsong' motive, both introduced in the sixth song. The remaining four are more abstract musical shapes whose meaning proves elusive and shifting: the graceful 'Mathilde' motive; the rising octave of the 'Exquisite Hour' motive, appearing on those words in the third song; the heraldic 'Avowal' motive from the end of the fifth song, introduced as the poet declares his love, and recalled in a more tender form in later songs; and the 'Lydia' motive, derived from his early *mélodie* quoted in the third song. These compact, malleable motives undergo a continuous development in the piano and voice, even joining in triple counterpoint in the fourth and fifth songs. The ending of 'J'allais par des chemins perfides' (no. 4), for example, combines the soaring octave of the Exquisite Hour motive in the voice, the rising scales of the Lydia motive in the pianist's left hand, and the graceful Mathilde motive in the right hand (see Example 9.2). Note how luxuriously the voice stretches out 'l'amour', in blissful disregard for metric regularity. Fauré's ceaselessly evolving

Example 9.2. Motivic counterpoint in Fauré, 'J'allais par des chemins perfides' (*La bonne chanson*), mm. 48–54

motives create an autonomous, nonverbal discourse that runs parallel to the poetic text but rarely mimics it, suggesting that pure language idealised by the Symbolists.

Fauré's motivic design complements the overall form of *La bonne chanson*, which divides roughly in half (5 + 4 songs). The first part fixates on three leitmotifs (Mathilde, Lydia, and Exquisite Hour), which emerge during the serene opening songs and enter into increasingly dense counterpoint in the turbulent fourth and fifth songs. The key scheme sinks stepwise to match this emotional descent – A♭-G-F♯-f♯-e. The arrival of the Avowal motive, after which the poet first addresses the beloved with the intimate *tu*, triumphantly closes the first part of the cycle. 'Avant que tu ne t'en ailles', which begins before dawn and ends with the glorious sunrise, inaugurates the second part. The Birdsong and Sun motives now appear and the first three motives all but vanish. And as the lovers enter the biological cycles of marriage and generation, the tonality ceases its stepwise descent and begins to rotate around a minor-third cycle, [e]-D♭-B♭-G-B♭.[9]

The fusion of human and natural music again plays a central role in Fauré's second Verlaine cycle, most obviously in 'Avant que tu ne t'en ailles'. The pantoum-like lyric interweaves two poems: a paean to the beloved, set as a slow chordal hymn; and excited exclamations at the new dawn, briskly accompanied by the Birdsong motive. In the final section, human and natural song unite in a single tempo, joining in one passionate flow. Avian music plays a broader role in the cosmological design of *La bonne chanson*. The final song begins with the Birdsong motive in an antiphonal duet, forming a complete pentatonic collection; yet this duet replicates the pentatonic outline of the cycle's opening theme, a polyphonic *chanson* that matches the chivalric imagery of 'Une Sainte en son auréole'. Fauré even spelled out this sublimation of human music in the coda of the penultimate song, 'N'est-ce pas?' The song closes with a pentatonic version of the Avowal motive, ending on a hovering F_5-G_5-D_5. The Avowal motive had emerged during the middle section on another reference to birdsong: 'Our two hearts, exhaling their peaceful tenderness, / Will be two nightingales that sing in the evening'. 'L'hiver a cessé' begins with the precise retrograde of the pentatonic cell, D_5-G_5-F_5, as the metaphoric song of the nightingales passes into real birdsong. The whole cosmos, Fauré seems to proclaim, rings with one transcendent music.

In its beauty, expressivity, technical fecundity, and metaphysical vision, *La bonne chanson* stands at the summit of Fauré's work as *mélodiste*. It is a wonder of creative and intellectual synthesis that reveals a composer and thinker at the height of his powers.

La chanson d'Ève, Op. 95

Fauré owed his next song cycle to two Belgian Symbolists. *La chanson d'Ève* originated in a ballad from his incidental music to Maurice Maeterlinck's *Pelléas et Mélisande*, produced in London in 1898. 'The King's Three Blind Daughters', sung by Mélisande at her spinning wheel, takes shape around a mysterious two-bar theme in sarabande rhythm, repeated throughout the song in the manner of a Baroque chaconne. In 1906 Fauré discovered *La chanson d'Ève* (1904) by Maeterlinck's classmate Charles Van Lerberghe and adapted Mélisande's ballad for the poem 'Crépuscule'. Later that year, he decided to create a song cycle from Van Lerberghe's collection and borrowed the ballad theme again for the first song, 'Paradis'. He worked on *La chanson d'Ève* even longer than *La bonne chanson*, completing the ten songs in 1910.

Van Lerberghe fashioned Eve as a poetess, the *Ur*-singer who gives voice to creation. The Symbolist epic falls into four parts, preceded by a prelude narrated posthumously by Eve. In *Premières paroles* (First Words), from which Fauré drew seven songs, Eve awakens and revels in her power to envoice creation. In *La tentation* (Temptation), she meets characters from pagan mythology – the Sirens, Venus, and Eros – who entice her to plumb the secrets of nature. Eve transgresses God's limits upon human knowledge in *La faute* (Original Sin), renouncing the spiritual realm and realising her unity with nature. She consummates her song in *Crépuscule* (Twilight) as she wills her own reabsorption into the cosmos.

La chanson d'Ève shares many poetic themes with *La bonne chanson*, not least an animistic world in which human and natural musics commingle. It traces another cycle, beginning at daybreak as Eve awakens and ending at nightfall as she dies. Op. 95 also begins with a Symbolist reflection on language, like the meditation on Mathilde's name in 'Une Sainte en son auréole': in 'Paradis', God institutes speech and directs Eve to name His creatures. Nevertheless, the two poets differ utterly in style and tone. Verlaine's preciosity and rhetorical virtuosity have no place in Van Lerberghe's limpid poem, a paragon of Symbolist discretion. The poet confined himself to a simple treasury of words and symbols that spin out in a diaphanous web and, inspired by the later Symbolists' *vers libéré*, he freely varied line lengths and scattered blank verse among the rhymes.

Fauré relished the challenge presented by this new poetic language (see the quote on p. 189), and the simplicity and reserve of his new songs departs radically from the extravagance of *La bonne chanson*. As Jean-Michel Nectoux summarised, 'the highly chromatic language, the wide, sweeping lines and the passionate excesses of an almost orchestral lyricism give way to a dreamscape in which the vocal line is modelled on the text, the harmony becomes taut and the texture lighter, denser, more transparently contrapuntal'.[10] Fauré also confined himself to two leitmotifs, which pervade five of the songs: the ethereal ostinato theme of Mélisande's ballad, and an undulating chromatic melody evoking the sensual delights of Eden.

La chanson d'Ève has inspired two notable readings by recent critics. Katherine Bergeron heard the cycle as an allegory for the fin-de-siècle *mélodie*, with its distinctive reticence and retreat from musical expressivity. In her interpretation, Eve's fall results from a desire for self-expression and representation, which emerges in the mimetic text-painting of 'Eau vivante' and 'Veilles-tu ma senteur de soleil?' (nos. 6 and 7). She atones for her transgression by dying in 'O Mort, poussière d'étoiles' (no. 10), and thus enacts 'the ultimate origin myth of modern French song'.[11] Bergeron's allegorical reading proves most convincing for songs like 'Prima verba' or 'L'aube blanche' (nos. 2 and 5), whose artless simplicity conforms to her prototype of the *mélodie*.

Carlo Caballero connected the narrative to Fauré's documented fascination with pantheism, a fashionable doctrine in the Third Republic. He noted that Fauré softened the biblical narrative with his selection of poems, avoiding any mention of temptation, sin, or the Fall. The pantheistic strain of *La chanson d'Ève* emerges in the final stanza of 'Roses ardentes' (no. 4):

And it is in you, supreme power,
Radiant sun,
That my soul itself
Attains its godhood!

This monistic theology transforms the biblical story: 'Unredeemed because never guilty, Eve does not transcend the world through personal immortality but rather returns to the world, is absorbed by it, becomes it'.[12] Caballero's argument is compelling, although we can locate pantheistic tendencies even earlier in Fauré's Verlaine cycles.

'Roses ardentes' also suggests the theological significance of Fauré's two motives. The song begins with Mélisande's theme in a learned contrapuntal texture, evoking the biblical God. The Phrygian tendencies of the theme, which avoids the second degree and cadences on the sixth degree, the modal dominant, enhances the sacred tone. In the final stanza, as Eve hails her pagan 'young god', the undulating motive from 'Paradis' reappears, rotating through a minor-third cycle. The first motive evokes purity and innocence, the aerial region of Eve's guardian angels; the second is lushly chromatic and sensual, suggesting the earthly realm to which the sirens tempt her. Ultimately, the second motive wins out, reappearing on the final page of the cycle as Eve surrenders herself to the cosmos.

A further interpretation emerges when we consider Fauré's puzzling treatment of leitmotifs in *La chanson d'Ève*. Unlike the labile, ceaselessly varied shapes of *La bonne chanson*, the twin leitmotifs of *La chanson d'Ève* are lapidary blocks that undergo precise operations – juxtaposition, truncation, ostinato, sequence. They never combine polyphonically but always occur separately or in a minor-major pairing. Indeed, Fauré's treatment grows increasingly rigid as the cycle progresses: in 'Dans un parfum de roses blanches' (no. 8), the chromatic motive rotates through both major- and minor-third cycles; and in 'Crépuscule' (no. 9), adapted from Mélisande's ballad, her theme returns to strict ostinato repetition. This angular, mechanistic treatment contrasts oddly with Van Lerberghe's delicate poetry.

The key to Fauré's new approach lies in the theatrical origin of his material. Fauré was immersed in the theatre when he wrote *La chanson d'Ève*: he had recently composed the lyric drama *Prométhée* (1900), and while writing the song cycle he was working on his opera *Pénélope* (1913). Mélisande's ballad is diegetic music, a stage song framed as performance. Like serenades or drinking songs, ballads do not directly express the feelings of the dramatic character; they thus lack the interiority of lyric poetry like *La bonne chanson*. The split consciousness of diegetic song served Fauré as a perfect metaphor for Eve's fall into self-awareness and estrangement from her own voice. In 'Crépuscule', the sound of her own singing wrings a lament from Eve:

Isle of oblivion, O paradise!
What cry in the night rends
Your voice that cradles me?

When Mélisande's theme first emerges in 'Paradis', it is spontaneous and exploratory, passing freely between singer and piano. By the last three songs of the cycle, as Eve realises her separation from the cosmos, both motives have frozen into lifeless ostinato patterns – that is, the original form of Fauré's stage song. On the last page, as Eve wills her dissolution into cosmic dust, the chromatic motive returns for its first complete rotation through a minor-third cycle. As she prays to be emptied 'like a golden amphora', the precise texture of Mélisande's ballad returns: *parlando* declamation above a repeating ostinato motive (see Example 9.3). The encroaching theatricality of Eve's singing thus signals her fatal separation from creation.

It also signals her consummation as a poet. Van Lerberghe's epic is, among other things, an allegory of poetry, in which the author must die to create the text. It begins with Eve's posthumous prelude and ends with a self-conscious reference to the book's title: 'She melts, sweetly, and completes *La chanson d'Ève*'. This idea is familiar from Roland Barthes' famous essay 'The Death of the Author' (1967), which celebrates a writing emancipated from transcendental source or meaning: 'the voice loses its origin, the author enters his own death, writing begins'.[13] Barthes drew his first examples from the Symbolists and their quest for a pure, self-contained language. This quest plays out musically across Fauré's cycle as Eve's song shifts from direct lyric expression, the native mode of

Example 9.3. Theatrical song in *La chanson d'Ève*
a) Fauré, 'The King's Three Blind Daughters' (incidental music to *Pelléas et Mélisande*), mm. 3–7
b) Fauré, 'O Mort, poussière d'étoiles' (*La chanson d'Ève*), mm. 18–19

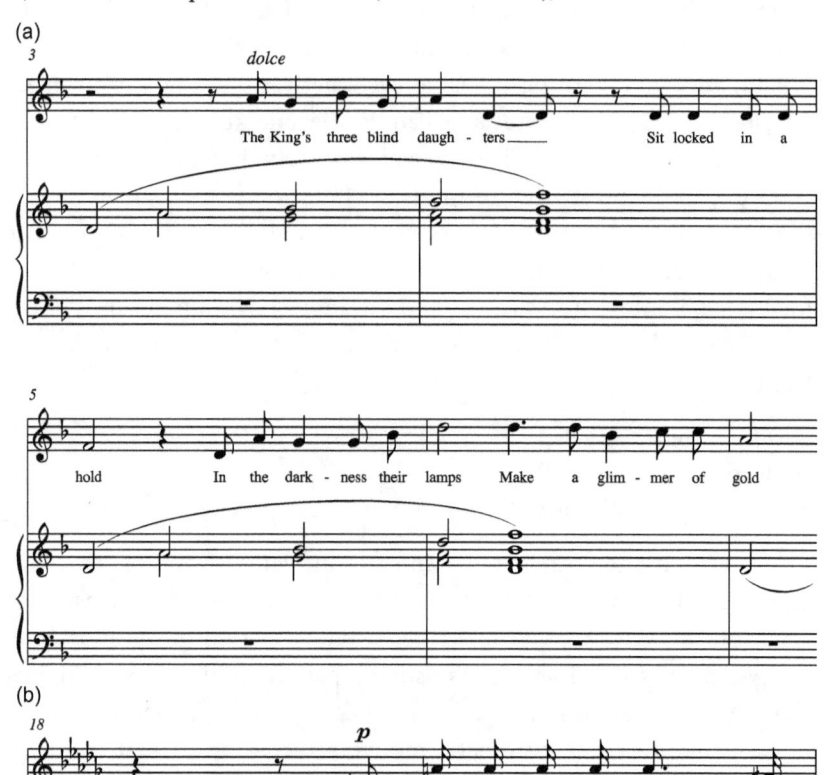

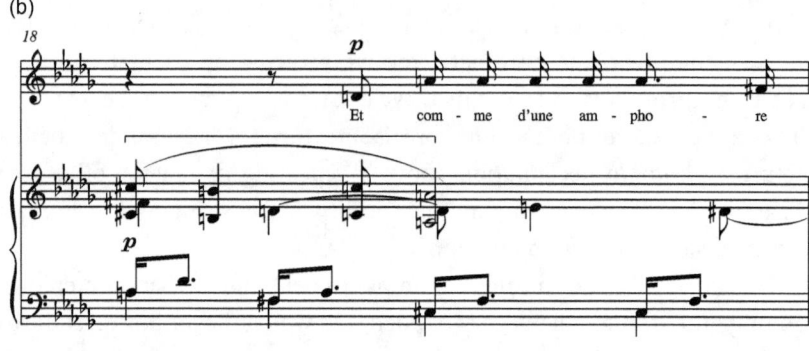

the *mélodie*, and crystallises in the form of diegetic stage song, detached from a subjective voice. *La chanson d'Ève* is an ingenious response to Symbolist poetics that should lay to rest the common notion of Fauré as a naïve reader of poetry.

Le jardin clos, Op. 106

In his last three song cycles, Fauré fundamentally rethought the genre. These sets cohere more loosely than his earlier cycles, with a unity that arises more from shared subject matter and ethos than a linear narrative. The balance between music and language has also shifted drastically. Gone are the leitmotifs, thematic recollections, and polyphonic texture that had created an autonomous musical discourse in the *Cinq mélodies*, *La bonne chanson*, and *La chanson d'Ève*. The piano now doubles the vocal line throughout in a rigid Baroque texture of bass, melody, and chordal filler. At the same time, the vocal line grows simpler and less expressive, often verging on psalmody, and is bound tightly to the poetic metre.

This change appears immediately in *Le jardin clos* (1914), Fauré's most elusive song cycle. He drew his eight poems from Van Lerberghe's early *Entrevisions* (*Glimpses*) of 1898, plucking texts from its three sections: *Jeux et songes* (*Games and Dreams*); *Le jardin clos* (*The Enclosed Garden*), based on verses from the Song of Songs; and *Sous le portique* (*Beneath the Portico*). Although he took his title from the middle section, Fauré set only three of the biblical poems, and his overall ordering can appear scattershot. Yet rather than dismiss *Le jardin clos* as a mere assemblage, we should read it in counterpoint with *La chanson d'Ève*. The two 'garden' cycles centre on women from the Old Testament, Eve and the dusky Sulamite of the Song of Songs, and both end with a meditation on a solitary woman's death. 'Inscription sur le sable' (Inscription in the Sand), a reflection on the traces left by a dead princess's diadem, recalls precise imagery from 'O Mort, poussière d'étoiles' – dust, dissolution, sublimation in song:

Altogether, with her robe and flowers,
She turned back to dust here,
And her soul, carried away elsewhere,
Was reborn in a song of light.

The Van Lerberghe cycles differ most sharply in Fauré's treatment of recurring material. *La chanson d'Ève* is governed by cycles: the ostinato of

Mélisande's ballad, the alternation of the two leitmotifs in 'Paradis', the sequential rotation through third cycles, and the procession of day and night. In *Le jardin clos*, Fauré mercilessly purged the music of repetition. Of the eight songs, only 'Je me poserai sur ton cœur' (no. 4) contains repeating thematic material, and the rest are through-composed. Sequences all but vanish, with only a handful of literal repetitions. *Le jardin clos* may revisit literary themes from *La chanson d'Ève*, but it embraces a radically different sense of musical time – spontaneous, fluid, unpredictable. Vladimir Jankélevitch justly compared the cycle to Henri Bergson's contemporary theory of *durée*, pure time unmeasured by spatial forms.[14]

Time, memory, the continuity of past and present – these are the central themes of *Le jardin clos*. Fauré wrote the cycle at a precarious historical moment at the onset of the First World War, and its composition dramatically straddled the opening hostilities: he began the cycle in the German town of Bad Ems then had to flee through Switzerland to reach France. In a letter from October 1914, Fauré mourned his country 'where so many regions are devastated, where houses are burned down, where there is shooting, where there is massacre!'[15] While Fauré could not have foreseen the cataclysm of the Great War, his song cycle betrays the anxiety of a graceful civilisation threatened with extinction.

Fauré took seriously the image of the enclosed garden, the *hortus conclusus* of medieval iconography derived from the Song of Songs. He chose the phrase as his title and foregrounded it in the first song, 'Exaucement', where the protagonist contemplates a slumbering maiden:

May your soul, calm and still
Like a fairy asleep in the enclosed garden,
With its sweet desire fulfilled,
Find joy and rest.

The palindromic key scheme of *Le jardin clos* also suggests an enclosed space. As Max Loppert noted, the cycle begins in C major, progressively adds sharps and flats until the fifth song, then reverts to simpler key signatures:[16]

C	F	G	E♭	D♭	E	G	F	e
—	♭	♯	♭♭♭	♭♭♭♭♭	♯♯♯♯	♯	♭	♯

At the heart of this tonal cloister lies 'Dans la nymphée' (no. 5), in the lush Fauréan key of D♭ major. In a grotto shrine consecrated to the nymphs, the speaker invokes the memory of another departed female:

Though your eyes see her not,
Know, in your soul, that she is there,
Divine and fair as in past days.

The song begins as a solemn incantation, accompanied by steady hieratic chords, but at the climax a sudden enharmonic flash of C♯ major illuminates the garden as the nymph reappears in memory. *Le jardin clos* is a sacred enclosure wherein a mysterious 'she' – slumbering fairy, bygone nymph, dead princess – lives on in imagination.

The cycle revels in equivocation, probing those elusive, indescribable 'glimpses' offered by Van Lerberghe. In four songs, the protagonist gazes upon a dreamer caught in the half-light between night and day, dream and reality. Fauré explored a different equivocation in 'Je me poserai sur ton cœur', which compares the lover to a bird hovering motionless over the sea as it beats against the wind. The refrain likewise perches over a $I^{6/4}$ chord, evoking both dynamism and repose. Linear counterpoint also contributes to the sense of ambivalence throughout *Le jardin clos*, with the bass line becoming a key source of expression. In 'Exaucement' and 'Je me poserai sur ton cœur,' the bass constantly moves out of sync with the harmony, creating a surprising amount of dissonance in the outwardly placid songs. In 'La messagère' (no. 3), the bounding motive in the left hand seems to respond to Van Lerberghe's text, depicting the joyous arrival of April. Yet the left hand abandons this mimetic pretence and begins to loop aimlessly in a sequence of interlocking thirds: the bass line reclaims the form of a leitmotif, but none of its meaning.

'Inscription sur le sable' closes the cycle on a bleak note, with syncopated chords for the broken diadem and a full bass descent through the Phrygian mode, token of dead antiquity. Yet signs of life remain in the desolate song. On words connoting timelessness – 'reborn', 'imperishable diamonds', 'eternal stones' – the singer soars to high notes. The voice reasserts its power in these flourishes, insisting on the living presence enshrined in the script.

Le jardin clos ends with the image of a broken circlet, a perfect metaphor for a work that breaks open the song cycle and scatters eight exquisite songs like jewels in the sand. The cycle invites us to immerse ourselves in the flux of time and memory, unencumbered by plots or musical repetition. Written on the cusp of world cataclysm, it pays poignant tribute to a culture and aesthetic that were fast slipping away.

Mirages, Op. 113, and *L'horizon chimérique*, Op. 121

Fauré's last song cycles, composed after the Armistice, breathe the new post-war air. The titles suggest a hazy seascape by Monet or perhaps a Debussy prelude, yet the lucid, sharply etched style of *Mirages* (1919) and *L'horizon chimérique* (1921) has little in common with impressionism. The shimmering mirage and vanishing horizon do not awaken visions of the beyond, as in Henri Duparc's 'L'invitation au voyage', but serve as limits on the poetic subject. Both cycles begin with a voyage, yet both return the protagonist safely to shore, prompting the wistful final line of *L'horizon chimérique*: 'For there are great unfulfilled departures within me'.

Fauré's 'voyage' cycles, with their call for restraint and moderation, reflect the new climate of neoclassicism, the backlash to Romanticism that emerged after the horrors of the Great War. The neoclassicists, spearheaded by Igor Stravinsky, renounced emotionalism, grandiosity, and mysticism, harkening back to the eighteenth century as an age of order, clarity, and objectivity. Many threads connected Fauré to the younger generation of composers. Elected president of Ravel's upstart Société musicale indépendante in 1910, he was also revered by Lili and Nadia Boulanger, and later, Les Six. Fauré's last song cycles are also, in a real sense, works of youth. Renée Baronne de Brimont was not yet forty when she published *Mirages*. As for Jean de la Ville de Mirmont, he died just shy of his twenty-eighth birthday, killed by a shell at Verneuil-en-Champagne, and *L'horizon chimérique* was published posthumously in 1920. Fauré also wrote his post-war cycles for young singers, Madeleine Grey and Charles Panzéra, both born in 1896.

In 1919, the same year that he composed *Mirages*, Fauré produced his most purely neoclassical work. *Masques et bergamasques*, a ballet comedy with a classical overture and suitably *ancien régime* songs and dances, anticipated by a year Stravinsky's *Pulcinella*, another pastiche based on the *commedia dell'arte*. Fauré revived another neoclassical strain in his last song cycles, the cult of Greek antiquity. *Mirages* is Fauré's most explicitly Hellenic work outside of his operas: 'Reflets dans l'eau' reworks the Narcissus myth, alluding to nymphs, fauns, and hamadryads, while 'Danseuse' brings to life a Grecian vase painting. *L'horizon chimérique* nods to the ancients with 'Diane, Séléné', which invokes the moon goddess by both Greek and Latin names.

Another curious feature allies Fauré's last cycles with neoclassicism: both works have four movements, comparable to the classical sonata cycle. The two song cycles begin and end with the same key or key signature and both have an intimate E♭-major 'slow movement' in third position. *Mirages* and *L'horizon chimérique* fall within Fauré's busiest period of chamber-music composition, 1917–24, during which he joined composers across Europe in returning to the classical genres, writing a violin sonata, two cello sonatas, a piano quintet, a piano trio, and a string quartet.

The first song of *Mirages*, 'Cygne sur l'eau', compares the protagonist's restless mind to a black swan setting forth on the water. Brimont's opening stanzas summon Symbolist commonplaces (swans, ennui, dreams, mirages), but a quoted voice pierces the mist in the fifth stanza, dissuading the swan from its journey: 'Now, I said: "Renounce, fair and illusory swan, / this slow voyage toward troubled destinations ... "' Fauré set the first stanza to music of striking purity and diatonic simplicity, but as the swan ventures forth in the third stanza the harmony falls under the sway of the octatonic scale, famously associated with Stravinsky. The bass ascends the symmetrical scale, rotating the harmony through F, G♯, B, and D minor (mm. 25–9). At the admonition of the poetic superego, the song returns to familiar diatonic waters, closing with a strict *da capo* reprise.

Fauré made a rare excursion into musical impressionism in 'Reflets dans l'eau' (no. 2), perhaps inspired by Debussy's piano piece of the same name. Broken arpeggios and an undulating melodic figure paint the fountain into which the nostalgic maiden gazes. The final stanza depicts the spreading ripples with Debussyan watercolours, and Fauré even used the proportions of the Golden Section favoured by the younger composer.[17] The ascending chromatic motive in the piano recalls the prelude to *Tristan und Isolde* (m. 35), drawing out the hidden death wish in the Narcissus-like protagonist, but another detached narration breaks the spell.

'Jardin nocturne' (no. 3) provides no relief from the moderate tempos of the first two songs, trading on a vocabulary of rising sequences and shifting enharmonic chords. Far more interesting is 'Danseuse' (no. 4), the most austere of all Fauré's songs. Brimont's ekphrastic poem brings to life a painted Greek vase, depicting a lithe dancer observed by a flute player. Fauré evoked this antique scene with a spare piano counterpoint, a dotted ostinato line against a dominant pedal, suggesting a flute accompanied by a cithara (see Example 9.4). Fauré's earlier music abounds in dances, but none sound remotely like 'Danseuse', whose jerky rhythm is as rigid and angular as the painted dancer's outstretched palms.

Bergeron has identified a quotation from the *Prélude à l'après-midi d'un faune* in mm. 44–51, where the pianist's inner line retraces the exact intervals of Debussy's famous flute solo. But the stiff dotted rhythm

Example 9.4. Fauré, 'Danseuse' (*Mirages*), mm. 1–6

denatures the lazy arabesque, a revision that Bergeron aptly compared to Vaslav Nijinsky's angular choreography for the *Prélude* (1912), itself inspired by Greek vase paintings. 'Danseuse', she concluded, resembles the style of a new generation: 'With its mechanical ostinato, denuded style, and squared-off phrases, it had more in common with the values of those "young ones" who belonged to [Jean] Cocteau's immediate circle'.[18]

L'horizon chimérique traces another interrupted voyage. In 'La mer est infinie', the protagonist imagines his dreams venturing upon the deep like seagulls; 'Je me suis embarqué' pictures him at sea on a real or imagined vessel; 'Diane, Séléné' lingers in this shipboard utopia; and in 'Vaisseaux, nous vous aurons aimés' he returns to land, confessing himself one of those 'whose desires are of the earth'. Tellingly, Fauré has reversed the poet's original narrative. La Ville de Mirmont began with texts expressing a longing for adventure, including Fauré's final song, and the cycle's first two songs come from the end of the book where the protagonist sets sail for distant climes. Unlike the poet, Fauré renounces the journey and remains wistfully on the quay.

The tonal plan of *L'horizon chimérique*, D-D♭-E♭-D, mirrors this journey of the mind. The cycle begins and ends in a sharp key, representing dry land, and modulates to flat keys during the voyage. The key scheme also describes a minute pendulum swing, inching a semitone to either side of D major before returning to equilibrium. The form is as orderly and balanced as the poet's prim alexandrines. *L'horizon chimérique* is Fauré's only song cycle to begin and end in the same key, a symmetry that reinforces the protagonist's decision to remain on *terra firma*.

'La mer est infinie' stands out for its vivid word-painting. The sunlit ocean sparkles throughout in rapid piano tremolos and the first phrase portrays the immensity of sea and sky with a steady octave ascent. The melody then capers like the tipsy seagulls before plunging an octave as if to swoop up a fish. At the climax of the song, as the protagonist surveys the infinite sea, melody and bass expand in contrary motion and the singer soars to a sustained high E before settling on a peaceful, rocking motive.

Fauré exploited the sharp-flat polarity to great effect in 'Je me suis embarqué', which evokes the roll and pitch of the deck with vigorous offbeat accents. The mention of land in the opening stanza prompts a brief sharp-side digression from D♭ and the song veers more dramatically into F♯ minor as the seafarer laments, 'My brothers, I have suffered on all of your continents'. F♯ minor bursts out with greater vehemence on the climactic cry, 'O my pain, my pain, where have I left you?' The return to D♭ sounds less convincing this time as the singer lingers on a dissonant B♭♭ before resolving the augmented triad – the sea offers a respite but no lasting peace.

'Diane, Séléné' grants a blessed reprieve, free from the pull of tide and wave. In this last and most beautiful of Fauré's Parnassian creations, the pale goddess beckons as an ideal of impassivity:

And my soul, always weary,
Always agitated
Aspires to the peace
Of your nocturnal flame.

Fauré's revived the Apollonian hymnody of 'Lydia' and 'Adieu' (*Poème d'un jour*) with steady *portato* chords and even a glinting Lydian fourth, but in a richer chromatic alloy. The interval of the fifth presides over 'Diane, Séléné', sanctifying the song with its perfect sonority.

'Vaisseaux, nous vous aurons aimés' unfolds as a broad 12/8 barcarolle after the sobering drop to D major and solid earth. It bears the same tempo marking as the first song, but the quadruple metre has absorbed the rolling maritime rhythms. An expansive augmented triad, D-F♯-B♭, expresses the protagonist's unstilled yearning as he laments, 'The setting sun has born away so many open sails', and again on the line 'But your call, in the depth of evening, fills me with despair'. The melody presses insistently against the upper note, but it cannot escape the tonic triad. While the previous songs all ended on the fifth degree, the melody now descends resolutely to the tonic, ending with a falling octave that closes the pitch space opened at the beginning of 'La mer est infinie'. With this decisive cadence, *L'horizon chimérique* ends a voyage that began in 1919 when the black swan ventured beyond its familiar shores.

La bonne chanson and *L'horizon chimérique* are Fauré's consummate song cycles, works from which we cannot dislodge a single song, and in which the expressive means and formal shape unite with the poetry to create a single compelling effect. Like all his cycles, they reveal a deep resonance with the evolving ideals of French poetry and music, expressed with astonishing originality and finesse. Fauré's individual songs will always hold their wonder, but it is the song cycles that best reveal the composer's mind.

Notes

1. Letter to Marie Fauré-Fremiet, 3 September 1906, in Gabriel Fauré, *Lettres intimes*, ed. Philippe Fauré-Fremiet (Paris: La Colombe, 1951), 127.
2. Readers can find a deeper exploration in my book *The Fauré Song Cycles: Poetry and Music, 1861–1921* (Oakland: University of California Press, 2020).
3. Henri Gauthier-Villars, *Les parnassiens* (Paris: Gauthier-Villars Imprimeur-Libraire, 1882), 37–42.
4. See Ulrich Linke, *Der französische Liederzyklus von 1866 bis 1914: Entwicklungen und Strukturen* (Franz Steiner Verlag, 2010), which includes a list of nineteenth- and twentieth-century French song cycles.
5. See Richard Cohn, *Audacious Euphony: Chromatic Harmony and the Triad's Second Nature* (New York: Oxford University Press, 2012), 59–81.
6. Louis Aguettant, 'Recontres avec Gabriel Fauré', ed. Jean-Michel Nectoux, *Études fauréennes*, 19 (1982), 6.
7. Marcel Proust to Pierre Lavallée, in *Correspondance*, vol. 1, ed. Philip Kolb (Paris: Plon, 1970), 338; *The Correspondence of Camille Saint-Saëns and Gabriel Fauré: Sixty Years of Friendship*, ed. Jean-Michel Nectoux, trans. J. Barrie Jones (Aldershot, UK, and Burlington, VT: Ashgate, 2004), 52, n. 75. Both sources are quoted in Caballero, *Fauré and French Musical Aesthetics* (Cambridge: Cambridge University Press, 2001), 148–9.
8. Maurice Ravel, 'Les mélodies', *La revue musicale*, 4, no. 11 (1922), 25.

9. For a discussion of Fauré's tonal scheme, see Klaus Strobel, *Das Liedschaffen Gabriel Faures* (Hamburg: Verlag Dr. Kovač, 2000), 142–3.
10. Jean-Michel Nectoux, *Gabriel Fauré: A Musical Life*, trans. Roger Nichols (Cambridge: Cambridge University Press, 1991), 366.
11. Katherine Bergeron, *Voice Lessons: French Mélodie in the Belle Époque* (New York: Oxford University Press, 2010), 51.
12. Caballero, *Fauré and French Musical Aesthetics*, 205.
13. Roland Barthes, 'The Death of the Author', in *Image, Music, Text*, trans. Stephen Heath (New York: Hill and Wang, 1977), 142.
14. Vladimir Jankélévitch, *Fauré et l'inexprimable* (Paris: Plon, 1974), 215.
15. Letter to Emmanuel and Jeanne Fauré-Fremiet, 15 October [1914], in Fauré, *Correspondance suivie de Lettres à Madame H.*, ed. Jean-Michel Nectoux (Paris: Fayard, 2015), 420.
16. Loppert, Max, 'A Neglected Garden', *Music and Musicians*, 21, no. 249 (1973), 44
17. See Roy Howat, *Debussy in Proportion: A Musical Analysis* (Cambridge: Cambridge University Press, 1983), 192–3.
18. Bergeron, *Voice Lessons*, 327.

10 | Debussy's Mature Songs

DENIS HERLIN

After the publication of the *Ariettes* (1888), Debussy composed forty *mélodies*, writing twenty-three in 1887–98 and seventeen others in 1903–15. Unlike the works conceived in his youth, most of these songs were published during his lifetime, excepting the two *mélodies* of the unfinished *Nuits blanches*.[1] The dates of composition, however, do not correspond to the publication dates of several of the collections (see Table 10.1). For example, the *Trois mélodies pour une voix avec accompagnement de piano sur des poèmes de Paul Verlaine* were completed in 1891 but only published by Hamelle in 1901. Likewise, *Fêtes galantes I*, completed around 1891–2, was issued by Fromont in 1903. When Durand became Debussy's main publisher, the gap between composition and publication finally disappeared. To these forty new songs we may add the revision in 1890–1 of six songs from the 1880s: 'Mandoline', 'Paysage sentimental', 'Romance' ('Voici que le printemps'), 'Fleur des blés', 'Romance' ('L'âme évaporée et souffrante'), and 'Les cloches' (revisions prompted, most likely, by Debussy's straitened finances), as well as his 1903 revision of the six *Ariettes* (1888), published by Fromont as *Ariettes oubliées*.

Structure of the Collections: From Polyptych to Triptych

With the exception of the *Cinq poèmes de Charles Baudelaire*, the four *Proses lyriques*, the unfinished project of the *Nuits blanches* (to include five songs), and a few isolated *mélodies*, the form that Debussy overwhelmingly favoured during this period was the triptych. He composed twenty-four songs in eight collections and assembled a ninth set, *Trois mélodies de Claude Debussy* (published in 1902), consisting of 'La belle au bois dormant' (1890) and revisions of two early works (see Table 10.1). As David Code has pointed out, 'scholars have tended to treat Debussy's songs individually, in isolation from their composed and published companions', no doubt because of the large number of individual songs he composed before 1885.[6] Although Debussy did not

Table 10.1. Chronology of Claude Debussy's composition and revision of songs, 1888–1915

Date of composition[2]	Title and dedicatee	Poet	Date of publication
1888, January 1889, January 1889, March 1889? 1887, December	*Cinq poèmes de Charles Baudelaire* (dedicatee: Étienne Dupin) I. Le balcon II. Harmonie du soir III. Le jet d'eau IV. Recueillement V. La mort des amants	Charles Baudelaire	1st edition, 1890 2nd edition without revisions (Durand), 1902 3rd revised edition (Durand), probably 1917
1890, revised version of an early song	Mandoline	Paul Verlaine	1st edition in *Revue illustrée*, in September 1890 (with a dedication to Marie Vasnier) 2nd edition (Durand), 1890
1890, July 1891, revised version of an early song 1891, revised version of an early song[3]	*Trois mélodies de Claude Debussy* I. La belle au bois dormant II. Romance ('Voici que le printemps') III. Paysage sentimental	Vincent Hyspa Paul Bourget Paul Bourget	1902 (Société nouvelle d'éditions musicales) 1st edition of no. III in *Revue illustrée*, in April 1891 (with a dedication to Jeanne Andrée)
1891, revised version of an early song?	Fleur des blés (dedicatee: Joséphine Deguingand)	André Girod	1891 (Girod)
1891, January or June[4]	Beau soir	Paul Bourget	1891 (Girod)
1891, revised version of early songs	I. Romance ('L'âme évaporée et souffrante') II. Les cloches	Paul Bourget	1891 (Durand)
1891, December[5]	*Trois mélodies pour une voix avec accompagnement de piano* I. La mer est plus belle que les cathédrales (dedicatee: Ernest Chausson) II. Le son du cor s'afflige vers les bois (dedicatee: Robert Godet) III. L'échelonnement des haies moutonne à l'infini (dedicatee: Robert Godet)	Paul Verlaine	1901 (Hamelle)

Table 10.1. (*cont.*)

Date of composition[2]	Title and dedicatee	Poet	Date of publication
1891–2?	*Fêtes galantes I* I. En sourdine (2nd version) (dedicatee: Geertrude Godet) II. Fantoches (dedicatee: Louise Fontaine) III. Clair de lune (2nd version) (dedicatee: Marie Fontaine)	Paul Verlaine	1903 (Fromont)
1892, February	Les Angélus	Grégoire Le Roy	1893 (Hamelle)
	Proses lyriques	Claude Debussy	1895 (Fromont)
1892?	I. De rêve (dedicatee: Vital Hocquet)		
1892?	II. De grève (dedicatee: Raymond Bonheur)		
1893, June	III. De fleurs (dedicatee: Jeanne Chausson)		
1893, August	IV. De soir (dedicatee: Henry Lerole)		
	Chansons de Bilitis (dedicatee: Alice Van Ysen-Peter)	Pierre Louÿs	1899 (Fromont)
1897, June	I. La flûte de Pan		
1897, August	II. La chevelure		
1898, August	III. Le tombeau des naïades		
	Nuits blanches	Claude Debussy	Unpublished during Debussy's lifetime, 1st edition, 2000 (Durand)
1898, July	I. Nuit sans fin		
1898, September	II. Lorsqu'elle est entrée		
1903, revised version of the *Ariettes* published by Girod in 1888	*Ariettes oubliées* (dedicatee: Mary Garden, unforgettable Mélisande) I. C'est l'extase II. Il pleure dans mon cœur III. L'ombre des arbres IV. Chevaux de bois V. Green VI. Spleen	Paul Verlaine	2nd revised edition, 1903 (Fromont)
1903, May	*Dans le Jardin*	Paul Gravolet	1905 (Hamelle)

Table 10.1. (cont.)

Date of composition[2]	Title and dedicatee	Poet	Date of publication
1903–4	*Trois chansons de France* (dedicatee: Emma Bardac, the future Madame Debussy)		1904 (Durand)
	I. Rondel	Charles d'Orléans	
	II. La grotte	Tristan L'Hermite	
	III. Rondel	Charles d'Orléans	
1904	*Fêtes galantes II* (dedicatee: Emma Bardac, the future Madame Debussy) I. Les ingénus II. Le faune III. Colloque sentimental (two versions)	Paul Verlaine	1904 (Durand)
1909–10	*Trois ballades de François Villon* I. Ballade de Villon à s'amye II. Ballade que Villon fait à la requeste de sa mère pour prier Nostre-Dame III. Ballade des femmes de Paris	François Villon	1910 (Durand)
	Le promenoir des deux amants (dedicatee: Emma Debussy)	Tristan L'Hermite	1910 (Durand)
1903–4	I. Auprès de cette grotte sombre (the same as II. La grotte in the *Trois chansons de France*)		
1910	II. Crois mon conseil, chère Climène		
1910	III. Je tremble en voyant ton visage		
1913	*Trois poèmes de Stéphane Mallarmé* (dedicatee: In memory of Stéphane Mallarmé, and in very respectful tribute to Geneviève Bonniot)	Stéphane Mallarmé	1913 (Durand)

Table 10.1. (cont.)

Date of composition[2]	Title and dedicatee	Poet	Date of publication
	I. Soupir II. Placet futile III. Éventail		
1915, December	Noël des enfants qui n'ont plus de maison	Claude Debussy	1915 (Durand)

explicitly discourage interpreters from excerpting the *mélodies* of his triptychs, he did complain to Durand in a letter of 1908 that a choir did not sing the *Trois chansons de Charles d'Orléans* in its entirety: 'Why two *Chansons* when there are three? What does this poor third one possess that it should be separated from its companions? God forbid that I have a bad temper, but I am too old to be forced to make a choice unjustified by any valid reason'.[7] Debussy himself regularly performed the full triptychs in concert from 1908 to 1917 with Maggie Teyte, Rose Féart, Ninon Vallin, and Claire Croiza, further evidence that he wished to keep the sets intact. While performers occasionally excerpted songs from *Ariettes oubliées* and *Proses lyriques*, they always respected the structure of the triptychs.

Code has noted that Debussy's turn to three-song collections coincided with the revival of the triptych in contemporary painting. He has traced unifying threads across Debussy's song triptychs, both musical and poetic, 'attending as much to his deployment (song by song) of textural, affective and mimetic devices as to the usual more narrowly technical (i.e., scalar, harmonic, motivic) ones'.[8] Code's analysis, culminating in the *Chansons de Bilitis*, suggests that by analysing the triptychs 'it is possible to recognise the progression from *Fêtes galantes I* through the three *Chansons de Bilitis* to *Fêtes galantes II* as a rich, three-stage interrogation of the expressive possibilities in Debussy's own musical languages during the most crucial years of his negotiation with the Wagnerian heritage'.[9]

Poetic Choices

The period 1888–1915 witnessed important changes in Debussy's poetic choices. Abandoning Paul Bourget and his favoured Parnassians Théodore de Banville and Leconte de Lisle, he turned to new poets, beginning with

Charles Baudelaire. From the 152 poems in the posthumous authorised edition of *Les fleurs du mal* (1868), Debussy chose only a handful for his *Cinq poèmes de Charles Baudelaire* (published 1890), yet he respected the order of the poet's six sections. The first four poems come from the first section, *Spleen et Idéal* – 'Le balcon' (no. 37), 'Harmonie du soir' (no. 48), 'Le jet d'eau' (no. 97), and 'Recueillement' (no. 104) – while the last, 'La mort des amants' (no. 156), belongs to the later section *La Mort*. 'Recueillement' and 'La mort des amants' are traditional sonnets (two quatrains followed by two tercets), albeit with crossed rhymes and, in the second poem, decasyllables rather than alexandrines. 'Le balcon' and 'Harmonie du soir', however, have more unusual forms whose repeating lines place greater constraints on the musical setting. In 'Le balcon', a poem par excellence about memory, each of the five-line stanzas recollects the first line at the end. As for 'Harmonie du soir', it resembles a pantoum, a Malaysian form in which, as Théodore de Banville explained in his famous poetic treatise, 'the second line of each stanza becomes the first line of the following stanza, and the fourth line of each stanza becomes the third line of the following stanza'.[10] 'Le jet d'eau' also features a refrain, but Debussy used a version of the poem published in *La Petite Revue* in July 1865 whose repeating stanza differs strikingly from the 1868 version:

La gerbe d'eau qui berce
Ses mille fleurs
Que la lune traverse
De ses lueurs
Tombe comme une averse
De larges pleurs.   (1865 version)

La gerbe épanouie
En mille fleurs
Où Phoebé réjouie
Met ses couleurs,
Tombe comme une pluie
De larges pleurs.   (1868 version)

The feminine rhymes of the 1865 version are mellower and richer (*-erce* instead of *-ie*), and Debussy would even soften Baudelaire's 'lueurs' ('rays') to 'pâleurs' ('paleness'). Despite his strong attraction to Baudelaire, whom he cited as his favourite poet in an 1889 questionnaire, Debussy set no more of his poems, paying tribute instead in two piano pieces.[11]

After this Baudelairean sojourn, Debussy returned to Paul Verlaine in the years 1890–1, composing the *Trois mélodies* and *Fêtes galantes I*. He would probably have abandoned Verlaine thereafter as well, had he not fallen in love with the amateur singer Emma Bardac in 1904, a love affair that prompted his composition of *Fêtes galantes II*. For the *Trois mélodies* of 1891, he took a brief respite from the Watteauian world of *Fêtes galantes* (1869) and focussed on *Sagesse* (1881), written after Verlaine's embrace of Catholicism. He chose three poems whose metres range from the decasyllabic ('Le son du cor s'afflige vers les bois') to the pentasyllabic ('La mer est plus belle') to the heptasyllabic ('L'échelonnement des haies').

After this return to Verlaine, which rekindled his youthful impulses, Debussy searched for other, more flexible poetic forms as he sought new approaches to the relationship between text and music. His impatience with traditional versification also led him to abandon *Rodrigue et Chimène*, his first operatic project from the years 1890–3: he was repelled by Catulle Mendès' alexandrines and octosyllables, which Paul Dukas dismissed as 'Parnassian bric-a-brac and Spanish barbarism mixed together'.[12] His discovery in 1893 of Maurice Maeterlinck's play *Pelléas et Mélisande* was decisive and coincided with his poetic experimentation of 1892–3 when he undertook to set his own poetry. The title of his self-authored song collection, *Proses lyriques*, is revealing: Debussy selected words, above all, for their power to awaken and call forth music. To this end, he used free verse, which retains the lines of traditional poetry but dispenses with regular metre and rhyme schemes. The genre was very much in vogue in the avant-garde circles of the 1890s, most notably with the French-American poet Francis Vielé-Griffin.[13] Debussy published the first two poems of *Proses lyriques* in the December 1892 issue of *Les entretiens politiques et littéraires*, edited by Vielé-Griffin and Henri de Régnier who seem to have revised the texts. When he undertook a second collection of *Proses lyriques* in 1898, *Nuits blanches*, Debussy again used free verse. Between these two collections, he set three of Pierre Louÿs' *Chansons de Bilitis* to music. Although published as prose poems, an early version of 'La chevelure' shows that Louÿs had originally conceived it in free verse.

After the Verlainian interlude of 1904, Debussy's literary tastes led him to authors from the Middle Ages (Charles d'Orléans and François Villon) and seventeenth century (Tristan L'Hermite). His interest in Charles d'Orléans dated from 1898 when he had set two unaccompanied four-part *chansons* for the amateur choir of his friends Lucien and Arthur Fontaine. For the *Trois chansons de France* (1904), Debussy chose two rondels by the poet-prince, a form revived by Banville in his third book of *Cariatides* (1842) and *Rondels* (1875). These poems consist of thirteen lines divided into three stanzas, two quatrains and a quinzain, in which the seventh and eighth lines always correspond to the first and second, and the thirteenth line to the first. The rhyme structure presents a further constraint: the first and third stanzas use *rimes embrassées* (*abba*), with an added fifth line in the latter, while the second stanza has *rimes croisées* (*abab*). The repeating form also limits each of the two rondels to only two rhymes (*-eau/-uie* and *-orte/-oir*), with the order of masculine and feminine rhymes reversed in the second. Debussy's second rondel will illustrate this demanding scheme, with capital letters indicating the repeating lines:

Pour ce que Plaisance est morte	A
Ce may, suis vestu de noir;	B
C'est grand pitié de véoir	b
Mon cœur qui s'en desconforte.	a
Je m'abille de la sorte	a
Que doy, pour faire devoir;	b
Pour ce que Plaisance est morte,	A
Ce may, suis vestu de noir.	B
Le temps ces nouvelles porte	a
Qui ne veut déduit avoir;	b
Mais par force de plouvoir	b
Fait des champs clorre la porte,	a
Pour ce que Plaisance est morte.	A

The text of 'La grotte', the second *mélodie* of the *Trois chansons de France*, comes from a long poetic ode by Tristan L'Hermite, 'Le promenoir des deux amants'. Of the twenty-eight quatrains, written in octosyllables with *rimes embrassées*, Debussy set the first, second, and fourth. In 1910, he recycled 'La grotte' as the first song of a triptych, *Le promenoir des deux amants*, named after L'Hermite's ode. He mined the ode for the remaining two songs, setting quatrains 14–6 in 'Crois mon conseil, chère Climène' and quatrains 22–4 in 'Je tremble en voyant ton visage'.

In that same year he undertook the *Trois ballades de François Villon*, a poet whose work he had discovered in 1903. The *ballade* follows a more or less rigorous pattern comprising three stanzas followed by a half-stanza, or *envoi*, which begins with a formal address – for example, 'Prince amoureux, des amans le greigneur' in the first *ballade*, or 'Prince, aux dames Parisiennes' in the third. Moreover, the number of syllables in the lines determines the length of the stanzas: in the third *ballade* the octosyllables yield stanzaic lengths of 8 + 8 + 8 + 4 lines, while the decasyllables of the second *ballade* correspond to a 10 + 10 + 10 + [7] scheme. As Debussy admitted in an inquiry conducted in March 1911, whimsically titled 'What should one set to music: Good Poetry or Bad, Poetry, Free Verse, or Prose?', he had considerable difficulty with Villon poetry's 'in following and rendering the rhythms while remaining freshly inspired'.[14]

With the exception of 'Noël des enfants qui n'ont plus de maison' (1915), a *pièce d'occasion* inspired by the First World War for which Debussy wrote both text and music, the composer reserved his final lyric energies for Stéphane Mallarmé, whose 'Apparition' he had set in his youth. The 1913 publication of a complete edition of the *Poésies* by the Nouvelle Revue Française undoubtedly prompted Debussy's return to the Mallarméan universe of 'L'après-midi d'un faune', which had inspired his celebrated *Prélude* composed in 1892–4. Whether it is 'Soupir' with its single phrase revived by the repetition of 'vers l'Azur' at the beginning of the second stanza, the *ancien régime* pastiche of 'Placet futile' (described by Mallarmé as a 'Louis XV sonnet'), or 'Éventail' with its playful personification of the decorative fan, these three poems offer an opportune space for Debussy's subtle and refined musical writing. The *Trois poèmes de Stéphane Mallarmé* (1913) achieve an almost perfect alliance between the Mallarméan word-music and its musical accompaniment, combined throughout with suppleness, brilliance, and elasticity. They epitomise the union of verse and music so dear to Mallarmé and soundly contradict Debussy's answer to the 1911 survey, in which he claimed to be 'more at ease with rhythmical prose, which allows us far greater freedom of movement'.[15] In point of fact, the composer abandoned the free-verse experiments of 1892–8 rather quickly and continued from 1904, albeit in a less intense way than in his youth, to set poems with more strictly codified forms.

Dedicatees

With the exception of the *Trois ballades de François Villon* and a few isolated *mélodies*, all of Debussy's later songs bear dedications. Strikingly, the composer dedicated most of them to a small circle of close acquaintances. It included friends such as Étienne Dupin (five songs), Robert Godet (two) and his wife Geertrude (one), and Vital Hocquet (one), as well as fellow composers like Raymond Bonheur, Ernest Chausson, and Chausson's wife Jeanne (one song each). He dedicated nine *mélodies* to his wife Emma Bardac, three to his probable lover Alice Van Ysen-Peter, one each to painter Henry Lerolle, Louise Fontaine, and Marie Fontaine, and six to his first Mélisande, soprano Mary Garden. Moreover, a tight network of marriage and kinship connected the dedicatees; Jeanne Chausson, for example, was the wife of Ernest Chausson, the sister of Marie Fontaine, and the sister-in-law of Henry Lerolle. He also dedicated the manuscripts of several *mélodies* to members of this intimate circle.

In short, Debussy seems to have regarded his songs less as publications for anonymous professionals than as offerings for a circle of sympathetic connoisseurs. This circle also boasted a number of accomplished amateur singers, including Marie Fontaine, Louise Fontaine, and Lucien Fontaine (who Debussy claimed sang like 'a sentimental bull').[16] And Emma Bardac-Debussy, a pupil of the famed teacher Eugénie Colonne for whose voice Gabriel Fauré composed his demanding cycle *La bonne chanson*, was a remarkable singer. The poet Albert Samain praised Emma's singing in a letter of 1896: 'She has a feeling for nuances and especially a purity of expression altogether rare'.[17] As with his early songs for Madame Vasnier, Debussy clearly tailored many of his later *mélodies* to specific female interpreters.

Cinq poèmes de Charles Baudelaire (1887–9)

After completing his *Ariettes*, Debussy turned to one of his favourite authors, Charles Baudelaire. Published in a print run of 150 copies, the *Cinq poèmes de Charles Baudelaire* gives no indication of the publisher; whatever copies were not given away were deposited in the offices of the Librairie de l'Art indépendant. The general appearance of this volume recalls the Symbolist publications brought out by this strange organisation, which Debussy frequented in the 1890s: a large format, cover page in simulated parchment, wide margins in blue, gold, and brown, generously spaced engraving, and blank pages inserted to allow each song to begin on a new page – in short, a deluxe edition for the 'happy few', presented with the refined taste that Debussy would display throughout his career. The *Cinq poèmes* are dedicated to Étienne Dupin, described by Robert Godet, one of Debussy's closest friends at the time, as 'a worldly young man who enjoyed considerable wealth and who was charming and elegant, cultivated, somewhat mysterious, and an assiduous reader of the medieval source book *The Golden Legend*'.[18] Debussy's dedication of this handsome score reflects his close relationship with Dupin, a musical enthusiast who twice accompanied Debussy and others on pilgrimages to Bayreuth, where they heard *Die Meistersinger* and *Parsifal* (1888) and *Tristan und Isolde* (1889).

Debussy's Wagnerian experience proved highly influential for the young composer's musical language during the time he composed the five Baudelaire songs. The piano writing is quasi-orchestral (indeed, Debussy orchestrated 'Le jet d'eau' in 1907), the voice is treated in almost instrumental fashion, and leitmotifs of a sort are employed along with a good deal of chromaticism. François de Médicis has noted reminiscences of and allusions to *Tristan*, *Parsifal*, *Die Walküre*, and *Götterdammerung* in 'La mort des amants' and especially 'Le balcon', 'with its ample proportions, its chromaticism, the at times powerfully declamatory character of its vocal line, and at the beginning of the melody, the intoxicating drive'.[19] In 'Harmonie du soir', Debussy even went so far as to impose upon the music the poetic form of the pantoum, recalling identical phrases for the repeating poetic lines. In 'Recueillement', Debussy employed the kind of recitative style that he later used so felicitously in *Pelléas et Mélisande*. After completing this cycle, however, Debussy would begin an ardent battle against the sorcery of this 'ghost of old Klingsor, otherwise known as Richard Wagner'.[20] His Baudelairean experience offered, as Code put it, 'an ideal textual forum to test the limits of his lyrical powers as he grappled head-on with the overweening model of Wagner'.[21] These songs would enchant Stéphane Mallarmé and prompted him to make the acquaintance of the talented young composer in order to propose that he add what the poet called 'un rien de musique' (just a bit of music) to a poem of his about the sensual experiences of a creature half-human, half-goat. This little 'rien' would, of course, become the refined and astonishing score known as the *Prélude à l'après-midi d'un faune*.

From *Fêtes galantes I* to the *Trois mélodies* (1891)

In 1891, after his time with Baudelaire and the parenthesis of 'La belle au bois dormant', Debussy returned to Verlaine. He revisited three of the poems from *Fêtes galantes* that he had set in 1882 ('En sourdine', 'Fantoches', and 'Clair de lune') and also selected three further poems from the third part of Verlaine's 1881 collection *Sagesse* ('La mer est plus belle que les cathédrales', 'Le son du cor s'afflige vers les bois', and 'L'échelonnement des haies'). His revisions of *Fêtes galantes I* were of two kinds: making modifications as he had earlier done for other songs, especially in the piano accompaniment, but also in the vocal part of *Fantoches*; and totally rewriting the music of 'En sourdine' and 'Clair de lune' such that the versions of 1891 have absolutely nothing in common musically with the versions of 1882. Compared to the Baudelaire songs, with their nearly orchestral piano writing, the accompaniment is much more transparent. The leitmotif technique is also abandoned, although in 'En sourdine' there is a recurring motif that one discovers at the end to be the song of the nightingale, 'the voice of our despair'. As Stephen Rumph has pointed out, Debussy's motto at the beginning of the song is supported by 'his most literal "Tristan" chord, identical in pitch content and spacing to Wagner's prototype'.[22]

In 'Clair de lune', Debussy employed longer notes suspended over continuous semiquavers to create a unique landscape of sound. What is more, he now delicately incorporated into the musical texture Verlaine's enjambment between the second and third stanzas in which the sentence flows across the break, a connection enhanced by the repetition of Verlaine's title:

Tout en chantant sur le mode mineur
L'amour vainqueur et la vie opportune,
Ils n'ont pas de croire à leur bonheur
Et leur chanson se mêle <u>au clair de lune</u>,   (Enjambment)

Au calme clair de lune triste et beau,
Qui fait rêver les oiseaux dans les arbres
Et sangloter d'extase les jets d'eau,
Les grands jets d'eau sveltes parmi les arbres.

Debussy matched Verlaine's enjambment with a half-step progression on the word 'lune', thus emphasising both the continuity and the change of mood between the two quatrains (see Example 10.1). Code has noted how the structure of key and tempo in *Fêtes galantes I* seems clearly 'painterly' in outline (five sharps–no sharps–five sharps, *Rêveusement lent–Allegretto scherzando–Très modéré*), as does the textual order (two poems of personal address frame one of objective description).[23]

The vocal and pianistic writing of the three new songs, now known as *Trois mélodies pour une voix avec accompagnement de piano sur des poèmes de Paul Verlaine*, seems conspicuously to foreshadow the environment of the opera Debussy would begin in the summer of 1893. The flow of 'La mer plus belle que les cathédrales' did not prevent the composer from weaving a dense harmonic tapestry in what is the sea-song of his career. 'Le son du cor

Example 10.1. Claude Debussy, 'Clair de lune' (*Fêtes galantes I*), mm. 19–22

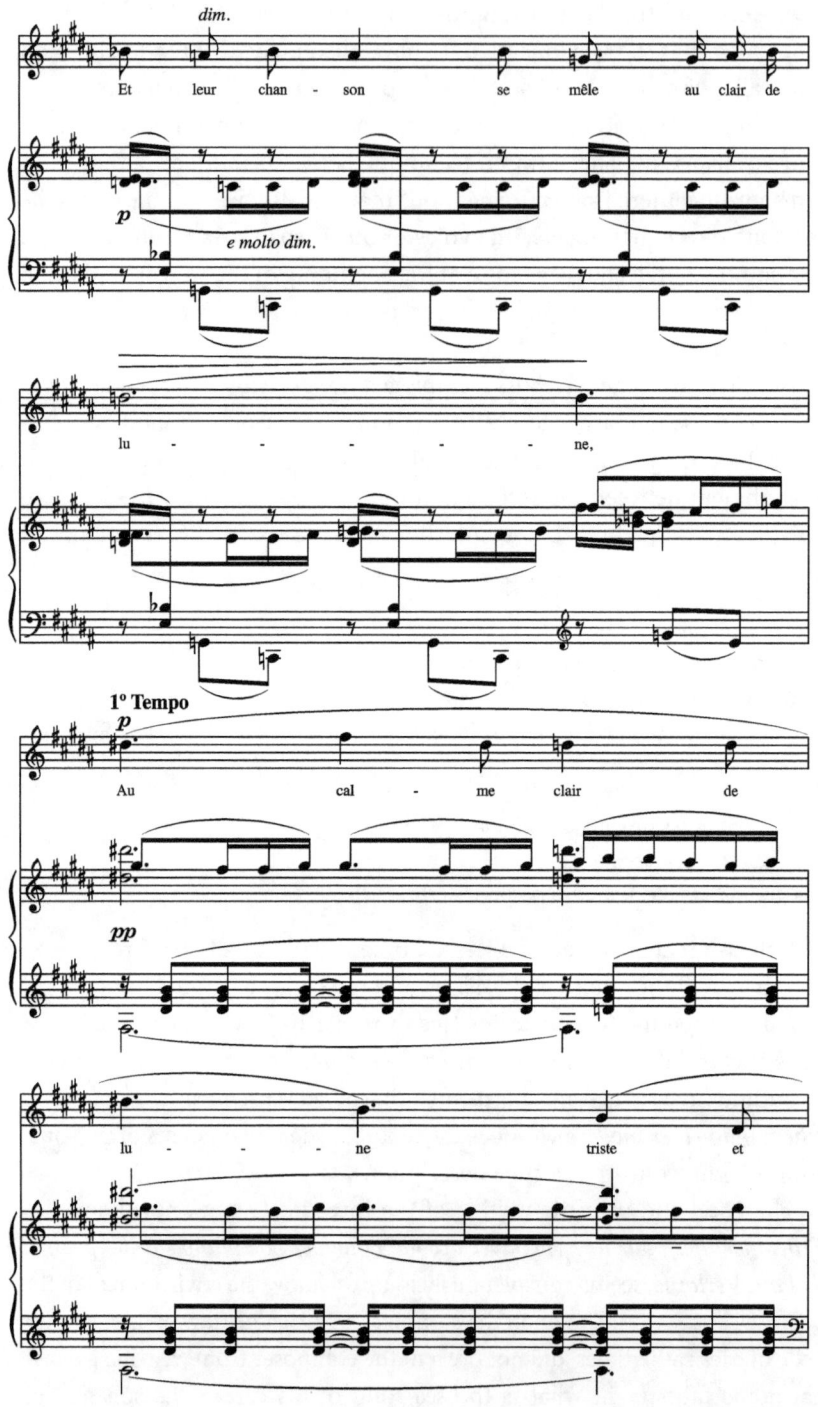

s'afflige vers les bois' reveals the quasi-parlando style that Debussy would perfect in *Pelléas et Mélisande*. And 'L'échelonnement des haies moutonne à l'infini' presages much of Debussy's piano writing of the first decade of the new century. As Debussy's close friend Pierre Louÿs would quip, these songs are 'Verlaine-like to the very ends of their quavers'.[24] The vocal writing is profoundly transformed by a newly restricted tessitura and a sensitive representation of the text. Although Julien Hamelle secured the rights to this publication in 1891, he did not publish it until 1901. Perhaps he felt that by comparison with the contemporary *mélodies* by Fauré (Hamelle was the older composer's principal publisher) Debussy's were too difficult.

'La belle au bois dormant' and 'Les angélus' (1890–2)

'La belle au bois dormant' (composed in 1890) is the setting of a poem by the artistic polymath Vincent Hyspa, a cabaret singer, actor, humourist, writer, and composer whom Debussy came to know during his years at the famous Chat Noir cabaret on Montmartre. The poem caricatures medieval poems, and Debussy responded with a through-composed setting flavoured with a droll piano ritornello based on 'Nous n'irons plus au bois', a nursery song he would reuse in one of the *Images* of 1894 and again in 'Jardins sous la pluie', the third of the *Estampes*. 'Les angélus', published by Hamelle in 1893, derives from a poetic collection by the Belgian writer Grégoire Le Roy, *Mon cœur pleure d'autrefois* (1889). Debussy composed the song in 1892, just a few months before starting work on the *Proses lyriques*. The piano accompaniment, with its continuous ostinato of four rising quavers, immediately evokes the sonority of the 'Christian matin bells', a sound that always fascinated the composer.

Proses lyriques (1892–3)

With the *Proses lyriques*, Debussy launched himself on an entirely new adventure, namely, setting his own poetry to music.[25] He made a deliberate choice to liberate himself from metric constraints – the alexandrines, octosyllables, and erudite heterometric stanzas of Banville, Verlaine, and Baudelaire. Debussy thus joined one of the favourite experiments of Symbolism: free verse. His first efforts at poetry, as the title of his four-song publication indicates, reflect the composer's preoccupation with the kind of verse best suited to musical setting. Determined not to be a slave to versification of any sort, he sought instead a kind of rhythmic prose attuned to his inner lyrical impulses. Each of the *Proses lyriques* – 'De rêve', 'De grève', 'De fleurs', and 'De soir' – is dedicated to one of the composer's close friends. He offered the first to Vital Hocquet, born Narcisse Lebeau and surprisingly enough a plumber. Debussy had met Hocquet at Le Chat Noir in the 1890s and stood witness at his marriage in 1892. The second song is dedicated to the composer Raymond Bonheur, whom Debussy also honoured with the dedication of the *Prélude à l'après-midi d'un faune*. He dedicated the third to Jeanne Chausson, wife of the well-known composer. And the fourth is dedicated to the painter Henry Lerolle, Chausson's brother-in-law and a very special friend. As he wrote to Chausson in early September 1893: 'I've just finished the last of the *Proses lyriques*, which is dedicated to H. Lerolle, first in order to please myself, and second in order not to go outside of a close circle of friendship'.[26]

The *Proses lyriques*, begun in late 1892 or early 1893, are all ample in length and vocal tessitura, with piano parts as orchestral as those of the Baudelaire songs. The first, 'De rêve', turns on strong contrasts like the opposition of the opening line, 'The night has a woman's softness', and the later evocation of the knights who 'have died in quest of the Grail'; the second, 'De grève', is a more regular, rippling sea-song such as Debussy had earlier conceived in 'La mer est plus belle que les cathédrales'. The poetry of the third song, 'De fleurs', recalls 'Serre d'ennui', one of Maurice Maeterlinck's *Serres chaudes* (Hothouses) that Ernest Chausson was setting in 1893. But Debussy's song reaches an almost suffocatingly intense harmonic density as it echoes the phrase 'hothouse of grief'. And the fourth song, 'De soir', revisits the poetic style of Jules Laforgue, much appreciated by Debussy, as it turns around upon itself at the image of those 'obstinate rounds' and 'trains that speed along'. Fromont published the *Proses lyriques* in 1895 with an Art Nouveau cover that suggests an entrelac of green branches, evoking the 'lassitude in desolate green' from 'De fleurs'. The cycle as a whole contains an unexpected musical variety. If it remains less well-known than other collections, the reason doubtless lies with Debussy's puzzling, even disconcerting poetry, even if, as Jean-Louis Leleu remarked, 'one cannot deny this literary component of the work a certain strength, linked to the precision with which the composer's imagination is expressed'.[27] The first two songs of the *Proses lyriques* premiered at the Société nationale de musique on 17 February 1894, with Thérèse Roger accompanied by Debussy on the piano.

The *Chansons de Bilitis* (1897–8)

Once he had completed a first version of *Pelléas et Mélisande* in 1895, Debussy chose to return to the intimate world of the *mélodie* and, for various reasons, to the *Chansons de Bilitis*. In 1893 he had become fast friends with the young writer Pierre Louÿs who would soon earn fame with such novels as *Aphrodite* (1896) and *La femme et le pantin* (1898), as well as with his erotic writings. Louÿs and Debussy were extremely devoted to one another for a period of three years and supported each other both materially and psychologically. After 1897, while continuing to correspond, they gradually went their separate ways. Louÿs was fanatical about music, especially Berlioz and Wagner, and his shared enthusiasms with Debussy could be as passionate as their disagreements. Contrary to received wisdom, Louÿs was not Debussy's literary mentor, although his circle of acquaintances, his erudition, and his artistic taste could only sharpen the intellectual curiosity of his musician friend, for whom Louÿs sincerely hoped to become the preferred librettist. Nevertheless, their attempts at collaboration on a *Cendrelune* and *Daphnis et Khloé* came to nothing. And despite their both frequenting Symbolist circles, the two men did not share the same artistic conceptions or needs. Still, Debussy very much liked the *Chansons de Bilitis*, which Louÿs published with the Librairie de l'Art indépendant at the end of 1894.

The book, to Louÿs' great delight, was a mystification, a bamboozlement, for the author boldly claimed on the title page that the poems were translations from an ancient tongue: 'Songs of Bilitis translated from the Greek, for the first time, by P.L.'. As a highly knowledgeable Hellenist, Louÿs could in fact have made such a translation, and he had proven as much when he brought out with the same publisher translations of *Scènes de la vie des courtisanes* by Lucien of Samosata and the poetry of Meleager of Gadara. To lend greater credence to his forgery, Louÿs prefaced the poems with an account of the life of 'Bilitis' in which he explains what was known about the poetess and even mentions the discovery by 'G. Heim' of her tomb, unearthed along a road near the ancient city of Amathus: 'The tomb, spacious and low, paved with limestone slabs, had four walls covered with plaques of black amphibolite on which were engraved in primitive capital letters all of the songs that one will read here except for the three epitaphs that decorate the sarcophagus'. If the subterfuge did not fool Louÿs' friends, others were taken in, especially academics, some of whom even claimed to know of Professor Heim's publication.

In June 1897 the composer completed the first song of the cycle, 'La flûte de Pan', whose third paragraph is especially suggestive: 'We have nothing to say to each other, so close have we become; but our songs seek to answer each other, and one by one our mouths unite on the flute'. One can only admire the extraordinary refinement of Debussy's musical language as he subtly evokes Pan's flute in the opening bar with the piano's simple rising and falling scale, marked *sans rigueur de rythme* (without strict rhythm), or as he so finely echoes the croaking of frogs near the end through a superimposition of triplets in the upper register of the piano upon a vacillating figure of diminished fifths and augmented fourths. The rhythm of the text-setting is remarkably fluid, unbound by the bar lines, and follows the supple rhythms of Louÿs' prose. For Katherine Bergeron, the song epitomises the modern *mélodie* in its understatement and freedom from rhetorical emphasis: 'Transcribing the *voix parlé*, Debussy dared to reunite song with its original accent and achieved an utterly modern form in the process: a dispassionate *mélodie*, without expression, without imitation, and almost entirely without melody'.[28]

Debussy intended to send 'La flûte de Pan' to the journal of wood engravers, *L'Image*, but Pierre Louÿs sent him a new poem not found in the 1895 edition. 'La chevelure' is deeply and frankly erotic. By the beginning of September, the music for the new poem was completed and appeared in October in *L'Image* with Art-Nouveau ornaments by Kees van Dongen whose foliage recalls the necklace of dark tresses so sensually painted in the poem. From Georges Rodenbach's 1892 novel *Bruges-la-morte* to the Tower Scene of *Pelléas et Mélisande* ('Mes longs cheveux'), *la chevelure*, hair, served as a potent emblem of the Symbolist movement. In 1898 Debussy completed the third and last member of the collection, 'Le tombeau des Naïades', a song suffused with profound disillusionment and sadness, no doubt a reflection of the darkness of the composer's existence during this difficult time. Among all of Debussy's *mélodies*, the *Chansons de Bilitis* arguably represents his subtlest evocation of an intimate atmosphere.

Nuits blanches (1898–9)

Until the year 2000, only a fragment copied on a single page of an album from 1900 attested to the existence of Debussy's *Nuits blanches* (*Sleepless Nights*). It remained unclear whether he had actually worked on this composition or whether, as with so many others, he had merely planned then abandoned the project. The recent discovery of the manuscripts proved that he did work on the set, which would have become a five-song cycle and a sequel to *Proses lyriques* with Debussy's own texts (he intended to call the set *Proses lyriques II*, with *Nuits blanches* as subtitle). Yet unlike the first *Proses lyriques*, which treat love, innocence, and distress in the manner of Jules Laforgue, the second *Proses lyriques* have a more intimate and personal character in which we find the unfulfilled desire to be loved, the suffering caused by waiting, and the deceit that always attends adultery. The second *mélodie* in particular, 'Lorsqu'elle est entrée', has distinct echoes of Golaud (*Pelléas et Mélisande*) and his pathological suspicion of his young bride.

Debussy had been living a particularly difficult life since 1897, as we have mentioned. His protector and publisher Georges Hartmann had failed to produce *Pelléas*, whose first version Debussy had completed in 1895. In addition to his ongoing financial burdens, his liaison with Gabrielle Dupont was becoming less satisfying, leading to their separation in 1898. It was in this climate of moral and material suffering that Debussy composed the two extant songs of *Nuits blanches*. On 14 July 1898, he wrote a long, confused, and discouraged letter to Georges Hartmann, not once mentioning the first of the *Nuits blanches*, even though he had completed the song on that very day:

I hardly need to tell you how much pleasure your letter gave me and how grateful I am for the affectionate patience you demonstrate in the face of my dilemma. Alas, nothing much has changed; 'something is rotten in the state of Denmark', as that elegant neurasthenic Hamlet puts it. With all the rest, my life is burdened with emotional problems, which means that it is the most miserable and complicated thing that I know of.[29]

The reasons that Debussy set aside these two songs are by no means clear. He was certainly at work on them again in 1899, because at one point he asked Hartmann to reserve some time for him on 1 May so that he could play the publisher a new *Nuit blanche*. Indeed, this phrase suggests the existence of a third song for the cycle, not yet discovered.

The tempo indications of the two songs (*Triste et Lent* and *Lent et douloureux*) recall the ambience of Act V of *Pelléas et Mélisande*, as does the use of 6/4, 'the measure par excellence of Pelléas'. The first *mélodie* is in a static movement punctuated by chords, except in mm. 14–16, while in the second the tempo gradually accelerates from m. 18. In both *mélodies*, the vocal range is wide and always starts in the middle range then gradually rises according to the meaning of the text. The subject of the poems and the tessitura suggest that Debussy intended this draft cycle for a male voice.

The second *mélodie*, longer than the first, plays on the tonal ambiguity in the piano's opening bars, setting up a suspicious and ambivalent atmosphere. The vocal line of 'Quand elle est entrée' oscillates between *parlando* declamation, especially at the beginning, and more lyrical passages. As François Le Roux has pointed out, the two songs come 'closer to a dramatic expressiveness than to the modesty associated with a traditional *mélodie*'.[30] Could it be that their tortured and suffering character led Debussy to abandon the publication of these *mélodies*? Be that as it may, the high quality of the first two songs is beyond dispute. They provide the missing links in a chain that stretches from the *Chansons de Bilitis* to the *Trois chansons de France*.

'Dans le jardin' (1903)

It is unclear why Debussy chose to set this poem extracted from *Les frissons* of Paul Gravollet, an actor at the Comédie française. Debussy's *mélodie* was published by Hamelle in 1903, the year of its composition, as was another song on a text by Gravollet composed by Debussy's friend Charles Levadé, suggesting that Levadé may have persuaded Debussy to set the poem. Many years later, Hamelle would assemble a collection entitled *Les frissons*, consisting of twenty-two *mélodies* by a variety of composers that included André Caplet, Paul Vidal, Maurice Ravel, Vincent d'Indy, and Xavier Leroux.

Trois chansons de France and *Fêtes galantes II* (1904)

Six years went by between the *Nuits blanches* of 1898 and Debussy's next song set, the *Trois chansons de France*. The intervening years saw two explosive events in the life of the composer: first, his marriage in October 1899 to the milliner Lilly Texier; and second, the newfound celebrity that resulted from the successful 1902 premiere of *Pelléas et Mélisande*, which reached more than one hundred performances at the Opéra-Comique during Debussy's lifetime. Aside from 'Dans le jardin', a revision of the 1888 *Ariettes*, and an unfinished setting of Dante Gabriel Rossetti's *La saulaie* (Louÿs' translation of *Willowwood*, planned for baritone and orchestra), Debussy had abandoned the *mélodie* after *Nuits blanches*, perhaps discouraged by the experience of setting his own texts. In 1904, however, he would compose two new cycles, *Trois chansons de*

France and *Fêtes galantes II*, in a burst of enthusiasm associated with an exciting new amatory encounter. Emma Bardac, his future wife, was a worldly woman from a Jewish family in Bordeaux, a talented amateur singer, and the wife of the banker Sigismond Bardac. Before any outward declaration of love, Debussy dedicated to Emma the *Trois chansons de France*. The first, 'Rondel', is characterised by 'a musical atmosphere of the Renaissance', a modal colour without 'worrying about archaism', as Charles Koechlin remarked.[31] The third song, another 'Rondel', is constructed on a rhythmic and melodic ostinato in the piano and embodies 'the natural flowering of the French Gregorian'.[32] 'La grotte', the middle song from Tristan L'Hermite's evocatively titled *Le promenoir des deux amants* (The Covered Walkway of the Two Lovers), clearly recalls the celebrated scene at the end of Act II of Debussy's opera where Pelléas and Mélisande descend to the grotto in search of Mélisande's lost ring. The vocal line of the *mélodie* creates a magnificently resonant landscape that turns on the almost obsessive rhythms, reminiscent of waves beating against pebbles.

The second collection of *Fêtes galantes* marked a new stage in Debussy's relationship with Emma Bardac, as we learn from the dedication of the first edition: 'To thank the month of June 1904, A.l.p.m.' – that is, 'à la petite mienne' (to my little darling), as Debussy called his new companion. The return to Verlaine was not coincidental as Emma greatly admired the poet's work. In returning to *Fêtes galantes*, Debussy was also returning, consciously or not, to earlier loves, in particular, his youthful passion for Madame Vasnier: in 1885 Debussy had thought of setting the last poem of the collection, 'Colloque sentimental'.[33] For Emma Bardac he would make two very different settings of the poem, although only the second was published during the composer's lifetime. The two settings share a recollection of the nightingale's song from 'En sourdine' in *Fêtes galantes I* at the moment when one of the interlocutors evokes previous passions – 'Do you remember our past raptures?' Even if both Debussy and Emma Bardac were attracted to this poem, the choice remains peculiar since the text evokes, with distinct cruelty, the disillusionment and disintegration of amorous emotions. This may explain why Debussy hesitated to include it in the cycle, which he had originally planned to begin with 'Le faune' and its astonishing left-hand rhythmic ostinato bordering on bitonality, followed by a setting of Baudelaire's brooding 'Crépuscule du soir'. In the end, Debussy decided to rely solely on Verlaine by opening the cycle with 'Les ingénus', which evokes a certain naive flirtatiousness, and to follow that song with 'Le faune'. The cycle comes to an end *triste et lent* (sadly and slowly) with the 'melancholic and distant' colours of 'Colloque sentimental'. After setting the 'lonely and icy' scene, the song continues in a dialogue punctuated by an inexorable syncopated piano rhythm enveloped, as Code put it, in 'fleeting surges of radiant post-Wagnerian harmony'.[34]

Le promenoir des deux amants and Trois ballades de François Villon (1910)

After concentrating on instrumental music for five years, Debussy returned to the *mélodie* with renewed fecundity in 1910. In that year he was able to deliver to his publisher two collections of songs, *Le promenoir des deux amants* and the *Trois ballades de François Villon*. Returning to his 1904 *Trois chansons de France*, the composer began *Le promenoir* with 'La grotte', but without the former title. He had no doubt purchased the new edition of Tristan L'Hermite's works, issued by the *Mercure de France* in 1909, and even the tumultuous state of his relationship with Emma did not deter his work on the new cycle, as his publisher Durand confirmed:

In my memory of the first hearings Debussy gave me of his works, I also remember *Le promenoir des deux amants*. Although he had only a composer's voice, the timbre was particularly warm and expressive; in short, it was an enchantment to hear. At that time, Debussy had great worries, and when I wondered why he had been able to compose this delightful work in his state of boredom, he replied: 'In the midst of drama, I feel at ease composing'. Needless to say, he was a lover of paradox. Yet there was a great deal of truth in his assertion.[35]

Debussy carefully selected his excerpts from the long ode as a way of reaffirming his love for Emma. In 'Crois mon conseil, chère Climène', Code has noted how 'the blithely innocent invitation that opens this central song leads, over rippling pianistic evocations of the "sighing Zephyr", to a powerful surge of suppressed passion at the invocation of a "rosy complexion" before it ends on a sensuous murmur'.[36] The cycle is a small masterpiece of refined prosody in music. Debussy dedicated it to Emma, now his wife and still his 'petite mienne', and Durand published it in August 1910. It was first performed in 1913 by the soprano Ninon Vallin with Debussy accompanying.

Debussy composed the *Trois ballades de François Villon* during same period, completing them in May 1910. As an avid reader, the composer had no doubt procured the reprint by Flammarion of the edition of the *Œuvres de François Villon* edited by Paul Lacroix. The first song provides an excellent illustration of the composer's craft as Debussy represents each one of the text's inflections while maintaining the organic unity of the iambic rhythms in the piano accompaniment. While certain archaic sonorities (open intervals, chant-like melodies) colour the second song, the third culminates in musical fireworks marked *Alerte et gai* (lively and cheerful). Departing from his customary procedure, Debussy made brilliant orchestrations of all three songs. Earlier he had orchestrated only 'Le jet d'eau' from the Baudelaire songs, and he had specifically rejected the idea of orchestrating two of his *Proses lyriques*. But the contrasting moods of the *Trois ballades*, which combine grief and regret with lightness and cheer (especially in the third song), and the intensity of the vocal line must have persuaded him to orchestrate the songs. The *Trois ballades de François Villon* remain the incarnation of Debussy's perfected melodic prowess, consummated by the murmuring refrain of the second song: 'In this faith, I wish to live and die'.

Trois poèmes de Stéphane Mallarmé (1913)

The genesis of the *Trois poèmes de Stéphane Mallarmé* dates from the summer of 1913 when Debussy had just completed the second book of *Préludes* and was working on the orchestration of *Jeux*. He thus reconnected with a poet who had made a lasting impression on the 'very silent musician', as Debussy styled himself, since the 1890s. After considering a second setting of 'Apparition', Debussy decided on 'Soupir' and 'Éventail', to which he would later add 'Placet futile'. Ironically, just as Debussy was working on these melodies, he learnt that Maurice Ravel had also set 'Soupir' and 'Placet futile'. As he wrote to his publisher in August 1913, 'this is an auto-suggestive phenomenon that ought to be investigated by the Académie de médecine'.[37] The matter was complicated, however, by the fact that Mallarmé's heirs refused to give permission for a second setting of the poems. Ravel's intervention to 'beg them to give Debussy their permission' helped to resolve the situation and avoid renewed animosity between the two musicians.[38]

Published in October 1913, the *Trois poèmes* received a mixed reception and were long neglected by biographers, critics, and performers, some even dismissing the work as uninspired.[39] Yet as Paolo Dal Molin and Jean-Louis Leleu have explained, Debussy set out 'to make different harmonic universes interact within the same piece, induced by the use of scales endowed with remarkable properties, and to base the logic of the musical discourse on the skilfully controlled shifts from one universe to another'.[40] Thanks to the highly refined range of dynamics, particularly in 'Soupir', situated between *pp* and *p* and in a medium range for the voice, Debussy followed the slightest inflections of the text with remarkable flexibility and did not hesitate to leave the voice unaccompanied at times (mm. 6–8 and 11–12 of 'Soupir'). In 'Éventail', the changes in tempo, reinforced by highly voluble piano writing, follow the whimsical movements of the animated object. As for 'Placet futile', Debussy suggested its eighteenth-century character by indicating 'Dans le mouvement d'un menuet lent', while avoiding outright pastiche. He used repeated rhythmic formulae (see, for example, mm. 1–2, 4–5, 7–9) mixed with highly ornamented passages (mm. 10–13), producing an exquisite miniature. Ninon Vallin premiered the *Trois poèmes de Stéphane Mallarmé* on 21 March 1914 at the Salle Gaveau accompanied by Debussy.

'Noël des enfants qui n'ont plus de maisons'

Debussy composed his last vocal work, the 'Noël des enfants qui n'ont plus de maisons', in early December 1915 in the midst of the First World War, prior to a surgical operation to relieve the physical suffering caused by his cancer. This occasional piece, for which he wrote the text, moves away from the realm of the *mélodie* and aims, above all, to denounce the horrors committed by the enemies of France. To this end, Debussy fashioned a discreet piano accompaniment, intended to emphasise the lyrics: 'Not a word must be lost of this text inspired by the rapacity of our enemies. This is my only way of waging war'.[41] He also wrote a two-part version for children's choir and piano, for which he had a marked preference: 'I dreamt of children's voices – women's voices immediately become deceptively dramatic. Or – what is worse: they sound like little girls!'[42] Published in December 1915, the 'Noël des enfants qui n'ont plus de maisons' was a great success, as the 9,000 copies printed by Durand during Debussy's lifetime attest. (By comparison, the print run during Debussy's lifetime of the *Trois ballades de François Villon* and the *Trois poèmes de Stéphane Mallarmé* amounted to only 800 copies.) Fully aware that the words appealed more than the music, he did not hesitate to write to Robert Godet:

At a matinée given in aid of the 'vêtement du prisonnier', I accompanied the *Noël des Enfants qui n'ont plus de maisons*. I had to give two encores ... This happened in a world of rich bourgeois with normally hard hearts! They were crying, dear friend, so much so that I wondered whether I should apologise to them! Should I thank the poet or the musician?[43]

Debussy accompanied the song in December 1916 for Jane Bathori, who he advised that it be 'sung as written, without any slurs or vocal effects', and accompanied Rose Féart on several occasions in March 1917.[44]

A Chimerical Quest

In a 1901 letter addressed to Paterne Berrichon, who had asked Debussy to set some poems by his brother-in-law Arthur Rimbaud, the composer made his thinking clear: 'I like [Rimbaud] far too much to have thought about encumbering him with the useless ornamentation of my music, no matter which of his texts it might be ... I would more easily see something inspired by Rimbaud'.[45] In a later letter of 29 November 1903, the composer wrote: 'If I had not forbidden myself to write songs, I would have been very happy to accept your permission to set several poems by the much-lamented Ch. De Sprimont. But at least I am able to enjoy the rare pleasure of possessing his works, thanks to your generosity'.[46] This assertion, no doubt dictated by a request he had hoped to avoid, would soon be rendered inaccurate by dint of the five song cycles that Debussy composed after 1903. Nevertheless, his aesthetic preference was for poets from the distant past (François Villon, Charles d'Orléans, Tristan L'Hermite) rather than his own time. His return to Verlaine in 1904 coincided with the burgeoning of his love for Emma Bardac, and it is conceivable that he was now inspired by the same sort of love he had experienced in his youth for Marie Vasnier, for whom he had also set Verlaine to music. Apart from the *Trois poèmes de Stéphane Mallarmé*, whose conception was associated with the publication of a new complete edition of the poet's work, Debussy began little by little to abandon the *mélodie*, which no longer matched his aspirations. His failure to complete *Nuits blanches* was no doubt due to his desire to find a new means by which to unite music and text. His aesthetic search led him instead to ponder works for the operatic stage, notably the two libretti after Edgar Allan Poe that never came to fruition but embodied his quest, however chimerical, for a perfect fusion of the universes of poetry and music.

Notes

1. The two *Nuits blanches* were published in 2000 by Durand, edited by Denis Herlin.
2. From the dates inscribed on the manuscripts.
3. For the chronology of this song, see David Grayson, '"Paysage sentimental": "Si doux, si triste, si dormant ... "', in *Debussy's Resonance*, ed. François de Médicis and Steven Huebner (Rochester: University of Rochester Press, 2018), 105–24.
4. Date on the title page of the autograph manuscript ('J. 91'), Paris, private collection.
5. Date on the sketch manuscript, now unlocated.
6. David Code, 'The "Song Triptych", Reflections on a Debussyan Genre', in *Debussy's Resonance*, ed. François de Médicis and Steven Huebner (Rochester: University of Rochester Press, 2018), 127.
7. Claude Debussy, *Correspondance (1872–1918)*, ed. François Lesure and Denis Herlin (Paris: Gallimard, 2005), 1133.
8. Code, 'The "Song Triptych"', 133.
9. Ibid., 166.
10. Théodore de Banville, *Petit traité de poésie française* (Paris: Charpentier, 1883), 247.
11. See Debussy, *Correspondance*, 68. Debussy entitled the fourth of his *Préludes* (Book 1), 'Les sons et les parfums tournent dans l'air du soir', a verse from 'Harmonie du soir'. In 1917, he named his final piano piece, *Les soirs illuminés par l'ardeur du charbon*, a verse from 'Le balcon'.
12. Paul Dukas, *Correspondance*, vol. 1, ed. Simon-Pierre Perret (Arles: Acte Sud/Palazzetto Bru Zane, 2018), 54–5.
13. See Denis Herlin, *Portraits et études* (Hildesheim: Georg Olms, 2021), 62–89.
14. Claude Debussy, *Monsieur Croche et autres écrits*, ed. François Lesure (Paris: Gallimard, 1987), 207.
15. Ibid.
16. Debussy, *Correspondance*, 221.
17. François Lesure, *Claude Debussy*, trans. and rev. Marie Rolf (Rochester: University of Rochester Press, 2019), 213.
18. Denis Herlin, *Portraits et études*, 135.
19. François de Médicis, *La maturation artistique de Debussy dans son contexte historique (1884–1902)* (Turnhout: Brepols, 2020), 352.
20. Debussy, *Correspondance*, 160.
21. David Code, *Claude Debussy* (London: Reaktion Books, 2010), 45.
22. Stephen Rumph, 'Debussy's *Trois chansons de Bilitis*: Song, Opera, and the Death of the Subject', *The Journal of Musicology*, 12, no. 4 (Autumn 1994), 489.
23. Code, 'The "Song Triptych"', 145–6.

24. Debussy, *Correspondance*, 611.
25. Herlin, *Portraits et études*, 62–78.
26. Debussy, *Correspondance*, 156.
27. Jean-Louis Leleu and Adrien Bruschini, '*Proses lyriques* de Debussy et *Serres chaudes* de Maeterlinck/Chausson, une mise en regard', in *Regards sur Debussy*, ed. Myriam Chimènes and Alexandra Laederich (Paris: Fayard, 2013), 175.
28. Katherine Bergeron, *Voice Lessons: French Mélodie in the Belle Époque* (New York: Oxford University Press, 2010), 170.
29. Debussy, *Correspondance*, 411.
30. François Le Roux and Romain Raynaldy, *Le chant intime* (Paris: Fayard, 2004), 125.
31. Charles Koechlin, 'La mélodie', in *Cinquante ans de musique française de 1874 à 1925*, ed. L. Rohozinski (Paris: Librairie de France, 1925), 36.
32. Ibid.
33. Debussy, *Correspondance*, 47.
34. Code, *Claude Debussy*, 172.
35. Jacques Durand, *Quelques souvenirs d'un éditeur de musique* (Paris: Durand, 1924), 124.
36. Code, *Claude Debussy*, 140.
37. Debussy, *Correspondance*, 1651.
38. See Maurice Ravel, *L'intégrale, Correspondance (1895–1937), écrits et entretiens*, ed. Manuel Cornejo (Paris: Le Passeur, 2018), 340–1.
39. See Paolo Dal Molin and Jean-Louis Leleu, *Les Trois Poèmes de Stéphane Mallarmé de Claude Debussy: Genèse et réception* (Lucca: Libreria musicale italiana, 2016), 57–102.
40. Ibid., viii.
41. Debussy's remark was reported by Henri Busser in *De Pelléas aux Indes galantes* ... (Paris: Fayard, 1955), 204. Busser added that Debussy refused to have *Noël* orchestrated.
42. Debussy, *Correspondance*, 2040.
43. Ibid., 2064.
44. Jane Bathori, *Sur l'interprétation des mélodies de Debussy* (Paris: Éditions ouvrières, 1953), 38.
45. Debussy, *Correspondance*, 588.
46. Unpublished letter to Pole Demade or Henry Carton de Wiart (Hôtel Drouot, 20–21 June 2019, no. 208).

11 | Ravel and His Contemporaries

EMILY KILPATRICK

In October 1897 the Parisian music critic Camille Bellaigue published a review article surveying various recent publications of French art song. Bellaigue lavished praise on the songs of Reynaldo Hahn: with the commendation, 'The disciple has gleaned from his master [Massenet] the secret of melodious murmuring', he singled out Hahn's Verlaine settings 'Offrande' and 'D'une prison' not just for their 'delicacy' and 'tenderness' but also for their masterful handling of vocal timbre and prosody.[1] Bellaigue's praise for Hahn came at the direct expense of Fauré, whose *La bonne chanson* he claimed to find 'horribly difficult'. 'At a certain point, ingeniousness becomes ignorance, refinement barbarity', he wrote, lamenting the 'sweetness' of the songs Fauré had composed a quarter of a century earlier.[2]

In that energetic wielding of the rear-view mirror, we may read a last-ditch effort to wrestle the *mélodie* back into a frame from which it was, with increasing determination, seeking to break free. By early in the new century *La bonne chanson* had been affirmed in multiple publications as the epitome of a new and distinctly French genre, a reimagining of the song cycle to rival Schubert and Schumann. In 1904 the critic Henry Fellot, surveying the repertory of contemporary 'Lieder français', remarked on a shift in the culture of song performance and lamented 'the last of the singing salons'.[3] In January 1907 Maurice Ravel's *Histoires naturelles* became the first *mélodies* to spark a veritable *scandale* at the Société nationale de musique, prompting lengthy review articles from almost all the leading critics and intellectuals. And in December of the same year Albert Roussel would write to the critic, poet, and impresario Jean-Aubry concerning a series of concerts organised to promote French music in Britain:

The fact that [Hahn's *mélodies*] are ubiquitous in the salons is not to their credit, though I must admit that Cortot finds the prosody of the *Études latines* remarkably good. But that is not sufficient to put Hahn on the same footing as Fauré or Chabrier, nor, above all, to turn that footing into a pedestal.[4]

In the space of a decade, art song had asserted a new place in French musical life: as a genre that could exploit the accomplished musicianship of professional and specialist performers, compel a measure of critical attention, and bolster a public profile. For decades the domain of the salon and the amateur, the *mélodie* was at last, and decisively, making its way onto the public stage.

Hahn, Koechlin, and the Rondel

Hahn's 'ubiquity' in the Parisian salons was established remarkably early. When *Le Figaro*, on 16 July 1890, hailed the advent of 'a delicate and original musician', he was not yet sixteen years old. A year later (1 July 1891), Hahn's 'Mai', 'Rêverie', and 'Si mes vers avaient des ailes' headed the list of songs recommended by the fashion magazine *La mode de style* for summer consumption ('evenings are long in the countryside!'). In 1893 Massenet arranged for the famous soprano Sybil Sanderson to give the premiere of his pupil's seven *Chansons grises*, and two years later his own publisher Heugel issued Hahn's first, immensely popular collection of twenty songs.

While in 1897 Bellaigue saw Massenet's imprint in the declamatory ease and intimacy of Hahn's *mélodies*, the very restraint of these early songs often marks a deliberate and daring contrast with the older composer. In 'Chant d'automne' (*Chansons grises*), for example, Hahn allows each line of Verlaine's short text to take on the same melodic shape, the sparse accompaniment barely expanding beyond three-voice textures and mostly contenting itself with a brief repeated piano figure that echoes the vocal phrase. The effect is to illuminate, with quiet immediacy, the key word 'monotone' (heard at the end of the first strophe), which serves as both synonym and sonorous mirror of the titular 'automne'. 'Offrande' is remarkable for its determined avoidance of harmonic resolution. It plays unrelentingly on a non-functional oscillation between second-inversion dominant-seventh and decorated diminished-seventh harmonies, and although the dominant is allowed briefly to resolve at the end of each strophe, Hahn reinstates it in the postlude, closing the song in the tonal limbo of the beginning. The piano part of the perennially beloved 'L'heure exquise' (*Chansons grises*) likewise circles around a single gesture, this time a languorous arpeggio; the key verb 'Rêvons' ('Let us dream') invites the vocal line to blossom from 'melodious murmuring' into the floated high phrases that conclude each strophe.

By the turn of the century, however – and notwithstanding Roussel's later reservations – a shift of compositional intent is discernible in Hahn's *mélodies*. Turning from the expressive lyricism of Verlaine, he became increasingly concerned with poetry that externalised its formal structures: the Parnassian clarity of Leconte de Lisle, the precision and wit of Théodore de Banville. In that changing focus we may read a deliberate move away from the salon toward a more experimental and rigorous frame.

In 1899 Hahn published a volume of twelve *Rondels* (nine for solo voice and three for mixed chorus), which juxtapose settings of Banville and Catulle Mendès with the most famous exponent of the rondel, Charles d'Orléans (1394–1465). A thirteen-line form built on two rhyme-sounds, the rondel comprises two quatrains, a quintain, and a clever metrical ploy: lines 1 and 2 are reprised as 7 and 8, then line 1 is repeated once more as the closing 13th. The refrain, appearing first as an antecedent, must thus return as a consequent phrase within the second quatrain, and then again as an effective coda.

These formal imperatives demand equivalent sophistication of musical structure and prosody. In Hahn's 'L'air', for example, the refrain ('Dans l'air s'en vont les ailes') is first heard beginning on the downbeat ('*Dans* l'air . . .');

while the second iteration begins the almost-identical rhythm from the quaver upbeat ('Dans *l'air* . . .').

The last line then augments the note values, reconfiguring the stresses a third time.

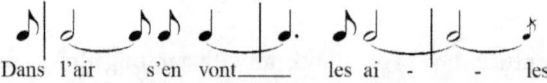

In the succeeding 'La Paix', not only do the three iterations of the refrain 'La Paix, au milieu des moissons' place the key word 'Paix' by turn on the first, second and fourth beats of the bar, Hahn underscores the declamatory play by setting the entire song on a single, repeated pitch (A_4).

Hahn prefaced his *Rondels* with an address to Louis Landry (*chef de chant* at the Opéra-Comique), set out in a mock-antique typeface that explicitly aligns the collection with the pre-Revolutionary classicism of the poetic form:

We have sometimes discussed declamation and musical prosody together; thus, I determined, in this little volume, to resolve a most subtle problem: I have attempted to demonstrate the mysterious relationships that exist between the natural inflections of the voice and harmony. For this, I chose the *rondel* – that is, a poem *in fixed form*, in which spoken recitation submits to certain rules, required and dictated by hearing and by instinct.

This emphasis on the strictness of his chosen poetry (and thus his songs) suggests that both the *Rondels* and the subsequent *Études latines* represent some deliberate 'rebranding', a shift from the lusciousness of the salon idiom to something more sculpted and intellectual.

Hahn's fascination with the rondel form was shared by his Conservatoire classmate Charles Koechlin, who devoted three opus groups (Opp. 1, 8, and 14) to Banville's *Rondels* (a collection of twenty-four poems published in 1875). Koechlin was later to reflect, in terms that echo Hahn's, that in these early songs, composed between 1890 and 1899, he 'sought, above all, the most faithful alliance of words and music, combined with a clear and precise form like that of the poetry – to which the music dared to add itself'.[5] Robert Orledge claims a purpose for Koechlin's *Rondels* that likewise draws near to Hahn's, observing a progression 'away from the salon towards his own original world' in the Op. 14 set in particular.[6] These last, more extended and symphonic songs, which Koechlin orchestrated in 1901, explore an increasingly varied harmonic and textural palette, from the densely Wagnerian 'Les métaux' (whose closing bars fleetingly but explicitly cite the 'anvil' leitmotif of *Das Rheingold*) to the simple clarity of Greek modes in the pantheistic 'La terre', via the distinctly *debussyste* 'L'eau', upon which Koechlin admitted the influence of 'De grève' (*Proses lyriques*).[7]

Curiously, Koechlin's rondels, like Hahn's, juxtapose solo and ensemble settings: the last four of the Op. 14 songs include optional female chorus. Hahn, like Koechlin, explored antique modalities, subtitling his 'Gardez le trait de la fenêtre' (a Charles d'Orléans setting) 'mode hypodorien'. Koechlin's Op. 8 *Rondels* even include one song, 'L'hiver', that pursues near-monotonal vocal lines (the first two quatrains lie almost entirely on E_4), with the refrain set to identical rhythms on each occurrence but beginning by turn from the first and third beats of the bar. Though no traced documentation shows a deliberate coordination, the dedication of Koechlin's 'Le midi' (Op. 14 no. 2) to Hahn suggests at least a quiet acknowledgement of the literary interests and musical preoccupations shared by these two very different composers.

Ravel's Early Songs

From his earliest songs Ravel, too, was testing the increasingly porous ground between poetry and song. A brief survey of his chosen poets lays bare the idiosyncrasies of Ravel's literary tastes, which range from Renaissance poets (Clément Marot, Pierre de Ronsard) to his close friends (Tristan Klingsor, Léon-Paul Fargue), via Symbolists (Émile Verhaeren, Henri de Régnier, Stéphane Mallarmé) and a brief early dabble with the Parnassians (the 1898 Leconte de Lisle setting 'Chanson du rouet'). Ravel appeared uninterested in Paul Bourget, Théodore de Banville, Armand Silvestre, and Victor Hugo; although he revered Charles Baudelaire, he never set him; and the brightest stars of the new century (Guillaume Apollinaire, Paul Valéry) did not tempt him. On the other hand, he was the first major composer to publish a Mallarmé setting and the only one to set Jules Renard; and at a time when Paris was flooded with *mélodies* on the more lyrical passages from Verlaine's *Fêtes galantes*, he was almost alone in selecting just the biting and brusque 'Sur l'herbe'. Ravel's earliest songs tellingly demonstrate the young composer's focussed explorations of musical and poetic structure, and the possibilities of their combination. The first of his *Deux épigrammes de Clément Marot*, 'D'Anne jouant de l'espinette', of December 1896, reimagines 'antique' sonorities in ways not dissimilar to Koechlin (whom he joined in Fauré's Conservatoire composition class in January 1898). If Koechlin's 'Le midi' evokes harpsichord textures and Rameau-like counterpoint (spiced with some naughtily unprepared dissonances), Ravel went so far as to designate the keyboard part of 'D'Anne jouant de l'espinette' for 'Clavecin ou piano'. The companion setting, 'D'Anne qui me jecta de la neige', dates from 1899. In his important *Petit traité de poésie française* (1872), Banville had singled out this poem as his exemplar for the poetic form of the ten-line *dizain*, observing that 'all the artifice and the glory of the poet lies in binding the strophe together precisely where it threatens to break in two, between the fifth and sixth lines'.[8] Here Marot propels us powerfully across that gap, with a breathless play of enjambment and assonance that is abruptly stalled by the question mark halfway through the seventh line:

Anne par jeu me jecta de la neige
Que je cuidoys froide, certainement:
Mais c'estoit feu, l'expérience en ay je,
Car embrasé, je fuz soubdainement.
Puis que le feu loge secretement
Dedans la neige, où trouveray je place
Pour n'ardre point? Anne, ta seule grace
Estaindre peult le feu que je sens bien
Non point par eau, par neige ne par glace
Mais par sentir ung feu pareil au mien.

Anne, in jest, threw snow at me
Which I certainly believed to be cold:
But what I felt was fire,
For I was suddenly set aflame
As fire lodges secretly
In the snow, where shall I find a place
Where I shall not burn? Anne, only your mercy
Can extinguish the fire that I truly feel,
Not by water, by snow or by ice,
But by feeling a fire that matches my own.

Ravel responded to the symmetry of Marot's *dizain* with an equivalent formal articulation, marking the poetic midpoint after m. 8 of his sixteen-bar song. As in the poem, however, there is some structural subtlety, for the changes of metre place the exact halfway mark of the song, counted by beats, at the *beginning* of m. 8 – just as the phrase first introduced in a more unstable, chromatic form at m. 6 regains the modal colouration of the opening. That phrase, cast first in chromatic then in diatonic guise, also represents the apex of the song's arch-form, which configures the motivic material as $(1 + 4) + 5 + (5 + 1)$ bars: in m. 11 the poet's question is answered with a restatement of the material of m. 2, accompanying the first iteration of Anne's name; the one-bar piano prelude returns as the postlude. If the five-bar divisions perhaps sketch a response to the 5 + 5-line form of the decasyllabic *dizain*, the slim musical arch also answers mirrored elements in Marot's poetic structure – the symmetry of the rhyme scheme (*ababbccdcd*), the echoing of the word 'par' across the first and last lines, and the plays of assonance that link the opening 'jeu'/'jecta' with the closing 'par'/'pareil'.

A poetic enjambment of equivalent structural and thematic significance characterises Mallarmé's 'Sainte', which Ravel set within weeks of 'D'Anne jouant de l'espinette'. The poem unfolds as a single long sentence, in which the first two quatrains each conjure a single image (the tarnished viol, the old book), but the third and fourth (reproduced below) are bound together through their sinuous evocation of the vivifying angel. The last line of the third quatrain is completed by the first line of the fourth: 'la délicate phalange // Du doigt ... ' In Heath Lees' reading, that delicate axis of the saint's fingertip symbolises the creation of a new, post-Wagnerian art, poetry (book) and music (viol) 'symbolically fused into one' across the artificial divide of the stanza break.[9] Poetic meaning is thus realised in the articulation of poetic structure:

À ce vitrage d'ostensoir
Que frôle une harpe par l'Ange
Formée avec son vol du soir
Pour la délicate phalange

Du doigt, que, sans le vieux santal
Ni le vieux livre, elle balance
Sur le plumage instrumental,
Musicienne du silence.

At this monstrance window
Brushed by a harp the Angel
Formed with her evening flight
For the delicate phalanx

Of the finger, that, without the old sandalwood
Without the old book, she balances
On the instrumental plumage,
Musician of silence.[10]

Ravel's emulation of Mallarmé's formal tension is meticulous. The poem unfolds above a regular 4/4 tread of Satie-like seventh and ninth chords, each quatrain offset with a single bar of 1/4. From the poetic midpoint (m. 16), a piano countermelody emerges to float above the voice, its two- and four-beat phrases cutting across the bar lines as the increasing plasticity of the poetry finds an answer in a more fluid play of vocal rhythm. The enjambment is carried in a single phrase, the break falling in a bar of 1/4 above the piano's bare bass crotchet (see Example 11.1). That single beat, with its abrupt modal shift, retrospectively illuminates the structural purpose of the earlier 1/4 bars, capturing the paradoxical melding and disjunction of the poem's pivotal phrase.

Example 11.1. Maurice Ravel, 'Sainte', mm. 20–24

In these early songs, then, we see Ravel responding to some of the same concerns that were motivating Koechlin and Hahn, especially in the integration of musical and poetic form. All three composers, too, were concurrently experimenting with allowing poetic declamation to shape or override melodic imperatives: Ravel's own experiment in vocal monotony, in the penultimate strophe of the bleak and unyielding Verhaeren setting 'Si morne!' (1898), is exactly contemporaneous with his colleagues' *Rondels*.

Shéhérazade and the Imagined Orient

In 1900, Ravel's friend Tristan Klingsor (Léon Leclère) published a long essay in *Le mercure de France* titled 'Les musiciens et les poètes contemporains'. He reflected there on some of the same concerns discussed above – structure, assonance, and the integration of musical and poetic form – while acknowledging the emergence into the public domain of what he saw as an essentially new musical imperative, reshaping both the composition and the performance of song:

> This *rapprochement* of true poetry and music is happening more and more: composers ... seek to penetrate the most intimate meaning of the poem, to complete it with the materials that best suit it; and it is precisely this quality, this fusion of the two arts, that is renewing singing, and which will be the defining feature of the modern *lied français*.[11]

Decades later Klingsor was to write that when Ravel came to set three poems from his collection *Shéhérazade* he 'took care to have me recite them out loud to him' before he began composing.[12] But Ravel's orchestral triptych *Shéhérazade* (1903) does not seek its 'fusion' in the overt alignment of song with spoken language, although it audibly responds to the expressive gestural and rhythmic patterns of its poetry. Instead, in *Shéhérazade* we find Ravel 'completing' Klingsor's exotic and sometimes erotic portraits with 'materials' that respond to the poetic narrative of wonders imagined and recounted.

The official premiere of Ravel's *Shéhérazade* came in 1904, but Roger Nichols notes that a first, private hearing of the songs might have been given late in 1903 at a gathering of the group of friends and artists known as the 'Apaches', with whom Ravel was closely associated from 1902, and which often met at Klingsor's house. The orchestral works of Balakirev, Rimsky-Korsakov, Borodin, and Musorgsky were particularly beloved and much played (in piano reduction) among the 'Apaches', and this 'taster' performance of *Shéhérazade* apparently saw the songs paired with Glazunov's *Fantaisie orientale*.[13] Though Ravel did not set it, he surely responded to another poem in Klingsor's collection, 'Les Djinns': 'All the djinns of the Orient are hidden, they say, / O Rimsky-Korsakov, in the instruments / That you conjure with a wave of your baton'.

Notwithstanding his friendship with Klingsor, the immediacy of Ravel's response to this poetry (which was likewise published in 1903) is perhaps surprising. He had already attempted one *Shéhérazade*, the 'ouverture de féerie' of 1898 that had been a major early failure, harshly criticised and rapidly withdrawn: the critic Henry Gauthier-Villars had described it as 'Rimsky fiddled with by a *debussyste*'.[14] But Klingsor's *Shéhérazade* offered a liberating twist, in its vision of an Orient that is imagined but never grasped: 'Asie' presents a series of pictures the poet would *like* to see, that he dreams not so much of experiencing as *retelling*. It was doubtless that poetic distance, with its touch of knowing irony, which allowed Ravel to revisit this tale-of-tales, the echoes of Rimsky now fainter and better assimilated into an increasingly individual command of musical architecture and orchestration.

This sinuous refraction of the real and the imagined is conjured in the tonal opposition of E♭ and D that anchors 'Asie', particularly the song's first thirty bars (to Fig. 5) and the equivalent final thirty (from Fig. 15^{-1}). At Figure 2 (which Peter Kaminsky terms 'the start of the song proper', the first ten bars serving as introduction[15]) the singer's D effectively splits to the pitches E♭ and D♭, in the E♭ minor-seventh harmony that underpins the first part of the catalogue of marvels; both pitches are maintained until Figure 5, notwithstanding the enharmonic shift at Figure 4. That harmonic foundation is regained at the song's climax (Fig. 15). At Figure 16, E♭ and D♭ coalesce back onto D, a pitch taken up in turn by the voice for the final line of text ('And then, later to return and retell my adventures to those intrigued by dreams ...'): as the lush textures contract to that sparse pedal note, the artful narration is left as the only 'real' experience. The postlude sees the D rediffused to E♭ and D♭, the textures of Figure 2 reprised to close the song in the dreamlike atmosphere of the opening.

Curiously, Charles Koechlin would recall that opening explicitly when he set Klingsor's *Shéhérazade* in his turn, almost twenty years later. In the early years of the First World War, Koechlin had set five of Klingsor's poems, which he published as his Op. 56; a larger group of eight followed in 1922–3, as Op. 84. The second song of this latter set, 'Le voyage', begins by citing 'Asie' so directly as to appear as if in quotation marks (see Example 11.2a–b). Like 'Asie', it then moves into a rolling triplet figure offset with semiquaver accents (see Example 11.2c; compare Ravel's Fig. 4^{-2} and Fig. 6).

There is an additional homage implicit in Koechlin's song, for Klingsor's 'Le voyage' is an explicit riposte to Charles Baudelaire's 'L'invitation au voyage' (and 'Le voyage', the long peroration that closes the 1861 *Les fleurs du mal*). 'Mais non, mieux vaut rester ici' ('But no, better off staying here'), Klingsor's poem begins, firmly refusing Baudelaire's proffered 'invitation'; it ends with the admission, 'For the fantasy is finer than reality / For the finest lands are those that one knows not, / And the finest voyage is one made in dream.' In Koechlin's setting that poignant conclusion mounts over quiet chords that move inexorably outward, their dissolution in the furthest registers of the keyboard capturing the fading not just of Klingsor's Orient but also of Baudelaire's isle of dreams.

Roussel's Harmonic Games

Against these depictions of an imagined East, Albert Roussel's three pairs of *Poèmes chinois* offer a fascinating counterpart, reflecting both his more tangible encounters with the 'exotic' and the progressive sharpening of his

Example 11.2. Charles Koechlin's homage to Ravel's *Shéhérazade*

a) Ravel, 'Asie' (*Shéhérazade*), mm. 1–2

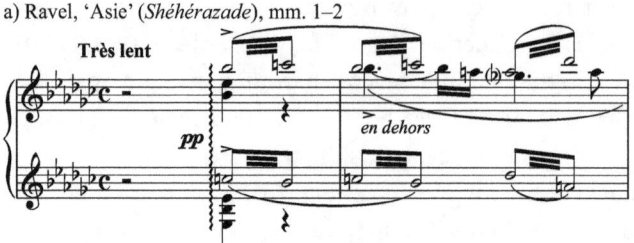

b) Charles Koechlin, 'Le voyage' (*Shéhérazade*, Op. 84, no. 2), mm. 1–2

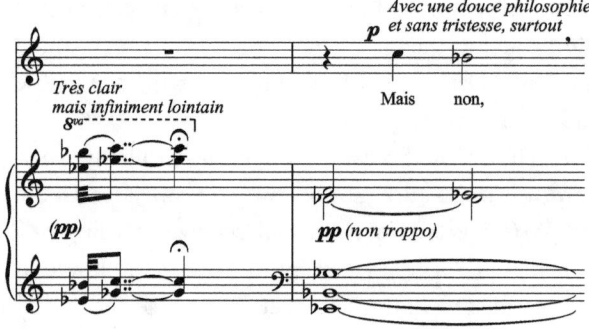

c) Koechlin, 'Le voyage', m. (4)

harmonic idiom. Roussel's lifelong fascination with the musics and cultures of South and East Asia was prompted by his voyages there in the 1890s as a young naval midshipman. His *Poèmes chinois*, which date respectively from 1907–8, 1927, and 1934 (Opp. 12, 35, and 47), set twice-translated poetry, ancient Chinese texts rendered into French via English by Henri-Pierre Roché. The first (Op. 12) pair plays with pentatony and bell-like textures in somewhat predictable ways, though their juxtaposition of black- and white-key pentatonic collections lends a characteristic harmonic spice. When he returned to the same poetry in 1927, Roussel employed similar textures but compressed his tonal strategy: rather than juxtaposing, 'Des fleurs font une broderie' (Op. 35 no. 1) *superimposes* white upon black keys. 'Vois, de belles filles' (Op. 47 no. 2) offers a final turn of the harmonic kaleidoscope, its black- and white-key oppositions now more abstracted and angular, in a setting that breathes a fleeting hint of jazz.

Roussel's distinctive harmonic language, and his taste for chromatic juxtapositions and superimpositions, is evident from his earliest works. The first harmony of his first published song, 'Le départ' (opening his Op. 3 Henri de Régnier settings of 1903), is strikingly dissonant, setting one major seventh ($D_2/C_3\sharp$) in the pianist's left hand against another (F_3/E_4) in the right. (Despite its biting aural effect, that sonority is most simply understood as a superimposition of the dominant triad upon the tonic.) In 'Le jardin mouillé' (Op. 3 no. 3), by contrast, destabilising chromatic threads are woven through an otherwise diatonic context. Opening in a shimmer of mingled tonic (C minor) and subdominant (F minor) harmony, at the vocal entry in m. 5, the texture is threaded with fleeting E♮s and B♮s: shorn of their leading-note function, those pitches become the spring for the chromatic middle section, which pulls towards E major. The closing strophe offers a further harmonic refraction, dropping into E major for a single bar before easing back into E♭ and thence to C minor (see Example 11.3). That multi-faceted chromaticism, from the tingle of single dissonant pitches to the structural opposition of tonalities, and their concentrated recapitulation, typifies Roussel's prismatic harmonic lens.

Rediscovering the *chanson populaire*

Meanwhile, on the heels of *Shéhérazade* Ravel had turned his attention to the music of a real and much closer East: the folksongs that would become his *Cinq mélodies populaires grecques*. The eventual third and fourth of these five songs were the first to be realised, in February 1904, for a lecture-recital on 'The songs of oppressed [Greek and Armenian] peoples'. Three further accompaniments written for that occasion are now lost, Ravel having apparently considered them too slight to retain.[16] Two years later, he composed three new arrangements for another lecture, this time on Greek popular song, given by his friend Michel-Dmitri Calvocoressi on 28 April 1906.

The accompaniments of all five of the final *Cinq mélodies populaires grecques* are anchored by pedal fifths that set in relief the modal colours of the vocal lines. Within that self-imposed gestural limitation, however, Ravel's

Example 11.3. Albert Roussel, 'Le jardin mouillé' (*Quatre poèmes de Régnier*, Op. 3), mm. 46–50

textures are markedly more interesting and pianistically challenging than most other contemporaneous folksong settings, in their variety (there are five textural shifts in the forty-five seconds of 'Quel galant m'est comparable' alone) and characteristic harmonic colourations. The latter part of 'Chansons des cueilleuses de lentisques', for example, progressively stacks fifth upon fifth, mounting from the bass tonic A_2 to $D\sharp_5$ – a progression that would return, lavishly extended, to open *Daphnis et Chloé* (1912). Equally noteworthy is the sounding A♭ dominant-seventh chord (enharmonically spelt as a German augmented sixth with $F\sharp_4$ rather than $G\flat_4$) superimposed on the pedal tonic G in mm. 13 and 17 (and similar) of 'Chanson de la mariée'.

This distinctive Phrygian gesture would return in a similar textural guise for another serenade, the entrance of the poet Gonzalve in Ravel's opera *L'heure espagnole*. It also dominates the last page of his 'Vocalise-étude en forme de habanera', composed as he was working on that opera in the spring of 1907. This attractive study was written for what became a long-running series of *Vocalise-Etudes*, compiled by Amédée-Louis Hettich under the auspices of Gabriel Fauré at the Paris Conservatoire. Alongside Ravel's vocalise, the second volume of this series also features Hahn's luscious 'Souvenirs de Constantinople', and two other offerings claiming to represent or reimagine 'authentic' folk materials: Pierre de Bréville's 'Maneh' (depicting the calls of boatmen on the Bosphorous) and Raoul Laparra's Basque-inspired 'Chanson des cyclades'. All these works reflect something of the newly internationalist outlook that shaped the *mélodie* in the decade or so preceding the First World War. As song came to command a place on the concert platform, composers – and historians and ethnomusicologists, too – became increasingly concerned with the elevation of folksong. Concert artists frequently programmed newly harmonised French and other folksongs, and in 1910 the Moscow-based Maison du lied organised a folksong-setting competition, in which Ravel carried off prizes in four categories. His Italian, French, Spanish, and 'Hebrew' songs were published collectively by Durand in 1925 as *Chants populaires*. Another pair of *Mélodies hébraïques* followed in 1914, settings of the sacred 'Kaddisch' and the folksong 'L'énigme éternelle'.

Pushing the Boundaries: *Histoires naturelles*

Ravel's close friend Hélène Jourdan-Morhange wryly observed that the texts he chose often seemed 'unsuited to being clothed with music'[17]: he plainly found an almost tactile satisfaction in the spikier contours of a language he would himself describe as 'not designed for poetry'.[18] His correspondence evinces his delight in comically, even childishly, repeated or juggled word-sounds: 'Kécèkécèkécèlà ?' (*Qu'est-ce que c'est que ça?*; What's that?), 'Ttan' (*ta tante*; your aunt), 'Douadouard' (for his brother Edouard). But Ravel's letters also reveal a gift for more lyrical plays of rhythm and assonance: early in 1906, for example, he wrote to a cousin of 'belles journées de gelée, qui font les forêts si féeriques' ('Beautiful frozen days, which make the forests so magical').[19] The evocative rhythms and alliteration there echo Ravel's first attempt at setting his own poetry in the song 'Noël des jouets' of 1905, with its delightful onomatopoeia of bleating sheep ('Dont la voix grêle bêle: / "Noël!"') and glittering Christmas-tree angels ('Qui cliquette en bruits symétriques' ['Jingling in symmetrical sounds']). 'Ravel knew how to see and to release the essential', reflected René Dumesnil in 1938, 'and to express it he always found the right word, not only by its precise meaning, but still more by its sonority'.[20]

It is hardly surprising that the poet of 'Noël des jouets' was attracted to the peculiarly expressive manipulation of metre and assonance in Jules Renard's *Histoires naturelles*, to which he turned in the autumn of 1906. In a 1911 reflection on text-setting, Ravel would describe Renard's prose-poetry as 'delicate, rhythmic, though rhythmic in a completely different way from classical verse'.[21] Often that rhythm is to be found at the level of paragraph rather than line or phrase. The plunge from heady metaphor to prosaic reality at the end of 'Le cygne', for example, is conveyed in the shift from long, ornate sentences to the near-monosyllabic closing phrases, which Ravel matches in the abrupt abandonment of the rippling piano textures for the brusque final chords:

Il s'épuise à pêcher de vains reflets, et peut-être qu'il mourra, victime de cette illusion, avant d'attraper un seul morceau de nuage.
Mais qu'est-ce que je dis?
Chaque fois qu'il plonge, il fouille du bec la vase nourrissante et ramène un ver.
Il engraisse comme une oie.

He exhausts himself in fishing for these empty reflections, and perhaps he will die, victim of this illusion, before having captured a single morsel of cloud.
But what am I saying?
Each time he dives, he digs with his beak into the nourishing mud and returns with a worm.
He is growing as fat as a goose.

Elsewhere, Renard deploys plays of assonance whose very articulation manifests their meaning. In the climactic line of 'Le martin-pêcheur' – 'Je ne respirais plus, tout fier d'être pris pour un arbre par un martin-pêcheur' ('I held my breath, so proud was I to be taken for a tree by a kingfisher') – the repeated 'r' sounds hold up the flow of text, literally compelling the performer to match the narrator's breathless tread. Ravel casts this as the most understated of musical climaxes, the *subitement ppp* in m. 15 curtailing the hesitant lyricism of the preceding phrase. Only later do we recognise it as such: in m. 18 the harmonic rhythm slackens; the narrator relaxes; the bird has flown.

The raucous reception accorded to *Histoires naturelles* at its January 1907 premiere was initially sparked by the perceived banality of the poetry itself: the singer Jane Bathori recalled that it was the first line of 'Le martin-pêcheur' – 'Ça n'a pas mordu, ce soir' ('Not a bite, this evening') – that prompted a veritable 'revolt'.[22] Equally radical was Ravel's setting of his texts, which prioritised the natural inflections of spoken language above the conventions of sung declamation: most strikingly, the songs elide or apocopate the mute 'e' (the schwa), which is traditionally articulated when sung. The press reaction was vociferous: was Ravel, critics wondered, trying to upend – or worse, mock – the tenets of art song performance and composition? Or were *Histoires naturelles* merely incompetent? But Ravel knew precisely what he was doing. Compositionally, the songs served (as he later acknowledged) as 'études' for *L'heure espagnole*; professionally, their much-debated premiere marked another decisive step towards the centre of French musical conversation. That Ravel achieved this through the medium of song is a remarkable testament to both the musical importance of *Histoires naturelles* and the increasing recognition of the *mélodie* as a genre of serious compositional endeavour.

In the spring of 1907, Ravel reshaped the naturalistic storytelling voice of *Histoires naturelles* into the mordant dialogue of 'Sur l'herbe'. Introducing the song in a letter to Jean-Aubry, he noted, 'as in *Histoires naturelles*, one must give the impression that one is almost not singing'.[23] Ravel was then putting the finishing touches to *L'heure espagnole*, in which a prefatory note explicitly instructs performers to 'speak, not sing' ('*dire*, plutôt que *chanter*'). But there is subtlety, and not a little irony, in Ravel's art of 'not singing'. Not for nothing did he select one of the only two poems in Verlaine's *Fêtes galantes* to incorporate musical notes (*solfège*). Conscientiously setting the words 'do, mi, sol, la, si' to the appropriate pitches, he underlines them with *tenuto* dashes that draw attention to a mockingly literal 'fusion' of text and music, as sung by an inebriated *abbé*. 'Look,' he says to the critics shocked by his *Histoires*, 'is *this* what you wanted?'

Trois poèmes de Stéphane Mallarmé and *Clairières dans le ciel*

Avant-garde experimentation in song arguably reached a pre-war peak in Ravel's *Trois poèmes de Stéphane Mallarmé*, composed in the spring and summer of 1913. On 2 April he wrote to the board of the Société musicale indépendante (founded in 1910 as a counterpart to the increasingly conservative Société nationale de musique), outlining a 'stupendous proposal for a scandalous concert'. The first two items on the programme – Schoenberg's *Pierrot lunaire* and Stravinsky's *Three Japanese Lyrics* – would 'make the audience howl', he wrote, but the last 'would send them out whistling tunes': '2 poésies de S. Mallarmé: Maurice Ravel'.[24] Two poems soon became three, and the 'concert scandaleux' took place on 14 January 1914, Ravel's songs programmed alongside Stravinsky's *Japanese Lyrics* and Maurice Delage's *Trois poèmes hindous*. (*Pierrot lunaire*, whose conception and ensemble had offered a prompt for all three composers, was not heard in Paris until 1922.)

Although Ravel's Mallarmé *Poèmes* represent some of his most abstruse harmonic language, they bear little resemblance to Schoenberg. Instead, every kind of musical process – form, timbre, texture, harmony, pitch – is brought to bear on the chiselled symbolism of Mallarmé's words. The third of his chosen poems, for example, 'Surgi de la croupe et du bond', depicts the ornate form of an empty vase, which holds neither water nor the flower towards which it aspires. Mallarmé sets that barrenness in stark relief by the richness and variety of allusion and metaphor with which he fills the imagined vase, its rigid poise traced through the formal contours of the sonnet, its promise evoked through the imagery of meeting lips and the final evocation of the rose, an ancient symbol of fulfilment and perfection.

The oft-observed 'still life' quality of the poem perhaps prompted Ravel's luminescent play of instrumental colour: 'Surgi de la croupe et du bond' is undoubtedly the most 'painterly' of his *Trois poèmes*.[25] He employs bass clarinet in this song alone (to striking effect in the closing bars), and makes the most extensive use of the piccolo, while relegating the strings to an almost exclusively colouristic role: indicated *sourdine* throughout, their lines mostly comprise *tremolandi*, harmonics, and sustained chords. The tonal plan equally suggests an element of visual thinking: the song is underpinned by the tritone opposition C/F♯, representing an exact division of the octave, and respectively the 'emptiest' and 'fullest' key signatures. Thus, the opening pedal C gives way to F♯ (via C♯) in m. 8, as the verb 's'interrompt' marks the end of the first poetic quatrain and the transition to the middle section; in the final bar of the song, the piano returns to the bass C as the voice sings the key word 'rose' on F♯$_4$. For the space of one quaver beat we hear the tritone – emptiness and plenitude – unadorned.

Perhaps most intriguingly, the symmetrical outlines of Mallarmé's vase also find equivalence in Ravel's manipulation of form and line. 'Surgi de la croupe' is the only one of his *Trois poèmes* to be cast in a loose ternary form. That basic architectural mirroring is reinforced through the very appearance of the score: the upward arabesques and sinuous melodic lines of the outer sections vividly suggest the leaping form of the vase. The corresponding blankness in the staves of the central passage, in which bell-like piano chimes resonate in near silence (the strings sound *pianissimo* chords in harmonics), contrasts with that more linear movement, the score both visually and aurally evocative of the empty belly of the vase. In a 1924 interview Ravel was to assert that in his *Trois poèmes* he had 'transposed the literary procedures of Mallarmé'.[26] We might usefully appropriate Alain Badiou's succinct appraisal of those procedures to describe Ravel's songs: 'what the poem says,' Badiou observes, 'it does'.[27]

One final work from the pre-war period may be viewed as a quiet but decisive culmination of two decades of probing compositional exploration, and an equally sophisticated – but entirely different – response to both musical and poetic Symbolism. If Fauré's *La bonne chanson* became a fulcrum for critical narratives of French art song at the dawn of the century, we might find that cycle's bookend in Lili Boulanger's *Clairières dans le ciel* (1914). Boulanger's first song ('Elle est descendue') is dedicated to Fauré and opens with some recognisably Fauréen textures and harmonic signatures, while the last song recapitulates thematic ideas from across the cycle, as Annegret Fauser observes, in the manner of *La bonne chanson*.[28]

Boulanger drew her thirteen poems from Francis Jammes' twenty-four-poem cycle *Tristesses* (which was published as part of his collection *Clairières dans le ciel* in 1906; Boulanger transferred that title to her cycle with the poet's permission). Nadia Boulanger asserted that her sister felt an intense affinity with the unnamed 'Elle' of Jammes' poetry, not least because the first letter of her name is pronounced *elle*.[29] What Nadia termed a 'fusion' is realised in Lili's cryptographic structures through the cycle: as Bonnie Jo Dopp has explored, the composer's well-documented self-identification with the number thirteen (likely springing from the number of letters in her name) underpins many of her structural choices and musical processes.[30] Thus, the central song – the lucky seventh – sets the thirteenth poem of Jammes' suite, 'Nous nous aimerons tant'; its first two pages each comprise a musical paragraph of thirteen bars; the central passage – the midpoint of the whole cycle – is suffused with thirteenth chords (see Example 11.4).

Boulanger's responsiveness to the language of musical Symbolism is most audible in the casting of certain half-diminished sonorities as unmistakable 'Tristan' chords, echoing Jammes' title *Tristesses*: in the third song, for example, that harmony is woven around the end of the opening phrase, 'Parfois, je suis *triste*'. (There is a nod here to Debussy's *Pelléas et Mélisande*, a work Boulanger revered: at the conclusion of the Act 4, Scene 4 love duet, Mélisande's admission 'Je suis triste ...' is similarly underscored with a 'Tristan' chord.) The sixth song, 'Si tout ceci n'est qu'un pauvre rêve', offers the most explicit response to *Tristan und Isolde*, the chromatically ascending gesture of Wagner's Prelude transformed into a thirteen-times-repeated ostinato.

For the listener, however, perhaps more striking is the gradual emergence of a three-note melodic cell across the latter part of the cycle, comprising a falling second and a rising fourth. That tiny gesture is first heard in its clearest motivic form across that midpoint of the seventh song (see Example 11.4, mm. 25–6). It is strongly present in the ninth, tenth, and eleventh songs, making more fleeting appearances in the shorter eighth and twelfth.[31] In the summative 'Demain fera un an', the motif is woven

Example 11.4. Lili Boulanger, 'Nous nous aimerons tant' (*Clairières dans le ciel*), mm. 17–26

through the texture in various guises before bursting through obsessively from m. 86, its three pitches (E-D-G) there sitting above a bass B♭ that completes another half-diminished chord.

Although it takes decisive shape only midway through the cycle, that motivic cell is fleetingly discernible much earlier on: it occurs in mm. 11–12 of the second song, 'Elle est gravement gaie' (highlighted with a tiny crescendo), in m. 2 of the third (on the same E-D-G that dominates the last song), and m. 6 of the fourth, 'Un poète disait'; a compressed, chromatic iteration of the same motif is buried midway through 'Si tout ceci' (from m. 21). The cumulative impact is remarkable: when the motif emerges more characteristically in 'Nous nous aimerons tant' it already seems familiar; in the final song it binds together Boulanger's sweeping musical narrative in a desperate, compulsive lament.

Post-War: Reflection and Restraint

Despite their extraordinary diversity, in the *mélodies* of the early 1900s there is a sense of common purpose: a focussed exploration of the conditions of song and singing, and a determination to elevate to the concert platform a genre that had long been bounded by the societal and artistic limitations of the salons. The songs that Ravel and his contemporaries composed in the post-war years are more disparate, created amid a fractured musical discourse and an ever-diversifying concert scene. They emerged, too, in tandem with technologies that would transform the consumption of art song: the concert artists of the 1920s left substantial recorded legacies, while Ravel's last songs (and Koechlin's) were composed in response to the new medium of film.

If the pre-war decade had seen composers testing ways to bring speech and song together, some of the *mélodies* of the 1920s suggest a questing experimentation in arguably an opposite, or at least a very different, direction. André Caplet's *Trois fables* on texts by La Fontaine (1919) represent, in Robert Orledge's assessment, a 'worthy comic successor' to Ravel's *Histoires naturelles*, but although they too play with 'naturalistic' declamation, Caplet would exaggerate his vocal inflections to a far greater degree.[32] The vocal line is spiked with ironic sixths, sevenths, and ninths, rapid changes of register, and deliberately exaggerated *quasi parlando*, the fusion of the spoken and singing voices almost grotesquely caricatured.

In other songs, we find vocal lines determined not so much by the inflections of the spoken text as by the more abstracted imperatives of counterpoint, in which voice and instruments are treated almost equivalently. Something of this quality characterises the outer songs of Ravel's *Chansons madécasses* (1925–6), whose linearity and restraint represent a marked shift of compositional perspective from the timbral and harmonic richness of the Mallarmé *Poèmes*. In 'Nahandove', it is the gradual accumulation of instrumental sound that drives the movement towards what is in every sense a climax; in the opening bars of 'Il est doux', Ravel's reluctance to employ the harmonic heft of the piano brings a coolness and distance in which the erotic and dramatic fervour of the first two songs is allowed to dissipate. The last bars of this third song, as Roger Nichols notes, recall the conclusion of 'Le grillon' (*Histoires naturelles*), two D♭-major endings with a sudden, almost cinematic 'pull-back' to a nocturnal landscape (the vocal lines in both songs also curve upwards from the tonic via a modal G♮).[33] But where the last bars of 'Le grillon' move through a series of fully articulated harmonies, 'Il est doux', typical of the 'pared-down' Ravel of the 1920s, offers just a bare fifth, now in the piano alone. Even this dissolves in the final three bars, whisking the harmonic rug out from beneath the singer's final, offhand command ('Allez, et préparez le repas').

Ravel's prompt for *Chansons madécasses* was a commission from the American philanthropist Elizabeth Sprague Coolidge, who left the choice of text to the composer. Discovering Évariste de Parny's *Chansons madécasses* when browsing the booksellers' stalls by the Seine, Ravel (according to his pupil Manuel Rosenthal) was delighted to have discovered this heady and remarkable blend of 'erotic and revolutionary' poetry.[34] Valérie Magdelaine-Andrianjafitrimo notes that Parny's assertion of the 'authentic' sources of his *Chansons madécasses* had no factual basis; the poems, first published in 1787, are entirely the invention of the Réunion-born poet.[35] But Parny's prefatory 'Avertissement' was prescient: writing of the warring Malgache peoples, their conflicts driven by the demands of European slave-traders, the poet observed 'without us, these people would be calm and content'. Those words were still resonating in 1925, when France was at the height of a conflict with another of its African colonial possessions, Morocco; it is thus unsurprising that at least one early performance of Ravel's 'Aoua !', with its repeated cry of 'Méfiez-vous des blancs' (Beware of the white men) prompted some outraged responses.[36] As it happens, the word 'Aoua !', which so dramatically characterises this central song, does not appear in Parny's poetry: Ravel, always fascinated by the possibilities of language-as-sound, added it himself.

The intertwining of voice and flute in 'Il est doux' most obviously echoes the duet of the Child and Princess from Ravel's newly completed opera *L'Enfant et les sortilèges* (1925). But other composers were exploring that timbral combination too: Caplet's 1924 setting of Rabindranath Tagore's 'Écoute, mon cœur' (*Corbeille de fruits*), for example, has the flute perform itself ('Listen, my heart / in his flute is the music / of the smell of wildflowers ...'). The first of Roussel's *Deux poèmes de Ronsard* (1924), 'Rossignol, mon mignon', is likewise for voice and flute alone. Here, Roussel casts the flute as the voice of the nightingale, twining around the hapless poet's song: 'While we both make the same music / Your love yields to the sweetness of your sounds, / But my own, who has taken my songs in aversion / Blocks her ears so as not to hear them.' His setting offers a calmly ironic distillation of those pre-war dialogues of speech and song: the poet now sings, but goes unheard. Meanwhile, Ravel's own 'Ronsard à son âme' (composed, like Roussel's 'Rossignol', for a *Revue musicale* initiative to mark the 400th anniversary of Ronsard's birth) constrains the piano part mostly to bare, modal fifths: Ravel joked that he liked it because he could keep one hand free for his cigarette.[37] The last bar of the song reprises the stacked fifths of 'Chanson des cueilleuses de lentisques' and *Daphnis et Chloé*, this time building from the bass A_1 all the way up to the treble $A\sharp_5$.

A Final Toast: *Don Quichotte à Dulcinée*

In 1932, Ravel received a commission to compose a trio of songs for a forthcoming film of *Don Quichotte*. In the event, he was unable to fulfil the task in time and the production went ahead with songs by Jacques Ibert instead. Only in 1933 did Ravel finish his *Don Quichotte à Dulcinée*, realising the stipulated serenade, heroic song, and comic song even though the film was no longer at stake. Perhaps he was simply hooked by the texts and the Spanish setting, or perhaps he was stung by this rare failure to meet a contract: while he composed slowly and painfully in the post-war years, he usually did deliver, albeit sometimes much later than anticipated.

The fluency and vigour of *Don Quichotte à Dulcinée* belies the composer's failing health, as he revelled one last time in the dance rhythms and harmonic colours of his beloved Spain. 'Chanson romanesque' is cast in alternating 3/4 and 6/8 metres of the *quajira*, while the rocking quintuple time of 'Chanson épique' nods to the Basque *zortzico*. 'Chanson à boire' is a lively *jota*, in which we hear a decided echo of Ravel's *Rapsodie espagnole* of 1907 (the spiralling trumpet figure at Fig. 3^{+2} and Fig. 8^{+2} reprises, at pitch, an equivalent gesture at Fig. 28^{-2} of the concluding 'Feria').

Ravel managed to orchestrate *Don Quichotte* and oversee Martial Singher's November 1934 recording (although Manuel Rosenthal later asserted that he had orchestrated the songs under the composer's guidance, Nichols asserts that the score is in Ravel's hand).[38] These were among the last professional tasks he was able to undertake. Forty years after completing his first song ('Ballade de la reine morte d'aimer' of 1893), with *Don Quichotte à Dulcinée* Ravel concluded a compositional career that had helped to propel the *mélodie* to the heart of French musical thought. Had it not been overshadowed by the tragic and desolate silence of his last years, we might imagine that Ravel would not have been dissatisfied to bow out with the Don's uninhibited toast: 'To joy!'

Notes

1. Camille Bellaigue, 'Revue musicale: Quelques chansons', *Revue des deux mondes*, 143, no. 4 (15 October 1897), 928.
2. Ibid., 934n.
3. Henry Fellot, 'Lieder français', *La revue musicale de Lyon*, 1, no. 23 (23 March 1904), 268.
4. Albert Roussel, *Lettres et écrits*, ed. Nicole Labelle (Paris: Flammarion, 1987), 32. On the emergence of the *mélodie* as a concert idiom, see Emily Kilpatrick, *French Art Song: History of a New Music, 1870–1914* (Rochester, NY: Rochester University Press, 2022), Chapters 9 and 11.
5. Aude Caillet, 'La mélodie selon Charles Koechlin: Protée et l'anti-sublime', in *Francis Poulenc et la voix: Texte et contexte*, ed. Alban Ramaut (Lyon: Symétrie, 2002), 41.
6. Robert Orledge, *Charles Koechlin (1867–1950): His Life and Works* (London: Harwood, 1989), 62.
7. Ibid., 60.
8. Banville, *Petit traité de poésie française*, revised ed. (Paris: Charpentier, 1881), 172. Ravel seemingly had a copy of the *Petit traité* to hand: Banville's exemplar for the *huitain* is 'D'Anne jouant l'espinette'.
9. Heath Lees, *Mallarmé and Wagner: Music and Poetic Language* (Aldershot: Ashgate, 2007), 141.
10. Translation by Rosemary Lloyd, in ibid., 137.
11. Klingsor, 'Les musiciens et les poètes contemporains', *Le mercure de France*, 36, no. 131 (November 1900), 444.
12. René Dumesnil, 'Maurice Ravel poète', *La revue musicale*, 19, no. 187 ('Hommage à Maurice Ravel', 1938), 125.
13. Roger Nichols, *Ravel* (New Haven and London: Yale University Press, 2011), 51.
14. 'L'Ouvreuse' [Henry Gauthier-Villars], *Garçon, l'audition!* (Paris: Simonis-Empis, 1901), 125.
15. Peter Kaminsky, 'Vocal Music and the Lures of Exoticism and Irony', in *The Cambridge Companion to Ravel*, ed. Deborah Mawer (Cambridge: Cambridge University Press, 2003), 166.
16. Nichols, *Ravel*, 51.
17. Hélène Jourdan-Morhange, *Ravel et nous* (Geneva: Milieu du monde, 1945), 134.
18. Arbie Orenstein (ed.), *A Ravel Reader: Correspondence, Articles, Interviews* (New York: Columbia University Press, 1990), 450.
19. Letter of 8 February 1906, in Manuel Cornejo (ed.), *Maurice Ravel: L'Intégrale: Correspondance (1895–1937), écrits et entretiens* (Paris: Le Passeur, 2018), 129.
20. Dumesnil, 'Maurice Ravel poète', 126.

21. Fernand Divoire et al., 'Sous la musique que faut-il mettre?', *Musica*, 102 (March 1911), 59.
22. Malou Haine, 'Cinq entretiens inédits de Jane Bathori avec Stéphane Audel', *Revue musicale de Suisse Romande*, 61, no. 2 (June 2008), 25.
23. Letter of 4 September 1907, in Cornejo (ed.), *Maurice Ravel: L'Intégrale*, 166.
24. Orenstein, *A Ravel Reader*, 135.
25. See for example Grahame Robb, *Unlocking Mallarmé* (New Haven and London: Yale University Press, 1996), 91.
26. Orenstein, *A Ravel Reader*, 433.
27. Alain Badiou, *Theory of the Subject*, trans. Bruno Bosteels (London: Continuum, 2009), 81. For a detailed analysis of Ravel's Mallarmé settings see Emily Kilpatrick, 'Ravel's *Trois Poèmes de Stéphane Mallarmé*: A Philosophy of Composition', *Music & Letters*, 101, no. 3 (2020), 512–43.
28. Annegret Fauser, 'Die Musik hinter der Legende: Lili Boulangers Liederzyklus *Clairières dans le ciel*', *Neue Zeitschrift für Musik*, 151 (November 1990), 11.
29. Léonie Rosenstiel, *The Life and Works of Lili Boulanger* (Cranbury, NJ: Associated University Presses, 1978), 96.
30. Bonnie Jo Dopp, 'Numerology and Cryptography in the Music of Lili Boulanger: The Hidden Programme in *Clairières dans le ciel*', *Musical Quarterly*, 78, no. 3 (Autumn 1994), 556–83.
31. See Fauser, 'Die Musik hinter der Legende', 12ff.
32. Robert Orledge, 'Caplet, André', *Grove Music Online*, 20 January 2001, www.oxfordmusiconline.com; accessed 11 October 2021.
33. Nichols, *Ravel*, 280.
34. Marcel Marnat (ed.), *Ravel: Souvenirs de Manuel Rosenthal* (Paris: Hazan, 1995), 119.
35. Valérie Magdelaine-Andrianjafitrimo, 'Les littératures réunionnaises: Entre francophonie et outre-mer', *Nouvelles études francophones*, 23, no. 1 (Spring 2008), 57.
36. Nichols, *Ravel*, 274.
37. Ibid., 256.
38. Ibid., 334; Marnat, *Ravel: Souvenirs de Manuel Rosenthal*, 180–81.

12 | Poulenc and His Circle: *Le style quotidien*

BYRON ADAMS

Thomas S. Kuhn's term 'paradigm shift', which originally referred to the idea of fundamental change in the history of science on the magnitude of the Copernican Revolution, has subsequently moved well beyond its original context into disciplines such as sociology, economics, and political science.[1] Although this expansion has served to dilute Kuhn's term somewhat, the concept remains evocative. The most recent historical paradigm shift of such importance is probably the First World War, whose catastrophic resonance can still be felt across modern human history.

Within music history, it is customary to view the birth of Modernism as a reflection of the paradigm shift that occurred during that conflict. Although a direct correlation is too facile given the complexity of aesthetic movements in fin-de-siècle Europe, a host of Modernist trends that represented a severe break from the past came to prominence during the war. Some of these movements, such as neoclassicism and Surrealism, held sway until the 1950s, while others, such as Cubism and Dada, were relatively short-lived. An examination of these movements and their impact on avant-garde music in early twentieth-century France reveals the wide-ranging cultural effects of this devastating socio-political paradigm shift. This chapter begins with the artistic milieu that rose to prominence during the First World War and proceeds to a discussion of the avant-garde musicians in the immediate post-war period, particularly, but not exclusively, those grouped together as 'Les Six'.

The latter part of this investigation focusses on Francis Poulenc, whose renown has exceeded that of any other French composer of his generation. One reason for Poulenc's commanding posthumous reputation is his expressive and sophisticated use of virtually all the musical and aesthetic trends of his time, so it is possible to compare his *mélodies*, for example, to those of his contemporaries in a mutually illuminating manner. Poulenc's *mélodies* have also been written about extensively, by the composer himself and by his recital partner, the baritone Pierre Bernac, as well as by a number of later authors. The lively survey by pianist and scholar Graham Johnson and extensively researched biographies by Carl B. Schmidt and Hervé Lacombe have made Poulenc's *mélodies* a natural lens through which to examine the ways in which twentieth-century French Modernism was manifested in song.

After 1914, the arts in France – plastic, literary, and musical – drew close to one another, engendering a heady period that literary critic Roger Shattuck celebrated in his volume *The Banquet Years* (1955). As Shattuck noted, the term 'Surrealism' itself was coined by the Polish-French poet Guillaume Apollinaire, who first employed it in a programme note written for the Ballets Russes production of *Parade*. Appearing during the week before the ballet's premiere on 18 May 1917 at the Théâtre du Châtelet, Apollinaire proclaimed that the ballet possessed 'a sort of sur-realism in which I see the point of departure for a series of manifestations of that New Spirit which ... promises to modify the arts and the conduct of life [*mœurs*] from top to bottom in a universal joyousness'.[2] A public manifestation of the avant-garde, *Parade* boasted music by Erik Satie, sets and costumes designed by Pablo Picasso, and choreography by Léonide Massine.

As Nancy Perloff comments, 'Many of the ballet's elements of varied repetition, musical quotation, brevity, and spoof were familiar from Satie's piano pieces of the 1910s ... *Parade* was Satie's first concert work to explore a popular language and his first to become known to a large French public'.[3] *Parade*'s chief revolutionary aspect was the juxtaposition of quotidian musical fragments placed in a dream-like, non-teleological context. Such juxtapositions evoked the Cubist canvases of Picasso and Georges Braque, on which everyday objects – a pipe, a newspaper, a hat – were divorced from their mundane associations, broken up, and viewed with new perspectives. This Cubist influence can also be seen in Apollinaire's own poetry; his experiments with typography in *Calligrammes* (1916, published in 1918) produced an effect akin to Picasso's paintings.

Regarding *Parade*, Mary E. Davis notes, 'Satie's score owed as much to the cabaret as the concert hall, blending ragtime with fugue and counterpoint to offend a range of musical constituencies, from devotees of *Schéherézade* to fans of *The Rite of Spring*'.[4] In addition, Satie's music seems to have been punctuated by the clatter of typewriters, the sharp reports of pistol shots, and the shrieks of whistles arising from the orchestra pit. Satie's jumble of allusions are a sonic analogue to Apollinaire's typographical experiments.

Satie's score was hardly the only radical element in *Parade*: the ten-foot-high Cubist costumes that Picasso designed for the two Managers astonished the audience. The ballet's scenario, a series of music hall 'turns', was the brainchild of author Jean Cocteau. Davis observes that Massine's choreography drew upon 'magic acts, dances, and tumbling routines of the circus', and the movements created for the Little American Girl were drawn from silent films.[5] Although the opening-night audience was largely hostile, Davis writes, 'At the same time, however, the ballet's transgression of the boundaries of high art and low culture was viewed in progressive circles as a harbinger of modernism'.[6]

In the decade preceding *Parade*, French art song – whether designated as *chanson* or *mélodie* – had begun to undergo a sea-change.[7] Maurice Ravel had signalled the demise of Symbolist aesthetics in French song with his cycle *Histoires naturelles* (1906), which Ravel's teacher Gabriel Fauré disapproved of for its musical innovations as well as for the selection of Jules Renard's mordant poetry. Nichols quotes Fauré's pupil Louis Aubert, who remembered that his teacher exclaimed, 'I'm very fond of Ravel. But I'm not happy with people setting stuff like that to music'.[8] Writing to Louis Laloy, Debussy was also dismissive: 'I agree with you Ravel is extraordinarily gifted, but what annoys me is the attitude he adopts of being a "conjuror", or rather a Fakir casting spells and making flowers burst out of chairs'.[9] Both Fauré and Debussy may well have intuited that these songs foretold a future for the *mélodie* with which they might not be in sympathy. The war accelerated the process that Ravel had set in motion, whether intentionally or not, with *Histoires naturelles*. Even Debussy, in his *Trois ballades de François Villon* (1910), and Fauré, in his last song cycle, *L'horizon chimérique* (1921), participated in several post-war developments such as brevity, speed, and transparent textures.

Albert Roussel (1869–1937) brought forth further changes to the *mélodie* with his *Deux mélodies*, Op. 19 (1918), and *Deux mélodies*, Op. 20 (1919). 'Sarabande', the second song of Op. 19, anticipates the use of Baroque dance forms that became fashionable during the 1920s. Nothing in Roussel's other songs, however, anticipates the sultry eroticism of 'Jazz dans la nuit', Op. 38 (1928), a setting of an evocative surrealistic poem by René Dommange. Roussel had been a naval officer in his youth and was recalled to service during the First World War, where he experienced the maelstrom at first hand. From the Front, he wrote prophetically to his wife, 'One will have to begin living again, on a new basis, which does not mean to say that all that was done before the war will be forgotten, but rather that everything done after it ought to be done differently'.[10]

Roussel was hardly the only one to foresee how different music would be after the conclusion of hostilities. Cocteau made the post-war break with fin-de-siècle aesthetics explicit in 1918 by writing *Le Coq et l'arlequin: Notes autour de la musique*. As Jann Pasler writes, 'By age twenty-nine, in writing *Le Coq et l'Arlequin*, he had figured out "what the public reproaches in you, cultivate it, that's who you are"'.[11] Cocteau attacks Wagner, Saint-Saëns, and the recently deceased Debussy, decrying 'the Debussy-ist abuse of "precious" titles ... Enough of clouds, of waves, of aquariums, of Ondines, of perfumes of the night; we need a music on the ground, AN EVERYDAY MUSIC'.[12] This manifesto is less radical, however, than it may have seemed at the time. Cocteau employs the peculiarly French literary genre of a short volume filled with pithy epigrams; he clearly took as his formal model the *Maximes* (1678) of François IV, duc de la Rochefoucauld. In such volumes, aphorisms, declarations, and paradoxes take on the force – if not the actuality – of truth due to their brevity: no explanation required.

Le Coq et l'arlequin is a product of its time, a patriotic exhortation designed to point the way toward a characteristically French music free of Germanic taint. Indeed, a strain of devotion to France runs through the work of avant-garde poets such as Apollinaire, Louis Aragon, and Paul Éluard. The very title of *Le Coq et l'arlequin* conjoins two signifiers of French nationalism: the confident cockerel, portrayed on the royal coat of arms of French kings for centuries, who literally rules the roost, alongside the ironical clown who is at once witty and melancholy.

During the war, even honoured émigré musicians became suspect. In a catty letter of 1916, Debussy characterised Stravinsky in unflattering terms: 'He claims to be a friend of mine because I've helped him climb a ladder from which he can hurl grenades – not all of which explode'.[13] Much the same could be said about the grenades that Cocteau lobs at Stravinsky and Debussy himself in *Le Coq et l'arlequin*: not all of them explode or inflict much damage on the intended targets. As Perloff notes, 'Satie may have echoed Cocteau's attacks on the imitative, formulaic Debussyites, but he diverged from the poet in his genuine respect for Debussy'.[14] None of the young composers who were associated with Cocteau and Satie rejected either Debussy or Stravinsky and many of their scores reflected the influence of one or the other – at times, both.

Cocteau dedicated *Le Coq et l'arlequin* to Georges Auric (1899–1983), an intellectual and musical prodigy who was just nineteen years old when the volume was published. Auric was already a welcome and established figure in intellectual Parisian salons as well as an assured composer. One of Auric's fascinating early scores is his song cycle *Huit poèmes de Jean Cocteau* (1918), the first of which is entitled 'Hommage à Erik Satie'. The poems by Cocteau that Auric set in this song cycle include two that were inspired by the painters Henri Rousseau (1844–1910) and Marie Laurencin (1883–1956), who designed the set and costumes for Poulenc's *Les biches* (1924). Jane Bathori sang the first performance of *Huit poèmes de Jean Cocteau* in 1917; this score was published in 1920. As Colin Roust observes,

'Following the *esprit nouveau* aesthetic and the aphorisms of *Le coq et l'arlequin*, the poetry is grounded in Cocteau's daily reality: several friends appear in the poems, as do scenes of Paris and war'.[15]

Auric's career was given a boost when, prompted by Cocteau, the music critic Henri Collet published two articles in *Comœdia* (16 and 23 January 1920) that used the Russian 'Mighty Five' as a precedent by which to hail the arrival of 'les six Français'.[16] Aside from Auric, Collet mentioned Louis Durey (1888–1979), Arthur Honegger (1892–1955), Darius Milhaud (1892–1974), Francis Poulenc (1899–1963), and Germaine Tailleferre (1892–1983). With the exceptions of Poulenc and Durey, these composers had all studied at the Paris Conservatoire. There was only one collaboration featuring all six, a set of piano pieces, *L'album des Six*; five of their number, excluding Durey, collaborated on a surrealistic ballet, *Les mariés de Tour Eiffel*, which was premiered on 18 June 1921 by the Ballets suédois with choreography by Jean Börlin.

Fissures in this collective appeared almost immediately, and at a certain point its public relations value began to pall. After a few years, Cocteau's marketing ploy became something of a poisoned chalice. In his autobiography, Milhaud wrote of his exasperation: what began as a publicity stunt became a pigeonhole, and, for Milhaud and Honegger at least, turned into a web of exaggerations from which they struggled to escape. There are two drawbacks to the survival of 'Les Six' as a concept: first, as Milhaud noted bitterly, the subsequent achievements of these six disparate composers were taken less than seriously due to their youthful high jinks.[17] As he recalled:

Quite arbitrarily [Collet] had chosen six names: Auric, Durey, Honegger, Poulenc, Tailleferre, and my own, merely because we knew one another, were good friends, and had figured on the same programs; quite irrespective of our different temperaments and wholly dissimilar characters. Auric and Poulenc were partisans of Cocteau's ideas, Honegger derived from the German romantics, and I from Mediterranean lyricism.[18]

(Notice the unconscious bias with which Milhaud excises Tailleferre, the only woman among Les Six, from the last sentence of this quotation.) Second, the relentless publicity surrounding Les Six overshadowed gifted contemporaries such as Marcelle de Manziarly (1899–1989) and Jean Françaix (1912–97), both of whom made significant contributions to French song.

Poulenc, alongside Auric and, for all his later equivocations, Milhaud, entered enthusiastically into the spirit of Cocteau's exaltation of the everyday. While Honegger collaborated with Cocteau on several projects, including the starkly modernist opera *Antigone* (1927) and the harmonically adventurous *Six poèsies de Jean Cocteau* (1924) for voice and piano, his love of Beethoven and Wagner found him out of step with the anti-Teutonic rhetoric of *Le Coq et l'arlequin*. The peripheral status of Durey and Tailleferre is often laid at the feet of their loyalty to Ravel, who was one of Cocteau's *bêtes noires*. The reality is more complex, however. Tailleferre's music was often the target of patronising critical dismissal that stressed its 'femininity' while ignoring its technical assurance and inventiveness. For example, James Harding cites Tailleferre's 'feminine discretion', which enabled her to 'adopt whatever seemed to be the prevailing tone'.[19] Durey's commitment to left-wing politics – he composed *Poèmes d'Ho Chi Minh* for voice and piano, Op. 69 in 1951, for example – meant that he was often snubbed by the French cultural establishment during the conservative Gaullist governments of the Fifth Republic. Durey's political convictions were the result of his miserable period of active service during the First World War. Later a prominent member of the intellectual Resistance during the German occupation, Durey declared, 'I am a Communist ... because it aims to abolish the inhuman division of society into classes.'[20]

As one of the aims of Cocteau's pamphlet was to promote Satie, it is unsurprising that Poulenc, Auric, and Milhaud were influenced in the early 1920s by the aesthetic of aphorism espoused during the war by both Satie and Stravinsky. Such concision is just one facet of what might be described profitably as Satie's *style quotidien*. A few years before the premiere of *Parade*, Satie's *Sports et divertissements* for piano (1914) crystalised his idiom. As Davis observes, 'In Satie's quest to yoke elements of high and low culture, *Sports et divertissements* represents a point of culmination, the moment at which the challenge of these boundaries evolves from stylistic feature to raison d'être'.[21] Aside from allusions to popular music, including American imports such as ragtime, these concise pieces are constructed by using short ostinatos to anchor the thematic material.

After 1914, Satie's songs, such as his *Trois mélodies* (1916), written for mezzo-soprano Jane Bathori, an indefatigable champion of the avant-garde, illustrate the skilful ways in which he adapted the techniques developed in *Sports et divertissements* to the composition of vocal music. For his *Trois mélodies*, Satie selected verse from three poets, all of whom were acquaintances: Léon-Paul Fargue (1876–1947); 'Mimi' Godebeska (1899–1949), whose poem was attributed to

'M. God'; and René Chalupt (1885–1957), who was inspired by *Alice in Wonderland*. Satie's masterpiece *Socrate* (1918), which is utterly *sui generis* and cannot therefore be classed as a *mélodie*, retains the ostinatos over which mosaic-like thematic fragments unfurl while eschewing any reference whatsoever to popular genres. Despite his unjustified reputation as an eccentric *farceur*, Satie could turn the extreme economy of his style to serious purposes, as in the 'Élégie' composed in memory of Debussy that comprises the first song of his *Quatres petites mélodies* (1920). Here Satie sets a short poem by the nineteenth-century poet Alphonse de Lamartine as a grief-stricken miniature whose disjunct vocal line and tonal ambiguity approach expressionism. It must be admitted, however, that such overt expressions of sombre emotion are more the exception than the rule in Satie's slender catalogue of *mélodies*. By the time that Satie composed the witty *Ludions* (1923), four short *mélodies* on Dada-like texts by Léon-Paul Fargue, his mastery of this idiom was complete. (A 'ludion' is a toy in which a small impish glass figurine is placed in a sealed container filled with water and made to do simple tricks.)

Auric's friendship with Satie had introduced him to the radical aesthetic of *Sports et divertissements*.[22] Auric's *Trois interludes* for voice and piano, begun in 1914 and finished the following year, was an early fruit of the cross-pollination that occurred between the teenaged Auric and the ageing Satie. Auric selected three poems by René Chalupt, whose verse Satie would set in 1916 as the last of his *Trois mélodies*. As Roust writes, 'Typically for Chalupt, the poems take an ironic look into the past'.[23] Roust detected lingering traces of Auric's youthful fondness for Ravel in these *mélodies*, but their concision and whimsy clearly reflect the marked influence of *Sports et divertissements*. Auric's *Trois interludes* were published in 1918, just in time to take advantage of the publicity that followed in the wake of *Le Coq et l'arlequin*.

Milhaud composed several examples of *le style quotidien* as well, most notably his *Catalogue des fleurs* for voice and piano (or seven instruments), Op. 60 (1920). For this little cycle, Milhaud chose poems by Lucien Daudet that were inspired by a catalogue of floral seeds; Daudet's verses are set to music whose surface ingenuousness conceals considerable technical and aesthetic sophistication. *Catalogue des fleurs* remains among Milhaud's most often performed song cycles, and as such represents an anomaly among his works in this genre. The baritone François Le Roux has remarked upon Milhaud's body of songs – all of which use texts of high quality – with sympathy and insight:

The relative lack of interest by singers in Milhaud's abundant vocal output stems from two factors. First, no particular poet seems to have fundamentally impacted on the general style of the composer; in other words, it seems to me that, for Milhaud, poetry was only one medium among many others that shaped his musical inspiration ... The second factor is that the voice is not an instrument that seemed to 'stimulate' the composer.[24]

For Poulenc, however, the voice so stimulated him that he completed some 157 *mélodies* over the course of his career.[25] Unsurprisingly, Poulenc's first true *mélodie*, 'Toréador' (1918, rev. 1932), sets a surrealistic and campy poem by Cocteau in which images of Venice and Spain jostle with mocking reminiscences of Bizet's *Carmen* in a carnivalesque farrago. (In *Le Coq et l'arlequin*, Cocteau writes: 'When Nietzsche praises "Carmen", he praises the crudity that our generation seeks in the music-hall'.[26]) Graham Johnson reports that Cocteau urged the teenaged composer to make the song 'bien <u>mais</u> moche' ('good but trashy').[27] Interestingly, this song was not published until 1932, by which time the composer had revised it.[28]

Poulenc's miniature song cycle *Le bestiaire, ou Cortège d'Orphée* (1919) is far more characteristic of his early style than 'Toréador'. Poulenc excerpted six poems from Apollinaire's eponymous 1911 volume of aphoristic poems dealing with animals. The cycle originally consisted of twelve *mélodies*, but Poulenc heeded Auric's advice and published half that number. (Roger Nichols has related that Auric's counsel concerning excising six songs from *Le bestiaire* was in accord with that of Poulenc's friend Raymonde Linossier, although the composer 'later chose to efface her part in this decision, for reasons that have never been satisfactorily explained'.)[29] Almost as precocious as Auric, the adolescent Poulenc had heard Apollinaire read aloud these poems at Adrienne Monnier's famous bookshop Le maison des Amis des livres. The young composer found that the experience of hearing the poet's voice was of crucial importance: 'The timbre of Apollinaire's voice, like that of his work as a whole, was both melancholy and cheerful'.[30] Even with Poulenc's reminiscences of Apollinaire, Satie's influence on *Le bestiaire* cannot be discounted. The final song, 'La carpe', features a chant-like vocal line floating above an ostinato that might have been taken directly from *Socrate* or one of Satie's late *mélodies*. By the time Poulenc composed *Le bestiaire*, he may have known Stravinsky's aphoristic *Three Japanese Lyrics* (1913) as well. As Nichols speculates, 'Poulenc must surely have heard [*Three Japanese Lyrics*] at the concert of the Société musicale indépendante on 14 January 1914'.[31]

In the same year that Poulenc composed *Le bestiaire*, Louis Durey finished a cycle in which he set all twenty-six poems found in Apollinaire's volume. As Johnson writes, 'Poulenc rather gallantly dedicated his own set to Durey, who was by no means a close friend'.[32] (The scion of a *haut-bourgeois* family, Poulenc never espoused progressive political views; he would hardly have approved of Durey's revolutionary left-wing convictions.) Aside from the length of Durey's *Le bestiaire*, Op. 17, the influence of Ravel, especially his *Ma mère l'oye* (1910), casts a heavy shadow over the music. (Durey's setting of Apollinaire's 'La chèvre du Thibet', for example, sounds so much like the first movement of Ravel's *Ma mère l'oye* as to approach plagiarism.) Many listeners may find that the succession of animals in Durey's cycle begins to blur together, as if all of them – dromedary, dolphin, and grasshopper – belong to the same species. By contrast, Poulenc's evocations of the denizens of Apollinaire's bestiary are as sharply drawn as an etching by Picasso. As Marc Wood notes, 'Durey's songs are more lyrical and less humorous and quirky than Poulenc's – in retrospect, Poulenc was perhaps right to pick and choose the most apposite poems rather than to aim for the completeness achieved by Durey'.[33] Durey follows the same procedure – with similar mixed result – in his song cycle using poems by Saint-Jean Perse (pseudonym of Alexis Leger, 1887–1975) titled *Images à Crusoé* (1918) for voice and an instrumental ensemble. One might argue further that Durey missed the point of the aesthetic of brevity by writing a long cycle of short songs. Poulenc's *Le bestiaire*, however, displays an incisive, inimitable idiom that impresses these songs on the listener's memory. Both Poulenc and Durey made instrumental versions of their respective cycles: Poulenc created his instrumental version in 1919, while Durey completed his instrumentation in 1965.[34]

In 1924, Poulenc, along with a host of other composers, celebrated the quatercentenary of Pierre de Ronsard's birth by composing *mélodies* to his verse. Unfortunately, Poulenc's *Poèmes de Ronsard* (1924–5) cannot be counted among his most successful songs. Auric exclaimed, 'I must tell you. Your Ronsard songs, apart from the beginning of the first one and the end of the last, that's not you. Believe me. You're not made for the classical poets. Stay with Apollinaire, set Max Jacob, Eluard [sic] and Reverdy'.[35] Auric's insightful advice posed a distinct challenge for Poulenc, since a major musical trend of the mid-1920s was a broad reinterpretation of the *ancien régime*. Pasler has located the origin of a renewed fascination with pre-revolutionary music in the 1880s: 'Simultaneously, aristocrats began to perform old dances, sometimes in period costumes, wigs and all, especially the stately pavane from the sixteenth and early seventeenth centuries and the elegant minuet that first appeared at the court of Louis XIV ... For republicans, the taste for bringing a modern perspective to old dances, which continued through 1900, reinforced interest in earlier models of French charm and grace.'[36] In fact, using musical styles and dance forms of the *ancien régime* as a signifier of French cultural identity assumed a new urgency during and immediately after the First World War. The success of Ravel's *Le tombeau de Couperin* (1919) testifies to the power that evocations of the *ancien régime* held during the post-war period. In *Le Coq et l'arlequin*, for example, Cocteau cites Couperin's practice of titling the dances in his *ordres* in order to defend Satie's use of droll titles in his work.[37]

François Couperin and his older contemporary, the poet Jean de La Fontaine, assumed an enormous importance for French composers during the period *entre-deux-guerres*. These two towering figures of the *ancien régime*, alongside composer and theorist Jean-Philippe Rameau, painter Antoine Watteau, and playwright Molière (né Jean-Baptiste Poquelin), became touchstones of French cultural patriotism in the 1920s. Invoking their achievements provided reassurance and inspiration during the labour and social unrest of the 1930s and the agony of the Occupation. Of course, admiration for these icons was nothing new, but the way in which they were admired changed significantly. Unlike evocations of the *ancien régime* by composers such as Fauré during the fin de siècle, the composers who rose to prominence in the 1920s and 1930s tended to avoid Symbolist intermediaries such as Verlaine. They chose to set earlier texts directly, following Debussy's precedent in his *Trois chansons de France* (1904) for which he selected texts by the medieval poet-prince Charles d'Orléans and the seventeenth-century author François Tristan L'Hermite. Following this trend, Poulenc chose verse by Charles d'Orléans for a touching *mélodie* 'Priez pour paix' (1938).

Debussy's *Trois chansons de France* are permeated by signifiers of antiquity such as modality and plainchant, but later composers such as Marcelle de Manziarly and Jean Françaix opted for an up-to-date neoclassical idiom when setting *ancien régime* poetry. Manziarly's sparkling *Trois fables de la Fontaine* (1935) owes more to Stravinsky than to either Debussy or Satie. In his cycle *L'adolescence clémentine* (1941), which was written for Bernac and Poulenc, Françaix set courtly verse by Clément Marot in a manner every bit as neoclassical as Manziarly's La Fontaine songs. *L'adolescence clémentine* exemplifies the composer's stylish *boulevardier* style, as far from evoking sixteenth-century French music as possible.

While Poulenc did allude to the eighteenth century in several of his instrumental scores during the 1920s and 1930s, such as the *Concert champêtre* for harpsichord and orchestra (1928), he deftly sidestepped the conundrum posed by Auric's criticism of his Ronsard songs by selecting anonymous bawdy poems drawn from two anthologies of sixteenth- and seventeenth-century verse published during the eighteenth century.[38] The texts of *Chansons gaillardes* (1926) are far from 'classics' of French poetry but do chime with the fashion for the *ancien régime* prevalent at the time. The eighteenth-century texts that Poulenc chose for the three vocal numbers in his 1924 ballet *Les biches* use similarly ribald poems; while descriptive of erotic dalliance, these poems, like those of *Chansons gaillardes*, are far from obscene. Commentators often characterise *Chansons gaillardes* as merely good-humoured obscenity, but this score encompasses sombre emotions as well: the second song, 'Chanson à boire', for example, contains a disturbing undercurrent of fatalism, while intimations of sinister masculine ruthlessness can be heard in the final 'Sérénade'.

Like Poulenc, Germaine Tailleferre chose texts from the *ancien régime* for her *Six chansons françaises*: poems by Voltaire, Gabriel-Charles de Larraignant, and Jean-François Sarrasin, alongside three anonymous fifteenth-century poems. These songs were written between June and August 1929, immediately after Tailleferre divorced her abusive husband, American cartoonist Ralph Barton.[39] All the poems in this cycle describe the indignities suffered by women at the hands of men. In a counter-intuitive aesthetic choice, Tailleferre set these poems to charming, seemingly light-hearted music. As Kiri L. Heel writes, 'Tailleferre's textual choices critique institutions of marriage and patriarchy . . . I find that the restrained neoclassical aesthetic of Tailleferre's musical settings of the *Six chansons françaises* in fact deepens the irony and detachment'.[40]

Tailleferre's *Six chansons françaises*, like *Chansons galliardes*, *Catalogues des fleurs*, *Ludions*, or, for that matter, *Histoires naturelles*, are settings of poems that either share a single author or at least evince a unified sensibility due to period. None of these cycles trace a narrative arc in the manner of Schubert's *Winterreise* (1828). Many of Poulenc's cycles rely on the sensibility of a single author in order to unify selected poems into a convincing entity. Poulenc followed this formula for two of his cycles that use poetry by Apollinaire: *Banalités* (1940) and *Calligrammes* (1948), in which Poulenc set the poet's avant-garde typographical innovations with considerable aplomb. As in *Le bestiaire*, Poulenc approached Apollinaire's Surrealism through his taste for demotic music. Poulenc sometimes explicitly connected his *mélodies* to popular French music through tempo markings such as found in the first song of *Banalités*, 'Chanson d'Orkenise', which is marked *Rondement, dans le style d'une chanson populaire*.

Poulenc and Auric did more than just produce concert music infused with popular styles; both published songs that became popular hits: Poulenc wrote 'Les chemins d'amour' (1940) for the celebrated chanteuse Yvonne Printemps (1894–1977), while Auric composed 'It's April Again' (1952) for the film *Moulin Rouge*. Poulenc's cycle *Chansons villageoises* (1942) is drenched in the style of French popular music – for the composer, any division between 'popular' and 'art' music was so fungible as to become irrelevant. (Poulenc originally conceived *Chansons villageoises* for orchestra, but the piano transcription was created and published in the same year as the orchestral score.) Poulenc did make one distinction between a *chanson* and a *mélodie*, however. In a 1947 talk about his songs, he mentioned the freedom with which he set the rustic and earthy verses by Maurice Fombeure in *Chansons villageoises*: 'The word "chanson", as I see it, refers to a style which, without being intrinsically folky, nevertheless suggests a completely free treatment of the text ... I repeat words, I cut them, I imply them even ... Maurice Chevalier's repertory taught me a lot in this respect'.[41]

From the 1930s onward, Poulenc's *mélodies* seldom reflected the sophisticated Stravinskian neoclassicism embraced by Manziarly and Françaix. Like *Six chansons françaises*, his two great song cycles of the 1930s, *Tel jour telle nuit* (1937) and the more diffuse *Fiançailles pour rire* (1939), deal with heterosexual relationships, but in a manner markedly different from Tailleferre's cycle. Eschewing the *ancien régime*, Poulenc selected contemporary texts by living poets whom he knew well: Paul Éluard, to whose poetry the composer returned repeatedly, and the glamorous Louise de Vilmorin.

Despite – or perhaps because of – the surrealistic juxtaposition of images that characterise the work of both poets, the basic premise of each cycle is quite clear. *Fiançailles pour rire* is a series of vignettes, erotic and melancholic by turn, told from the perspective of a highly intelligent *femme du monde*, while in *Tel jour telle nuit* a man narrates his experience as part of a married couple. *Fiançailles pour rire* concludes in voluptuous regret; *Tel jour telle nuit* ends with the couple making love after having turned out the bedroom lamp. (While theoretically a woman could sing *Tel jour telle nuit* and a man could sing *Fiançailles pour rire*, to do so would be counter to the composer's conception of these scores.) Although Poulenc professed to dislike Fauré's music, the similarities between *Tel jour telle nuit* and Fauré's *La bonne chanson* (1894), also a nine-song cycle narrated by an ardent fiancé and ending in fulfilment, cannot be dismissed out of hand (Poulenc and Bernac featured *La bonne chanson* on their recitals).[42]

Tel jour telle nuit is justly considered by many biographers as the summit of Poulenc's achievement as a composer of *mélodies*. Through his selection of nine poems from Éluard's volume *Les yeux fertiles* (1936), Poulenc fashioned a narrative that unfolds over a single emotionally tumultuous day, surely the reason why Poulenc chose *Tel jour telle nuit* over the three other titles supplied to him by Éluard.[43] By relating the musical materials of the first and last *mélodies*, and by deriving thematic material found in all the songs from the first one, Poulenc created a seamless musical and narrative continuity.

One aspect of Poulenc's œuvre as a song composer is his constant renewal of procedures, even if thematic fragments are repeated from *mélodie* to *mélodie* – or from work to work – over decades. For example, the opening theme of 'Hymne', the second of his *Trois pièces pour piano* (1918–28, rev. 1953), which is itself cribbed from Stravinsky's *Sérénade en la* (1925), returns over thirty years later at the beginning of the Gloria (1960). As William W. Austin observed, 'No piece of his as a whole resembles any model, while no single phrase is either original or obscure', and he further marvelled at the 'mysterious unity of his best smaller compositions'.[44] Part of the expressive power of *Tel jour telle nuit* derives from the ways in which Poulenc's music mirrors Éluard's evocative language: 'a dead horse with a child as master', or 'an impoverished blade of wild grass'. It was Poulenc's good fortune that his bourgeois father forbade him to study at the Conservatoire, as his freedom from preconceptions, allied to his precocious intellectual development among avant-garde poets and painters, enabled him to respond to the poetry and painting of his time with an insight born of personal experience. In 1956, Poulenc composed *Le travail du peintre*, a cycle for which he selected seven poems from Éluard's volume *Voir* (1948), each poem inspired by a different modernist artist.[45]

Poulenc created a musical idiom analogous to Surrealism, as well as a technique that enabled him to illumine the complex poetry of Apollinaire and Éluard. He employed a variety of harmonic resources to do so. Ned Rorem once observed, 'Take Chopin's dominant sevenths, Ravel's major sevenths, Fauré's plain triads, Debussy's minor ninths, Mussorgsky's augmented fourths. Filter these through Satie by way of the added sixth chords of vaudeville ... blend in a pint of Couperin to a quart of Stravinsky, and you get the harmony of Poulenc.'[46] Paradoxically, Poulenc's eclecticism created, through the force of his musical personality, the 'mysterious unity' that Austin found in his music.

Example 12.1. Francis Poulenc, 'Bonne journée' (*Tel jour telle nuit*), mm. 1–4

While an extended analysis of *Tel jour telle nuit* is outside the scope of this chapter, some observations about 'Bonne journée', the first *mélodie* of the nine that comprise *Tel jour telle nuit*, may shine a light on Poulenc's compositional practice. 'Bonne journée' is cast in C major/minor, and the flickering between modes creates an analogue to the ambiguity of Éluard's verse. This ambiguity is deepened musically by recurrent Lydian inflections in mm. 1, 14, 15, and 29 (see Example 12.1). Using C major/minor enables movement through mixture to F minor (m. 7): here the tonal instability is disorienting, matching the unexpected images of the text. (This passage can be heard either in the Aeolian mode or natural minor scale.) Poulenc modulates through double mixture into the even darker key area of E♭ minor (m. 17) at the words, 'One who passed / His shadow transformed into a mouse / Darted into the gutter.' The most double-edged, even ironic, musical qualification of certain lines is created through the octatonic scale, which is implicit in the Lydian inflection of the opening phrase. Poulenc's deployment of octatonicism qualifies Éluard's image of a 'great wide sky' (m. 23): the tonal instability here suggests not just a wide but a darkening sky. The same octatonic collection reappears in mm. 25–6, adding a touch of unreality to the line 'A distant shore where no one lands'.[47] While the music returns to the minor tonic in m. 29, the resolution to the main key in the final measures is preceded by a dominant chord compromised by an unresolved 4-3 suspension (m. 39). The final six measures consist of a C-G dyad over a tonic pedal in which the third is absent: the song ends in neither major nor minor but still hovering between the two. In m. 43, the final cadence is clouded by a B♭, creating a Mixolydian tonic seventh chord reminiscent of the alleluias in the third movement of Stravinsky's *Symphonie de psaumes* (1930).[48]

All of the chords in Rorem's list (and more) can be found in 'Bonne journée': supersaturated chords of the seventh, ninth, and thirteenth (such as

Example 12.2. Poulenc, 'Sanglots' (*Banalités*), mm. 15–18

at m. 32, a V^{13} modified by both a flat ninth and a flat thirteenth); altered German augmented sixth chords (m. 31); chromatically altered chords, particularly favouring altered fifths, both raised and lowered (see m. 25, the V^{13} of V with a lowered fifth in C, an octatonic collection that reappears at the climax in m. 37); secondary dominants as well as secondary diminished-seventh chords, always of the dominant (see, for example, the third beat of m. 38); and a common-tone diminished seventh on the raised fourth degree during the course of an octatonic passage (m. 23). Plain triads, such as at the imperfect authentic cadence that establishes the modulation to E♭ minor, create moments of harmonic stability amid the chromatically altered chords. (Remarkably, Poulenc uses mostly unadulterated triads to depict existential alienation in the sixth song of the cycle, 'Une herbe pauvre'.) Despite the richness of these chords, Poulenc ensures continuity in 'Bonne journée' through elegant voice-leading, by reinterpreting and extending the opening Lydian ascent in the voice part (mm. 14, 24, 29), and by the relentless tread of quavers in the piano part – no rubato allowed.

Several of Poulenc's cycles end in tears. One thinks of 'Fleurs', the final song of *Fiançailles pour rire*, or 'Sanglots' ('Sobs'), the *mélodie* that concludes *Banalités*: 'My poor heart, my broken heart'. Poulenc is never self-indulgent when turning towards tragedy: he remained loyal to the economy of means that he inherited from Satie and Stravinsky. In 'Sanglots', he expresses the despair of Apollinaire's line, 'This is the song of dreamers / Who tore out their heart' through a common-tone modulation in m. 17 that moves without transition from the opening tonal centre, F♯ minor, to E♭ minor (see Example 12.2). The connection between the two keys is made more explicit by the frequent use of the raised sixth degree in F♯ minor – as D♯, it is a Dorian inflection as well as enharmonic to E♭ minor – and the bare fifths of the tonic triad without a third (mm. 15 and 16). This prepares the tonic F♯ to be reinterpreted enharmonically as the mediant G♭ of the new key centre. Poulenc needed only a single well-placed triad to reveal a vista of profound suffering.

By contrast, *Tel jour telle nuit* ends with a vision of erotic and emotional consummation. Like 'Bonne journée' cast in C major/minor, this final *mélodie*, 'Nous avons fait la nuit' ('We have created the night'), concludes like Schumann's *Dichterliebe* with an extended postlude for the piano; the ambiguous Lydian inflections of the first song have been banished from this *mélodie* as well as from its postlude. The Mixolydian tonic cadence that closed the first song remains, but in this context evokes the hope for the constant renewal of love implied by the final line: 'A stranger just like you just like / All that I love / Which is forever new'.

Some commentators have pointed out the paradox of the homosexual Poulenc composing such an eloquent hymn to a heterosexual union. However, *Tel jour telle nuit* was begun in 1936, the year in which, upset by the death of a colleague, the composer Pierre-Octave Ferroud, Poulenc made a pilgrimage to the ancient shrine of Rocamadour with Pierre Bernac and the choral conductor Yvonne Gouverné, both devout Catholics.[49] Poulenc had been baptised, catechised, and confirmed as a Catholic, but had lapsed from his faith. At Rocamadour, he returned to Catholicism with an ardent and unflagging devotion. To be clear, Poulenc did not 'convert', nor was he 'reconverted', to Catholicism, as some biographers claim: he simply returned to his childhood faith. In this regard, Nichols quotes Yvonne Gouverné: 'On ne fait pas de retour à la foi' ('One does not return to the faith').[50] Poulenc conceived of *Tel jour telle nuit* in November 1936, just four months after he completed his first piece of religious music, *Litanies à la Vierge Noir* for women's (or treble) chorus and organ.

This chronology can illumine the rapturous final *mélodie* of *Tel jour telle nuit*: for a practising Catholic, marriage – even an unconventional marriage such as that between Éluard and his wife Nusch (née Maria Benz) – is a sacrament of the Church. Poulenc's active homosexuality, still considered a sin by the Church, here took a secondary place to the faith that empowered him to express the sacral beauty of a great poet's marriage. Poulenc composed many superb *mélodies* after *Tel jour telle nuit*, but he rarely matched the depth of emotion and formal perfection of this lapidary cycle.

Notes

The author thanks Stephen Rumph, Jann Pasler, Colin Roust, Mary E. Davis, Marcus Desmond Harmon, Rama C. Bauer, and David Conte for their assistance in the creation of this chapter, which is dedicated to the memory of Geoffrey Ford.

1. Thomas S. Kuhn, *The Structure of Scientific Revolutions* (Chicago: University of Chicago Press, 1962).
2. Quoted in Roger Shattuck, *The Banquet Years: The Origins of the Avant-Garde in France 1885 to World War I*, rev. ed. (New York: Vintage Books, 1968), 294.
3. Nancy Perloff, *Art and the Everyday: Popular Entertainment and the Circle of Erik Satie* (Oxford: Clarendon Press, 1991), 112.
4. Mary E. Davis, 'Modernity à la mode: Popular Culture and Avant-Gardism in Erik Satie's *Sports et divertissements*,' *The Musical Quarterly*, 83, no. 3 (Autumn 1999), 430.
5. Ibid.
6. Ibid.
7. For a useful discussion of the natures of the *mélodie* and the *chanson*, see François Le Roux and Romain Raynaldy, *Le Chant Intime: The Interpretation of French Mélodie*, trans. Sylvia Kahan (New York: Oxford University Press, 2021), 13–18.
8. Roger Nichols, *Ravel* (New Haven and London: Yale University Press, 2011), 89–90.
9. Claude Debussy, *Letters*, ed. François Lesure and Roger Nichols, trans. Roger Nichols (Cambridge, MA: Harvard University Press, 1987), 178.
10. Norman Demuth, *Albert Roussel: A Study* (London: United Music Publishers, 1947), 23.
11. Jann Pasler, 'New Music as Confrontation: The Musical Spaces of Jean Cocteau's Identity', *The Musical Quarterly*, 75, no. 3 (Autumn 1991), 255.
12. Jean Cocteau, *Le Coq et l'arlequin: Notes autour de la musique avec un portrait de l'auteur et deux monogrammes par P. Picasso* (Paris: Éditions de la Sirène, 1918), 26, 32. For an English translation, see Jean Cocteau, *The Cock and the Harlequin: Notes Concerning Music*, trans. Rollo H. Myers (London: The Egoist Press, 1921).
13. Debussy, *Letters*, 312.
14. Perloff, *Art and the Everyday*, 13.
15. Colin Roust, *Georges Auric: A Life in Music and Politics* (Oxford and New York: Oxford University Press, 2020), 35.
16. Henri Collet, 'Un livre de Rimsky-Korsakov et un livre de Jean Cocteau – Les cinq russes, les six français et Erik Satie', *Comœdia* (16 January 1920). The first page of Collet's article is reproduced in Roust, *Auric*, 46.
17. Darius Milhaud, *Notes without Music*, trans. Donald Evans (New York: Alfred A. Knopf, 1953), 124.
18. Ibid., 97.

19. James Harding, *The Ox on the Roof: Scenes from Musical Life in Paris in the Twenties* (London: Macdonald and Company, 1972), 69.
20. Quoted in Harding, *The Ox on the Roof*, 241. Ho Chi Minh (1890–1969) was a Vietnamese Marxist-Leninist revolutionary who was President of North Vietnam from 1945 until his death in 1969.
21. Davis, 'Modernity à la mode', 434.
22. In 1979, Auric wrote about his first meeting and initial friendship with Satie; see Robert Orledge, *Satie Remembered* (Portland, OR: Amadeus Press, 1995), 113–17.
23. Roust, *Auric*, 28.
24. Le Roux, *Le Chant Intime*, 211.
25. Excluded from this number are the single vocal duet, *Colloque* (FP108, 1940), two songs discarded from *Le bestiare* (FP15b) and the tiny 'Vive Nadia' (FP167, 1956), which is more a musical birthday card than a *mélodie*.
26. Cocteau, *Cock and the Harlequin*, trans. Meyers, 14.
27. Graham Johnson, *Poulenc: The Life in the Songs* (New York and London: Liveright Publishing Co., 2020), 17.
28. Although some might argue that the third movement of Poulenc's *Rapsodie nègre* (FP3, 1917) should be considered the composer's first song, this is rather a sung interlude in an otherwise instrumental composition.
29. Roger Nichols, *Poulenc: A Biography* (New Haven: Yale University Press, 2020), 32.
30. Francis Poulenc, *Articles and Interviews: Notes from the Heart*, ed. Nicholas Southon and trans. Roger Nichols (London and New York: Routledge, 2014), 107.
31. Nichols, *Poulenc*, 23.
32. Johnson, *Poulenc*, 20.
33. Marc Wood, 'Louis Durey: homme de tête', *The Musical Times*, 141, no. 1873 (Winter 2000), 44.
34. Ibid.
35. Poulenc, *Notes from the Heart*, 211–12.
36. Jann Pasler, *Composing the Citizen: Music as Public Utility in Third Republic France* (Berkeley, Los Angeles, London: University of California Press, 2009), 502, 504.
37. Cocteau, *Le Coq et l'arlequin*, 27.
38. For a discussion of the origins of these texts as well as Bernac's prudishness concerning them, see Johnson, *Poulenc*, 60–62.
39. Kiri L. Heel, 'Trauma and Recovery in Germaine Tailleferre's *Six chansons françaises* (1929)', *Women in Music: A Journal of Gender and Culture*, 15 (2011), 38. Tailleferre produced two versions of this cycle simultaneously, one for voice and piano and the other for voice and orchestra.
40. Ibid., 46, 50.
41. Poulenc, *Notes from the Heart*, 109.

42. See Johnson, *Poulenc*, 233, 241. In 1928, Poulenc mentioned *La bonne chanson* in the pages of *Arts Phoniques*, a journal devoted to reviews of gramophone recordings; see Nichols, *Poulenc*, 81–2.
43. Johnson, *Poulenc*, 154.
44. William W. Austin, *Music in the 20th Century: From Debussy through Stravinsky* (New York and London: W. W. Norton and Company, 1966), 517.
45. See Johnson, *Poulenc*, 387–412.
46. Ned Rorem, *Setting the Tone: Essays and a Diary* (New York: Coward-McCann, 1983), 276.
47. The octatonic collection that Poulenc uses in these passages corresponds to Messiaen's Third Mode of Limited Transposition: alternating whole and half steps starting on C.
48. Igor Stravinsky, *Symphonie de psaumes*, new revision 1948 (London: Boosey & Hawkes Music Publishers, 1948), 27; see movement III, mm. 1–3.
49. Johnson, *Poulenc*, 153–4.
50. Nichols, *Poulenc*, 121.

13 | Olivier Messiaen

STEPHEN BROAD AND DAVID EVANS

We might not immediately think of Olivier Messiaen (1908–92) as an important composer of vocal music and *mélodies*, yet he himself regarded his works for voice as especially significant in his output. Begun in the early 1970s, the gigantic opera *Saint François d'Assise* dominated the last phase of his compositional career, but some years before, in conversation with Antoine Goléa, Messiaen had highlighted his earlier vocal cycles of the 1930s and 1940s as music of which he was particularly proud. Goléa clearly thought that this pride was not misplaced, calling these works 'sublime' and affirming their significance by reference to the particular qualities he saw in song as a genre: 'Song is the most intimate, the most profound cry of humankind. For the musician, it is the essential test; it is doubtless through song that he expresses his personal life, both in the most mysterious and the most obvious way'.[1] In this chapter, we consider the musical, poetic, and personal significance of Messiaen's earlier vocal music, beginning with the *Trois Mélodies* of 1930, which belong in the salon, and tracing the rapid evolution of his *mélodies* through the chamber cantata *La Mort du Nombre* (1930) and the song cycles *Poèmes pour Mi* (1936), *Chants de Terre et de Ciel* (1938) and *Harawi: Chant d'amour et de mort* (1945). The song cycles make considerable demands on both singer and pianist, and they are rarely performed, Messiaen being far better known for works such as *Quatuor pour la fin du temps* (1940), the piano pieces of *Vingt Regards sur l'Enfant-Jésus* (1944), or the *Turangalîla-symphonie* (1948). Yet no history of French art song can be complete without serious consideration of vocal works with which, as Graham Johnson argues, 'the *mélodie* in the form we know it ceases to exist'.[2]

Roger Smalley sums up the paradoxes of Messiaen's distinctive musical world with the pithy observation that 'the emotional scope of Wagner is wedded to a musical language derived from Debussy'.[3] Smalley was almost certainly thinking of the uninhibited emotional ecstasies and mystical *longueurs* of works like the *Vingt Regards sur L'Enfant-Jésus*, but there are further parallels with Wagner, most obviously the extended temporal plan of many of Messiaen's key works from *La Nativité du Seigneur* (1935, solo organ) onwards. Then there is Messiaen's professed love of *Tristan und*

Isolde and *Parsifal*, and his coinage of the sobriquet 'Tristan Trilogy' for three of his works of the 1940s – *Harawi*, *Turangalîla-symphonie*, and *Cinq Rechants* (1948) – that consider in very different ways an overwhelming earthly love consummated in death. Particularly relevant to a discussion of Messiaen's *mélodies* is his propensity to tackle musical composition in the same spirit of *Gesamtkunstwerk* as Wagner. This came to prominence most clearly in *St François d'Assise*, with its careful stage and design directions (including a detailed colour plan), and 'authorised' productions, but it is also evident in the way Messiaen couched his music in paratext: quotations that follow movement titles (which he occasionally declaimed before performance) and explanatory prefaces. The most obvious connection with Wagner, however, is Messiaen's practice of writing his own texts for vocal works.

For Graham Johnson, this sets Messiaen apart from some of the traditions of French art song: he 'did not write *mélodies* in the accepted sense of the term … Of collaboration with others, the essential raison d'être of the *mélodie* composer who enters a poet's world in order to give it a new depth and dimension, there is scarcely a sign'.[4] While Johnson is right to highlight the important fact that Messiaen, as composer-and-poet, produced his own song texts, we would question his view that 'Messiaen's vocal music does not represent the meeting of the musical world with the literary' or that 'the words do not make much of a difference to what happens'.[5] On the contrary, through the course of the early *mélodies*, the interplay of text and music is carefully crafted, as Messiaen told Claude Samuel:

I think I write rather well for the voice because I sing it myself. Obviously, I've a horrible composer's voice, but I nonetheless understand the theatre stage … I also understand problems of diction, the phonetic value of vowels and consonants, the importance of breathing, where to breathe, and the different registers of the voice.[6]

Indeed, of the text of *Cinq Rechants* – 'half surrealist French, half invented language' according to Messiaen – he observes that he used 'words invented for their phonetic qualities, words whose vowels and consonants are specifically chosen to correspond to certain rhythms and certain registers of the voice'.[7]

Messiaen's heightened sensitivity to language is hardly surprising, since he came from a family with a heady literary heritage. His father Pierre Messiaen was a teacher of English at the Lycée Charlemagne in central Paris who translated the complete works of Shakespeare and wrote critical studies of major French poets. Far more important, though, to Messiaen's personal narrative was his mother, the poet Cécile Sauvage, whom he adored and whose work lay at the very centre of his sense of self. While pregnant with Messiaen, her first child, Sauvage wrote an extraordinary collection of poems, *L'Âme en bourgeon* (1910), in which maternal pride in creation and delight at a profound connection with the irrepressible generative force of nature is tempered by a painful sense of postpartum loss and grief for the child's mortality: 'My being is a closed-up house / From which a dead man has just been taken'.[8] In response to Goléa's opening question, 'Who are you, Olivier Messiaen?', the composer first talks about the crucial role played by his mother in forming his poetic sensibility, identifying in her work 'a taste for observing natural phenomena and a richness in the imagery that must have inspired my love of shimmering sounds [*chatoiement sonore*] and my love of birdsong'.[9]

Messiaen went so far as to claim that 'the greatest influence I received was that of my mother, an influence all the more extraordinary in that it preceded my birth' and suggested that *L'Âme en bourgeon* 'influenced my whole destiny'.[10] One poem, 'Here you are, my little lover', articulates an extraordinary proximity between mother and son:

You love me, we caress each other ...
Good day, my little statue
Of blood, of joy, of naked flesh.
My little double, my emotion,
It is myself whom I touch as I grasp your fingers ...
I am you.[11]

In 1917 Sauvage describes her relationship with her elder son as a fairy tale in which her poetry plays a part:

We are two very pure little lovers, living a private life animated by all the beautiful songs of his youthful dream-world, a life of light and gold in which the only shadow is that of my maternal melancholy ... I have read *L'Âme en bourgeon* with him. 'These grasshoppers, these bees, they're all for you', I told him. 'Mummy', he said, 'You're as much of a poet as Shakespeare'.[12]

Poetry, therefore, was central to Messiaen's personal and cultural life – in *Technique de mon langage musical* (1944) he lists his influences as his mother, his wife, William Shakespeare, Paul Claudel, Pierre Reverdy, Paul Éluard, and the Roman Catholic authors Ernest Hello and Blessed Columba Marmion.[13] Indeed, the texts Messiaen wrote for his songs juxtapose imagery reminiscent of Surrealist poets with religious motifs, a combination which, as he tells Goléa, he finds perfectly natural since 'the truths of faith contain a certain surrealist poetry, which I have always been careful not to dismiss'.[14] Messiaen was a versatile and confident writer in a number of distinct modes, writing evocative and often detailed programme notes for his music, sustaining a side career in music journalism in the years before the Second World War, and writing two treatises on his musical language. The first, *Technique de mon langage musical*, is a strikingly unusual work, setting out and carefully curating his musical techniques and influences with copious musical examples; the second, left incomplete at his death in 1992, is a vast seven-volume compendium of techniques and source material, the *Traité de rythme, de couleur et d'ornithologie*. We should, therefore, see his writing of texts for vocal music – words *in* music – in the context of both a sophisticated erudition and a great outpouring of words *on* music.

Messiaen's earliest *mélodies* are no longer available to us: the *Deux ballades de Villon* (1921) were composed as student works but never published, and in the absence of a manuscript we do not know for which voice they were written. Nonetheless, Messiaen often noted them in work lists (including the one provided in *Technique de mon langage musical*), suggesting that he may have wished to draw attention to the lineage with Debussy that the setting might indicate. Messiaen's Villon, however, is quite different from Debussy's. In *Trois ballades de François Villon* (1910), Debussy set a poem bemoaning the cruelty of a former lover, a prayer on behalf of the poet's aged mother, and a humorous ode to the conversational skills of Parisian women, while Messiaen chose 'Épître à ses amis' and 'Ballade des pendus', texts which deal, albeit in Villon's typically playful manner, with the Christian virtues of charity and forgiveness.

Trois Mélodies (1930)

The earliest songs by Messiaen to which we have access are the *Trois Mélodies*, composed in the summer of 1930 and first performed at no less venue than the Société nationale de musique in February 1931. Written for soprano and piano, these three songs were described by Sherlaw Johnson as 'slight' and 'hardly typical of the composer's mature style', but there is no mistaking these very earliest works for any other composer.[15] Although the sound world is altogether simpler and the textures less dense than those found in his later music, Messiaen's use of his characteristic 'modes of limited transposition' marks them out immediately. The modes of limited transposition, also known as symmetrical modes, are scales made up of small repeated patterns of intervals (such as tone-semitone) such that each scale has fewer transpositions than the twelve transpositions that may be made of the major mode. The whole-tone scale (tone-tone) and octatonic scales (tone-semitone) are examples of such modes that have been widely used by other composers, but Messiaen sought out less-used examples and deployed them in a characteristic way throughout his career. These songs are interesting in a number of respects, both historically, because they were among the most frequently performed of all Messiaen's music in the 1930s and therefore shaped the way he was understood by audiences and contemporaries in that phase of his career; and in the context of his later vocal music, because they contain the sole example of Messiaen's setting the words of another poet.

The two outer songs of the set – 'Pourquoi?' and 'La fiancée perdue' – have texts by Messiaen, while the central song, 'Le sourire', is a short poem by Messiaen's mother, who had died three years previously in 1927.[16] With 'Le sourire' embodying great calm, the surrounding songs seem almost to act as a setting in the sense of jewellery, with Sauvage's poem the gemstone at the centre. 'Pourquoi?' laments a loss of receptivity to the beauty of the world; 'Le sourire' is an expression of the profound effect of love; and 'La fiancée perdue' is a short prayer commending a woman to God, ending with the plea 'give her rest, Jesus'. It is not too difficult, then, to imagine that the recent death of Sauvage shaped the programme that the three songs unfold when performed together. Correspondence between Messiaen and his Conservatoire friend Denis Joly gives a sense of the significance for Messiaen of the summer anniversary of his mother's death: '26 August is approaching. You know what sad memories it calls to my mind. For every day I see the poetry and the radiance with which my mother surrounded herself and those who lived with her!'[17] Sauvage's text stands in some contrast to those that Messiaen himself composed for the outer songs: 'Le sourire' establishes a delicate counterpoint between a metrical frame and semantic units that work across that frame in a series of linked images. It is simple and direct, avoiding extravagant imagery and thereby drawing attention to the central image of a kiss on the soul which draws from the speaker a smile which trembles, perhaps at the intensity of the emotion, or in sensual anticipation. Messiaen works with the text in the manner of the traditional *mélodiste*, using a melodic style reminiscent of plainchant whose simplicity matches the text. The introduction of an additional, unanticipated rest before the final 'tremble' is especially effective.

Messiaen's own texts draw on a repertoire of imagery familiar from Symbolist poetry, some of which he had already used in the titles of his *Préludes*. 'Les sons impalpables du rêve', 'Un reflet dans le vent', and 'Cloches d'angoisse et larmes d'adieu' directly echo Debussy's use of the same source material in piano pieces such as 'Les sons et les parfums tournent dans l'air du soir', 'Le vent dans la plaine', 'Reflets dans l'eau', and 'Cloches à travers les feuilles'. Messiaen's texts for both songs deploy the simple rhetorical device of a repeated phrase that is also repeated, with variation, in the melody:

Pourquoi les oiseaux de l'air
Pourquoi les reflets de l'eau
Pourquoi les nuages du ciel ... ('Pourquoi?')

C'est la douce fiancée
C'est l'ange de la bonté
C'est l'après-midi ensoleillé ... ('La fiancée perdue').

The interplay of text and music is especially effective in 'Pourquoi?', the process operating in both directions: the repeated 'pourquoi' has an internal structure created by the ejectives 'p' and 'qu' and the diphthong 'oi', which modulates the simple quaver-crotchet rhythm and is full of expressive potential in performance, as the word's sounding-structure inflects the music. We also see this process of inflection operating in the other direction in the final repetitions of 'pourquoi', which are given a clear shape and meaning only in the way the musical phrase unfolds.

La Mort du Nombre (1930)

Although *La Mort du Nombre* was premiered after the *Trois Mélodies*, we cannot be sure of the order of composition: both were composed in the summer of 1930. *La Mort* is a curious work: difficult to categorise in a satisfactory way, it is a short cantata with two souls represented by a male and a female voice, accompanied by piano and violin. Remarkably, it is the sole instance of Messiaen's writing for male voice in the art-song context, which in *La Mort* represents a soul impatiently yearning for a heavenly realm of which the angelic female voice offers the promise. The story unfolds through contrasting sections. The male voice recounts how by showing him the vision of a blinding, all-consuming light she inspired in him a yearning for transcendence and impatience with his earthly condition: 'Let time and space die!' ('Meurent le temps et l'espace!'). The female voice assures him of an imminent release – 'the weight of multiplicity will die' ('le poids du nombre sera mort') – as their souls become one, bound together in song, rising toward the light of an eternal spring. In the sections for the male voice, Messiaen uses chromatic transpositions of his modes to create a sense of drama, while the final apotheosis is resolutely tonal, ending with a climactic high B from the soprano, as the violin sounds over ecstatic rippling passagework in the piano. As with the *Trois Mélodies*, we might infer an autobiographical programme in *La Mort* that relates to the death of Sauvage, although the desire for a transcendent union of two souls in a 'trembling ecstasy' may also reflect a spiritual transposition of Messiaen's romantic relationship with violinist Claire Delbos, whom he married in 1932 and with whom he gave recitals in the early 1930s.

La Mort received its first performance at another Parisian chamber music society, the Société musicale indépendante, a month after the premiere of the *Mélodies*. It presented some logistical challenges for the young Messiaen, including a significant churn of personnel in the run up to the performance, though as in the premiere of the *Mélodies* Messiaen himself played the piano. *La Mort* received a mixed reception, with some reasonable criticism of the stark contrast between the different sound worlds of the two souls. Messiaen composed both words and music, and much of the imagery adds a cosmic, Mallarméan dimension to the romantic idealism of Symbolist verse. Just as there were connections between the imagery of the *Mélodies* and the titles of Messiaen's *Préludes*, so *La Mort* uses similar imagery, intensified to match the more dramatic context. The 'sunny afternoon' of the *Trois Mélodies* becomes in *La Mort* a source of light 'so dazzling that I can see nothing else', and where 'Le sourire' ended on 'my smile trembles', *La Mort* closes with the words 'clear smile, pure gaze, trembling ecstasy', uttered by the angelic female soul. Octave displacements in the vocal lines underline key ideas: 'serene soul', 'flower', 'clouds', 'suffering', and at the climax, 'eternal spring'.

The title *La Mort du Nombre* has been translated and understood in different ways, which relate to the aesthetic and the spiritual, and to the relationship between the two. Some scholars have drawn a parallel with Messiaen's developing rhythmic processes – since one meaning of *nombre* is 'metre', the title has been read as presaging the supposed freedom of his rhythmic techniques, a reading which has also been frequently made of the title of the more famous *Quartet for the End of Time*.[18] *La Mort*, though, predates Messiaen's rhythmic innovations, which only come into their own with the organ cycle *La Nativité du Seigneur* some five years later, and it is, for Messiaen, rather four-square in its approach to rhythm. In the text of *La Mort*, the notion of *nombre* is synonymous with an earthly multiplicity which contrasts painfully with divine unity, an opposition which may be traced back to the theological aspect of nineteenth-century French poetics, as Charles Baudelaire writes in his essay on Victor Hugo: 'How did the *one* Father engender duality, and ultimately transform Himself into a countless population of numbers? Mystery! Will, or could, the infinite totality of numbers one day return to the original unity? Mystery!'[19] The continuing importance of *nombre* to avant-garde ideas on poetics was cemented in Mallarmé's experimental poem *Un coup de dés jamais n'abolira le hasard* (1897). Here 'the unique Number which can be no other' appears to offer a clue to what this infamously difficult meditation on humankind's place in the cosmos might mean, and Messiaen's text uses the same vocabulary to articulate heavenly transcendence.[20] A similar imbrication of theological and aesthetic questions may be observed in the title of the third of Messiaen's *Préludes*, 'Le Nombre léger' (The Light Number), which contrasts with 'le poids du nombre', or 'the weight of numbers', from which *La Mort* imagines an escape. This *Prélude* is a light-hearted and exuberant little piece, almost a tribute to Ravel with its near-quotation of his *Jeux d'eau*, and also almost entirely four-square rhythmically.

In other respects, *La Mort* is rooted in two musical antecedents: the prosody of plainchant, which we hear in the male soul's opening lines, and the chromaticism and emotional drama of Wagner, which is introduced in the male soul's tormented second stanza and transformed in the apotheosis into a reworking of the *Liebestod* from Wagner's *Tristan und Isolde*. This reworking preserves not only the musical rhetoric of Wagner's original but also its harmonies (and key), with the violin taking over from the female singer as a sort of supernaturally extended voice that has broken free of the weight of earthly existence and no longer needs to breathe. *La Mort*, then, offers a very concrete example of the connection that Smalley drew between Messiaen and Wagner.

Towards the Vocal Cycles

Messiaen was certainly not the first French composer to unite the 'emotional scope of Wagner' with a language 'derived from Debussy'; indeed, Smalley could have been writing about Messiaen's principal composition teacher at the Paris Conservatoire, Paul Dukas, whose surviving music also represents a bridge between those composers' compositional worlds. Dukas' trick, strongly in evidence in his most famous work, *L'apprenti sorcier* (1897), was to use chromatic auxiliary notes and rapid modulations in phrases built up from the whole-tone scale, creating the tension of Wagner's chromaticism within a harmonic context that also alludes to Debussy.

Dukas used this approach in his opera *Ariane et Barbe-bleue*, which Messiaen heard at the Paris Opéra in the early months of 1935. Messiaen's enthusiasm for *Ariane* goes beyond a dutiful student's appreciation of his teacher's masterwork: in an article for *La revue musicale*, he expounded at length on the merits of the opera, reading it (perhaps surprisingly) as a Christian allegory. There is no doubt that *Ariane* made a huge impression on Messiaen. His article was written at the behest of the journal's editor in the summer of 1935 while Messiaen was working on the organ cycle *La Nativité du Seigneur* in Grenoble. Not only did *La Nativité* mark a significant step forward in the development of Messiaen's rhythmic techniques but it was also the first of his long-form meditations, extended multi-part works tackling a particular theme from a variety of perspectives over a long duration. Messiaen would go on to make this approach his own, writing in such forms for the organ in *Les Corps Glorieux* (1939), *Méditations sur le mystère de la Sainte Trinité* (1969), and *Livre du Saint Sacrement* (1984), for piano in *Visions de L'Amen* (1943) and *Vingt Regards sur L'Enfant-Jésus*, and for orchestra in *Turangalîla-symphonie*. It is not immediately apparent, however, that such an approach would work in the world of art song. How could a singer be expected to sustain continuously a virtuosic solo line over similar durations? In Messiaen's essay on *Ariane*, the answer was clear: here was a work that made terrific demands on an individual voice. The singer who plays Ariane must sustain a demanding vocal role and carry the entire drama, and Messiaen had seen the young dramatic soprano Marcelle Bunlet do exactly that in the performances at the Opéra. It is not too difficult to imagine that the path to Messiaen's three major song cycles, *Poèmes pour Mi*, *Chants de terre et de ciel*, and *Harawi*, became clear in the summer of 1935: Bunlet's range and stamina would allow him to transfer the technical and aesthetic innovations of *La Nativité* into the vocal realm.

Poèmes pour Mi (1936)

While the *Trois Mélodies* and *La Mort du Nombre* are worthy contributions to the *mélodie*, Messiaen's first vocal cycle, *Poèmes pour Mi*, opens a new chapter for the concept of the genre. Composed for Bunlet and first performed by her on 28 April 1937, it celebrates the sacrament of marriage and is dedicated to Delbos, whom Messiaen affectionately called 'Mi'. In a curious and compelling echo of Messiaen's mother's writing poems on maternity during her pregnancy with him, Delbos composed a cycle of eight songs (*L'Âme en bourgeon*, 1937) to texts from that very volume while pregnant with their first child, Pascal.[21] Delbos took as her texts excerpts from eight different poems, available in the Table ronde (2002) edition: 'L'Agneau', 'Mon cœur revient à son printemps', 'Je suis là', 'Te voilà hors de l'alvéole', 'Je savais que ce serait toi', 'Il est né', 'Te voilà, mon petit amant', and 'Ai-je pu t'appeler de l'ombre'. Several of the texts chosen by Delbos articulate the darker side of Sauvage's vision of maternity, featuring striking lines such as 'Your heart will tremble as it anticipates death' (p. 63), and 'Now he is born. I am alone, I feel / The horrifying emptiness of my own blood' (p. 69). Delbos also published five songs in 1935 under the title *Primevère*, using texts by Sauvage from an unfinished, unpublished volume of the same name (1913), also available in the Table ronde edition: 'Le long de mes genoux', 'J'ai peur d'être laide', 'Mais je suis belle d'être aimée', 'Je suis née à l'amour', and 'Dans ma robe à bouquets bleus'. These five poems are adjacent in *Primevère* to the short text which Messiaen used for 'Le sourire'.

Like *La Nativité*, *Poèmes pour Mi* comprises nine interrelated meditations which vary in length and complexity to give the cycle a compelling narrative arc, demonstrating variety within an overall thematic unity. The first, third, and sixth songs continue the transcendent ecstasies of *La Mort* as the lovers leave the earth behind, becoming one with the divine: 'Action de grâces' thanks God for the gift of love, which provides a revelation of truth, grace, and light; 'La maison' looks forward to the moment when 'we will leave our bodies / . . . We will contemplate the Truth in pure, young, eternally luminous bodies'; and in 'Ta voix', the voice of the beloved, a 'springtime bird awakening', sings of an eternal happiness in the Holy Trinity. The second and eighth songs, 'Paysage' and 'Le collier', contain striking images and turns of phrase reminiscent of Reverdy, such as 'The lake like a great blue jewel', an image of the beloved as 'green and blue like the landscape', and a description of her embrace as a 'light morning rainbow', 'a necklace of renewal, smile and grace', 'a curved landscape, marrying the cool morning air'. Moments of drama come in the fourth song, 'Épouvante', which warns of bloodied fragments of memories noisily pursuing the beloved into the darkness, and 'Les deux guerriers', in which the armour-clad soldiers, 'From two become one', take a town by storm: 'Fire into the sky your arrows of dawn's devotion'. The final song, 'Prière exaucée', describes the speaker's heart as a bell, which he exhorts to toll out a final hymn of praise to the Lord: 'Ring out, my heart!' Two long melismas highlight the phrases most important to this sense of resolution: on 'âme' (soul) in 'my soul will be cured', and 'joie' (joy) in the final line 'joy has returned'.

Bunlet's qualities as a singer allowed Messiaen to write in a way that is completely different from the salon-friendly *mélodies*. Across the two books of four and five songs, there are examples of the same felicitous vocal writing that was seen in the earlier works, but alongside it we find longer chant-like passages, more complex rhythmic work, extended virtuosic vocalise, emotive exclamation ('ha, ha, ha, ha, ha, ha, ho!' in 'Épouvante'), and a sense of drama that totally eclipses that of *La Mort*. Stylistically, the cycle opens with the same technique Messiaen used in 'Pourquoi?', namely, multiplying noun phrases while delaying the arrival of the verb:

The Sky,
And the water ...
And the earth, and the mountains ...
And the light ...
And an eye ...

This creates a sense of syntactic anticipation, while repetition of whole lines of text is a prominent feature in six of the nine songs. In a sense, the longer form provides the space for Messiaen to experiment with different approaches to vocal writing, but it also requires a variety of approaches to sustain interest across a larger structure. It is also striking that this work considering the sacrament of marriage from a man's perspective, and specifically Messiaen's, is written for female voice. This, and the titular dedication to Delbos, places Messiaen's unique focus on the spiritual dimension of personal experience front and centre in the *Poèmes*, an approach he would repeat in *Chants de Terre et de Ciel*.

The premiere of *Poèmes pour Mi* was given at yet another chamber music society, La Spirale, a group in which Messiaen played an important committee role. It was preceded by the premiere of Delbos' *L'Âme en bourgeon*, performed like the *Poèmes* by Bunlet and Messiaen. Although the two cycles contrast in a number of respects – most particularly in the harmonic worlds they inhabit – there are points of contact in the incantatory vocal writing and in the way the piano parts often offer a sort of commentary on the vocal line, interjecting or responding between individual vocal phrases rather than offering more traditional support. One critic, Roger Vinteuil, suggested a deep bond between the two cycles, doubtless aware of the multiple symmetries they presented when performed together: 'I don't know why, but it seems to me that some deep connection binds this cycle to the previous one: the same impression of the serious, noble, religious aspects of the great realities of life'.[22] The striking new aspects of vocal writing in the *Poèmes* grow from seeds that were sown in *Trois mélodies* and *La Mort*. The long, incantatory quasi-recitatives that are the major feature of the first *Poème*, 'Action de grâces', recur in 'Paysage', 'La maison', and 'Les deux guerriers', while 'Prière exaucée' can be seen as an extension of the male soul's opening phrase in *La Mort* and the simple chant-like melody of 'Le sourire', but they grow enormously in dimension and significance. Centred on a reciting note (or 'tenor'), they are notated exactly, but are naturally inflected rhythmically by the text. In 'Action de grâces', almost every phrase begins with a rest: knowing Messiaen's deep love for and knowledge of *Pelléas et Mélisande*, it is tempting to draw a comparison not only with the traditions of plainchant but also with Debussy's vocal writing in that opera, in which phrases that begin with rests are very common, as, for example, in the opening scene.

In 'Action de grâces', we find evidence of how Messiaen's text and music work together. Each successive melisma in this *poème*, leading up to the long and highly virtuosic 'alleluias' that are the climax, is built on a more 'open' vowel – moving from [ɔ] to [i] to [ɛ] to [a] – as the imagery moves from the worldly, via the spiritual, to the cosmic and universal. Not only does this tonal transformation mirror the imagery, but it also supports the singer in the vocal acrobatics of the 'alleluias', of which Johnson opines, 'since Purcell, there has never been a more extraordinary and extended "alleluia" in song'.[23] Whereas the violin took over the role of voice at the climax of *La Mort*, 'singing' in supernaturally extended phrases, these alleluias bring that sense of magical extension to the voice itself, with the breaths worked out and marked in the score by Messiaen in such a way as to conceal them as far as possible.

The *Poèmes pour Mi* were orchestrated by Messiaen in 1937, with the first song performed as a stand-alone item in June 1937 at a concert of La Jeune France, the loose and short-lived affiliation which Messiaen formed in 1936 with André Jolivet, Jean-Yves Daniel-Lesur, and Yves Baudrier. Although the orchestral version was published by Durand in 1939, the cycle was not performed complete in that form until 1946. The orchestral reworking introduces a wider range of colour into the accompaniments, including several that are reminiscent of organ voicings; it also transforms the context of the music from the chamber recital to the orchestral concert. Messiaen orchestrated neither the *Chants de Terre et de Ciel* nor *Harawi*, and Sherlaw Johnson comments that their orchestration would have been superfluous, given the wider palette of colour Messiaen achieves in those works with piano alone.[24] It is, however, tempting to speculate whether Messiaen considered the changed context of an orchestral performance to be effective. The larger venues required, for example, reduce the intimacy that characterises all three cycles and lessen the close-quarters impact of the bravura 'dramatic soprano' at the most dramatic moments. It might, therefore, be argued that the orchestration of *Poèmes* was an experiment that Messiaen chose not to repeat. Nonetheless, the currently available edition of the *Poèmes* in its piano version is incorrectly described as 'pour Grand Soprano dramatique et Orchestre' with a 'réduction pour Chant et Piano': this 'réduction' is the accompaniment as originally composed.

At the time of the Spirale performance that saw the premieres of *Poèmes pour Mi* and *L'Âme en bourgeon*, Delbos was six months pregnant with their son Pascal, who would be born on 14 July 1937. Roger Nichols goes so far as to speculate on 'the purely personal satisfaction that Messiaen derives from writing both *La Nativité* and *Poèmes pour Mi* as cycles of nine pieces because nine is the number symbolic of maternity'.[25] Certainly, while Messiaen writes himself into a tradition that includes composers such as Debussy, Ravel, and Wagner, it is striking how, in parallel with this musical lineage, both he and Delbos explicitly foreground in their respective cycles, *Poèmes pour Mi* and *L'Âme en bourgeon*, a sense of familial cultural inheritance, both by setting Sauvage's texts and by drawing, as she had done, on their intimate family experience for their compositional raw materials. The following summer, with baby Pascal a year old, Messiaen turned to a second long-form cycle: whereas the *Poèmes* was a mystical meditation on the sacrament of marriage, this next cycle centred on the experience of parenthood.

Chants de Terre et de Ciel (1938)

Originally performed under the title *Prismes*, this cycle was almost immediately renamed *Chants de Terre et de Ciel*, reflecting the by now familiar juxtaposition of Messiaen's personal and spiritual preoccupations. The programme is clearly self-referential, with the first song titled 'Bail avec Mi' and the third and fourth dedicated 'to my little Pascal', referred to by his familial nickname 'bébé-Pilule'. Messiaen, the bereaved son of the *Mélodies* and *La Mort* and the husband of *Poèmes*, has now become a father whose voice, as in *Poèmes*, is conveyed by a soprano. The songs for Pascal, 'Danse du bébé-Pilule' and 'Arc-en-ciel d'innocence', describe playing with his infant son, dancing, laughing, and throwing him up in the air: 'let's do it again, a hundred times!'. The first, second, and sixth songs explore the same themes of transcendence and resurrection as *La Mort* and *Poèmes*. 'Bail avec Mi' considers marriage as a welcome state of earthly companionship, foregrounding the brightness and luminescence found in earlier songs – 'little ball of sunshine, a complement to my earth' – but it is a transient state, *bail* meaning 'lease', or temporary contract of residence. 'Antienne du silence' turns to the next life – 'Let me breathe in the silence of the heavens, Alleluia' – while the final song expresses faith in resurrection after death: 'Clothe yourself in light / I am reborn ... I rise toward you, my Father, towards you, my God'.

Key images from previous songs reappear in *Chants* and are recontextualised in fascinating ways, especially in the songs for Pascal. The lake that represented the beloved in 'Paysage' (*Poèmes*) is here applied to the child's mother: 'Her perpetual yes was a tranquil lake'. The springtime bird, a metaphor for the beloved's voice in 'Ta voix' (*Poèmes*), now articulates the child's exuberance: 'All the light birds took flight from your hands', 'casting birds into your toothless mouth'. And the smile of 'Le sourire' (*Mélodies*) is linked to the child's joyful, natural musicality: 'Smile, smile, how you sing / Singing, singing taught you to smile', 'weave, weave vocalises around the silence'. The echoes of Surrealist poetics are more pronounced in *Chants*, and certain turns of phrase recall Reverdy or Éluard: 'Our hands of earth / For weaving the atmosphere' ('Bail avec Mi'), 'It's the alphabet of laughter at your mother's fingertips' ('Danse du bébé-Pilule'), 'Attach to your slender wrists the rainbows of innocence / That have fallen from your eyes' ('Arc-en-ciel d'innocence'), or the description of anguish as 'an unheard of beast, eating, slavering in my chest', as the speaker's body becomes a bell – 'my bones vibrate' – tolling out midnight: 'nine, ten, eleven, twelve' ('Minuit pile et face'). Messiaen's mother is also present, discernible in 'Danse du bébé-Pilule' in a remarkable piece of rhythmic remembrance. As the father evokes his son's mother, it is as if his thoughts turn to his own mother, the most powerful presence in his early life and work, and at this point the free verse text is punctuated several times by alexandrines, the canonical twelve-syllable line of French poetic tradition which Sauvage used frequently. In 'Danse du bébé-Pilule', they are grouped in twos and threes, and they stand out thanks to their regular 6 + 6 syllabic structure. For example:

C'est l'alphabet du rire // aux doigts de ta maman
Son oui perpétuel // était un lac tranquille ...
Et la présence verte // et l'œil de ta maman
En effeuillant une heure // autour de mon sourire[26]

Given the scarcity of such clearly identifiable metrical lines in Messiaen's free verse texts, this offers a compelling suggestion of how present his own childhood memories were at this early stage in his experience of fatherhood. Indeed, in 'Minuit pile et face' the father seems to identify so strongly with the child that in a moment of existential anguish reminiscent of 'Épouvante' (*Poèmes*) he fantasises: 'Oh to fall asleep, small! ... / My hand beneath my ear, in a tiny nightshirt'.

The step forward in musical terms from *Poèmes* is immediately apparent: this is an even more ambitious work, drawing on a wider range of musical and poetic references and making even greater demands on the soloist and pianist alike. Bunlet and Messiaen gave the first performance on 23 January 1939 at a concert of Le Triton in Paris, after which the critic Pierre Capdevielle, a colleague of Messiaen's at the music fortnightly *Le Monde musical*, gave an excoriating review of music that he clearly considered a step too far:

Examine your conscience, and ask yourself, Olivier Messiaen, if you have not sinned through pride, through a hubristic desire to surpass yourself by disguising your intimate thoughts beneath the trappings of a pseudo-theological double language. You doubtless know as well as I do what God thinks of that.[27]

Following Capdevielle's outburst, the editors of *Le Monde musical* invited Messiaen to respond, and he did this in a good-natured article in which he describes himself as 'the author of the poems and the music' and defends the theological perspective underpinning his imagery. Finally, he turns to his musical language, arguing:

It is not extravagant! I have studied harmony, fugue, and composition long enough to be able to claim I know what I'm doing! ... I have, moreover, appreciated certain pages by Schoenberg, Jolivet, certain French or Russian popular melodies. If you bear in mind, in addition, that I love Massenet, because he is tonal, well-harmonised, you will have some idea of my style. As for those who rail against my so-called dissonances, I declare quite simply that I am not dissonant: they should wash out their ears![28]

Although the total duration of *Chants* is almost identical to that of *Poèmes* and the text is only slightly longer, there are fewer individual songs within the set (six as opposed to nine), meaning that there is greater scope for Messiaen to develop both his musical and his poetic ideas within each song.

Just as in *Poèmes*, the vocal antecedent of plainchant is strongly in evidence across the cycle, and there are several long melismas on 'alleluia' in the second and sixth songs. As with the textual imagery, however, the vocal writing has expanded, and while the reciting notes or tenors of *Poèmes* are still in evidence, they are joined by a much more sophisticated use of melodic figures, based around subsets of Messiaen's modes of limited transposition. As Sherlaw Johnson pointed out: 'The melodic behaviour of the various notes of the mode becomes specialised so that the mode is best described by a melodic formula rather than by a scale. In this respect it resembles the modes of plainsong, where melodic formulae can be crucial in defining the mode, and the *râgas* of Classical Indian music'.[29] These figures are subject to constant alteration – expansion, contraction, embellishment, and deformation – and the effect is to create a vocalise with a strong identity that is nonetheless continuously evolving, as seen in the second song, 'Antienne du silence'. This technique permits a greater sense of forward movement and allows the piano part to operate as a more complex commentary on the vocal line, providing three independent polyphonic lines built on related subsets of the same mode. As Jane Manning observes, 'the tuning has to be scrupulous, despite other challenges of breath capacity and rhythm'.[30]

Messiaen had experimented with simple vocables – 'ho' and 'ha' – in the fourth *Poème*, 'Épouvante', to express a fear bordering on hysteria. In 'Danse du bébé-Pilule', he explores this approach further, but in the very different context of tender infant-directed speech and a baby's pre-speech verbalising. Alongside the gentle vocables 'ma', 'io', and 'ha', the latter transformed through the musical setting from the sobbing of 'Épouvante' into a light giggle, Messiaen uses the non-lexical vocables of French folk song, 'malonlanlaine', that could come from the mouth of baby or parent. The opening of 'Danse du bébé-Pilule' is described by Messiaen as an 'artificial folksong' and this description, along with the nonsense words and vocables, might raise an expectation of simplicity.[31] In reality, however, the song grows from a simple and apparently metrical opening into an extended, playful, and ametrical vocalise, radiantly supported by the piano in some of the most straightforwardly joyous of all Messiaen's music. Both the decorative harmony and the harmonic sequences deployed look forward to the 'Chant d'amour' movements of *Turangalîla-symphonie*, but Messiaen also incorporates a short but clear allusion to Debussy's 'The Little Shepherd' (*Children's Corner*), immediately before the innocently ravishing phrase that is the intimate centre of the work: 'Can you sing more deliciously?' ('Pouvez-vous chanter plus délicieusement?').

Harawi: Chant d'amour et de mort (1945)

The cast of characters in the unfolding story of Messiaen's *mélodies* expands with each new work we encounter: his mother is the key figure in *Trois Mélodies*, joined perhaps by Delbos in *La Mort du Nombre*; Delbos and Bunlet together inspire *Poèmes pour Mi*, and in *Chants de Terre et de Ciel* Pascal appears; Wagner, we might say, stands in the background throughout. All are present in *Harawi*, the last of Messiaen's song cycles, joined by yet another new figure: the young pianist Yvonne Loriod, who had been a student of Messiaen on his return to occupied Paris in 1941. Her extraordinary, transcendent facility at the keyboard had the same effect on Messiaen's writing for piano as Bunlet's expressive range and vocal stamina had on his writing for voice. Initially, Messiaen wrote for Loriod the first piano part of the duo *Visions de L'Amen* (1943), a virtuosic decoration of the simpler second part which he composed for himself and played with her in the premiere. Then came in quick succession the solo piano part in *Trois Petites Liturgies de la Présence Divine* (1943–4) and the monumental twenty movements of *Vingt regards sur L'Enfant-Jésus*. While *Poèmes* and *Chants* were significant works of extended duration which made considerable demands of the voice, *Harawi* marks a further radical expansion in scale, scope, and ambition, not only for the voice but also for the piano. Although Messiaen himself gave the first performance, the experience of writing for Loriod had unlocked vastly greater possibilities in his writing for the instrument. The twelve songs of *Harawi* last around an hour in total and there are numerous extended piano interludes that are by turns hypnotic and dazzling. Alongside this, the vocal demands extend even beyond those of *Chants* – as Jane Manning writes, 'piano and voice together undertake an epic adventure'.[32] From a technical perspective, then, *Harawi* harnesses the combined potential of Bunlet and Loriod, to startling effect.

It would be wrong, however, to imagine that the two women occupy equivalent places in *Harawi*. Whereas Messiaen's relationship with Bunlet was professional, his meeting and working with Loriod, who would much later become his second wife, brought a further complication to a period of unprecedented emotional turmoil. Around 1943 Delbos began to show signs of a serious and intermittently disabling mental disorder. While she was sometimes able to participate in family life, the periods of respite from her condition seem to have become increasingly rare through the mid-1940s. Finally, an operation that was planned to treat her condition went badly wrong, leaving her confined to a hospice and requiring constant care.

Messiaen's relationship with Loriod at this time is a matter of speculation, but one can imagine the painful dilemma of a devout Catholic devoted to an increasingly distant and withdrawn wife, attracted musically and emotionally toward another woman, caring for a young son – and all this against the backdrop of the privations of a world war and its aftermath. Loriod would later summarise her relationship with Messiaen in the long period of Delbos' decline before her death in 1959 as an 'impossible love'.[33]

Messiaen's description of *Harawi* as part one of a 'Tristan Trilogy' that also includes *Cinq Rechants* and the *Turangalîla-symphonie* reminds us again of Wagner, but Messiaen explores the *Tristan* idea in these works not so much as a drama of passion but rather as a parable of a love that aspires towards, and finds its ultimate consummation in, death. The twelve songs create a narrative arc familiar from *La Mort du Nombre*. The lovers meet at midnight – the 'banc de minuit' of 'La ville qui dormait, toi' recalls Act 2 of Wagner's *Tristan und Isolde* where the lovers lie down on a grassy bank – to contemplate the vertiginous abyss of the cosmos ('Montagnes') and the dance of the stars ('Doundou tchil'). In 'L'Amour de Piroutcha', the heroine offers herself to her lover as ashes ('ta petite cendre, pour toi'), while he responds with the remarkable request 'Cut off my head', and juxtaposes the key terms of the drama: 'love, death'. The lovers then shed their earthly forms, dissolving into the universal play of atoms: in 'Répétition planétaire' they enter a whirling, spiralling staircase ('escalier tournant, tourbillon'), a recurrent symbol from this point onwards; in 'Adieu' they bid each other farewell before being reborn in 'Syllabes': 'oh my heaven, you are flowering'. In the ninth song, the lovers are reunited in death and 'the silence of the infinite' as the young man declares: 'Let us invent the love of the world / To search for ourselves, to cry for ourselves, to dream for ourselves, to find ourselves'.[34] At this moment of communion, a 'fan of birdsong' appears, which in the next song becomes 'all the birds of the stars'. There is time for one final dance among the swirling nebulas in 'Katchi-katchi les étoiles' during which the man reiterates his yearning for the ecstasy of death, echoing *La Mort du Nombre* – 'Cut off my head, its number is rolling in blood' ('Coupe-moi la tête, son chiffre roule dans le sang') – before the final song, 'Dans le noir', plunges us into the black of night.

For *Harawi*, Messiaen drew on the work of ethnomusicologists Raoul and Marguerite Béclard d'Harcourt, taking the title from a type of Peruvian folksong that tells the story of doomed love and adapting the musical theme that recurs throughout the cycle from one quoted in their 1925 study of the music of the Incas.[35] Indeed, Messiaen told Goléa that, in his opinion,

'Peruvian music contains the most beautiful folk melodies in the world'.[36] Thematic and linguistic elements from South American civilisations coexist in *Harawi* with Messiaen's familiar brand of Catholic mysticism, as in the recurrent description of the female protagonist Piroutcha as a green dove. While Messiaen suggested that this was a Mayan sacred symbol for the beloved, the dove is also a Christian symbol of peace, and in Christian colour symbolism green represents the power of everlasting life. It has been observed that, in terms of the development of his compositional techniques, Messiaen rarely rejects aspects of his earlier music, as many twentieth-century composers did, but rather continually extends and enriches his previous techniques, integrating new approaches into a highly coherent 'musical language'.[37] The same could be said of his approach to text in *Harawi*, in which the Andean sources commingle with his familiar preoccupations. Messiaen retains key symbols from the earlier songs, such as flowers and stars, and further develops the Surrealism of *Chants* with opaque, inventive images: 'The kneeling stone carries its dark masters', 'In hoods pulled tight the pines hasten towards the dark' ('Montagnes'). While writing *Harawi*, Messiaen was avidly reading Reverdy and Éluard as well as a work by André Breton on Surrealism and painting; the tenth song, 'Amour oiseau d'étoile', was written in response to a Surrealist canvas of 1937 by Sir Roland Penrose, *Seeing Is Believing (L'île invisible)*, which Messiaen claimed was a symbol for the whole of *Harawi*.[38] Most strikingly of all, perhaps, the cycle foregrounds quite dramatically a technique that had been seen only in embryonic form in earlier works such as 'Épouvante' (*Poèmes*) and 'Danse du bébé-Pilule' (*Chants*): the use of text principally for its sounding structure.

The fourth, sixth, eighth, and eleventh songs feature Quechua words, nonsense vocables, and onomatopoeia, thereby untethering, for a European audience at least, the sound of the words from their semantic meaning. Some of the Quechua words may also be onomatopoeic, such as 'katchikatchi', which Messiaen claimed was a French transliteration of the word for grasshopper (it also reminds us of the continued influence of the natural images instilled in him by his mother). Messiaen may also have invented 'Quechua' words in the way that he later did in *Cinq Rechants*, blurring the boundary between onomatopoeia, in which sound and sense are bound together, and units of pure sound. In *Harawi*, these unfamiliar words are repeated extensively, making a significant contribution to the rhythmic effect while also rendering interpretation uncertain. Sherlaw Johnson, for example, suggests that 'Doundou tchil' is an onomatopoeic representation of the ankle-bells of Peruvian dancers, that syllable sequences such as

'Toungou, toungou, ma pa, na ma, ma pa, na ma, ma pa, kahipipas' or 'Ma pa na ahi tchil ahi o lila mapu pampahika adoundoutchil' act as a kind of 'black magic ritual' invoking cosmic dissolution, and that the 'pia, pia, pia' section of 'Syllabes', which lasts for over five pages of music, reproduces the cries of apes from Peruvian legend.[39] Certainly, where the gentle nonsense words of *Chants de Terre et de Ciel* ('Io, Io, malonlanlaine') drew us into the innocently magical world of the infant, the non-semantic text in *Harawi* produces a powerful sense of magical incantation, offering a disorientating glimpse of the more-than-human. Yet while the violin part at the apotheosis of *La Mort* took us beyond earthly experience in an affirmation of everlasting life, the sense of linguistic and cosmic dissolution in *Harawi* is altogether more sinister and less theologically certain.

The interleaving of sections of semantic text in 'Doundou tchil' with pure vocables marks a contrast between the worldly realm of the lovers and the mystery of wider creation. The boundary separating these worlds then dissolves in the litanies of 'Répétition planétaire' and the orgiastic repetitions of 'Syllabes', leading to an ecstatic spiralling of atoms – 'electrons, ants, arrows' – in 'Katchikatchi les étoiles', where Messiaen deploys all the various approaches to text that he has used up to this point: familiar bodily images ('hands of my hair'), surrealist juxtapositions ('Dilate space gaudy rainbow of time'), and exclamations of pure sound ('Tou, *ahi! isc*, mani'). Alongside this dissolution of words into syllables, the frequent accumulation of noun phrases may perhaps be read as a syntactic illustration of the lovers' bodily dissolution and recomposition. As in 'Pourquoi' (*Trois Mélodies*) and 'Action de grâces' (*Poèmes*), the first two songs feature no main clause, instead building a chain of noun phrases that float free of any explanatory syntactic relationship other than parataxis. These fragments then reappear across all twelve songs, as if language itself, like the lovers, were dissolving in order to be reconfigured. Key images such as the 'double violet', 'green dove', 'clear pearl', or 'the number five for you' recur throughout, and the phrase 'You, of flower, of fruit, of heaven, and of water' in the second song returns in the seventh, ninth, and twelfth, each time with variations. The crucial symbol of this universal whirling, the cosmic staircase, also spirals through several incarnations in the ninth song: 'staircase of time … staircase of heaven … staircase of water'. The overall effect of this linguistic fragmentation is compelling, yet disorientating, and rather than achieving a lasting sense of joyous union for the lovers, the conclusion of the cycle is strongly marked by an impression of chaos and fear.

The final song of *Harawi* is perhaps the darkest moment in Messiaen's entire output, fittingly entitled 'Dans le noir', and it represents, for Johnson, 'one of the most exceptional pieces in French vocal music'.[40] Images of the beloved from the first two songs – 'green dove', 'clear pearl' – reappear, but they are preceded each time by 'In the darkness', as descending piano chords, blurred by the pedal, evoke a total dissolution. Just as Messiaen used octave displacements to underline the key ideas of *La Mort du Nombre*, the interval of a minor third is important throughout *Harawi*, used to underline key images relating to the beloved, as well as the name Piroutcha in 'Doundou Tchil' and her direct speech in 'L'amour de Piroutcha'. As the cycle ends on a moment of desolate ambiguity, a rising major sixth performed without words ('à bouche fermée') provides an inversion of the falling minor third that has recurred throughout. This inversion of minor third to major sixth has the practical consequence that the vocal part remains within reasonable range of a dramatic soprano, but it also adds to the ambiguity of the cycle's end: is this a distant echo of the beloved, or does it mark her absence? The lovers of *Harawi* experience the overwhelming force of love as a cosmic cataclysm, but in the death to which they eagerly submit, they seem to become so subsumed into the cosmos that they simply disappear.

While it is tempting to imagine *Harawi* as a covert love-song to the young Loriod, and this is certainly the attractive interpretation that Goléa made, the sense of tragedy in the final song may also point to an anguished foretelling of the death of Delbos.[41] That her final departure came only after another fifteen years of decline only adds to the poignancy of *Harawi*.

Messiaen's song cycles are epic in all senses of the word, from their scale and musical ambition to the themes they tackle and the sheer challenge they present to the singer and pianist who, in Manning's words, undertake the adventure together. Nonetheless, recalling Goléa's assessment of song forms, they are profoundly intimate, bound as they are with the intense experiences of Messiaen's unfolding personal circumstances in the 1930s and 1940s. While they may not be *mélodies* in the usual sense of the term, they look back to some of its conventions and traditions, while being at the same time strikingly new in other respects. Messiaen, as composer and poet, blending pure sound and imagery, makes a highly significant contribution to the twentieth-century *mélodie*.

Notes

1. Antoine Goléa, *Rencontres avec Olivier Messiaen* (Paris: René Julliard, 1960), 119. All translations from the French are our own.
2. Graham Johnson and Richard Stokes, *A French Song Companion* (Oxford: Oxford University Press, 2000), xxvii.
3. Roger Smalley, 'Debussy and Messiaen', *The Musical Times*, 109 (February 1968), 128.
4. Johnson and Stokes, *A French Song Companion*, 313.
5. Ibid., 313 and 314.
6. Claude Samuel, *Entretiens avec Olivier Messiaen* (Paris: Pierre Belfond, 1967), 145.
7. Samuel, *Entretiens avec Olivier Messiaen*, 148.
8. Cécile Sauvage, *Œuvres complètes* (Paris: La Table ronde, 2002), 65. *L'âme en bourgeon*, or *The Soul in Bud*, took its title from the pet name which Sauvage, in her letters to her husband, used to refer to her son *in utero* (ibid., 244, 254–5, and 257).
9. Goléa, *Rencontres avec Olivier Messiaen*, 19–20.
10. Samuel, *Entretiens avec Olivier Messiaen*, 121 and 10.
11. Sauvage, *Œuvres complètes*, 71.
12. Ibid., 243–4.
13. Messiaen, *Technique de mon langage musical* (Paris: Alphonse Leduc, 1944), 4.
14. Goléa, *Rencontres avec Olivier Messiaen*, 39.
15. Robert Sherlaw Johnson, *Messiaen* (London: J. M. Dent & Sons, 1975), 55.
16. Taken from the unfinished volume *Primevère*, in *Œuvres complètes*, 167.
17. F-Pn, *Département de la musique*, L. a. *Messiaen*. (Letter sent 17 August 1929.)
18. Paul Griffiths, *Olivier Messiaen and the Music of Time* (London: Faber, 1985), Chapter 2.
19. Charles Baudelaire, *Œuvres complètes*, vol. 2, ed. Claude Pichois (Paris: Gallimard, 'Bibliothèque de la Pléiade', 1975), 137 (original italics).
20. Stéphane Mallarmé, *Œuvres complètes*, vol. 1, ed. Bertrand Marchal (Paris: Gallimard, 'Bibliothèque de la Pléiade', 1998), 372–3.
21. See Claire Delbos, *L'âme en bourgeon* (Paris: Fortin, 2009).
22. Roger Vinteuil, 'La Spirale (28 avril)', *Le Ménestrel* (7 May 1937), 147–8.
23. Johnson and Stokes, *A French Song Companion*, 314–5.
24. Sherlaw Johnson, *Messiaen*, 58.
25. Roger Nichols, *Messiaen* (Oxford: Oxford University Press, 1986), 25.
26. The other alexandrines which appear in 'Danse du bébé-Pilule' are 'Douceur des escaliers, surprise au coin des portes', 'Tous les oiseaux légers s'envolaient de tes mains', 'Oiseaux légers, cailloux, refrains, crème légère', 'Ton petit nez levé vers le bleu qui s'avale', 'Ourlant de cris dorés les horizons de verre'.

27. Pierre Capdevielle, 'Le Triton Ferraud – Jaubert – Tomasi – Ol. Messiaen', *Le Monde musical* (31 January 1939), 26.
28. Olivier Messiaen, 'Autour d'une Parution', *Le Monde musical* (30 April 1939), 35.
29. Sherlaw Johnson, *Messiaen*, 59.
30. Jane Manning, 'The Songs and Song Cycles', in *The Messiaen Companion*, ed. Peter Hill (London: Faber, 1994), 129.
31. Olivier Messiaen, *Technique de mon langage musical: Texte avec exemples musicaux* (Paris: Leduc, 2000), 33.
32. Jane Manning, 'The Songs and Song Cycles', in *The Messiaen Companion*, ed. Peter Hill (London: Faber, 1994), 136.
33. Hill and Simeone, *Messiaen*, 229.
34. This recalls Rimbaud's famous assertion, 'L'amour est à réinventer', from *Une saison en enfer*, in *Poésies*, ed. Louis Forestier (Paris: Gallimard, 1999), 188.
35. R. and M. Béclard d'Harcourt, *La Musique des Incas et ses survivances* (Paris: Paul Geuthner, 1925), in Hill and Simeone, *Messiaen*, 156.
36. Goléa, *Rencontres avec Olivier Messiaen*, 149. Goléa provides a detailed, enthusiastic appreciation of all twelve songs of *Harawi* (158–74), in which, he suggests, 'the poems, the most beautiful of all that Messiaen wrote, are perhaps even more important, more significant, than the music' (174).
37. See, for example, Sherlaw Johnson, *Messiaen*, 191.
38. Goléa, *Rencontres avec Olivier Messiaen*, 155–6.
39. Sherlaw Johnson, *Messiaen*, 80–1.
40. Johnson and Stokes, *A French Song Companion*, 316.
41. Goléa, *Rencontres avec Olivier Messiaen*, 150–6.

14 | Interpreting French Art Song

FRANÇOIS LE ROUX

Starting with Personal Memories

For many children of my generation, when only radio was available, singing with other members of my family was customary and for me a joy. Even when travelling by car, we all sang a vast repertory of French *chansons*. They were folk songs of the past and songs of contemporary popular singers heard on the radio. Most of them in the 1950s and 1960s had a strong link with the tradition of classical poetry, and by listening to them one learnt rhymes, melodies, and how to pronounce well while singing. I remember clearly some of these songs even today: 'Le loup, la biche et le chevalier' (The Wolf, the Doe, and the Knight) by Henri Salvador, on a poem by Maurice Pon from 1950, and 'L'eau vive' (Running Water) by Guy Béart, who wrote both poem and music in 1958. This last song is particularly memorable to me. The first verse is 'Ma petite est comme l'eau' (My darling is like water); I remember asking my mother, 'What is an "écomelo" [ekɔmølo]?', which is what I had understood. Many years later, as a professional performer, I still take this first question as a sign of concern about the perception of a sung text by a fresh ear: not to take for granted what an audience will get from a live performance. It surely was an early sign of my interest in the sonorities of the French language and its characteristics (mute e [ə], rhyme, etc.), but not yet of the fact that this verse, 'Ma petite est comme l'eau', is a heptasyllable, a rarity in French *chanson*, which usually has a basic octosyllabic verse to cope with! Although many of Victor Hugo's poems titled 'chanson' have seven-syllable lines, for example, 'S'il est un charmant gazon', set by Gabriel Fauré, César Franck, Franz Liszt, and many other composers, eight syllables is usual for the French *chanson*.

Later at college I had the chance to work with distinguished teachers in French language courses (combined, as was the custom in those days, with studies of what was called 'lettres classiques', including ancient Greek and Latin). Most of them were connoisseurs of poetry. And I worked with an outstanding music teacher, a great pianist (we later would perform recitals together) who is the person who strongly suggested that I could become a professional musician. With this double influence, I was undoubtedly prepared to try out the art forms where poetry and music could meet. However, it is when I started to study singing seriously that all these elements came together in my mind. Undoubtedly, as well, learning other languages at the same time at university – German, Italian, Russian (English had been the only foreign language I had studied in secondary school) – made me conscious of the specific musicality of my native language. I then decided to listen to prominent ambassador singers of the *mélodie* genre. And almost immediately I found their way of singing *mélodie* mannered and old-fashioned, as if presenting an element of a moribund (if not already dead) culture. Would it not be possible to make the genre sound lively, connected to young generations, without transforming its essence? My younger sister Claire had said to me when I decided to start vocal studies, 'Too bad that you are going to change your naturally beautiful voice into a manufactured sound!' This remark has driven me ever since toward deepening work both on the form and meaning of all songs, whatever the language, without fabricating the sound. I realise now that the classical education these singers of former generations were given comprised cultural elements that were no longer known to the public, such as the rules of poetry; any classical composer knew these by heart. But what could be a way of sounding 'natural' without undermining the cultural specificities of the *mélodie*, called by philosopher Roland Barthes (1915–80) 'the celebration of the cultured French language'?[1]

One of my first decisions was to avoid 'rolling the *r*', in order to have a way of singing close to 'normal people' (that is, popular singers of the 1970s), as I always had before as a child, long before my voice had changed from treble (very high) to baritone. Another was to keep in mind the inner music of the French language and to pay attention to all the elements of a *mélodie* at the same time: music, poem, vocal sonorities (assonances, colours). In the masterclasses I took, attention was concentrated more on the meaning of a poem, the emotion it carried, and how to connect it to one's own experience. Right enough, but not sufficient to understand why a composer would choose a certain interpretation, a certain phrasing, a general sound ...

The first *mélodie* I sang, for my final examination at college ('baccalauréat', nicknamed 'bachot' or 'bac'), was 'Priez pour paix', composed in 1938 by Francis Poulenc and based on old poetry of the fifteenth century by Duke Charles d'Orléans. It is one of the very few songs by Poulenc available in two keys, the original being in C minor and the transposed version in F minor. I sang the original one. I have never understood why publishers set aside some versions, even when they are in the composer's original chosen tonality, and in this case giving the singer a very easy range ($B\flat_3$-$B\flat_4$). Although Poulenc himself declared that he would rather set poets whose voice he had heard – Guillaume Apollinaire, Louis Aragon, Jean Cocteau, Colette, Paul Éluard, Max Jacob, Jaboune, or Louise de Vilmorin – and gave less credit to his settings of older poetry, I have always heard in his settings of Pierre de Ronsard or d'Orléans his recognisable personal voice and style, rooted perhaps in a trace of historical nostalgia and melancholy. Ronsard is buried by the Prieuré Saint-Cosme near Tours, while the Duke d'Orléans' castle was in Blois, both cities not too far from Poulenc's chosen home in Noizay along the Loire Valley. Biographical elements do not directly guide a singer's interpretation, but they can certainly help to avoid mistakes. And when you are aware of such details it enriches the singing. I think it is not irrelevant to know that the sea Fauré loved and depicted in his last cycle, *L'horizon chimérique*, is not the ocean that Debussy depicted in 'La mer est plus belle que les cathédrales' in his *Trois mélodies sur des poèmes de Paul Verlaine*. Debussy went often to Normandy and the Basque country, where he enjoyed the marine atmosphere and the stormy, impressive strength of the sea. Fauré loved Venice and the lagoon, and certainly the barcarolle rhythm associated with it, not the tremulous roar of the ocean. These are just remarks or 'endnotes', but any such tiny detail can bring light to the interpretation.

It is thanks to Craig Rutenberg, an American pianist working at the Paris Opera Studio of which I was a member at the end of the 1970s (and later a brilliant coach at the Paris Opera, then at the Metropolitan Opera), that I was offered a recital in a Spring Festival in Poitiers. I sang a carefully chosen selection of Schubert *Lieder*. The following year at the same venue we decided (Craig's guidance was essential, being in permanent contact with Pierre Bernac, among others) on a whole Fauré programme, shared with soprano Dominique Lebrun, another member of the Paris Opera Studio – my second recital of French *mélodie*! (The first was a recital of the complete Duparc songs with my college music teacher Nicole Aubert Cazalet at the end of 1979. It took place at the Opera House in Tours and remains a wonderful memory.) Dare I say that compared to the Schubert evening the Fauré recital was much more challenging? I was not then comprehending the style, the lines of Fauré songs, and my inclination towards French poetry did not help me as much as I had first thought. I now understand what was for me totally new in those days: Fauré treated the voice like a string instrument, demanding specific bowing and use of vibration as if he were writing for a violin. This is, I think, unique in the French song repertoire. When I sang the Duparc songs a few months earlier, I had felt myself much more 'at home'; later Debussy would become 'my home', or at least one of them. Nowadays, as people like to classify things, they say that there are two 'schools', the Fauréan and Debussyan. For my part, I like to offer this perspective: after having selected a poem, Fauré would learn it by heart then close the book and compose the song – music above all! Debussy, after choosing a poem, would have it on the piano while composing, always going back to it, trying to find the rhythmically closest enunciation in music – poetry first!

Form and Content

From very early on I thought of poet Paul Verlaine (1844–96) as the champion of musicality in French poetry. And indeed, he is certainly one of the most frequently chosen by French composers up to the present day. I have found more than a hundred different songs on his untitled poem from *La bonne chanson* (1870) beginning 'La lune blanche' (often named by composers 'L'heure exquise'), if one includes the translated versions set to music in English, German (for instance, Richard Dehmel's 'Helle Nacht'), or Russian (for example, Valeri Bryusov's 'Имесяц белый')!

Comparing different musical versions of the same Verlaine poem has been a key to my understanding of the interpretation of *mélodie*. Starting from a single poem, one can decipher how composers have a different (or similar) perception of a text. The too-frequent attitude of a singer is, I have noticed, to look for a personal feeling about the song. That is perfectly all right for a *chanson* where the singer is centre stage and, as such, often cited before the composer and the poet by radio commentators. (For example, Joseph Kosma's 'Autumn Leaves', which in France is often announced as 'Les feuilles mortes d'Yves Montand' (or 'de Juliette Gréco', or any popular singer).) A composer has already conceived a personal interpretation of the poem he or she sets to music, long before a performer starts working on the song. And it is the path the composer has taken that a good recitalist has to find (recreate) in order to be faithful both to the composer and the poet.

What is most striking among the repertoire of French *mélodies* is how often the most formerly elaborate poems have interested composers. Many would certainly say that Fauré did not always choose the best poets of his time, but if we look at the form of the poems he chose, they always contain an element of challenge for him to face, be it reiteration of words or enjambments.

Victor Hugo (1802–85) was the key poet for composers born in the nineteenth century. Take, for instance, his 'Le pas d'armes du Roi Jean' (1828), a real poetic *tour de force* with verses of only three syllables but alternating feminine and masculine rhymes. Camille Saint-Saëns took up the challenge in 1852, setting the poem as a narrative song or *ballade*, and he preserved Hugo's Romantic spirit although he left out more than half of the poem.

Yes, French poetry is formal, and yes, its strict demands were known to all composers of the golden age of the *mélodie* from Berlioz to Poulenc. Poulenc's first known (though unpublished) song, composed when he was fourteen, is incidentally on a poem by Victor Hugo, 'Viens! – une flûte invisible', set by many composers before him, including Saint-Saëns and André Caplet. French composers even privileged the most restricted form of all, the French sonnet, with its fourteen verses (only alexandrine verses or decasyllables) distributed into two quatrains followed by two tercets. A composer forgotten today, Jules Duprato (1827–92) even completed a *Livre des sonnets*, a book of twenty songs composed on sonnets by fifteen different poets from diverse times: Vincent Voiture (1597–1648) is the oldest, Jules Truffier (1856–1943) the most recent. The score was published in Paris by Heugel around 1864.

More recently, Henri Dutilleux (1916–2013) has composed four *Sonnets de Jean Cassou*; 'La geôle' (The Jail) was composed in 1944 and the other three in 1954. He told me that for 'J'ai rêvé que je vous portais entre mes bras' (I dreamt that I was carrying you in my arms) he had decided to take each twelve-syllable alexandrine as a series of twelve different tones and to therefore write dodecaphonic serial music! As shown in Example 14.1, the singer's first twelve notes are G, B♭, D, A, E, D♭, A♭, F, C, B, F♯, E♭. Dutilleux kept this idea for both quatrains, plus two verses, then let the rest run more freely.

The alexandrine verse in classical versification is submitted to the hemistich rule, allowing only one possible cut in the middle of each verse and forming thus two symmetrical parts of six syllables. This rule evolved later, as we can see in the Cassou verse presented in Example 14.1 where a caesura in the middle would make no sense, separating the subject from the verb – 'J'ai rêvé que je vous // portais entre mes bras'. Dutilleux phrased the line, as shown above, in two uneven parts – 'J'ai rêvé que je vous portais // entre mes bras'. As in Fauré, the *legato* sign applies to the complete verse, but the rhythm clearly shows where to take a breath.

Example 14.1. Tone row in Henri Dutilleux, 'J'ai rêvé que je vous portais entre mes bras' (*Sonnets de Jean Cassou*), mm. 1–4

Prosody

I have always been accustomed to counting the syllables of the poem set to music each time I have to experiment with the phrasing of a song, whether the composer has marked it or has failed to give any clear indication. And even today I advise my students to pay attention first to the poem as printed in the book (this is my practice, notwithstanding that one must provide them with the poem if it is difficult to find), and to recite it before singing with a neutral ear in order to experience physically the musicality of the text itself. Then, still with the same neutral ear, I have them try while reading the song to perceive the phrasing that the composer has decided to achieve, serving the poem.

Let us take an example, and a famous one, to show how decisions that we do not perceive immediately have been taken by the composer: Baudelaire's celebrated 'La vie antérieure' (Past Life) in the setting by Duparc (his last published song, 1884). The piano introduction lasts exactly six beats (one and a half bars of 4/4) like a hexasyllable. All the strong beats are placed carefully, and the phrasing by Duparc is never duplicated (I underline these strong syllables for the first quatrain):

J'ai long-temps ha-bi-té sous de vas-tes por-ti-ques
Que les so-leils ma-rins tei-gnaient de mil-le feux,
Et que leurs grands pi-liers, droits et ma-jes-tu-eux,
Ren-daient pa-reils, le soir, aux grot-tes ba-sal-ti-ques.

Les houles, en roulant les images des cieux,
Mêlaient d'une façon solennelle et mystique
Les tout-puissants accords de leur riche musique
Aux couleurs du couchant reflété par mes yeux.

C'est là que j'ai vécu dans les voluptés calmes,
Au milieu de l'azur, des vagues, des splendeurs
Et des esclaves nus, tout imprégnés d'odeurs,

Qui me rafraîchissaient le front avec des palmes,
Et dont l'unique soin était d'approfondir
Le secret douloureux qui me faisait languir.

The piano introduction is a kind of a march on the same note (B♭ in the original tonality of E♭ major); in the orchestrated version, a trumpet even plays this repeated note. The first sung phrase starts on the same note, keeping the same momentum, and the position of the first syllable on the third beat establishes a solemnity in the declamation. All the upbeats have been clearly marked rhythmically: 'long-temps' and 'por-tiques' show the same pattern, as do 'ha-bi-té' and 'sous de vas-'. The feminine ending of the first verse is the same syllable as the first one of the following verse: '-que' and 'Que'. There are only two rhymes for both quatrains. The first quatrain has two feminine rhymes '-i-que' [i-kə], for 'portiques' and 'basaltiques', embracing two masculine endings, '-eux' [ø], for 'feux' and 'majestueux'; the second has the same rhymes, but inverted as the masculine rich rhyme 'ieu' [iø] of 'cieux' and 'yeux' now embraces 'mystique' and 'musique'. Feminine and masculine endings have to be well contrasted by the singer in order not to make the same phrasing end unchanged. The contrast is clearly established between the solemn declamation Duparc writes for the first quatrain, portraying an almost majestic portico with columns, and the long, sliding phrasing for the second, depicting the surface of the sea with its *crescendo* and *agitato*, ending with a great wave in the piano part. This effect is difficult to achieve for both singer and pianist: the marking *un peu plus vite* at the start of the second quatrain asks for restraint before moving forward, the 'attente' (expectation) of which Leconte de Lisle wrote in another poem set by Duparc, 'Phydilé', being rewarded only if no excitement is shown ahead of time! The climax at the beginning of the first tercet is extraordinary as Duparc makes a single amendment to Baudelaire's poem, repeating 'C'est là': the first time, it is isolated in an almost Promethean and glorious affirmation (with a great C-major chord played *ff* at the piano); the second time, it is linked in a classical hexasyllable preparing the change of mood, phrased in two hemistichs – 'C'est là que j'ai vécu / Dans les voluptés calmes'. Then the dreamy evocation of remembered sensations (sight, smell, etc.) is marked by caesuras (not breathing stops!) before, on the penultimate verse, changing to a mood of spleen. A general remark: all composers have used rests as marks of phrasing, not of breathing! I like to tell my students that song composers normally love singers (and work closely with good ones) and let them decide for themselves where to take a breath. They would never dare write: *You MUST take a breath here!*

Let me focus on the penultimate verse. How does Duparc treat the hemistich? It is not a pressing question for the singer, who would choose whatever he or she thinks best in matters of breathing, often opting for 'Et dont l'u-ni-que soin é-tait / d'ap-pro-fon-dir', which means cutting the verse into an octosyllable and four-syllable word. But let us watch exactly what happens musically (see Example 14.2). The first five syllables are sung on an A♭ in the original key (F in the version for medium voice), and then the melody rises a half step between 'unique' and 'soin'. Then, on the new A♮ (or F♯) there are five syllables *recto tono*, and the melody rises another half step between '-fon' and '-dir', making exactly symmetrical hexasyllables:

Et don't l'u-ni-que (half step) soin // était d'ap-pro-fon-(half step)-dir

Having noticed this, you can only perform the hemistich the way it has been thoroughly elaborated by Duparc. Moreover, this most musical alexandrine verse, comprising nine different vowels, is emblematic of the care composers put into their examination of a poem!

Example 14.2. Henri Duparc, 'La vie antérieure', mm. 44–8

Many singers would certainly see this is as accessory and of little importance compared to the depth of the mood and feeling that Baudelaire is expressing. On the contrary, I see it as an example of attention and respect to both poetic and musical composition. To keep looking for what is perhaps not at once perceptible, but could help the audience to follow the music and the text and understand a 'work of art', should be a respectful rule.

A Permanent Self-Questioning

Deepening our understanding of a *mélodie* is always rewarding, at least intellectually; there are certain meanings that keep their secrets if you do not have the chance to find a reference to illuminate the composition. Let me take two examples from Poulenc's wonderful songs that Pierre Bernac did not totally explain in his books, although he certainly knew about these elements – for him, it was perhaps too obvious, or unnecessary, to spell out.

I would like to start with the cycle *Deux poèmes d'Aragon* (1943). Louis Aragon made two *tours de force* in these poems: each octosyllable of C ends with a single rhyme, [se] (Poulenc makes the difference, for his part, between masculine and feminine rhymes, adding a note for each mute e of the feminine *-ée*); and each decasyllable of 'Fêtes galantes' begins (except the last) with the indefinite pronoun *on* [õ]. Poulenc's indication at the start of 'Fêtes galantes', *Incroyablement vite dans le style des chansons-scies de café-concert*, should perhaps be clarified: it means singing with extraordinary speed, as if no stop could be allowed, while piling up different ideas. Poulenc also adds elements to evoke a slang Parisian accent: *exagérez la muette* above m. 7 (meaning: sing the mute e at the end of the word 'voi-ri-e' as an accentuated and opened [œ]), and the accent in m. 28 on the last syllable of 'chaussu-res'. To keep that *café-concert* feeling, he does not write a note for the second syllable of 'qua-tre' (although specifically written in the poem), therefore making of the last decasyllable a nonasyllable: 'Et fuir la vie à la six-quat'-deux'.

About 'Fêtes galantes' Bernac wrote, 'This ludicrous and cynical poem recalls, in the form of parody, the hard days of the occupation – the many kinds of restrictions, the deterioration of certain expressions and certain true values'.[2] For singers today it is informative, yes, but who knows in detail nowadays what Aragon was referring to in the poem? What is a 'marlou'? The translation in Bernac's book is 'brat', which is fine, although it does not give the historicity of the term (nowadays, in France, instead of *marlou*, one would maybe say *caïra*, which is slang for *racaille*). What are the 'mots jetés à la voirie'? Certainly the three words forming the motto of the French Revolution: 'Liberté, Égalité, Fraternité'. And opposed to them, what are the 'mots élevés au pavois'? The three words of the motto that the Vichy regime established under Marshal Pétain, ominously echoing the German 'Arbeit macht frei' on the gates of Auschwitz: 'Travail, Famille, Patrie' (Work, Family, Fatherland). It is not obvious for a singer, French or not!

And what about 'On voit des lascars que les longs nez gênent?' The translation given in Bernac's book is 'You see wily fellows whose long noses hinder them'. I do not quite agree with this, as the verse is clearly talking about how people regard Jews as a nuisance; the Jewish population was said by the Vichy regime to be easily detectable through their physical features, and especially their long aquiline noses, as in a propaganda exhibition called 'Le juif et la France' displayed from September 1941 to January 1942 in Paris. I would propose, therefore, asking students if the period of composition means something to them, and if not giving an explanation. It would take some time, but time well spent!

Example 14.3. Francis Poulenc, 'Aussi bien que les cigales' (*Calligrammes*), piano postlude

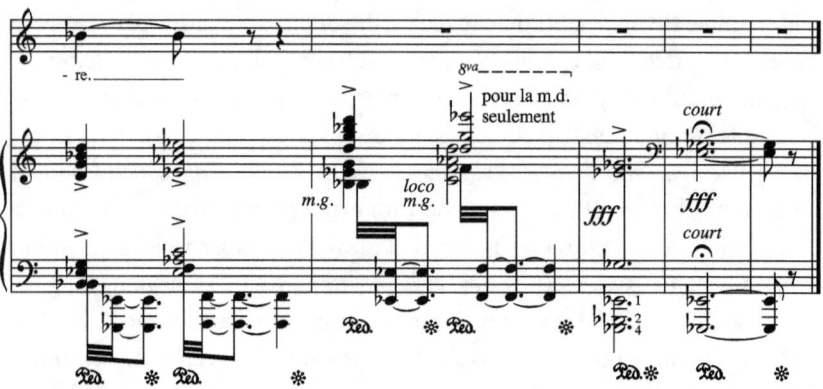

In the penultimate number of Poulenc's great cycle of seven songs *Calligrammes* (1948), the ending chords at the piano sound like blasts, especially the last E♭-minor chord (see Example 14.3). For a long time, I did not understand why such a *fff* was indicated by the composer, as the poem ends on the verse 'La joie adorable de la paix solaire' (The loveable joy of the sun-filled peace). Poulenc mentioned only a parallel with a chord in his ballet *Les animaux modèles* (composed in 1948 on poems by Jean de La Fontaine). It was only in 2013 when I acquired a new biography of Apollinaire that I understood: the word *cigales* refers indeed to cicadas of Provence, but it also served in World War I as a nickname for a certain type of hand grenade that made a terrifying whistle before exploding.[3] Apollinaire was playing on both meanings throughout the poem and Poulenc, a former *bleuet* who had finished his military service at the end of World War I, certainly knew what it meant (as did Bernac, I suppose). Young recruits were named *bleuets* in France because of their light blue uniforms. Three paintings of the composer by the famous portrait painter Jacques-Emile Blanche (1861–1942) show us Poulenc in the *bleuet* uniform. The most famous hangs in the Musée des Beaux-Arts in Tours, donated by Poulenc's heirs. The subtitle of Apollinaire's work *Calligrammes* is *Poèmes de la paix et de la guerre* (Poems of Peace and War).

To Be Decided ... or Not

Another question is very often raised: why do composers change the text of a poem, be it changing a word or omitting elements of a verse, and thereby alter its form? Indeed, it is quite intriguing when it comes to Fauré, who made many drastic changes in his *mélodies*, particularly to poems by Verlaine. Personally, I have decided to go back to the original poem whenever it produces no musical change to the notes or rhythms in the song. For instance, in 'C'est l'extase' (last song of the *Cinq mélodies 'de Venise'*), Fauré wrote: 'Cela ressemble au **bruit** doux' (It resembles the soft noise), thus erasing totally the poetic figure of oxymoron, associating opposite meanings and sounds, which Verlaine expressively opted for: 'Cela ressemble au **cri** doux' (It resembles the soft scream). A full knowledge of both poetic and musical content and style allows one, I think, to make such a decision.

Another famous poem by Verlaine, 'Clair de lune', has most of the time been performed in musical settings with no consideration for one of the basic rules of French poetic style: the rich rhyme rule. Rich rhymes include not only the last sound but at least the last two sounds of a verse, here between the first line, 'Votre âme est un paysage choisi' (Your soul is like a choice landscape), ending with *choisi* [ʃwazi]), and the third line, 'Jouant du luth et dansant et quasi' (Playing the lute, and dancing, and almost). The rule thus dictates that one should sing [kwazi]. Alas, most people sing [kazi], perhaps because of the enjambment (the running of the sense and syntax of one line into the next) that links 'quasi' with 'Triste' (that is, 'almost sad'). The importance of this rich rhyme is totally forgotten. I do think that any composer of Verlaine's time, and until at least the beginning of World War I, knew the poetic rule. I like to say to students, as a half-nonsensical joke, 'If you know the rules, you may decide to ignore them; if you don't, you have no right to break any of them'.

Sometimes perplexity changes into stupefaction when a composer known to be scrupulously faithful to the poetic text is found ignoring a rule or tradition. For instance, how is it possible that Poulenc omitted a word in Apollinaire's 'Rosemonde' (1954)? The penultimate octosyllable of Apollinaire's *Alcools* is 'Puis lentement je m'en allai'; Poulenc has written 'Puis lentement je m'allai' (a heptasyllable, unlike the other verses of the poem). It is in the manuscript of the song as well as the edition.[4] In point of fact, this error comes from the edition Poulenc used (probably the first from 1912); it is only in the later critical editions of Apollinaire's poetry, after 1960, that someone 'corrected' the verse to a balanced octosyllable, matching the rest of the poem. And Bernac, who premiered the song, does not say anything about this strange occurrence. Finally, it shows that Poulenc was so faithful to the poet's 'œuvre' that he did not notice (or consider relevant) this omission. Here, then, the singer should not be 'more of a royalist than the king' (*plus royaliste que le roi*), as a common French saying has it. Besides, as it is not possible to add the missing syllable in the music, at least for me (I have tried out different things with no success!), one has to assume this 'mistake' in singing.

Conclusion

The French attitude about what is called the performing arts, since at least Verlaine, has been to consider that the formal aspect has to do with the meaning of a text, or a situation, and that nothing could be taken as accessory. For performers, the *mélodie* lies in that sense at the heart of this concern. I think this explains why a type of poetry that does not express directly one's emotion, be it pain, sorrow, or happiness, has been privileged by French composers. The undetermined feeling named *spleen* by Baudelaire and then Verlaine is the mysterious element that poetry and, above all, music tries to capture in a way that everybody can share and perceive, but not exactly like the German *Sehnsucht* (longing). A kind of universal human connection to the world, hard to describe ... Verlaine has provided some keys in certain poems. In the untitled 'Écoutez la chanson bien douce' from the 1881 collection *Sagesse*, set to music by Ernest Chausson (1898) and Nadia Boulanger (1905) among others, Verlaine wrote, 'Elle [la chanson] est discrète, elle est légère: / Un frisson d'eau sur de la mousse' (It is discreet, it is light: / A shiver of water on the moss). Lightness and discretion are the keywords, with a very soft evocation of sound (water shivering). And in his 'Art poétique' (*Jadis et naguère*, 1882), which begins with 'De la musique avant toute chose' (Music before all), he writes, 'Rien de plus cher que la chanson grise / Où l'indécis au précis se joint'. The unspoken, the undetermined, in a word, the mystery of the world, is what counts; the expression is neither a definition nor an explanation, but a quest. We recitalists are explorers of the unknown!

Notes

1. Roland Barthes, *L'obvie et l'obtus: Essais critiques III* (Paris: Éditions du Seuil, 1982), 249.
2. Pierre Bernac, *Francis Poulenc: The Man and His Songs*, trans. Winifred Radford (London: Victor Gollancz, 1977), 189.
3. Laurence Campa, *Guillaume Apollinaire* (Paris: Gallimard, 2013), 634.
4. The manuscript, which belonged to Pierre Bernac, has been in the Pierpont Morgan Library since 1985.

Guide to Further Reading

General Studies

Bergeron, Katherine. *Voice Lessons: French Mélodie in the Belle Epoque*, New York, Oxford University Press, 2009

Faure, Michel and Vincent Vivès. *Histoire et poétique de la mélodie française*, Paris, CNRS, 2000

Fauser, Annegret. *Der Orchestergesang in Frankreich zwischen 1870 und 1920*, Laaber, Laaber Verlag, 1994

Flothuis, Marius. '… *exprimer l'inexprimable* … ': *Essai sur la mélodie française depuis Duparc en dix-neuf chapitres et huit digressions*, Amsterdam and Atlanta, Rodopi, 1996

Johnson, Graham. *A French Song Companion*, with translations by Richard Stokes, New York, Oxford University Press, 2000

Kilpatrick, Emily. *French Art Song: History of a New Music, 1870–1914*, Rochester, University of Rochester Press, 2022

Linke, Ulrich. *Der französische Liederzyklus von 1866 bis 1914*, Stuttgart, Franz Steiner Verlag, 2010

French Poetic History

Abbott, Helen. *Baudelaire in Song 1880–1930*, Oxford, Oxford University Press, 2017

Balakian, Anna. *The Symbolist Movement: A Critical Reappraisal*, New York, New York University, 1977

Caws, Mary Ann. *The Poetry of Dada and Surrealism: Aragon, Breton, Tzara, Éluard & Desnos*, Princeton, Princeton University Press, 1970

Illouz, Jean-Nicolas. *Le Symbolisme*, Paris, LGF/Le Livre de Poche, 2004

Martino, Pierre. *Parnasse et symbolisme (1850–1900)*, Paris, Armand Colin, 1954

Murat, Michel. *Le Surréalisme*, Paris, LGF/Le Livre de Poche, 2013

Porter, Laurence. *The Crisis of French Symbolism*, Ithaca, Cornell University Press, 1990

Prendergast, Christopher (ed.). *Nineteenth-Century French Poetry: Introductions to Close Readings*, Cambridge, Cambridge University Press, 1990

Schultz, Gretchen. *The Gendered Lyric: Subjectivity and Difference in Nineteenth-Century French Poetry* [on Romanticism and the Parnassian school], West Lafayette, IN, Purdue University Press, 1999

Shaw, Mary Lewis. *The Cambridge Introduction to French Poetry*, Cambridge, Cambridge University Press, 2003

French Versification

Hunter, David. *Understanding French Verse: A Guide for Singers*, New York, Oxford University Press, 2005

Scott, Clive. *French Verse-Art: A Study*, Cambridge, Cambridge University Press, 1980

Romance and Early *Mélodie*

Cheng, William. 'The French Romance and the Sexual Traffic of Musical Mimicry', *19th-Century Music*, 35, no. 1 (2011), 34–71

Messina, Kitti. 'Mélodie et romance au milieu du XIXe siècle: Points communs et divergences', *Revue de musicologie*, 94 (2008), 59–90

Noske, Frits. *French Song from Berlioz to Duparc: The Origin and Development of the Mélodie*, trans. Rita Benton, New York, Dover Publications, 1970

Romagnesi, Antoine. *L'art de chanter les romances, les chansonnettes et les nocturnes et généralement toute la musique du salon*, Paris, Chez l'Auteur, 1846

Tunley, David. *Singers, Salons, and Songs: A Background to French Song, 1830–1870*, Aldershot, Ashgate, 2002

Hector Berlioz

Abbott, Helen. 'Singing and Difference: The Case of Gautier and Berlioz Re-Examined', *French Studies*, 71, no. 1 (2017), 31–47

Bloom, Peter. 'In the Shadows of *Les Nuits d'été*'. In *Berlioz Studies*, edited by Peter Bloom, 81–111, Cambridge, Cambridge University Press, 1992

Fauser, Annegret. 'The Songs'. In *The Cambridge Companion to Berlioz*, edited by Peter Bloom, 108–24, Cambridge, Cambridge University Press, 2000

Reuter, Evelyn. 'Berlioz mélodiste', *La revue musicale*, 233 (special issue, *Hector Berlioz 1803–1869*, 1956), 31–37

Rodgers, Stephen. 'Miniatures of a Monumentalist: Berlioz's *Romances*, 1842–1850', *Nineteenth-Century Music Review*, 10, no. 1 (2013), 119–49

Rushton, Julian. 'Berlioz and *Irlande*: From Romance to Mélodie'. In *Irish Musical Studies: The Maynooth International Musicological Conference 1995*, Part

Two, edited by Patrick F. Devine and Harry White, 224–40, Dublin, Four
Courts Press, 1996
'*Les Nuits d'été*: Cycle or Collection?' In *Berlioz Studies*, edited by Peter Bloom,
112–35, Cambridge, Cambridge University Press, 1992

Lili Boulanger

Dopp, Bonnie Jo. 'Numerology and Cryptography in the Music of Lili Boulanger:
The Hidden Programme in *Clairières dans le ciel*', *Musical Quarterly*, 78, no.
3 (Autumn 1994), 556–83
Fauser, Annegret. 'Die Musik hinter der Legende: Lili Boulangers Liederzyklus
Clairières dans le ciel', *Neue Zeitschrift für Musik*, 151 (November 1990),
9–14
Giesbrecht-Schutte, Sabine. 'Lili Boulanger: "Clairières dans le Ciel" – ästhetischer
Ausdruck und musikalische Form', *Die Musikforschung*, 47, no. 4, 384–402

Ernest Chausson

Bretaudeau, Isabelle. *Les mélodies de Chausson: Un parcours de l'intime*, Arles,
Actes Sud, 1999

Claude Debussy

Bergeron, Katherine. 'The Echo, the Cry, the Death of Lovers', *19th-Century Music*,
18, no. 2 (1994), 136–51
Bruschini, Adrien and Jean-Louis Leleu. '*Proses lyriques* de Debussy et *Serres
chaudes* de Maeterlinck/Chausson, une mise en regard'. In *Regards sur
Debussy*, edited by Myriam Chimènes and Alexandra Laederich, 377–84,
Paris, Fayard, 2013
Cobb, Margaret (ed.). *The Poetic Debussy: A Collection of His Song Texts and
Selected Letters*, Rochester, University of Rochester Press, 1994
Code, David. 'The "Song Triptych": Reflections on a Debussyan Genre'. In
Debussy's Resonance, edited by François de Médicis and Steven Huebner,
127–74, Rochester, University of Rochester Press, 2018
Dal Molin, Paolo and Jean-Louis Leleu. *Les Trois Poèmes de Stéphane Mallarmé de
Claude Debussy: Genèse et reception*, Lucca, Libreria musicale italiana, 2016
Grayson, David. '"Paysage sentimental": "Si doux, si triste, si dormant ... "'. In
Debussy's Resonance, edited by François de Médicis and Steven Huebner,
105–24, Rochester, University of Rochester Press, 2018

Herlin, Denis. 'Des *Proses lyriques* aux *Nuits blanches* ou Debussy et la tentation poétique'. In *Claude Debussy: Portraits et études*, Hildesheim, Georg Olms, 2021, 62–89

'From Debussy's Studio: The Little-Known Autograph of *De Rêve*, the First of the *Proses lyriques* (1892)', *Notes*, 70, no. 4 (September 2014), 9–34

'The Kunkelmann Manuscripts: New Sources for Early Mélodies by Claude Debussy'. In *Debussy's Resonance*, edited by François de Médicis and Steven Huebner, 57–104, Rochester, University of Rochester Press, 2018

Johnson, Julian. 'Present Absence: Debussy, Song, and the Art of (Dis)appearing', *19th-Century Music*, 40, no. 3 (2017), 239–56

'Vertige!: Debussy, Mallarmé, and the Edge of Language'. In *Debussy's Resonance*, edited by François de Médicis and Steven Huebner, 66–92, Rochester, University of Rochester Press, 2018

Rolf, Marie. 'Debussy's Mallarmé Songs'. In *Debussy Studies,* edited by Richard Langham Smith, 179–200, Cambridge, Cambridge University Press, 2007

'Debussy's Settings of Verlaine's "En sourdine"'. In *Perspectives on Music*, edited by Dave Oliphant and Thomas Zigal, 205–33, Austin, Texas, Humanities Research Center, The University of Texas at Austin, 1985

'Oriental and Iberian Resonances in Early Debussy Songs'. In *Debussy's Resonance*, edited by François de Médicis and Steven Huebner, 272–98, Rochester, University of Rochester Press, 2018

'Semantic and Structural Issues in Debussy's Mallarmé Songs'. In *Debussy Studies*, edited by Richard Langham Smith, 179–200, Cambridge, Cambridge University Press, 1997

Rumph, Stephen. 'Debussy's *Trois chansons de Bilitis*: Song, Opera, and the Death of the Subject', *The Journal of Musicology*, 12, no. 4 (1994), 464–90

Wenk, Arthur. *Claude Debussy and the Poets*, Berkeley, University of California Press, 1976

Youens, Susan. 'To Tell a Tale: Symbolist Narrative in Debussy's *Fêtes galantes II*', *Nineteenth-Century French Studies*, 16, no. 1/2 (1987–8), 180–91

Henri Duparc

Escobar, Angélia Minero. '"Anywhere out of the World": Escapism in Baudelaire-Duparc's "L'invitation au voyage"', *Ars lyrica*, 15 (2005), 103–25

Moore, Stacey. '*Mort exquise*: Representations of Ecstasy in the Songs of Duparc and Fauré'. In *Regarding Fauré*, edited by Tom Gordon, 273–96, Amsterdam, Gordon & Breach, 1999

Northcote, Sydney. *The Songs of Henri Duparc*, London, Dobson, 1949

Pau, Andrew. 'Plagal Systems in the Songs of Fauré and Duparc', *Theory and Practice*, 41 (2016), 81–111

Stricker, Rémy. *Les mélodies de Duparc*, Paris, Actes Sud, 1994

Gabriel Fauré

Abbott, Helen. 'Poetic Time and Space, or What Fauré Learns from Baudelaire'. In *Time and Space in Words and Music*, edited by Mario Dunkel, Emily Petermann, and Burkhard Sauerwald, 137–49, Frankfurt, Peter Lang, 2012

Caron, Sylvain. 'Hiérachie et homogénéité dans *Le jardin clos* de Fauré'. In *Musique et modernité en France, 1900–1945*, edited by Sylvain Caron, François de Médicis, and Michel Duchesneau, 237–54, Montreal, Presses de l'Université de Montréal, 2006

Howat, Roy and Emily Kilpatrick. 'Editorial Challenges in the Early Songs of Gabriel Fauré', *Notes*, 68, no. 2 (December 2011), 239–83

  'Gabriel Fauré's Middle-Period Songs, Editorial Quandaries, and the Chimera of the "Original Key"', *Journal of the Royal Musical Association*, 139, no. 2 (2014), 303–37

  'Wagnérisme de Fauré: *Pénélope* (1913) et les mélodies'. In *Wagner, 1913–2013, Ruptures et Continuité*, edited by Marie-Cécile Leblanc and Danièle Pistone, 25–38, Paris, Presses de la Sorbonne-Nouvelle, 2015

Jankélévitch, Vladimir. *Gabriel Fauré: Ses mélodies, son esthétique*, Paris, Librairie Plon, 1938

Johnson, Graham. *Gabriel Fauré: The Songs and Their Poets*, Farnham, Ashgate, 2009

Loppert, Max. 'A Neglected Garden' [*Le jardin clos*], *Music and Musicians*, 21, no. 249 (1973), 42–4

Molino, Jean. 'Poesie et musique: *L'Horizon chimerique*, de Jean de la Ville de Mirmont à Gabriel Faure', *Intersections*, 31, no. 1 (2010), 100–62

Orledge, Robert. 'A Voyage of Discovery into Fauré's Song Cycle *Mirages*'. In *Regarding Fauré*, edited by Tom Gordon, 333–67, Amsterdam, Gordon and Breach, 1999

Porter, Laurence. 'Text versus Music in the French Art Song: Debussy, Fauré, and Verlaine's "Mandoline"', *Nineteenth-Century French Studies*, 12, nos. 1/2 (1983–4), 138–44

Rumph, Stephen. 'Fauré and the Effable: Theatricality, Reflection, and Semiosis in the *Mélodies*', *Journal of the American Musicological Society*, 68, no. 3 (2015), 497–558

  The Fauré Song Cycles: Poetry and Music, 1861–1921, Oakland, University of California Press, 2020

Strobel, Klaus. *Das Liedschaffen Gabriel Faures*, Hamburg, Kovac, 2000

Augusta Holmès

Olivier, Brigitte. *Les mélodies d'Augusta Holmès*, Arles, Actes Sud, 2003

Charles Koechlin

Caillet, Aude. 'La mélodie selon Charles Koechlin: Protée et l'anti-sublime'. In *Francis Poulenc et la voix: Texte et contexte*, edited by Alban Ramaut, 35–48, Lyon, Symétrie, 2002

Olivier Messiaen

Manning, Jane. 'The Songs and Song Cycles'. In *The Messiaen Companion*, edited by Peter Hill, 105–56, London, Faber, 1994

Sholl, Robert. 'Love, Mad Love and the "point sublime": The Surrealist Poetics of Messiaen's *Harawi*'. In *Messiaen Studies*, edited by Robert Sholl, 34–62, Cambridge, Cambridge University Press, 2007

Francis Poulenc

Bernac, Pierre. *Francis Poulenc: The Man and His Songs*, London, Kahn and Averill, 2001

Johnson, Graham. *Poulenc: The Life in the Songs*, New York, Liveright Publishing Corporation, 2020

Poulenc, Francis. *Journal de mes mélodies*, edited by Renaud Machart, Paris, Cicero éditeurs/Éditions Salabert, 1993

Maurice Ravel

Gut, Serge. 'Permanence et transformation des structures mélodiques grecques antiques dans les *Mélodies populaires grecques* de Maurice Ravel'. *Revue de Musicologie*, 84, no. 2 (1998), 263–76

Huebner, Steven. 'Ravel's Poetics: Literary Currents, Classical Takes'. In *Unmasking Ravel: New Perspectives on the Music*, edited by Peter Kaminsky, 9–40, Rochester, University of Rochester Press, 2011

Kaminsky, Peter. 'Of Children, Princesses, Dreams and Isomorphisms: Text-Music Transformation in Ravel's Vocal Works', *Music Analysis*, 19, no. 1 (March 2000), 29–68

  'Vocal Music and the Lures of Exoticism and Irony'. In *The Cambridge Companion to Ravel*, edited by Deborah Mawer, 162–87, Cambridge, Cambridge University Press, 2003

Kilpatrick, Emily. 'Ravel's *Trois poèmes de Stéphane Mallarmé*: A Philosophy of Composition', *Music & Letters*, 101, no. 3 (2020), 512–43

Revuluri, Sindhumathi. 'Maurice Ravel's *Chants populaires* and the Exotic Within'. In *Rethinking Difference in Music Scholarship*, edited by Olivia Ashley Bloechi, Melanie Diane Lowe, and Jeffrey Kallberg, 238–59, Cambridge, Cambridge University Press, 2015

Camille Saint-Saëns

Fauser, Annegret. 'What's in a Song? Camille Saint-Saëns's *Mélodies*'. In *Camille Saint-Saëns and His World*, edited by Jann Pasler, 210–29, Princeton, Princeton University Press, 2012

Interpretation of French Art Song

Bathori, Jane. *On the Interpretation of the Mélodies of Claude Debussy*, trans. Linda Laurent, Stuyvesant, NY, Pendragon Press, 1998
Bernac, Pierre. *The Interpretation of French Art Song*, New York, Norton, 1978
Croiza, Claire. *The Singer as Interpreter: Claire Croiza's Master Classes*, trans. Betty Bannerman, London, Gollancz, 1989
Hahn, Reynaldo. *Du chant*, Paris, Lafitte, 1920
Le Roux, François. *Le chant intime: The Interpretation of French Mélodie*, trans. Sylvia Kahan, New York, Oxford University Press, 2021
Panzéra, Charles. *50 mélodies françaises: Leçons de style et d'interprétation = 50 French Songs: Lessons in Style and Interpretation* [bilingual], Brussels, Schott, 1964

Salon Culture and Patronage

Adlard, Emma. 'Interior Time: Debussy, "Fêtes galantes" and the Salon of Marguerite de Saint-Marceaux', *The Musical Quarterly*, 96, no. 2 (2013), 178–218
Brooks, Jeanice. 'Nadia Boulanger and the Salon of the Princesse de Polignac', *Journal of the American Musicological Society*, 46, no. 3 (1993), 415–68
Chimènes, Myriam. *Mécènes et musiciens: Du salon au concert à Paris sous la IIIe République*, Paris, Fayard, 2004
Epstein, Louis K. *The Creative Labor of Music Patronage in Interwar France*, Woodbridge, Boydell & Brewer, 2022
Kahan, Sylvia. *Music's Modern Muse: A Life of Winnaretta Singer*, Rochester, University of Rochester Press, 2004

'Patrons and Society: Gabriel Fauré's "Other" Career in the Paris and London Music Salons'. In *Fauré Studies*, edited by Carlo Caballero and Stephen Rumph, 13–34, Cambridge, Cambridge University Press, 2021

Pasler, Jann. 'Comtesse Greffulhe as Entrepreneur: Negotiating Class, Gender, and Nation'. In the *Musician as Entrepreneur, 1700–1914: Managers, Charlatans, and Idealists*, edited by William Weber, 221–55, Bloomington, Indiana Press, 2004

Ross, James. 'Music in the French Salon'. In *French Music since Berlioz*, edited by Richard Langham Smith and Caroline Potter, 91–115, Aldershot, Ashgate, 2006

Tardif, Cécile. 'Fauré and the Salon'. In *Regarding Fauré*, edited by Tom Gordon, 1–14, Amsterdam, Gordon & Breach, 1999

Performers

Borchard, Beatrix. *Pauline Viardot-Garcia: Fülle des Lebens*, Cologne, Weimar, and Vienna, Böhlau, 2016

Howat, Roy and Emily Kilpatrick. 'Gabriel Fauré's Middle-Period Songs, Editorial Quandaries, and the Chimera of the "Original Key"', *Journal of the Royal Musical Association*, 139, no. 2 (2014), 303–37

Laurent, Linda. 'The Performer as Catalyst: The Role of the Singer Jane Bathori (1877–1970) in the Careers of Debussy, Ravel, "Les Six" and Their Contemporaries in Paris, 1904–1926', PhD dissertation, New York University, 1982

Nectoux, Jean-Michel. 'Fauré: Voice, Style and Vocality', trans. Tom Gordon. In *Regarding Fauré*, edited by Tom Gordon, 369–402, Amsterdam, Gordon & Breach, 1999

Schwab, Catharine Mary. 'The *Mélodie française moderne*: An Expression of Music, Poetry, and Prosody in *fin-de-siècle* France, and Its Performance in the Recitals of Jane Bathori (1877–1970) and Claire Croiza (1882–1946)', PhD dissertation, University of Michigan, 1991

Zwang, Gérard. *Mémoires d'une chanteuse française: La vie et les amours de Madeleine Grey*, Paris, L'Harmattan, 2008

Scholarly Editions

Berlioz, Hector. *New Edition of the Complete Works*, vol. 13: *Songs for Solo Voice and Orchestra*, ed. Ian Kemp, and vol. 15: *Songs for 1, 2, or 3 Voices and Keyboard*, ed. Ian Rumbold, Kassel, Bärenreiter, 1975, 2005

Debussy, Claude. *Œuvres complétes de Claude Debussy*, series 2, vol. 2: *Mélodies (1882–1887)*, ed. Marie Rolf, and series 2, vol. 4: *Mélodies (1892–1915)*, ed. Denis Herlin, Durand, 2016, 2024

Songs of Claude Debussy, 2 vols, edited by James Briscoe, Milwaukee, Hal Leonard, 1993

Duparc, Henri. *Complete Songs*, edited by Roger Nichols, London, Edition Peters, 2005

Fauré, Gabriel. *Complete Songs*, edited by Roy Howat and Emily Kilpatrick, 5 vols, Leipzig and London, Edition Peters, 2013–22

French Romantic Song [facsimile], edited by David Tunley, 6 vols, New York, Garland, 1994–5

Online Resources

www.imslp.org (International Music Score Library Project)
    Open archive of musical scores, including most of the essential French art song repertoire

www.oxfordlieder.co.uk
    Poetic texts and expert translations of international art song, as well as information on poets, composers, and performances

www.melodiefrancaise.com
    Website of the Académie Francis Poulenc, including thousands of scores of *romances*, *mélodies*, and *chansons*

Index

Abbott, Helen, 20
Adam, Adolphe, 39
Adorno, Theodor, 13–14
Apollinaire, Guillaume, 265, 271, 274
   Alcools, 16
   Calligrammes, 16
Aragon, Louis, 17, 315
Auric, Georges
   Huit poèmes de Jean Cocteau, 267–8
   'It's April Again', 275
   Trois interludes, 270

Bach, Johann Sebastian, 72, 79, 97, 112
Baïf, Jean-Antoine de, 13
Ballif, Claude, 16
Banville, Théodore de, 221, 242, 243, 244
Barthes, Roland, xxi, 1, 2, 18, 203, 307
Baudelaire, Charles, xxi, 249, 290
   correspondances, 196
   song settings, 155, 162, 164, 219
Bellaigue, Camille, 240
Belle Époque, xxi, xxii
Bergeron, Katherine, 201, 209
Bergson, Henri, 206
Berlioz, Hector
   Goethe, Johann Wolfgang von, settings of, 44–5
   Irlande, 45–7
      'Elégie', 47
      'L'Origine de la Harpe', 46
      'Le Coucher du soleil', 46
   'La captive', 41, 42, 50
   'La mort d'Ophélie', 55
   'Le dépit de la bergère', 43–4
   'Le jeune pâtre breton', 48–9
   'Le matin', 55
   'Le montagnard exilé', 44
   'Le pêcheur', 47–8
   Lélio, 47
   'Les champs', 55
   Les Nuits d'été, 11–12
      'Absence', 53–4
      cyclic coherence, 51
      'L'île inconnue', 54
      'Le Spectre de la rose', 51–3
      'Sur les lagunes', 53
      through-composition, 51
   'Petit oiseau', 55
   Receuil de romances, 41
   'Zaide', 55
Bernac, Pierre, 20, 264, 315
Bertin, Louise, 56
Bizet, Georges, 178
   'Adieu à Suzon', 82–3
   'Adieux de l'hôtesse arabe', 81–2
   Carmen, 117, 164, 271
   'Douce mer', 84
   'Guitare', 80–1
   'La coccinelle', 83
   'Rose d'amour', 84
Bonis, Mel, 165
Bordes, Charles
   Paysages tristes, 164
Borodin, Alexander, 248
Bouchor, Maurice, 156
Boulanger, Lili, 169, 208
   Clairières dans le ciel, 257–9
      cryptography, 257
      motivic structure, 257–9
      Tristan und Isolde, allusions to, 259
   'Dans l'immense tristesse', 179
Boulanger, Nadia, 208
Boulez, Pierre, 18
Bréville, Pierre de, 165
Brimont, Renée de, 177, 208
Bunlet, Marcelle, 291, 293, 297, 299
Burke, Edmund, 7

Caballero, Carlo, 202
café-concert, 161
Calvocoressi, Michel-Dmitri, 251
Canal, Marguerite, 169, 178
Caplet, André
   'Écoute, mon cœur' (*Corbeille de fruits*), 260
   Trois fables, 259
Castillon, Alexis de, 165

Chabrier, Emmanuel, 93
  'Ballade des gros dindons', 163
  Gwendoline, 163
  'L'invitation au voyage', 162
  'Les cigales', 163
  'Pastorale des cochons roses', 163
  'Sérénade de Ruy Blas', 162
  'Sommation irrespectueuse', 162–3
  'Tes yeux bleus', 163
  'Villanelle des petits canards', 163
Chalupt, René, 270
Chaminade, Cécile, 169, 179
Chang-Chi, 17
chanson, 251–3, 275, 306
Chateaubriand, René de, 7, 10
Chausson, Ernest
  'Amour d'antan', 156
  'Apaisement', 157
  'Cantique à l'épouse', 161
  Chanson perpétuelle, 161
  Chansons de Shakespeare, 160
  'Dans la forêt du charme et de l'enchantement', 161
  Deux mélodies, 161
  'Hébé', 156
  'L'aveu', 157
  'La caravane', 157
  'La cigale', 157
  'La pluie', 157
  'Le colibri', 156
  'Les morts', 157
  'Nanny', 156
  'Nocturne', 156
  'Nos souvenirs', 156
  Poème de l'amour et de la mer, 157–8
  'Printemps triste', 156
  'Sérénade', 157
  'Sérénade italienne', 156
  Serres chaudes, 16, 158–60
  song cycle, conception of, 160
  Trois lieder, 160
Chaynes, Charles, 17
Chenier, André, 35
Chopin, Frédéric, 101
Claudel, Paul, 16
Cocteau, Jean, 210, 265
  Le Coq et l'arlequin: Notes autour de la musique, 266–7, 271
Collet, Henri, 268
Conservatoire, 184, 276, 290
Coolidge, Elizabeth Sprague, 260
Cubism, 264, 265

Dada, 16, 264, 270
Debussy, Claude, 267, 270
  Ariettes (*Ariettes oubliées*), 96, 136
    'C'est l'extase', 196
    'Spleen', 136–41
  Banville, Théodore de, settings of, 115–16
  Bardac, Emma, 233
  Caprice, 121–5
  Chansons de Bilitis, 218, 229–30
    'La chevelure', 230
    'La flûte de Pan', 230
  Cinq poèmes de Charles Baudelaire, 16, 219, 223–4
    Wagner, Richard, influence of, 223–4
  'Clair de lune' (1882), 126–30
  'Dans le jardin', 232
  early songs
    Parnassianism, 114–15
    poets, choice of, 113, 114–20
    prosody and text-setting, 125, 126–7, 139
    stylistic development, influence on, 141–3
  Fêtes galantes I, 224–5
    'Clair de lune', 131–6, 225
  Fêtes galantes II
    'Colloque sentimentale', 233–4
  'Flots, palmes, sables', 117
  'La belle au bois dormant', 227
  Le promenoir des deux amants, 221, 234
  'Les angélus', 227
  literary formation, 111–13
  mature songs
    dedicatees, 222–3
    poets, choice of, 218–22
    publication history, 214–18
    triptych form, 214–18
  'Noël des enfants qui n'ont plus des maisons', 236–7
  'Nuit d'étoiles', 116
  Nuits blanches, 230–2
  Pelléas et Mélisande, 141, 220, 227, 230, 231, 233, 257
  poet, 227–8
  Prélude à l'après-midi d'un faune, 132, 141, 209, 222, 224, 290
  Proses lyriques, 227–8
    'De grève', 243
  Recueil Vasnier, 126, 182
  'Rondel chinois', 117
  'Séguidille', 117
  text-setting, comparison with Fauré, Gabriel, 309

Debussy, Claude *(cont.)*
   Trois ballades de François Villon, 221–2, 234–5, 266, 286
   Trois chansons de France, 220–1, 232–3, 273
   Trois mélodies sur des poèmes de Paul Verlaine, 227, 308
   Trois poèmes de Stéphane Mallarmé, 222, 235–6
   Vasnier, Marie, 112, 119, 121, *See mélodie*, singers
   'Zéphyr', 118
Decadence, 16, 156, 158
Delage, Maurice
   Trois chants de la jungle, 16
   Trois poèmes hindous, 255
Delbos, Claire, 178–9, 292
   L'Âme en bourgeon, 179, 292, 293
   Primevère, 178–9, 292
Denya, Marcelle, 168
Desbordes-Valmore, Marceline, 8, 39, 178
Diderot, Denis, 7
Donizetti, Gaetano, 56
Duchambge, Pauline, 39, 179
Dukas, Paul
   Ariane et Barbe-bleue, 291
   L'apprenti sorcier, 291
Duparc, Henri, 93
   'Au pays où se fait la guerre', 151–2
   'Chanson triste', 151
   'Élégie', 153
   'Extase', 153
   'L'invitation au voyage', xxi, 3, 152–3, 164
   'La fuite', 151
   'La vague et la cloche', 153
   'La vie antérieure', 154–5, 312–14
   'Lamento', 154
   'Le galop', 151
   'Le manoir de Rosemonde', 154
   'Phydilé', 148, 154
   'Romance de Mignon', 151
   'Sérénade', 151
   'Sérénade florentine', 154
   'Soupir', 151
   'Testament', 154
Durey, Louis
   Images à Crusoé, 272
   Le bestiaire, 272
   Poèmes d'Ho Chi Minh, 269
Dutilleux, Henri
   'J'ai rêvé que je vous portais entre mes bras' (*Sonnets de Jean Cassou*), 310

Éluard, Paul, 17

Fargue, Léon-Paul, 270
Farrenc, Louise, 56
Fauré, Gabriel
   'Accompagnement', 181
   'Au bord de l'eau', 96
   Bardac, Emma, 198, *See mélodie*, singers
   Baudelaire, Charles, settings of, 92–4
      'Chant d'automne', 93, 104
      implicit cycle, 93
      Wagner, Richard, influence on, 92–3
   'C'est la paix', 102
   'Chanson', 97
   Cinq mélodies 'de Venise', 180, 194–7
      'À Clymène', 196
      'C'est l'extase', 196–7, 317
      common motive, 195–6
      cyclic unity, 194
      diegetic music, 195
      'En sourdine', 196
      'Green', 104, 108
      'Mandoline', 195
   'Clair de lune', 3, 96, 103, 106, 126, 195, 317
   Golden Section, 209
   Hugo, Victor, settings of, 94
      implicit cycle, 94
      'L'absent', 102
      'L'aurore', 75, 99
      'Le papillon et la fleur', 94, 98
      'Mai', 94
      'Puisque j'ai mis ma lèvre', 75, 94
      'S'il est un charmant gazon' ('Rêve d'amour'), 94, 101
   'Ici-bas!', 96, 107
   L'horizon chimérique, 266, 308
      cyclic design, 210–11
      Parnassianism, 211
      word-painting, 211
   La bonne chanson, xxii, 16, 181, 197–200
      cyclic design, 197, 199
      leitmotifs, 198–9
      natural and human music, fusion of, 200
      reception, 198, 240, 257
   La chanson d'Ève, 200–5
      compositional history, 200
      leitmotivic design, 202–3
      pantheism, 202
      theatricality, 203–5
   'La rose', 105
   'Le don silencieux', 97

Le jardin clos, 205–7
    hortus conclusus, 206
    key structure, 206–7
    time and memory, 205–6, 207
Leconte de Lisle, settings of
    'La rose', 95
    'Le parfum impérissable', 95
    'Les roses d'Ispahan', 95
    'Lydia', 95
    'Nell', 95
'Les berceaux', 104
Masques et bergamasques, 208
Mirages, 208–10
    'Danseuse', 177
    Debussy, Claude, tribute to, 209
    octatonicism, 209
neoclassicism, 208–9, 266
'Nocturne', 107
Parnassianism, relation to, 190–1
Pavane, 96
pianistic style, 105–6
Poème d'un jour, 191–4
    cyclic design, 192–4
    key structure, 191
poets, choice of, 91–2, 189
'Prison', 103
prosody and text-setting, 98–9, 102–3, 196
Silvestre, Armand, settings of, 96–7
singers, 104–5
song cycle
    complementary pairings, 190
    conception of, 189–90, 205
'Spleen', 104
Symbolism, response to, 194–5, 198–9, 201, 203–5
tempo, 107–8
text-setting, comparison with Debussy, Claude, 309
transposition, 106–7
Vocalise-Études, 106
Wagner, Richard, influence of, 195–6
word-painting, 103–4
First World War, xxi, xxii, 16, 206, 236, 264, 273, 316
Françaix, Jean, 268
Franck, César, 178
    cyclic form, 158, 165
    'La procession', 150, 164
    'Lied', 147–8
    'Souvenance', 150
Franco-Prussian War, xxi, 66, 146

Gauthier-Villars, Henri, 248
Gautier, Théophile, 50, 157, 173
    aestheticism, 12, 190
    La Comédie de la mort (1838), 11, 50
Golden Section, 137
Goncharova, Natalia, 170
Gounod, Charles, 12, 60
    'À une jeune grecque', 72
    'Ce que je suis sans toi', 63–6
    'Le soir', 67
    'Le vallon', 66–7
    'Ma belle amie est morte', 70
    operas, relation to *mélodies*, 66–7
    poets, choice of, 70–2
    religious songs, 72
    'Venise', 70
Grandmougin, Charles, 191
Granval, Clémence de, 169
Grétry, André, 41

Hahn, Reynaldo, 56
    'Chant d'automne' (*Chansons grises*), 241
    Études latines, 240
    'L'heure exquise' (*Chansons grises*), 241
    'Offrande', 241
    Rondels, 242–3
        'L'air', 242
        'La Paix', 243
Hanslick, Eduard, 13
Herder, Johann Gottfried, 7
Holmès, Augusta, 165, 168, 173
    'Berceuse', 174
    'Le ruban rose', 176
    Les chants de la Kytharède, 176–7
    'Les griffes d'or', 174
    'Noel', 174
    Wagner, Richard, influence of, 173, 176
Honegger, Arthur
    Six poésies de Jean Cocteau, 269
Hugo, Victor, 41, 70, 74, 162, 310
    Les orientales (1829), 11, 41, 73, 80
    song settings, 11
Huysmans, J. K., 96

Ibert, Jacques, 261
Indy, Vincent d'
    'L'amour et la crâne', 164
    'Lied maritime', 164

Jammes, Francis, 16, 257
Jankélévitch, Vladimir, 14, 206

Jeune France, 18, 294
Johnson, Graham, 20, 264
Joyce, James, 17

Kant, Immanuel, 7
Klingsor, Tristan (Léon Leclère), 247
Koechlin, Charles
   Rondels, 243–4
   Shéhérazade, 249
Kuhn, Thomas S., 264

L'Hermite, Tristan, 13, 234
La Fontaine, Jean de, 35
La Ville de Mirmont, Jean de, 208
Laforgue, Jules, 228
Lahor, Jean, 157
Lamartine, Alphonse de, 67, 270
   'Le lac', 9
   mélodie, influence on, 8–11
language, French
   mélodie, influence on, xxi, 2–3
   phonology, 5
   political significance of, 3–5
Leconte de Lisle, Charles Marie René, 13, 117, 190
Lekeu, Guillaume
   Trois poèmes, 165
Les Six, 18, 208, 264, 268–9
Lied, xxi, 1, 40, 61, 89
   mélodie, contrast with, 2–3, 7–8
lied français, 248
Li-Ho, 17
Liszt, Franz, 56, 101, 170
Lorca, Federico García, 17
Louÿs, Pierre, 227, 229

Mâche, François-Bernard, 17
Maeterlinck, Maurice, 158, 228
   Pelléas et Mélisande, 92, 200
Mallarmé, Stéphane, 16, 114, 169, 195, 222, 224, 235, 246
   settings of, 14, 255–6
   Un coup de dés jamais n'abolira le hasard, 290
Manziarly, Marcelle de, 268
   Trois fables de la Fontaine, 273
Marot, Clément, 119, 244, 273
Martini, Jean-Paul Égide
   'Romance du chevrier' (Plaisir d'amour), 40–1
Massenet, Jules, 155, 241
   'Enchantement', 87
   'Septembre', 85–7

song cycles, 88–9
   Poème d'avril, 88–9, 191
Mauclair, Camille, 168
Mauté de Fleurville, Mathilde, 103
mélodie
   after 1970, 18
   ancien régime, evocation of, 79, 96, 115–16, 236, 244–5, 272–4
   animals, songs about, 83, 163–4, 253–5, 271–2
   antiquity, evocation of, 208, 209, 211, 229–30
   chamber, 161, 255–6, 272
   decline of, 17–18
   foreign poets, translations of, 17
   gendering of, 89, 168
   lesbian poets, settings of, 177–8
   Lied, contrast with, 2–3
   linguistic culture of, xxi, 2–3
   medieval poets, settings of, 13, 172–3, 220–2
   name, origins of, 1–2
   orchestral, 11–12, 51, 157, 243, 247–9, 275, 294–5
   orientalism, 76–9, 81–2, 95, 103, 117, 247–51, 255, 259–60, See Hugo, Victor, Les orientales (1829)
   poetic milieu, 20
   poetic voice, 7–8, 10, 13
   professionalisation, 240–1
   Renaissance poets, settings of, 13, 17, 70, 79, 171–2, 242–4, 260–1
   singers, 183–6
      Bagès de Trigny, Maurice, 105
      Bardac, Emma, 105, 223
      Bathori, Jane, 105, 183–4, 254, 269
      Bernac, Pierre, 183, 273
      Croiza, Claire, 103, 105, 106, 107, 183–5
      Girette, Emilie, 105
      Grey, Madeleine, 105, 208
      Guilbert, Yvette, 185
      Michaud, Janine, 185
      Miolan-Carvalho, Caroline, 104
      Panzéra, Charles, 105, 183, 208
      Raunay, Jeanne, 105
      Souzay, Gérard, 185
      Vasnier, Marie, 112, 117, 121, 182–3
      Viardot, Pauline, 50
   Spain, evocation of, 50, 55, 72, 80, 117, 173, 252, 261, 271
   understatement, xxi–xxii, 15, 131, 230, 318
Mendès, Catulle, 242
Messiaen, Olivier
   author, 286

Chants de Terre et de Ciel, 179, 295–8
   'Chant du bébé-Pilule', 298
Debussy, Claude, influence on, 286, 288, 294, 298
Delbos, Claire, 295
Deux ballades de Villon, 286
Dukas, Paul, influence on, 290–1
Harawi: Chant d'amour et de mort, 299–303
   'Dans le noir', 303
   folksong, South American, 300–1
   'Tristan' trilogy, 300
La Mort du Nombre, 288–90
literary background, 284–6
Loriod, Yvonne, 299–300
modes of limited transposition, 286–7, 289, 298
Poèmes pour Mi, 179, 291–5
   'Action de grâces', 294
   cyclic design, 292–3
   orchestration, 294–5
Quatuor pour la fin du temps, 289
râga, 298
Sauvage, Cécile, 285, 287, 295
St François d'Assise, 284
Symbolism, influence of, 288, 289
Trois Mélodies, 286–8
   'Le sourire', 287
   'Pourquoi?', 288
vocal music, importance to, 283
Wagner, Richard, influence on, 283–4, 290, 300
Meyerbeer, Giacomo, 56, 61
Milhaud, Darius, 17
   Catalogue des fleurs, 270–1
modality, 151, 156, 157, 163, 194, 207
modernism, 264–7
Monpou, Hippolyte, 41
Montesquiou, Robert de, 96, 194
Moore, Thomas, 2, 45
Mozart, Wolfgang Amadeus, 40
   Don Giovanni, 163
Musorgsky, Modest, 159, 248
Musset, Alfred de, 173

neoclassicism, 6, 264
Niedermeyer, Louis
   'Le lac', 9–10, 41
Nietzsche, Friedrich, 15
Noailles, Anna, Comtesse de, 178
Nourrit, Adolphe, 47, 61

Orléans, Charles d', 220, 242

Paris Commune, 102
Paris Conservatoire, 146, 155, 268
Parnassianism, xxii, 16, 76, 177, 190–1
   Le Parnasse contemporain, 114, 190
Parny, Évariste de, 17, 260
Perlemuter, Vlado, 107
Picasso, Pablo, 265
Pierné, Gabriel, 165
Pisan, Christine de, 172
plagal progressions, 149, 152–3
plainchant, 290, 298
Poe, Edgar Allan, 237
poetic form, French
   ballade, 221–2
   couplets, 27–8, 136–7
   dizain, 29, 119, 244–5
   huitain, 29
   pantoum, 200, 219, 224
   prose poem, 37, 227–8, 230–2, 253–5
   quatrain
      rimes croisées vs *rimes embrassées*, 28–9
   quinzain, 29
   rondel, 32, 117, 220–1, 242–4
   sixain (sestet), 29, 30, 121–2
   sonnet, 30–1, 155, 310, 312–13
   tercet, 29
   triolet, 118
   typography, 30
poetic metre, French, 5
   alexandrin trimètre, 35
   alexandrine, 6, 24–5, 98, 310, 313
   decasyllable, 25–6
   enjambment, 225, 246
   mute e, 22–4
   octosyllable, 26
   shorter lines, 27
   syllabic structure, 21–4, 311
   vers composés vs *vers simples*, 24
   vers impairs, 27
   vers libre, 35–6, 220
      history, 35
Poulenc, Francis, 16, 17, 56, 162
   Banalités, xxii, 274
      'Chanson d'Orkenise', 275
      'Sanglots', 278–9
   Calligrammes, 274, 316
   Catholicism, 279
   Chansons galliardes, 274
      'Chanson à boire', 274
      'Sérénade', 274
   Chansons villageoises, 275
   Deux poèmes d'Aragon, 315
      'Fêtes galantes', –315

Poulenc, Francis *(cont.)*
　Fiançailles pour rire, 275
　harmonic idiom, 276–8
　homosexuality, 279
　'La grenouillère', 15
　Le bestiaire, 164, 271–2
　　'La carpe', 271
　Le travail du peintre, 276
　'Les chemins d'amour', 275
　Poèmes de Ronsard, 184, 272
　popular style, 274–5
　'Priez pour paix', 273, 307–8
　'Rosemonde', 317
　song cycle, conception of, 274–5
　Surrealism, affinity with, 276
　Tel jour telle nuit, 275–9
　　'Bonne journée', 277–8
　　'Une herbe pauvre', 278
　'Toréador', 271
Proust, Marcel, 96, 198
Puget, Loïsa, 60, 62, 168

Quicherat, Louis, 5, 32

r, rolled, 307
Ravel, Maurice, 61, 63, 161, 198, 235, 269
　Chansons madécasses, 17, 183, 259–60
　Chants populaires, 253
　Cinq mélodies populaires grecques, 251–2
　Daphnis et Chloé, 252, 261
　Deux épigrammes de Clément Marot
　　'D'Anne qui me jecta de la neige', 244–5
　　'D'Anne jouant de l'espinette', 244
　Don Quichotte à Dulcinée, 261
　Histoires naturelles, 15, 164, 183, 253–5, 259
　　'Le cygne', 254
　　'Le martin-pêcheur', 254
　　reception, 254–5, 266
　L'heure espagnole, 252, 255
　Le tombeau de Couperin, 273
　Ma mère l'oye, 272
　Mélodies hébraïques, 253
　'Noël des jouets', 253
　poets, choice of, 244
　'Ronsard à son âme', 261
　'Sainte', 246
　Shéhérazade, 183, 247–9
　'Si morne!', 247
　'Sur l'herbe', 255
　Trois poèmes de Stéphane Mallarmé, 16, 183, 255–6
　　'Surgi de la coupe et du bond', 256
　Vocalise-étude en forme de habanera, 252

Renard, Jules, 253
Revue wagnérienne, La, 195
rhyme, French
　assonance, 33
　degree, 33–4
　gender, 168
　rime riche, 33, 317
Rimbaud, Arthur, 103, 194, 237
　settings of, 14
Rimsky-Korsakov, Nikolai, 248
romance
　ancestry, 40–1
　characteristics, 60–1
　marketing, 38, 39, 60
　mélodie, coexistence with, 42, 56
　mélodie, contrast with, 38–9, 61–3
　subgenres, 38, 60
Romanticism, 6–8, 16
Ronsard, Pierre de, 13, 169, 170, 272
Ropartz, Guy
　Quatre poèmes d'après l'Intermezzo de Heine, 164–5
　Veilles de départ, 165
Rossini, Gioacchino, 56
Rousseau, Jean-Jacques, 7
Roussel, Albert, 17
　Deux mélodies, 266
　harmonic idiom, 249–51
　'Jazz dans la nuit', 266
　'Le départ', 251
　'Le jardin mouillé', 251
　Poèmes chinois, 249–51
　'Rossignol, mon mignon' (Deux poèmes de Ronsard), 260

Saint-Saëns, Camille, 41, 63, 198, 266
　Cinq poèmes de Ronsard, 79
　'Guitare', 73–4
　'L'attente', 75
　'La cloche', 74
　'La mort d'Ophélie', 74
　'Le lever de la lune', 74
　'Le matin', 75
　'Le pas d'armes du Roi Jean', 11, 74, 310
　Mélodies persanes, 76–9
　　'Sabre en main', 78
　'Puisque j'ai mis ma lèvre', 75
　'Si vous n'avez rien à me dire', 75
　'Violons dans le soir', 178
salonnières, influence of
　Bardac, Emma, 181
　Girette, Emilie, 181
　Greffulhe, Elisabeth, Comtesse, 180

Saint-Marceaux, Marguerite de, 180
Singer, Winnaretta, 180
Vasnier, Marie, 182–3
Sanderson, Sybil, 241
Sartre, Jean-Paul, 16
Satie, Erik, 246, 267
Parade, 265–6
Quatre petites mélodies, 270
Socrate, 270
Sports et divertissements, 269, 270
Trois mélodies, 269–70
Sauvage, Cécile, 178–9
L'Âme en bourgeon, 285
Primevère, 292
Schiller, Johann Christoph Friedrich von, 7
Schmitt, Florent, 168
Schoenberg, Arnold
Pierrot lunaire, 255
Schubert, Franz Peter, 39, 40, 47, 61, 66, 67
'Erlkönig', xxii, 83, 151, 154
Schumann, Robert, 75
Dichterliebe, xxii, 279
Frauenliebe und -leben, 179
Second Empire, 13, 190
Second World War, 17, 300
Shattuck, Roger, 265
Shostakovich, Dmitri, 16
Silvestre, Armand, 88, 173
Société musicale indépendante, 183, 208, 255, 271, 289
Société nationale de musique, 105, 146, 161, 228, 255, 286
Franco-Prussian War, response to, 12–13
influence on *mélodie*, 13
song cycle, history in France, 189
Staël, Germaine de, 7
Stravinsky, Igor, 277
Pulcinella, 208
The Rite of Spring, 265
Three Japanese Lyrics, 183, 255, 271
sublime, 7–8

Surrealism, xxii, 16, 264, 265, 274, 275, 285, 301
composers, influence on, 16–17
Symbolism, xxii, 16, 120, 157, 223, 257
music, idea of, 194–5
synaesthesia, 196

Tagore, Rabindranath, 17
Tailleferre, Germaine, 268, 269
Six chansons françaises, 274

Van Lerberghe, Charles, 200
Verlaine, Paul, 10, 103, 126, 157, 161, 220, 309
biography, 194
'Clair de lune', 14
mélodie, influence on, 13–15
Viardot, Pauline, 67, 68, 92, 169, 170–3, 185, 191
'Bonjour mon cœur', 170–1
'Seulette', 172–3
Vichy, 315
Vierne, Louis, 178
Villon, François, 13, 217, 220, 221, 234
Vilmorin, Louise de, 178
Vivien, Renée, 177

Wagner, Richard, 56, 153, 266, 283
chromaticism, contrast with Franckist school, 147–9
Der Ring des Nibelungen, 195, 243
France, reception in, 146–7
Franckist school, influence on, 146, 153, 163
Gesamtkunstwerk, 284
Liebestod, 161, 290
musical prose, 196
Parsifal, 158, 164, 284
reception, France, 195
Siegfried Idyll, 195
Tristan und Isolde, 153, 154, 158, 179, 209, 284, 300
Weitzmann transformation, 192, 196

For EU product safety concerns, contact us at Calle de José Abascal, 56–1°, 28003 Madrid, Spain or eugpsr@cambridge.org.

www.ingramcontent.com/pod-product-compliance
Lightning Source LLC
LaVergne TN
LVHW081523060526
838200LV00044B/1985